The Sensuous Immortals

The Sensuous Immortals

A Selection of
Sculptures from the Pan-Asian Collection

Pratapaditya Pal

Los Angeles County Museum of Art

Distributed by The MIT Press
Cambridge, Massachusetts, and London, England

Published by the
Los Angeles County Museum of Art
5905 Wilshire Boulevard
Los Angeles, California

Exhibition Dates
Los Angeles County Museum of Art
25 October 1977–15 January 1978
Seattle Art Museum
9 March–23 April 1978
Denver Art Museum
26 May–30 July 1978
William Rockhill Nelson Gallery, Kansas City
15 September–29 October 1978

Library of Congress Cataloging in Publication Data

Pal, Pratapaditya.
The sensuous immortals.
Includes bibliographical references.
1. Sculpture—South Asia—Exhibitions.
2. Sculpture—Asia, Southeastern—Exhibitions.
I. Los Angeles Co., Calif. Museum of Art, Los Angeles.
II. Title.
NB1000.P34
732'.4'074019494
77–2619
ISBN 0–87587–079–1 (LACMA, softbound)
ISBN 0–262–16068–4 (MIT Press, hardbound)

Cover (detail) **45. Lovers (Mithuna)**

Contents

Acknowledgments

This extraordinary collection of sculptures was formed over the last decade and a half by a person who wishes to remain anonymous. While scholars and connoisseurs have admired a few of the sculptures included in previous exhibitions, this is the first time that so large a selection from the enormous Pan-Asian collection has been presented to the public. There is no doubt in my mind that it is by far the most important and comprehensive collection of South and Southeast Asian sculptures in private hands today. I am particularly happy to have been associated with the assemblage of so outstanding a collection and am grateful for the opportunity of presenting it to the public.

The logistical problems in organizing this exhibition over the last five years have been enormous. Almost every department in the museum has been involved in one way or another and mere words can hardly express my deep sense of gratitude and appreciation for the ungrudging cooperation I have received throughout this project. In particular, I would like to mention Ben Johnson and his staff (Conservation), Jim Kenion and his staff (Technical Services), Pat Nauert and her staff (Registrar), Ed Cornachio and his staff (Photography), Jeanne D'Andrea and her staff (Exhibitions and Publications), and George Hernandez and his staff (Construction). We would also like to acknowledge the cooperation of the Oriental Department of the Denver Art Museum where part of the Pan-Asian collection has resided for years.

The efficiency and diligence of my own staff members have been exemplary. Cathy Glynn and Virginia Dofflemyer have been associated with the project almost from its very inception. Gloria Carroll has been alone responsible for preparing the typescript of the catalog for the editor. A special word of appreciation is due Ms. Dofflemyer, who along with several extraordinarily assiduous volunteers has cheerfully coordinated the documentation and photography of the collection. In addition, she has helped me generously with her knowledge of Cambodian and Thai sculptures, although I assume all responsibility for any errors. I would also like to acknowledge the help I have received from Dr. Vidya Dehejia of New Delhi and from Gautamvajra Vajracharya in deciphering some of the inscriptions.

Finally, a few words about the diacritical marks. Since the catalog is intended primarily for a general audience, we have tried to burden the text with as few accent marks as possible. I have therefore eliminated all marks from those Sanskrit words that are included in Webster's Seventh New Collegiate Dictionary without accents.

Pratapaditya Pal
Senior Curator of Indian and Islamic Art

Collector's Preface

It is with a deep sense of gratitude that the collector wishes to express his sincere appreciation to the museums participating in this exhibition. Special thanks, naturally, are due to the Los Angeles County Museum of Art—to its Trustees and to so many on its talented staff—for initiating and organizing this exhibition and supervising the production of this beautifully composed catalog.

It has become axiomatic to view a private assemblage of art works as the result of collaboration between scholars, dealers, and the collector. The Pan-Asian collection, from which these sculptures have been selected, reinforces this truism. The objects in the collection bear witness to the taste and connoisseurship of a large number of scholars and dealers alike: a litany of so many in fact that it becomes impossible to list them all, despite the fact that each one of them deserves a large measure of gratitude.

Among the specialists whose help has been invaluable are Emma C. Bunker, Virginia Dofflemyer, Catherine Glynn, and Mary Lanius. Also Laurence Sickman, Dr. Diran Dohanian, and Fong Chow. In particular I would like to thank Dr. Aschwin Lippe.

Among dealers from Europe as well as America on whom the collector has particularly relied are Claude de Marteau (Brussels), Adrian Maynard (London), Isidor Kahane (Zurich), Jean-Michel Beurdeley (Paris), and James Goldie. In New York, Mrs. Nasli Heeramaneck in association with her late husband, Doris Wiener, Mr. and Mrs. J. J. Klejman, R. H. Ellsworth, Peter Marks, and William H. Wolff were especially helpful.

The sculptures in this exhibition have been immeasurably enhanced by the painstaking labors of the Los Angeles Museum's Conservation Department under the inspired supervision of its director, Ben Johnson. In many cases the appeal of the stones and bronzes, when cleaned or remounted, has been considerably increased. The extraordinarily sensitive and vibrant photography of Edward Cornachio and his staff adorns this publication in so evident a manner as to render any further praise superfluous. Without the efficiency of the Los Angeles Museum's Registrar, Pat Nauert, and her staff, this exhibition could never have been realized.

The above acknowledgments notwithstanding, one man, Dr. Pratapaditya Pal, has been the catalyst of this exhibition. In the past decade he has guided the evolution of the collection with skill, tact, and devotion. The prodigality of Dr. Pal's advice, his forbearance in the coordination of all the elements involved in the preparation of this exhibition, the evocative brilliance and informativeness of his text for the present catalog—all this and much more summon from the collector his deepest admiration and gratitude. In the selection of the objects to be included in this exhibition, it was a measure of the profound influence of Dr. Pal's taste and discrimination upon the collector that no meaningful disagreement arose.

If the viewers of the show and the readers of this catalog derive pleasure from their contact with these sculptures, it will be due to the instinctive appeal of works of art executed by believers in any humanistic creed. The spiritual inspiration of the nameless sculptors represented here imbues their work with an imposing presence and a contemplative as well as a physical vitality. But it is probably those figures in which a deity's compassion is most lovingly expressed that will generate the greatest enjoyment. And is that not as it should be, since in the final analysis love and compassion are what religion is all about.

When Love came there, his flower-bow ready stringing,
With fair Desire, his consort, at his side,
The forest creatures showed the passion springing
In every bridegroom's heart towards his bride. . . .

Yet Shiva still remained in meditation
Absorbed, although he heard the singing elves:
Can anything have power of perturbation
Of souls completely masters of themselves?

Kālidāsa[1]

Introduction

The sculptures represented in this collection are from several nations of South and Southeast Asia that cover almost half the continent. The time in which they were created is also vast, spanning almost two millennia between the second century B.C. and the seventeenth century A.D. Most of the sculptures were rendered between the first and the thirteenth century A.D. in regions that are now known as Pakistan, India, Nepal, Tibet, Sri Lanka, Indonesia, Burma, Thailand, Cambodia, and Vietnam. In the days when the sculptures were executed, many different kingdoms and empires flourished and disappeared with little relation to the current national boundaries. For example, the name Nepal once applied only to the Kathmandu Valley, which occupies a very small area of the country known today as Nepal, and Pakistan was created as a state as recently as 1947. In the region known as Indochina several kingdoms rose and fell in different areas, some well within the confines of today's political states, others extending far beyond the present boundaries. Until the end of the first millennium A.D. part of Thailand comprised the kingdom of Dvāravatī and the Thais who have now given their name to the country arrived there relatively late. From Chinese sources we know that at least two successive kingdoms—Fu-nan and Chen-la—flourished before the emergence of the Kāmbuja kingdom in the sixth century, which during its heyday expanded far beyond the borders of modern Cambodia. There was no political entity known as Vietnam, but Champā was the principal kingdom that prospered around the modern region of Hue.

If the political map of South and Southeast Asia was once so decidedly different, the ethnic diversity of the region was even greater.[2] The Indian subcontinent was a mosaic of many different ethnic and tribal peoples, the vast majority of whom, including the Dravidians of the south, had come under the influence of the Brahmanic tradition by the fifth century A.D. This same Brahmanic or Sanskritic tradition was transplanted at about the same time across both land and sea to the Indonesian islands and the Indochinese peninsula, where it was received with remarkable enthusiasm by people who belonged to totally different ethnic stock and cultural backgrounds. Whether they spoke Mon, Khmer, Cham, Melanesian, or Burmese, they adopted Sanskrit, the language of India, as their official court language, just as Hinduism and Buddhism became their principal religions. However, both religions were considerably modified according to local spiritual needs and pre-existing religious beliefs.

Thus, while a general knowledge of the two religions is necessary to comprehend the meaning of these sculptures, we must also remember that many of the religious concepts that evolved outside of India cannot be understood simply in terms of their Indian models. Nonetheless, the basic philosophical assumptions and religious tenets of Hinduism and Buddhism remained valid whether in Nepal, Tibet, Dvāravatī, Kāmbuja, or Java. With one or two exceptions (see no. 63), all the sculptures included here were created to serve a religious purpose, either to be worshiped as icons in temples, monasteries, or domestic shrines or to embellish the walls of religious buildings where they also conveyed a didactic message.

Hinduism is a blanket term derived from *Hindu*, a word that originally had no religious connotation. It was used mainly by the Persians in ancient times to denote the people who lived on and beyond the banks of the river Sindhu, or Indus. Thus, in fifth-century India every inhabitant of the subcontinent was a Hindu, irrespective of his spiritual beliefs. In Islamic India (after the twelfth century) the word gradually came to denote both race and religion, and in British India it acquired its exclusively religious usage in order to distinguish all Indians who were not Buddhist, Parsee, Jaina, Muslim, Christian, or Jewish.

Essentially, a Hindu is a polytheist who believes in many different gods and goddesses, although Hindu philosophy declares them to be manifestations of a supreme principle known as Brahman. Hence, a more appropriate term for the religion is *Brāhmaṇyadharma* or Brahmanism. Philosophically, this Brahman is beyond description and without form (*nirākāra*) or qualities (*nirguṇa*). However, such abstract notions held little or no meaning for a people that had always worshiped visible images and symbols, both natural and man-made. As a result, countless gods and godlings populate the world of Indian mythology and these have provided the artists with an inexhaustible repertoire. Among the millions of Hindu deities, three concepts predominate and each has inspired a major religious system. These three are known as Siva, Vishnu, and Devī or Sakti, and their followers are referred to as Saiva, Vaishnava, and Sakta, respectively.[3]

Saivas regard Siva as the Brahman and he is primarily worshiped by his phallic symbol known as the *linga*. In most Saiva temples, whether in India, Nepal, Java, or Cambodia, the principal icon is a linga, which generally has a stylized form and may or may not be provided with one or more faces of the god (see no. 130). When shown in human shape, Siva is conceived as an ascetic with stylized matted hair adorned with the moon and serpents, and with the third eye and two or more arms holding, among other emblems, the trident. In North Indian images, he is often depicted with an erect phallus, but almost never in South India, and rarely, if ever, in Cambodia, Java, or Vietnam. It may be pointed out that while the linga by itself is a fertility symbol that emphasizes Siva's erotic role, by contrast his erection signifies his ascetic aspect, for according to an ancient Indian belief, seminal retention (urdhvaretas) leads to the sublimation of the virile force into yogic power.[4] Siva is regarded as the lord of all animals (paśupati), but his favorite is the bull, known as Nandi. Also considered to be the originator of all performing arts, he is often represented dancing (see no. 77), or playing a stringed instrument known as the vina (see no. 67). Although Siva has a permanent home in the Himalayas, on the snow-covered peaks of Mt. Kailasa, he is more frequently found roaming around cemeteries, naked and ash covered, in the company of his ghoulish, gnomelike attendants known as ganas. When he is angry, he is known as Rudra or Bhairava (see no. 86), the form closely associated with the cemetery.

Even though Siva is the archetypal wandering ascetic or yogi, who has little use for the phenomenal world, or samsara, he also has a wife and a family. His wife is known variously as Satī, Pārvatī, Umā, or Gaurī, and they have two sons—Gaṇeśa and Kumāra (also called Skanda or Kārttikeya). Much later, in Bengal, the family was expanded by the addition of Lakshmī and Sarasvatī, the goddesses of wealth and wisdom, respectively, as their daughters. In both the mythological and poetic traditions Siva and Pārvatī are regarded as the divine exemplars of human love and are often represented in art (see no. 28) surrounded by their family, watching the antics of their sons and other attendants. Gaṇeśa, the god of auspiciousness, is one of the most important of the Indian gods, while Kumāra, the god of war, is far less popular.

As Siva is to the Saivas, so Vishnu is to the Vaishnavas. As the bard in the Mahābhārata, one of the two great Indian epics, eulogizes:

I bow to the Primeval person, the Lord, widely invoked and lauded, who is the True, the One-Syllabled Brahman, manifest and unmanifest, everlasting, at once the existent and the non-existent, creator of things high and low. I bow to Him who is the Ancient One, supreme, imperishable, blissful and blessing, the most desirable Viṣṇu, faultless and resplendent, who is Kṛṣṇa Hṛṣikeśa, the preceptor of all creatures, those that move and those that move not; the God Hari.[5]

Vishnuism has remained the most openly syncretistic of all the various Hindu religious systems and has continuously assimilated innumerable cults and sects. Its history, therefore, is a complex one. Simply stated, two rather different currents, one Vedic and the other non-Vedic, swelled the stream that came to be known as Vaishnavadharma or Vishnuism. The name is derived from Vishnu, the cosmic god of the Vedas, who came to be regarded as the preserver of the universe in later Hinduism. He is also a solar deity and is intimately associated with kingship, which is why he is invariably represented as a majestic figure in sculptured images (see nos. 51, 72). However, by the fourth century many different beliefs, deities, and cults, which probably had totally independent origins, had been assimilated into Vishnuism. This process was made relatively simple by the concept of avatars, which states that whenever the world is threatened by evil, Vishnu, the preserver, assumes the role of savior and comes down (avatīrṇa) to earth in a suitable form. Typically, therefore, the Vaishnavas claimed that Vedavyāsa, the mythical author of the Mahābhārata; Rāma, the Aryan hero of the epic Rāmāyaṇa; Kapila, the legendary founder of the important philosophical school of Sāṃkhya; and Buddha Śākyamuni, the founder of Buddhism, are all avatars of Vishnu. It was this spirit of syncretism that brought within its fold the cult of Krishna with its emphasis on personal devotion and mysticism. Indeed, the dark romantic hero of the cowherders of Vrindavan is the antipode of Vishnu, the fair cosmic god of sacrifice and sovereignty, yet the two came to be assimilated completely, and ultimately the cult of the mystical Krishna became central to Vishnuism.

In the evolution of Hinduism the religious system known as Śāktadharma or Saktism, which glorifies the Great Goddess as the source of all energy, is rather a late development, although the concept of a Magna Mater goes back at least as far as the neolithic period. Originally, the Great Goddess was a symbol of fertility in predominantly agricultural societies. This aspect of fecundity and abundance has remained basic to the Indian concept of the goddess, whether Hindu, Buddhist, or Jaina, and accounts for much of the voluptuousness of the female form, both divine and human, in Indian sculpture. Apart from the diverse fertility and earth goddesses who were worshiped in various though closely related forms in different neolithic agricultural communities, there appear to have been other goddesses who were venerated by hunting tribes living in remote mountains and forests away from the centers of civilization.[6] Appropriate to a hunting community, they were apparently bloodthirsty goddesses of a bellicose rather than benevolent nature. Both the agricultural earth goddess and the militant hunting goddess were invoked and appeased with bloody sacrifices and sexual orgies.

The Sakta religion seems to have been profoundly influenced by the Sāṃkhya philosophical system. Unlike Vedanta, which advocates monism, Sāṃkhya is a dualist theory stating that both the manifest and the unmanifest worlds were created by Prakritī for the sake of Purusha. Prakritī is regarded as a sort of active first principle, while Purusha is a passive spectator or simply a catalytic agent. Since the word purusha means "man" and prakritī is loosely equated with nature or woman, it is easy to see why the abstract concept of Prakritī was signified by a goddess.

Basic to the concept of the Great Goddess of Hinduism is the idea that as the embodiment of all energy (sakti), she is the source of all creation. This idea was manifested in the form known as Durgā, as described in the Devīmāhātmya of the Mārkaṇḍeyapurāṇa. In order to destroy Mahishāsura, who was threatening the earth, all the gods created a goddess out of their combined energy. She came to be known by many names, such as Durgā, Kātyāyanī, and finally, after her destruction of Mahishāsura, Mahishāsuramardinī. This is by far the most familiar of the goddess's forms and Indian sculptors, as well as those of Nepal and Java, have created some of the most dynamic images of this manifestation (see nos. 31, 103). Almost equally popular is another militant and more bloodthirsty emanation known as Chāmuṇḍā or Kālī (see no. 48), who was originally an awe-inspiring tribal goddess and was later absorbed into the Sanskritic tradition. It is somewhat curious that this goddess of destruction was added to a group of mother goddesses who from fairly early times were worshiped during childbirth and for the protection of the young. Subsequently, under the influence of the concept of sakti, each of these mother goddesses came to be regarded as the energy residing in one of the major gods.[7] Thus, Indrāṇī is the energy of the Vedic god Indra, Māheśvarī of Maheśvara, or Siva, Kaumārī of Kumāra, and so on. Sometimes they are identified by modern scholars as the consorts of the respective gods, but this is incorrect. Innumerable other goddesses were also assimilated into the Hindu pantheon and all are deemed to be manifestations of the Great Goddess, who appears originally to have been worshiped in a numinous stone.

The pervasive influence of the concept of the Great Goddess is evident in the fact that virtually no Indian religion, sect, or cult seems to have remained untouched by it. Every god has his consort and, for example, Siva and Vishnu are rarely represented without their wives, Pārvatī and Lakshmī. This inseparability of the male and female aspects of the godhead is most appropriately expressed by the fifth-century Sanskrit poet Kālidāsa, in the *Raghuvaṁśa*:

For the right understanding (or the proper knowledge) of words, and their meanings, I bow down to Pārvatī and Parameśvara, the greatest of the gods, who are the parents of the universe (or creation) and the perpetual relation (or constant union) between whom is as close as the one subsisting between words and their meanings.[8]

The influence of the Great Goddess concept was not limited only to Hinduism, but also permeated both Buddhism and Jinaism (commonly known as Jainism), as we will presently discuss.

Buddhism began as a simple monastic religion in the fifth century B.C. Soon after the death of Buddha Śākyamuni, his followers organized themselves into a monastic order and established a theology based on the collected words of their master. To begin with it was a religion that used no human images and the stupa served as the principal votive symbol. Although there were lay disciples, the monks and the monasteries remained the focal point and the primary emphasis was on introspection, meditation, moderation, and charity. By the second century B.C., however, Buddhism seems to have come under the influence of other cultic practices and began to employ in its monuments figurative images of nature spirits, such as *yakshas* and *yakshīs*, of gods and goddesses such as Sūrya and Śrī-Lakshmī, and of guardian deities as well as other divinities. By the second century A.D. further radical changes occurred: the Buddha Śākyamuni was deified and his image became the most

potent symbol for the Buddhists, replacing the stupa in importance. An early form of Buddhism, known as Theravada, or the doctrine of the elders, is still practiced in Sri Lanka, Thailand, Burma, and to a lesser extent in Cambodia, Laos, and Vietnam. Theravada iconography is relatively simple, consisting mostly of images of the Buddha, which are worshiped in temples within a monastic complex. It is rather curious that in none of these countries did they adopt the rich imagery universally employed in all early Buddhist monuments in India.

Sometime in the first century A.D. a major schism occurred within the Buddhist church that resulted in the creation of a new school known as Mahayana. The most significant doctrine put forward by this school is that of the bodhisattva, which had far-reaching consequences for both religion and art. There was no disagreement among the elders and the dissenters regarding the ultimate objective, which is to attain nirvana, a concept that is basically the same as the Hindu *moksha* or the Jaina *kaivalya*. All major Indian philosophical systems believe in rebirth, the theory that a human being is born again and again on this earth in one form or another, with the ultimate goal being extinction (nirvana) or release (*moksha*) from the chain of rebirth. Where the Mahayana dissenters differed from their elders was in the method of attaining nirvana. Probably influenced by the Vaishnava concept of grace or salvation, they declared that to attain one's own enlightenment was essentially a selfish or egocentric act and that it was more noble to help others, particularly the unfortunate, toward the right path. Such a savior is called a bodhisattva, and once this concept was adopted it was like opening Pandora's box, for now bodhisattvas could be created ad infinitum and supplicated for salvation, just as the Vaishnavas worshiped Vishnu or the Saivas worshiped Siva in order to achieve *moksha* or whatever material benefits they desired. That is precisely what happened, and a vast Buddhist pantheon developed over the centuries, often mirroring ideas and forms in the Hindu pantheon.

By the seventh century, all major religious systems in India, including Buddhism, had absorbed many of the peculiar and non-Vedic rites, rituals, mystical and sexo-yogic practices, and magical ceremonies that had been in vogue in different parts of the country from ancient times. The scriptures of these newly diversified, expanded, and syncretistic religious systems, which form the basis of today's Hinduism, were characterized by the generic term *tantra* in order to distinguish them from the earlier sacred literature of the Aryans known as *veda*, which was considered to be sacrosanct and therefore immutable. That form of Buddhism which was strongly influenced by tantra came generally to be known as Vajrayana, which believes in an ultimate principle called Ādi-Buddha, or Vajradhara, from which emanated the five Tathāgatas known as Amoghasiddhi, Amitābha, Akshobhya, Ratnasambhava, and Vairochana. It appears that in early Buddhist literature each of these terms denoted an abstract quality of the Buddha Śākyamuni. For instance, Amitābha means "infinite light," Akshobhya means "one who is indestructible," etc. Since the Mahayana believed in the transcendental nature of the Buddha, it was easy to multiply the number of Buddhas, or Tathāgatas, as they are alternately known. The figure five was presumably selected because the universe was believed to be constituted of five elements, each of which was symbolized by a portion of the Ādi-Buddha. Then, because of the Indian's compulsive need to classify everything, all the other bodhisattvas, gods, and goddesses were assigned to one of these five Tathāgatas. Often in Vajrayana Buddhist images a tiny image of the parental Tathāgata is attached to the crown of the figure, announcing the family to which the figure belongs. As with the Hindu pantheon, the gods are classified into families, with the male and female deities paired as partners.

The influence of tantrism on later Buddhism is manifested in a strong emphasis on knowledge and in the dominant role of the goddess. Like the Hindus, the Buddhists address all goddesses by the generic term Bhagavatī and the difference in their representations is so blurred that unless the context is quite clear it is often difficult to distinguish between Hindu and Buddhist goddesses. Both gods and goddesses of tantric Hinduism and Buddhism are frequently provided with multiple limbs, have similar names, and often embody analogous concepts. However, there are certain differences between Hindu and Buddhist goddesses that are important.

The word *sakti* should not be applied to a Buddhist goddess, although most modern scholars do so commonly. She is not a bundle of energy as the Hindu goddess is, but a symbol of knowledge or wisdom (*prajñā*). Hence, in tantric Buddhist texts she is referred to as *prajñā*, never as *sakti*. Moreover, unlike the Hindu goddess, Prajñā is passive and inert and is activated only by the male, who symbolizes *karuṇā* or "compassion," in Mahayana Buddhism and *upāya*, or "method," in Vajrayana Buddhism. It is as a result of the union between the active male Upāya and the passive female Prajñā that ultimate enlightenment, or Bodhi-chitta, is realized. In art this idea is often expressed by the sexual embrace of a god and a goddess, as we encounter in several examples here (nos. 105, 110–11). Such explicit sexual imagery involving the principal deities, however, is rare in Hindu art.

Although the Jaina religion was less popular than Buddhism in ancient India, it is not only an older religion but also outlived Buddhism there. Curiously, however, the Jainas apparently were not as interested in spreading their faith beyond the subcontinent as were the Buddhists and the Hindus, and Jinaism has remained confined within India. Today it is concentrated mostly in the states of Rajasthan, Gujarat, and Karnataka, but, like Buddhism, it seems to have originated in Bihar. There are other similarities between the two religions, but there are important differences as well. Both are regarded as heterodox religious systems by orthodox Hindus.

The word Jaina is derived from *jina*, meaning "conqueror." The Jaina religion recognizes twenty-four Jinas who are more commonly known as Tīrthaṃkara, which means "one who helps to ford the river of phenomenal existence" (samsara). All the Tīrthaṃkaras are supposed to have been historical figures, but the last and greatest of them was Mahāvīra, who was a contemporary of Buddha Śākyamuni. Mahāvīra is also said to have been a friend of King Bimbisāra of Magadha and of his son Ajātaśatru. Like

Buddhism, Jinaism has monastic orders and lay worshipers; unlike Hinduism, in which a temple need not play an essential role, Jinaism revolves around the temple. Like both the Hindus and the Buddhists, the Jainas employ elaborate rituals in their worship. Sometime around the first century A.D. a schism developed in the Jaina religion, as it did in that of the Buddhists, and thereafter Jinaism split into two principal sects known as Śvetāmbara ("white-clad") and Digambara ("sky-clad"). What is significant for us is that in their art the Śvetāmbara images of Tīrthaṃkaras are always clothed and may also be ornamented, while the Digambara images are invariably naked. Other differences between the two sects seem to occur mostly in terms of rituals. For example, the Śvetāmbaras use very little water to bathe their images, but Digambaras wash their images far more elaborately.

Essentially, Jinaism is atheistic in that it does not believe in a supreme being. This, however, did not prevent the adoption of image worship, particularly in the deification of the Tīrthaṃkaras. As a matter of fact, although the Jaina pantheon ultimately adopted innumerable gods and goddesses from both Hindu and Buddhist mythology and created still others, all of them remain subservient to the twenty-four Tīrthaṃkaras, the gods and goddesses serving merely as attendants. Images of the Tīrthaṃkaras invariably follow one of two formulas: they are either shown seated in meditation (see no. 50) or standing rigidly in the posture known as *kāyotsarga* (see no. 18). They never carry any objects in their hands but can be recognized from their animal emblems (*lāñchhana*), their attendants known as *yakshas* and *yakshīs*, and the tree, when it is represented, associated with each. The tree is an essential element of the ascetic tradition and is frequently included in depictions of ascetics and teachers, as for instance, the Buddha Śākyamuni (see no. 54), Jaina Tīrthaṃkaras, and Siva in his role as a teacher (see no. 76).

The primary features of a Tīrthaṃkara figure are his serenity, his youthful body with long arms stretching down to the knees, and the auspicious symbol *śrīvatsa* marked on his chest, although this last is not encountered in every image and is also an important emblem of Vishnu. In contrast to this austere figure, his attendant gods and goddesses embody alluring physical charms in the typical Indian fashion. Perhaps this contrast was intended to indicate the superiority of a Tīrthaṃkara even over the gods, who are still shackled by the bondage of desire and pleasure in their mythical world, whereas the Tīrthaṃkara has attained complete freedom.

Despite their philosophical and theological differences, all the religious systems in Indian Asia share certain similar concepts and rituals. Moreover, despite the iconographic differences of their images, certain basic aesthetic principles and motifs are common to their artistic representations. First of all, the artist's personal religious beliefs had nothing to do with his professional duties, for he worked for patrons of all different faiths. Thus, one day he might have been called on to carve an image of Vishnu and the next day one of Buddha. Since it was impossible for him to know the iconography of all the many gods and goddesses of the different faiths he usually worked in close association with a priest or a monk who would give him the necessary guidance, often based on detailed iconographic descriptions of the deities provided in manuals of liturgy and iconography. In most cases the theologian was responsible only for giving the artist a basic concept to be developed according to the aesthetic norms he had learned, the style he had acquired, and the motifs he had added to his repertoire. A glance at the sculptures will reveal that irrespective of their sectarian differences, most deities have similar thrones, sit on lotuses, and are given flaming nimbi; the gestures and postures are common to all and frequently the same emblems are held by different divinities in various combinations. Furthermore, all the deities are similarly dressed, crowned, and ornamented, the designs differing from one regional school to another, but not from one religion to another.

Apart from such iconographic similarities there are also certain conceptual and aesthetic considerations that are common to Indian sculptures no matter which religious system they serve. Yoga, for instance, has played an important role in the formulation of the imagery of the gods and goddesses and is common to Hinduism, Buddhism, and Jinaism. The historical Buddha Śākyamuni, the transcendental Tathāgatas, and all the Jaina Tīrthaṁkaras are always represented as ideal yogis engaged in meditation, whether seated or standing (see nos. 18, 50, 54). Even other Buddhist gods of the Vajrayana pantheon are portrayed as imperturbable yogis (see nos. 27, 52), as are two of the more important Hindu gods, Siva and Brahma (see nos. 36, 42, 76). Both Siva and Brahma are, of course, archetypal yogis or ascetics who usually have matted hair and carry the various paraphernalia of yogis. More significantly, since yoga is considered the best means of attaining control over both body and mind, the relaxed and supple body of a perfect yogi provided the sculptor with the ideal form for his gods. In contrast to the muscular bodies of the Greco-Roman gods, those of their Indian counterparts seem smooth, relaxed, and strong. They exude a vitality that emanates from inner tranquility rather than physical power and the achievement of this inner harmony is one of the principal aims of yoga. As the *Īśa Upanishad* states: "He [the Self] encircled all, bright, incorporeal, scatheless, without muscles, pure, untouched by evil...."[9]

At the same time, however, Indian sculpture reflects an ambivalence that is characteristic of all Indian mythology, literature, music, and art, that is, the celebration of the sensuous even though the intent is spiritual. The gods and goddesses are spiritual entities, but their forms are often blatantly sensuous, if not erotic. This is probably the feature of Indian religious art that most distinguishes the tradition from all other forms of religious art. Youthfulness is also regarded as an essential feature, and indeed this is true of all Indian gods and goddesses, even of the ascetic Jaina Tīrthaṁkaras. As the *Vishṇudharmottarapurāṇa*, a text compiled not later than the seventh century, tells us regarding Hindu gods:

The principal face should not be triangular and oblique. It should be square and full. It should be serene and have good auspicious marks. Long, circular, oblique and triangular shapes should be avoided for the welfare of people. In the case of gods, hair should be shown in eye-lashes and eye-brows.

The remaining limbs should be free from hair. *Their forms should represent youthful figures of persons 16 years of age.*[10]

That similar injunctions were also followed by the Buddhists is evident from typical descriptions of the bodhisattva Mañjuśrī, which state that he is sixteen years of age, adorned with princely ornaments and attire, and displays the sentiment of love (*śriṅgāra*).

The same idea is expressed more poetically by Purushottama in a charming verse:

May this youth, the scion of the Buddha, long protect you, whom the nymphs of heaven view in different ways: with loud acclaim when he is armed with sword, most thoughtfully when he comes with manuscript, playfully when he is a child, but when he is most beautiful, with Love.[11]

In such verses we not only note the emphasis on the perennial youthfulness of the gods, but also the ambivalence between the sensuous and the ascetic. A glance at the sculptures leaves no doubt as to how successful the Indian artist was in expressing this ambivalence.

Age and death are the misfortunes of mortals, but gods and goddesses are immortal and hence there was little or no justification for portraying them as elderly. Sometimes a god such as Brahma or Agni is represented with a beard, but never as decrepit or infirm. The semi-nude forms of the females are disturbingly desirable and seem more to celebrate life than to renounce it. Not only all the gods, but such mortal saints as the Buddha Śākyamuni and the Tīrthaṁkaras are portrayed as ageless beings (see nos. 50, 54), and even in the scenes of the Buddha's death (see no. 12), he is shown not as the octogenarian he actually was, but as a tranquil youth whose body has remained unaffected by time.

This emphasis on youth and sensuousness remained the sine qua non of all religious sculptures created not only in Nepal and Tibet, but also in Java, Thailand, and Cambodia. However, the sculptors in Southeast Asia appear to have used greater restraint, for their forms are not quite as voluptuous as those of the Indian artist. The frank eroticism of some Indian images, particularly of *yakshīs*, celestial nymphs, and lovers in dalliance (*mithuna*), which play so pervasive a role in embellishing Indian temples, is more understated in Southeast Asian temples. When such subjects are used, as in the great friezes of standing or dancing nymphs at Angkor Wat, the forms are more stylized and, as a result, they appear to be delicately elegant but somewhat aloof.

Also basic to the Indian aesthetic tradition is the close relationship between the visual and performing arts, particularly dance and drama. Those who are familiar with classical Indian dancing, such as Bharata Nāṭyam or Kathākali, will easily recognize the profound influence exerted by the form of dance on sculpture. Not only did the sculptors borrow specific themes from the dancer's repertoire, but the underlying rhythm in Indian sculptural form is essentially similar to the dancer's rhythm. The postures and gestures of the figures, whether mortal or divine, are closely related to those used in the dance and they often have the same theatrical effect. This is hardly surprising in view of the advice constantly repeated in texts on aesthetics that before artists can be successful they must thoroughly study both dance and drama. This is clearly stated in the following dialogue between Vajra, the interlocutor, and the sage Mārkaṇḍeya in the *Vishṇudharmottara*:

Vajra:
O sinless one, how should I make the forms of gods so that the image made according to rules may always manifest [the deity]?

Mārkaṇḍeya:
He who does not know the canon of painting [*citrasūtram*] can never know the canon of image-making [*pratimā lakṣaṇam*].

Vajra then requests Mārkaṇḍeya to teach him the art of painting, but the sage replies, "It is very difficult to know the canon of painting without the canon of dance, because O king, in both, the world is to be represented."[12]

Finally, a few words about the relationship between nature and art may be relevant. It can be generally stated that the primary concern of Indian sculpture is with the human body, mostly as divine manifestation. Whenever a form of nature is employed in sculpture, it is used primarily as a symbol. For instance, almost every deity is placed upon a lotus, which is regarded as the flower par excellence in India and hence an appropriate support for divine beings. Flowers or their petals are strewn over steles because a floral shower is regarded as indicative of divine presence. In the hands of some deities, flowers often serve as symbols of grace and beauty or of fertility. Held by Vishnu, the lotus is a solar symbol and perhaps even one of fertility; in the hands of the Hindu goddess Lakshmī or the Buddhist Tārā it signifies beauty and fertility; and carried by a king as a nosegay it is symbolic of royal playfulness. Other deities stand or sit below trees whose symbolic significance may vary from one figure to another. An ascetic god such as Śiva or Buddha sits below a tree that symbolizes wisdom; elsewhere, it may represent a wish-fulfilling tree (*kalpavriksha*); and generally when a tree is associated with a woman, whether mortal or divine, it announces the intimate relationship between nature and woman and also functions as a fertility symbol. The sculptural form itself often expresses vegetative abundance, and as we look at the swaying, curvaceous figures with their surging sensuality, we are at once reminded of the lush vegetation of the tropical world. The forms expand like fruit-laden branches, exuding a rhythmic vitality that is essentially organic.

It has already been established that as both Hinduism and Buddhism were transplanted in the different regions of Asia they were modified and transformed by local spiritual needs and existing religious ideas about which we know very little. As one might expect, it seems that the closer the region is to the Indian subcontinent the stronger are the religious and cultural ties. Since only a few bronzes in this collection are from Sri Lanka and Burma, and they all represent the Buddha (see nos. 91, 92), it will be unnecessary to discuss the religious peculiarities of these areas. Although there are many more bronzes from Nepal represented here, most of them conform to concepts evolved in India. The angry form

of the bodhisattva Mañjuśrī (see no. 97) does seem to be a local variation, for nothing similar is known from India. The charming bronze representing Vajrapāṇi with Vajrapurusha (no. 93) derives ultimately from a Gupta model, but the Nepali artists seem to have been particularly fond of this image type and continued to reproduce it even after its usage was discontinued in India. The influence of the art of the Gupta period appears to have been strongly felt in Nepal, and even as late as the tenth–eleventh centuries we find bronzes (see nos. 94, 95) that are astonishingly reminiscent of Gupta-style works. After the eleventh century we frequently encounter images, particularly those expressing tantric ideas, that have a local origin, although the aesthetics are those that prevailed in India.

Numerous bronzes representing Hindu and Jaina deities found their way into Tibet and were reverently placed on temple altars, but Buddhism, particularly Vajrayana, is the most important religious force in the country. There is no doubt that of all Asians influenced by Indian ideas, the Tibetans were the most assiduous in adhering to the original Indian iconographic and aesthetic norms. Indeed, innumerable deities described in Indian Buddhist texts are known today only from images made by pious Tibetan Buddhists. However, when Buddhism arrived in Tibet in the seventh century, various forms of shamanism and animism were flourishing there, and in order to survive Buddhism had to adopt many of these beliefs. Later these primitive and tribal religious ideas, along with others borrowed from the imported religion, formed the basis of the religion known as Bon-po, which still survives in parts of the country. As a result of this intermixture, Tibetan Buddhism, known also as Lamaism because of the predominance of the monks, or lamas, displays a marked predilection for oracles, the occult, and demons. The Lamaist pantheon is the richer for it, and the artists evolved new forms that are especially dynamic and expressive of the Tibetan psyche. Moreover, Tibetans reveal a strong inclination to apotheosize their saints and reincarnated lamas, and hence the artists developed a tradition of idealistic portraiture that is also uniquely Tibetan.

Although Hinduism was not unknown in Thailand, the country has remained predominantly Buddhist. And since, as in Sri Lanka, Theravada Buddhism prevails, the image of the Buddha is the principal motif in Thai art. As a matter of fact, all the Thai sculptures included here represent the Buddha. The Buddha images of the ancient Dvāravatī kingdom (see no. 126) are the closest to the Indian models, revealing particularly the influences of the Sarnath and the Ajanta schools.

It must be stressed that since there is no historical record of the pattern of migration from India, it is almost impossible to cite precise stylistic sources for the artistic traditions of Southeast Asia.[13] Nevertheless, at least one small stele with the Buddha has been found in Thailand that must have been taken there all the way from Sarnath.[14] Whatever the exact source, it is clear that the artists responsible for carving the earliest sculptures, whether in Dvāravatī, the kingdom of Fu-nan in Cambodia, or the Dieng plateau in Java, were remarkably original, even from the beginning. Indeed, it is curious that the earliest Hindu or Buddhist images so far recovered from each region of Southeast Asia deviate so significantly from their Indian models, which would be unthinkable if the artists were from India. On the other hand, if the artists were local inhabitants, then we are left with the question of how they could have mastered the tradition so rapidly. Since no early sculpture shows any hesitancy, and even assuming that the artists were all geniuses, how did they understand and reinterpret a different, rather sophisticated artistic and religious tradition with such self-confidence in so short a period of time? These questions cannot be answered here, but they must be kept in mind as one admires the brilliant artistic creations by the unknown sculptors of the Dvāravatī, Kāmbuja, and Śailendra kingdoms.

Hinduism and Mahayana Buddhism both flourished in Java and Cambodia (today the latter is predominantly Buddhist, the former is Islamic). Both religions underwent transmutations in the two countries and influenced one another in a way that was quite unlike their interaction in India. In both countries the belief in the cosmic mountain Sumeru appears to have been particularly strong and to have had a profound influence on their religious architecture, as can be seen from a glance at their temples, such as Angkor Wat in Cambodia and Borobudur in Java. Secondly, as in Tibet, apotheosis played an important role in Cambodia and possibly to a lesser extent in Java; not only were all kings considered to be living gods and identified with the personal deities of their choice, but even lesser mortals, such as members of the royal families, ministers, and religious preceptors, were all deified after their death and their images consecrated in temples. Generally, however, these statues, whether in bronze or stone, were not portraits at all, but idealized images of particular gods or goddesses with whom the deceased were identified. Thus, the extraordinarily beautiful image of Umā (no. 146) may at the same time represent a princess, but her form and features are not at all individualized. Most Cambodian temples, and possibly those of Central Java as well, are therefore funerary monuments in which the central image often represented both a god and a mortal donor, while other divine statues depicted deceased members of the donor's family. This cult, known as *devarāja* ("god-king"), was not unknown in India, but it reached a climax in ancient Kāmbujadeśa (Cambodia).

Apart from such fundamental conceptual differences between the arts of India and those of Cambodia and Java, there are other variations in both iconography and style. Iconographic differences are too tedious and detailed to warrant a discussion here, but a few words regarding the stylistic variations may be appropriate.

Most of the Javanese sculptures in the collection were made in the ninth and tenth centuries. It is generally assumed that the art of Java at this time was strongly influenced by that of the Pāla empire in Bihar and Bengal. The most important Buddhist strongholds within the Pāla empire were Nalanda and Vikramaśila in Bihar and Paharpur in Bengal. We know that a Śailendra king built a hostel for Javanese monks and pilgrims at Nalanda for which the Pāla king provided a grant of five villages. It must also be remembered that other Śailendra kings built a similar hostel at Nagapattinam in the Tamil country and that the Javanese must have traded with the entire coastal region of eastern India from the Bay of Bengal down to Sri Lanka. Thus, if monks and pilgrims as well as merchants of both countries carried images with them to Java, the Javanese artists must have had a great variety of styles at their disposal.

The temple designs of the Prambanam Valley in Java, where most of the Śailendra monuments are concentrated, undeniably reflect strong influences of the temples of Vikramaśila and Paharpur, and the bronzes are stylistically similar to those found at Nalanda and Kurkihar, but there are also differences that are so subtle they are more easily perceived than described. At the same time, Javanese sculptures with their somewhat heavy proportions and smooth modeling appear to be closer to Orissan sculptures than to the more slender and naturalistically modeled Bihar and Bengali sculptures. The sensuousness of Javanese sculptures is more gentle and even when the images are provided with more than two arms to emphasize their divine omnipotence, they retain a human scale. In the words of Coomaraswamy, "the rich and gracious forms . . . bespeak an infinitely luxurious rather than a profoundly spiritual or energized experience . . . the fullness of its forms is an expression of static wealth rather than the volume that denotes the outward radiation of power."[15]

From the very beginning, Cambodian sculptures have revealed certain fundamental differences from their Indian models. It is generally believed that the early sculptures of the Pre-Angkor period (550–800) show influences of the art of the Gupta period (300–600). Although this is true to an extent, there are certain characteristics of Pre-Angkor sculptures, as exemplified by the superbly modeled Vishnu head (no. 137) and the delightful Gaṇeśa (no. 136), that are distinctly local. The most conspicuous of these is the fact that most Pre-Angkor sculptures are freestanding and thus modeled in the round. This preference for fully carved figures, especially those intended as icons for worship rather than for didactic use on temple walls, continued among the Cambodian artists even during the Angkor period (800–1400). Indian sculptures, on the other hand, are rarely modeled in the round and are generally attached to a stele. Certainly if the first sculptors in the kingdom of Fu-nan had been from India, they would have followed the method in which they were adept rather than deviate so radically; yet even during the initial phase of Indian influence, the modeling of Pre-Angkor sculptures is distinctly different from Indian prototypes. The different planes and joints of the body were far more articulately defined by the Pre-Angkor sculptors than by their colleagues in India. The modulation of the surface is still subtle, but the substructure is far more evident than in Indian sculpture. Pre-Angkor sculptures are remarkably unencumbered; except for a short loincloth for the males and a longer skirt for the females, all the forms of ornaments and rich details that so delighted the Indian artists were eschewed by Cambodian sculptors. Vishnu's crown is a starkly plain miter, while Gaṇeśa looks almost naked without any ornaments. Although ornamentation does increase in time and by the tenth century the gods wear elaborate crowns and some of the goddesses are given rich jewelry, the form is never enmeshed with intricately carved ornaments as it is in India. Finally, one reason why Cambodian sculptures are not quite as overtly sensuous as their Indian forebears is their rigid composition. This becomes clear if we compare the tenth-century Cambodian Umā (no. 146) with her near-contemporary Indian counterparts (nos. 66 a and b). Elegant as the Cambodian lady is, the hieratic frontality of her posture puts her at a slight disadvantage beside her Indian sister, who thrusts her hips out provocatively and is far more animated and voluptuous. The Cambodian sculptors seem to have expressed the sense of movement with restraint, and consequently their sculptural forms exhibit more noble grandeur than sinuous motion.

Greater restraint is also evident in the use of multiple limbs and heads in the sculptures of Southeast Asia. From very early times Indians have freely embellished their figures with additional arms and heads, and in the case of Vajrayana deities also legs, apparently to convey the cosmic nature of their deities. While it may seem strange to us that omnipotent and omniscient divinities should need additional limbs, for the Indians they demonstrate precisely the difference between divine powers and human limitations. Not only did the Indian sculptors delight in endowing their figures with additional limbs, but it is remarkable how aesthetically successful the result is. The sculptors of Nepal and Tibet also had a deep empathy for this principle of multiplication, but those of Southeast Asia seem not to have been entirely comfortable with it. Even where they did use multiple arms and heads (see no. 147), the additions look like contrived appendages rather than the seemingly naturalistic growths they appear to be in Indian sculptures.

While some scholars have plausibly attempted to relate the early sculptures of Indochina to specific Indian styles, the problem is still unresolved. However, there can be little doubt that the fundamental religious and aesthetic ideas that shaped the sculptural traditions of Southeast Asia originated on the Indian subcontinent. While influences continued to percolate intermittently throughout the history of Kāmbuja, Champā, and Java, of the successive kingdoms of Sukhothai and Ayuthya in Thailand and of Pagan in Burma, there was considerable cultural and political intermingling among these kingdoms themselves. It is not uncommon, therefore, to find influences of the art of Dvāravatī on that of Pre-Angkor Cambodia, or to encounter strong Pre-Angkor features in the Prakon Chai bronzes (nos. 127–29), or to see notable characteristics of the Śrīvijaya style of the Malay peninsula in the art of the Dvāravatī kingdom, and even of Cambodia. In the ninth and tenth centuries sculptors in the Indochinese peninsula must also have been conscious of the great monuments raised under the auspices of the Śailendra dynasty in Java. During the twelfth and thirteenth centuries Thailand was both politically and culturally dominated by the Khmer civilization of Cambodia, so that scholars speak of Khmer or Khmerizing styles in Thailand. Several bronzes in the collection are rendered in this Khmerized style (nos. 132–33). A truly distinctive national Thai style appeared only after the emergence of the Ayuthya kingdom following the dissolution of the Kāmbuja kingdom in Cambodia.

In this age when cults are more frequently formed around individual artists than around the works they create, it may seem odd that we know almost nothing about these sculptors. The situation in ancient Indian Asia was analogous to that in medieval Europe: the artist was part of a guild or atelier and very likely the profession was hereditary. Few, if any, works are actually signed, for it was believed that the artist was simply an instrument for Viśvakarmā, the divine artist, who was ultimately responsible for all art and architecture. In this sense, no matter what the actual social status of the artist every imager was considered divine, for as Dante expressed it so aptly, "He who would paint a [divine] figure, if he cannot be it, cannot paint it."[16] Similar ideas are also expressed in ancient Indian texts which repeatedly state that the mortal artist merely imitates the divine model. In the *Mahābhārata*, for instance, when Krishna commands the architect Maya to build a palace for the Pāṇḍava brothers he explicitly states that the structure is to follow the designs of the gods. Since the artist was considered to be divinely inspired during the act of creation, his own ego would naturally have to be sublimated and hence his name was deemed quite unimportant.

Although today the traditional artist does not belong to the upper echelon of a caste-structured society, there is evidence to believe that such was not always the case. Certainly many priests and monks were talented artists and many Tibetan monks to this day are excellent painters. It was also customary in ancient India for princes and the nobility to learn the art of painting, and we do know that at least two Cambodian monarchs were sculptors. The Prah Ko inscription of Indravarman clearly tells us that in the year 878, the king installed three images of Siva and three of Devī which were made by him (*svaśilparachita*).[17] The illustrious king Yaśovarman also appears to have been a sculptor, for in two of his inscriptions he claims to have sculptured an image of Siva-Śarvāṇī (Umā-Maheśvara) and of Siva.[18] It may further be mentioned that A-ni-ko, the Nepali sculptor who gained eminence at the court of the Chinese emperor Kublai Khan, was also said to have belonged to the royal family of Nepal. Other artists in India are known to have risen to high political offices, while we have historical information that in Tibet eminent monk-teachers, many of whom were talented artists, supervised and participated in the execution of the temple designs.

Even though so little is known about the sculptors who were responsible for producing such a wealth of beautiful forms, it would be wrong to assume that they were not human beings deeply concerned with the problems and challenges presented by their work. But, involved as they were in capturing in stone or bronze something of the divine essence, the image was more important to them than the artistic process. Furthermore, the artist was not required or expected to express the transient emotions of the world of mortals, but rather the mysterious spirit and abiding truths that underlie both nature and the cosmos. It is therefore a measure of the universal appeal of these sensuous forms that a Western collector should be so captivated by their alluring charm and their profound spiritual meaning.

1.
J. Brough, trans. and ed., *Poems from Sanskrit*, Baltimore, 1968, pp. 109–10. Translated from Kālidāsa's *Kumāra-sambhava*.

2.
For a lucid introduction to the history and culture of Southeast Asia, read G. Coedes, *The Making of Southeast Asia*, Berkeley and Los Angeles, 1969.

3.
For an authoritative discussion of Hindu religious systems, see J. Gonda, *Les religions de l'Inde*, 3 vols., Paris, 1962, 1965, 1966.

4.
For a detailed discussion, see W. O'Flaherty, *Asceticism and Eroticism in the Mythology of Śiva*, London, 1973.

5.
J. A. B. van Buitnen, trans. and ed., *The Mahābhārata*, Chicago and London, 1973, I, pp. 20–21.

6.
A similar synthesis also occurred in ancient Greece when the concept of Athena *Polias*, the goddess of agriculture, was fused with that of the warrior maiden, Athena *Parthenos*. See J. J. Pollitt, *Art and Experience in Classical Greece*, Cambridge, 1972, p. 71.

7.
Originally the six mothers were worshiped to protect a newly born infant, one mother for each of the six nights immediately after birth. These six mothers have nothing to do with the later concept of eight mothers who are regarded as the sakti of eight important gods. The number eight here probably represents the eight constituents of Prakritī according to the Sāṁkhya system. It is also interesting to note that in classical Sāṁkhya the number of constituents is said to be sixteen and curiously the number of mother goddesses was also increased to sixteen.

8.
G. R. Nandargikar, *The Raghuvaṁśa of Kālidāsa*, Delhi, Patna, and Varanasi, 1971, p. 2 in *nāgarī* numeral.

9.
J. B. Alphonso-Karkala, ed., *An Anthology of Indian Literature*, Harmondsworth, 1971, p. 66.

10.
P. Shah, ed., *Viṣṇudharmottara-purāṇa Third Khaṇḍa*, Baroda, 1961, II, p. 109.

11.
Ingalls, p. 67.

12.
Shah, *Viṣṇudharmottara-purāṇa*, p. 3.

13.
For discussions of precise Indian sources for Southeast Asian art, see M. Bénisti, *Rapports entre le premier art khmer et l'art indien*, 2 vols., Paris, 1970, and S. J. O'Connor, *Hindu Gods of Peninsular Siam*, Ascona, 1972.

14.
Boisselier and Beurdeley, p. 69, fig. 39.

15.
Coomaraswamy, p. 204.

16.
As quoted by A. K. Coomaraswamy, "The Intellectual Operation in Indian Art," *Journal of the Indian Society of Oriental Art*, III, no. 1, 1935, p. 9.

17.
R. C. Majumdar, ed., *Inscriptions of Kāmbuja*, Calcutta, 1953, p. 64.

18.
Ibid., pp. 86, 140. It is strange that this important information has escaped the attention of scholars who have written on Cambodian art.

Glossary

Abhayamudrā
Gesture denoting reassurance.

Añjalīmudrā
Basically the same as *namaskāramudrā*. Literally means "gesture of offering."

Ardhaparyaṅkāsana
A posture in which one leg extends to the ground and the other is folded toward the extended leg.

Bhūmisparśamudrā
A specifically Buddhist gesture in which the right hand is extended to touch (*sparśa*) the earth (*bhūmi*). Buddha Śākyamuni is said to have made this gesture as he became enlightened below the Bodhi tree after having resisted the temptation of Māra, the Buddhist god of desire. Since there was no one else around, he called on the earth to witness his victory over Māra.

Dharmachakrapravartanamudrā
A special gesture invented by the Buddhists to express the first sermon taught by the Buddha. The gesture is also given to the Hindu Lakuliśa, an avatar of Siva, and to Prajñāpāramitā and Chundā, both Buddhist goddesses.

Dhyānamudrā
Gesture of meditation in which both hands, with palms facing up, are placed on the lap.

Jñānamudrā
Gesture of wisdom similar to *vyākhānamudrā*.

Kāyotsarga
A posture in which the figure stands erect with arms extended rigidly down to the knees.

Khaṭṭvāṅga
Literally "the limb of a cot," presumably the leg used as a makeshift weapon.

Kinnara
A mythical creature with an avian body but a human head.

Kīrttimukha
Literally "face of glory." Represented as a stylized lion's head, it is generally regarded as an auspicious symbol by all religions. In Indonesia the motif is known as *kāla*.

Lalitāsana
Posture of sitting with one leg placed parallel to the ground and the other pendant.

Nāga
Literally "serpent." Often in Indian art a *nāga* is represented in anthropomorphic form with a serpent's hood attached to the head.

Namaskāramudrā
Gesture of hands with enjoined palms expressing a greeting or reverence.

Samapada
Posture with the feet placed close together and the weight of the body evenly distributed over both legs.

Sampot
Loincloth worn by male figures in Southeast Asian sculptures.

Sarong
Long skirt worn by female figures in Southeast Asian sculptures.

Siṁhakarṇamudrā
Literally "lion's ear gesture," in which the position of the hand seems to imitate the shape of a lion's ear.

Sukhāsana
Posture of comfort, basically the same as *lalitāsana*.

Tarjanīmudrā
Gesture of admonition with the index finger raised.

Tathāgatavandanāmudrā
Gesture of adoring a Tathāgata.

Tribhaṅga
Posture with the body flexed at three places along the vertical axis, somewhat similar to an *s*.

Urṇā
A tuft of hair between the eyebrows, generally indicated by a dot and considered a supernatural sign of greatness.

Ushṇīsha
The cranial bump on the Buddha's head, signifying supernatural wisdom.

Vajrahuṁkāramudrā
A gesture in which the two hands cross each other at the wrists and are held against the chest, sometimes holding the bell and the thunderbolt.

Varadamudrā
Gesture of the hand signifying charity or the bestowing of gifts.

Vyākhyāṇamudrā
Gesture of teaching or exposition.

The sculptures are arranged chronologically through A.D. 600 irrespective of their provenance. The period between 200 B.C. and A.D. 300 can be characterized as the formative or early classical phase of Indian sculpture. The three centuries between A.D. 300 and 600 are generally regarded as the classical period, during which certain artistic norms were universally established across the northern and central regions of the subcontinent. These standards remained valid for artists throughout the next period stretching from the seventh through the thirteenth century. This long period is generally designated by historians as "medieval." The gradual evolution of regionalism that ultimately came to be identified with the development of the various vernacular languages had its genesis during this period. The final culmination of this process can be seen in the states that constitute today's India, not including Pakistan and Bangladesh. The sculptures created during the "medieval" period are therefore grouped by the major states recognized in India. It must be pointed out, however, that considering that so little is known about the exact findspots of the sculptures, the provenances suggested here are based primarily on the types of stone and a broad analysis of styles. Within this period and within each state, the sculptures are arranged chronologically.

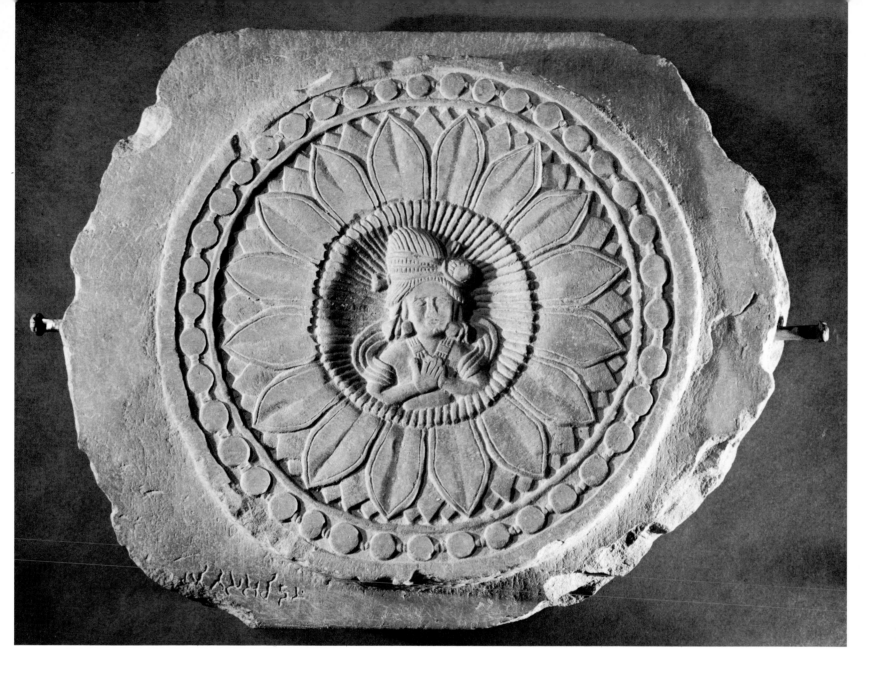

1. Crossbar from a Railing
Madhya Pradesh, Bharhut
2nd century B.C.
Red sandstone
h: 22 in. (55.9 cm.)
w: 26 in. (66.0 cm.)

The greater part of this slightly bulging slab is decorated with a lotus medallion enclosed by a string of pearls. From the center the figure of a man emerges, his hands disposed in *namaskāramudrā*. Very likely he represents a celestial being engaged in adoring the Buddha, although it is not impossible that the bust portrays the donor. Bedecked with ornaments, he is distinguished by an imposing turban and billowing scarf. This type of medallion was a popular motif for decorating the crossbars of the railings that surrounded the great stupa at Bharhut. The inscription reads: "... *mitasa suchi dānam*." ("This crossbar [*suchi*] is the gift of ... mitra.")

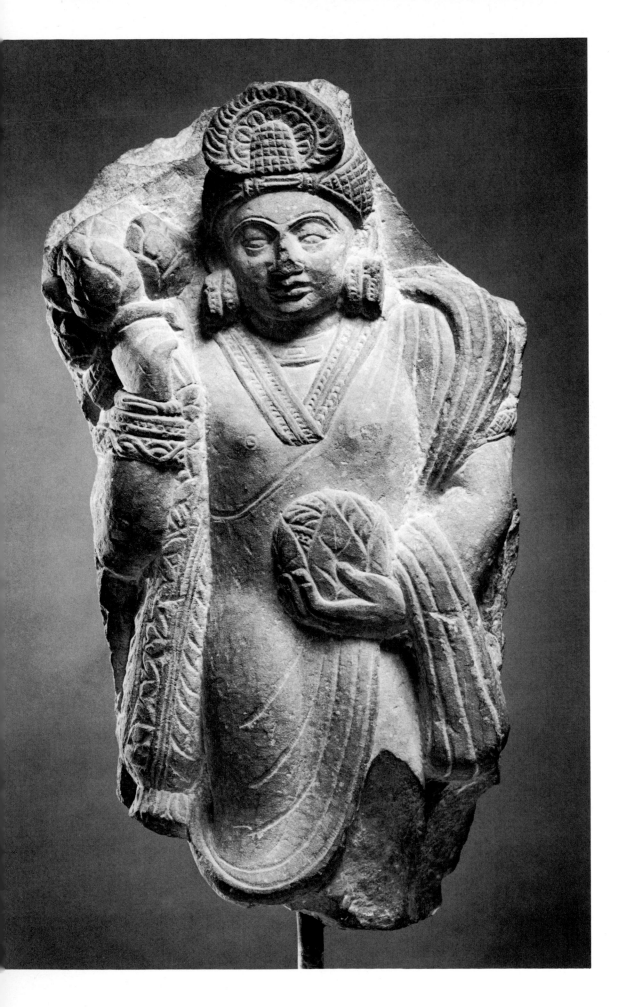

2. Portrait of a Donor
Uttar Pradesh, Mathura
1st century
Spotted red sandstone
h: 19½ in. (49.5 cm.)

Such donor figures holding floral
offerings are quite common in the art
of the Kushān period (A.D. 1–300) at
Mathura, but they are more frequently dressed in Scythian attire,
whereas this one wears the native
dhoti and shawl. Although they may
represent particular donors, generally
such sculptures are idealized. The
treatment of the bunch of lotuses
supported by a long, thick, decorated
stem is characteristic of these figures,
as is the form of the turban. The
details of the turban are rendered in a
rather distinctive fashion, somewhat
flat and cursory. One wonders if this is
indicative of a date earlier than the
first century, which the shallowness of
the relief also suggests.

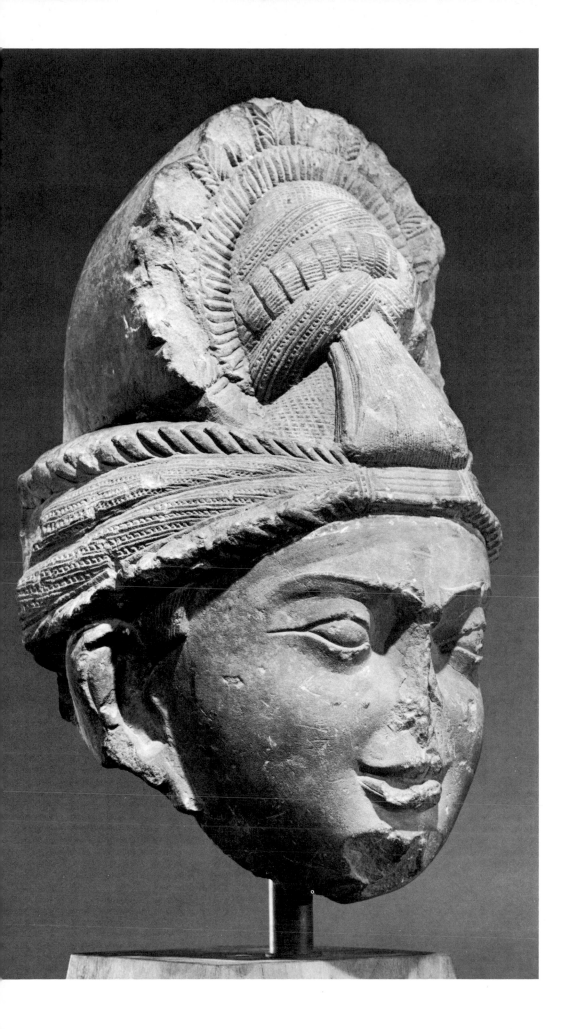

3. Head of a Bodhisattva
Uttar Pradesh, Mathura region
2nd century
Spotted red sandstone
h: 20 in. (50.8 cm.)

This imposing head once belonged to a larger than life-size figure of a bodhisattva, and although the nose and the chin are damaged, we can still discern the smiling countenance frequently encountered in Buddha and bodhisattva figures of Kushān Mathura. Also typical of the period is the enormous turban that considerably enhances the majestic effect. That the figure was enshrined and viewed only from the front seems evident from the summary treatment of the turban and the head at the back. Details of the front, however, are rendered carefully and the medallion looks like a strikingly elegant appendage.

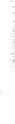

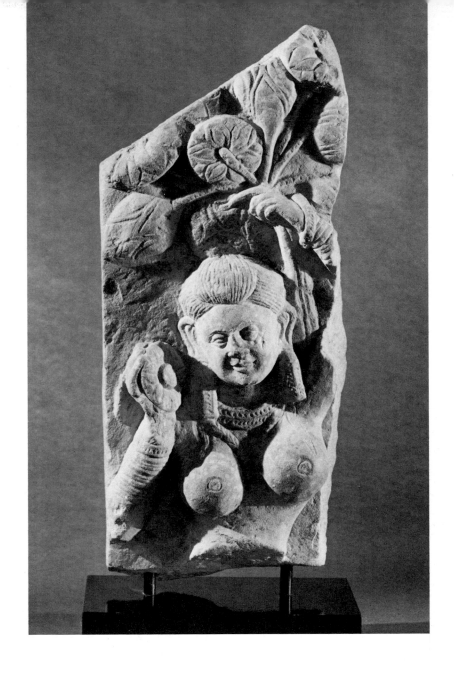

4. A Yakshī
Uttar Pradesh, Mathura
2nd century
Spotted pink sandstone
h: 18 5/16 in. (46.5 cm.)

This fragment carved with a charming
female bust was probably part of a
railing upright or post. Unabashedly
displaying her physical charms, she
holds a stylized lotus in her right hand,
while her left grasps another bunch
of lotuses, both buds and full-blown
flowers. Richly ornamented with
heavy jewels, she also has an elegantly
modish coiffure.

Such abundantly endowed females
frequently seen embellishing
the pillars of railings in early Buddhist
art are known as *yakshīs*, generally
regarded as nature or fertility goddesses. Often they are shown in association with trees, but because of the
lotuses, this particular yakshī seems to
be associated with water. Possibly we
are looking at a water nymph emerging from the water like Venus or like the
Hindu goddess Śrī-Lakshmī, who also
came from the ocean and was taken by
Vishnu as his wife.

Published: *Indische Kunst*, no. 45, pl. 9.

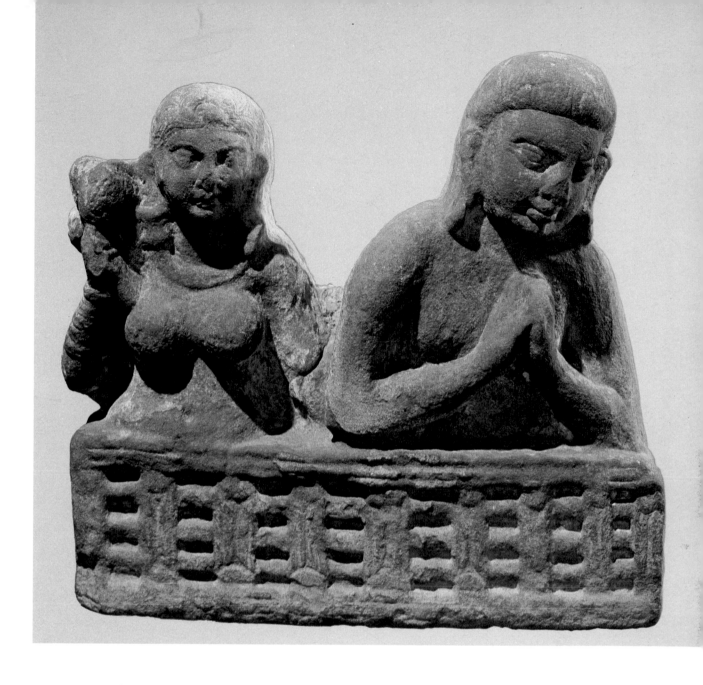

5. Two Devotees
Uttar Pradesh, Mathura region
2nd century
Spotted red sandstone
h : 11 in. (28.0 cm.)

A couple leans over a balustrade in a devotional attitude. Judging by the position of the male, the object of veneration was below and to his left. His hands are engaged in the gesture of adoration and she carries a bunch of flowers. The piece may have served as the capital of a pillar of either a Jaina or a Buddhist railing, as we know from other similar fragments found at Mathura. During the Kushān period around Mathura such capitals were usually carved into charming and naturalistic representations of couples engaged in various mundane activities (cf. Rosenfield, 1966, p. 30).

6. Two Youthful Figures

Afghanistan, Hadda
Ca. 300
Stucco, with light traces of polychrome
h: (a) 9¾ in. (24.8 cm.)
(b) 10½ in. (26.6 cm.)

Figures such as these, distinguished
by smiling, boyish faces and graceful
postures, are usually identified as
young monks in the service of the
Buddha. One of the figures (a) holds a
thunderbolt in his right hand and the
end of his garment in his left. The
other figure (b) points with his right
hand to a skull in his left. In addition to
the dhoti, the figure with the thunderbolt wears a tunic and a toga like a
Roman. He must, therefore, represent
Vajrapāṇi, the thunderbolt-bearer,
who is a frequent companion of the
Buddha in Gandhāran art (see nos.
11, 12). Almost an identical representation of Vajrapāṇi occurs in a Hadda
relief depicting an incident from the
Buddha's life (see J. J. Barthous, *Les
fouilles de Hadda*, Paris and Brussels,
1930, III, pl. 40a). The figure holding
the skull (b) has his right arm and belly
bare and his earlobes are elongated,
like those of the Buddha. Since
extended earlobes are regarded as one
of the signs of a superhuman being, the
figure may not be just an ordinary
monk. In any event, his attitude
obviously reflects that he is contem-
plating the transitoriness of life. For
other similar skull-bearing monks, see
ibid., pls. 39 a and b.

Originally polychromed, these
two figurines are among the finest of
the Hadda stucco statuettes. Because
the artist modeled them directly with
his fingers, the forms are particularly
sensitive and lively.

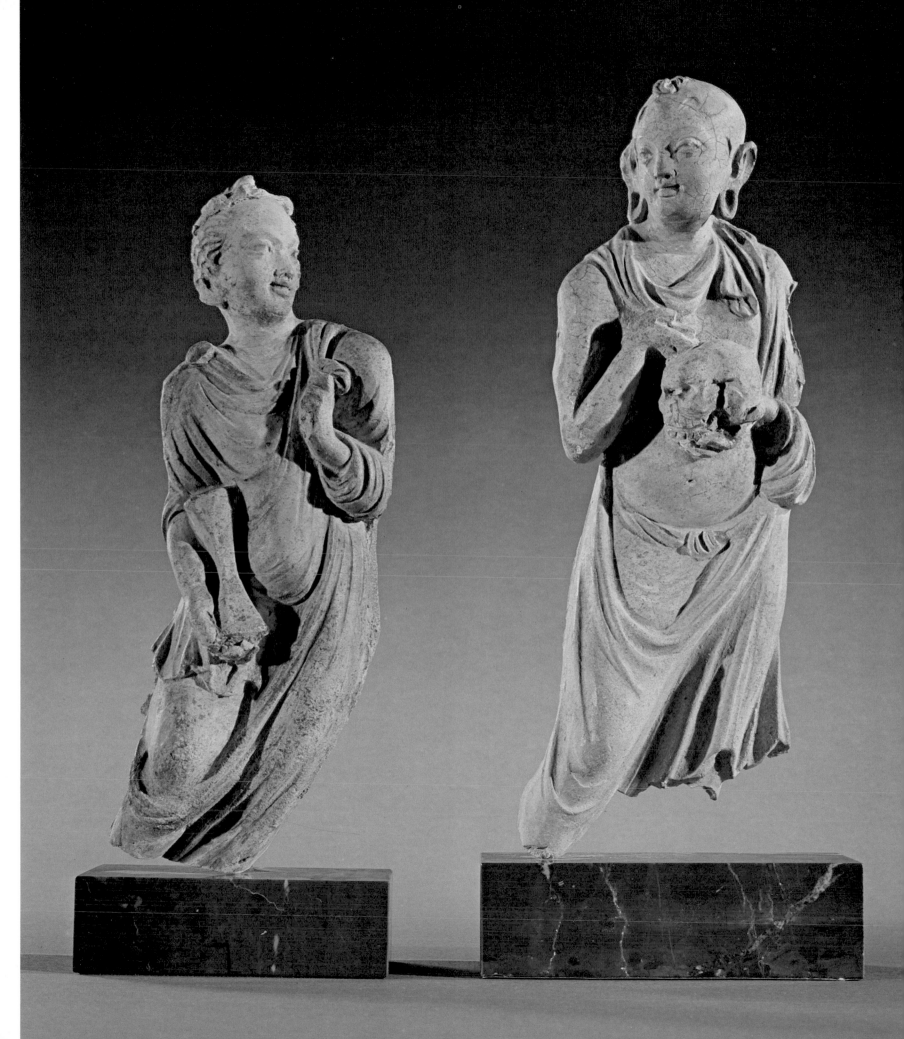

7. Head of the Buddha Śākyamuni

Pakistan, Mardan district (?)
2nd–3rd century
Gray schist
h: 19 in. (48.2 cm.)

During the period when this sculpture was created, the northern parts of present Pakistan and the southern parts of Afghanistan comprised the region known as Gandhāra. It formed the heartland of the Kushān empire and benefited economically from the northern trade along the silk route. The region was strongly Buddhist and developed a distinctive school of art that was heavily influenced by Greco-Roman, Iranian, and Central Asian traditions. Provincial Roman styles, however, appear to predominate, and there seems little doubt that with the decline of the Roman empire the artists from the Roman provinces of West Asia moved to this region, attracted by rich Buddhist patrons and the Kushān emperors themselves.

Slightly larger than life size, this well-preserved head is a fine example of the technical proficiency of the Gandhāran sculptor. The thick moustache added above the upper lip is characteristic of many Gandhāran Buddha images. The *urṇā* between the eyebrows is a prominent dot, and the *ushṇīsha* crowning the head is secured by a band at the base. The locks above the *urṇā* are arranged in what is described as "the almond-shape form."

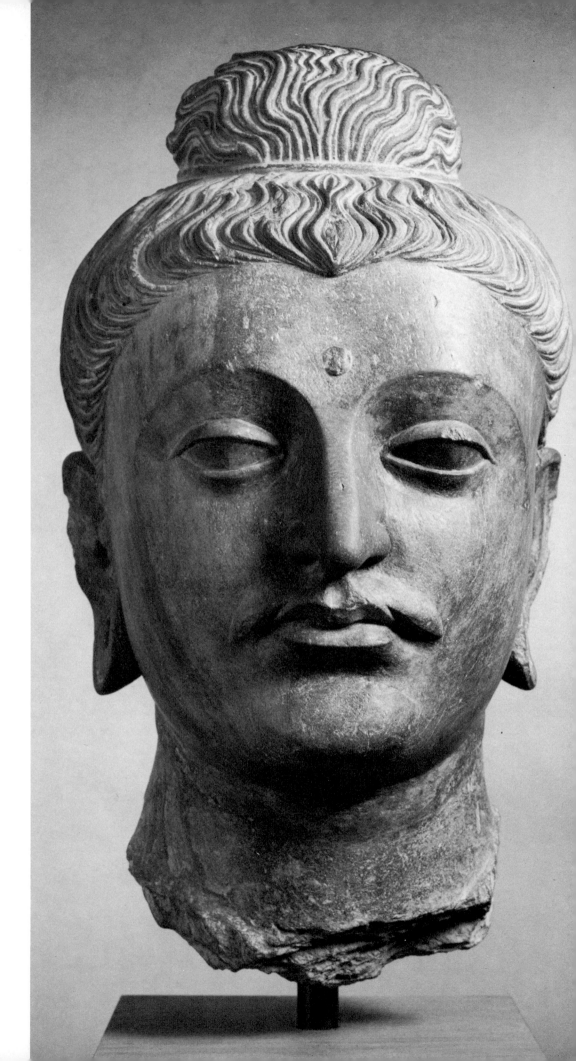

8. Bodhisattva Maitreya

Pakistan
2nd–3rd century
Gray schist
h: 48 in. (121.8 cm.)

Elaborately ornamented and draped,
this thickset figure with slightly swayed
hips stands on a richly carved pedestal.
The hair on his head, set off by a plain
nimbus, is tied in a bow and adorned
with strings of pearls. In addition to
four necklaces, he wears several
charm boxes attached to a string that
goes around his body diagonally.
Such protective charm boxes are still
frequently worn by Indians, but it is
surprising that a divine being would
need them. His left hand holds a pot,
which would identify him as Maitreya,
the future Buddha. The pedestal is
rendered as a pillared shrine with
devotees worshiping what appear to be
the three jewels (*triratna*) symbolizing
the Buddha, Dharma (the religion),
and Samgha (the monastery).

The figure admirably demonstrates the hybrid nature of the
Gandhāran style, combining the
naturalism of the Roman aesthetic
with iconographic elements that are
purely Indian. Typical of Roman
sculptures, much emphasis is placed on
the volume and folds of the dhoti and
the swirling shawl, elements that held
no fascination for subsequent Indian
schools of sculpture. Such Gandhāran
statues, impressive as they are, have
more of a physical than a spiritual
impact. This figure is stylistically very
close to another in the Karachi
Museum (Ingholt and Lyons, fig. 290).

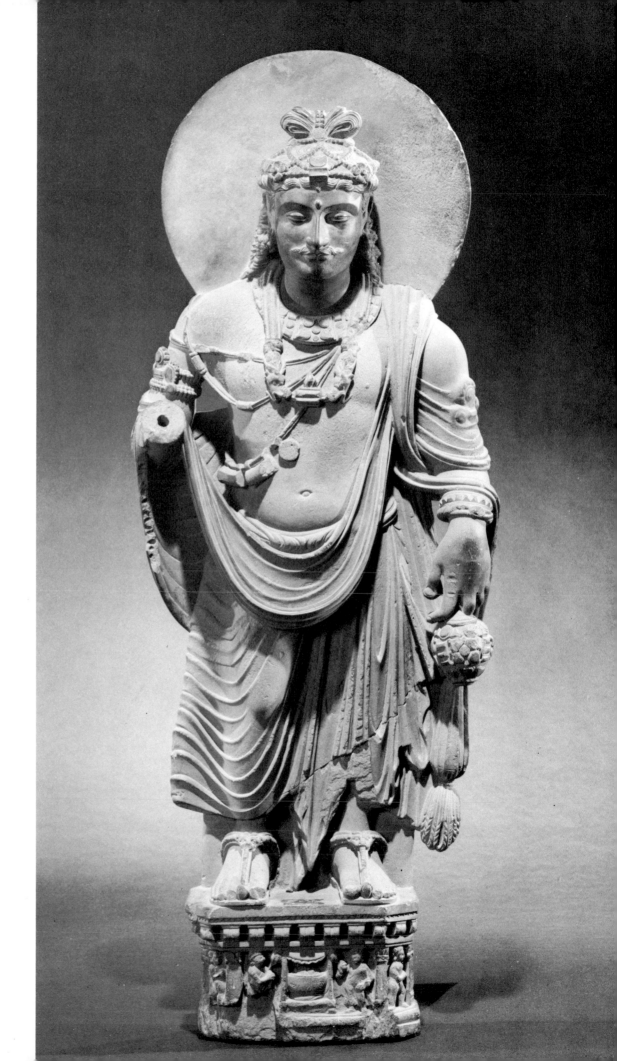

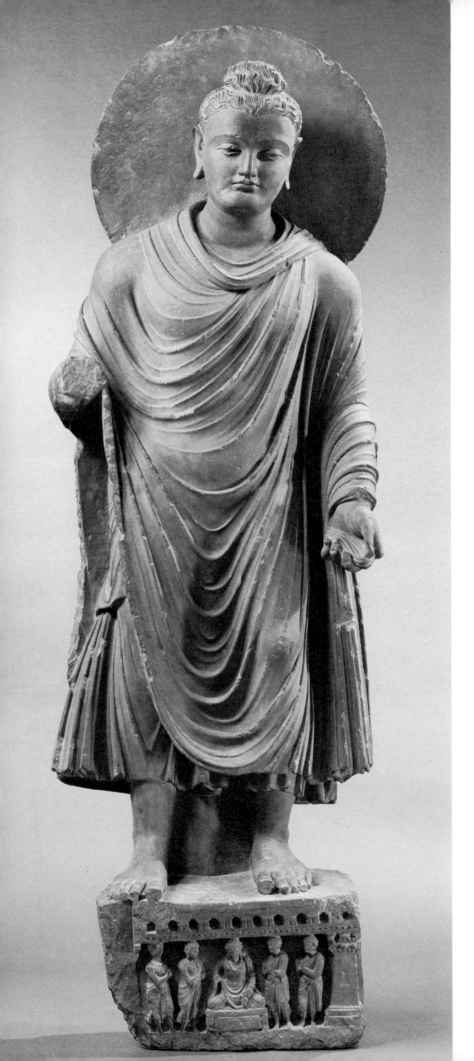

9. Buddha Śākyamuni

Pakistan, Mardan district (?)
3rd century
Gray schist
h: 61 in. (155.0 cm.)

In this classic Gandhāran-type statue, the Buddha is depicted as an ideal monk-teacher. His broken right hand must once have displayed the *abhayamudrā*; his left hand delicately grasps the end of his shawl. Three of his supernatural signs of greatness— the *urṇā* between the eyebrows, the elongated earlobes, and the *ushṇīsha*— are clearly delineated. Typical of the Gandhāran manner, the hair is indicated by wavy lines and the volume of the garments by heavy folds. The nimbus is plain and circular, but the base is decorated with a row of medallions and a sawtooth molding; at the sides only one of the Corinthian columns remains. Within the columns a bodhisattva in the meditation posture is worshiped by four figures, one of whom appears to be a monk, the others to be lay persons. The bodhisattva holds a waterpot in his left hand and may represent Maitreya, the future Buddha (see no. 8).

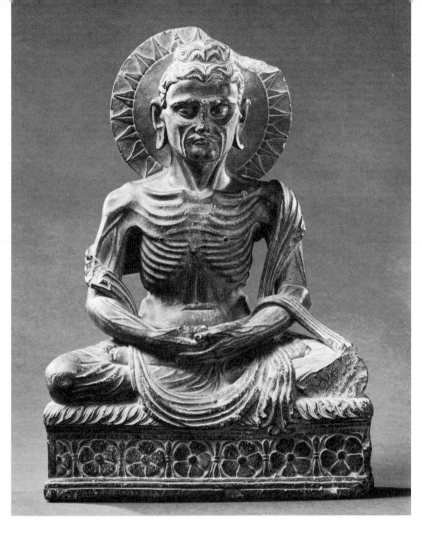

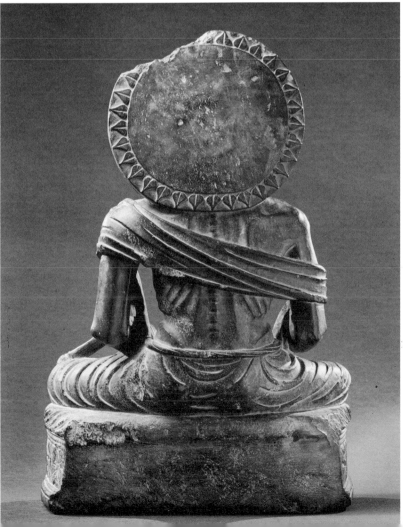

10. Emaciated Śākyamuni

Pakistan, Peshawar region
3rd century
Gray schist
h: 20½ in. (52.0 cm.)

In his *Buddhacharita* (*Life of the Buddha*), Aśvaghosha, a poet who probably lived in the first century A.D., writes:

For six years, vainly trying to attain merit, he practiced self-mortification, performing many rules of abstinence, hard for a man to carry out. . . . But the emaciation which was produced in his body by that asceticism became positive fatness through the splendour which invested him. . . . Having only skin and bone remaining, with his fat, flesh and blood entirely wasted, yet, though diminished, grandeur like the ocean. . . .

(F. Max Muller, ed., *Buddhist Mahâyâna Texts*, Delhi, 1965, p. 133.)

Descriptions like this inspired the artists of Gandhāra to create a number of sculptures depicting the emaciated Śākyamuni. Following the strong Hellenistic aesthetic tradition of the region, the representations are unusually realistic and the sculptors seem certainly to have been familiar with human anatomy. The nimbus is decorated with a motif that looks like pipal leaves. An almost identical motif adorns the nimbus behind the Buddha's head in the well-known Kaṇishka reliquary (Ingholt and Lyons, fig. 494), and that of a seated Buddha in the Brundage collection (ibid., pl. XI 3). The rosette along the base occurs on several sculptures from the Peshawar and Taxila regions (ibid., figs. 195, 292, 450), but most notably in a representation of Pañchika (ibid., fig. 339), which seems to be stylistically similar to the emaciated Śākyamuni.

11. The Great Farewell

Pakistan
3rd–4th century
Gray schist
h: 12⅝ in. (32.0 cm.)
w: 13¼ in. (33.6 cm.)

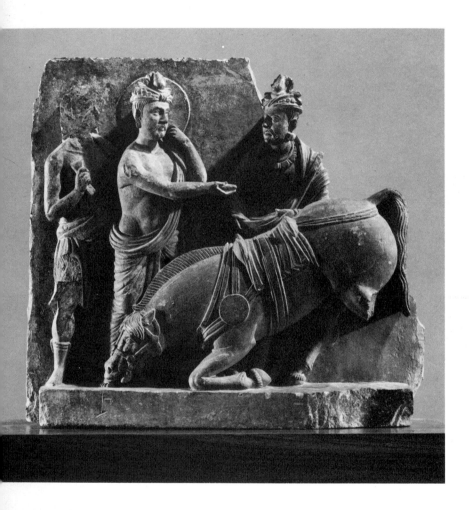

Although Śākyamuni's farewell to his loyal groom, Chandaka, and his horse, Kaṇṭhaka, is one of the most touching moments in the master's life, very few representations of the subject have survived. In this partially preserved relief, we see the nimbate figure of Śākyamuni extending his arm to hand over his jewels to Chandaka, who spreads out his shawl to receive them. Śākyamuni's torso is bare and behind him stands Vajrapāṇi, his divine guardian. The most arresting figure in the composition, however, is that of the horse, who kneels on his forelegs to touch his master's feet and thereby emphasizes the poignancy of the occasion. In the words of Aśvaghosha, on hearing Śākyamuni's farewell address, Kaṇṭhaka, "the noblest of steeds, licked his feet with his tongue and dropped hot tears." It is interesting to note that the inclusion of Vajrapāṇi, whose figure is modeled after the Greco-Roman Hercules in most reliefs portraying incidents from the life of the Buddha, is a peculiarity of Gandhāran sculptures and is not recorded in any known text. Noteworthy also is the fact that both Śākyamuni and his groom are given the same type of elaborate tiara.

12. The Death of the Buddha Śākyamun[

Pakistan
3rd century
Gray schist with remains of paint
h: 26 in. (66.0 cm.)
w: 26 in. (66.0 cm.)

This square high-relief slab shows the physical death of the Buddha Śākyamuni at Kusinara. Commonly, the death of the Buddha is known as *mahāpariṇirvāṇa*, since the incident took place long after his enlightenment at Bodhgaya where, in fact, he had already attained nirvana. In this relief, following the conventional formula, the fully clothed figure of the Buddha lies on a couch, his head and right hand resting on a pillow. The artist has not forgotten to add a halo behind the master's head. Among the grief-stricken companions, Vajrapāṇi is the bearded figure at the Buddha's feet and the meditating monk with his back toward the viewer is Subhadra, the last convert, whose water pouch is suspended from a tripod. The trees above, one of which is now broken, are meant to represent the forest of *śāla* trees where the Buddha died. A woman, probably representing a *yakshī* or the spirit of the tree, emerges from the surviving tree.

The *mahāpariṇirvāṇa* of the Buddha was a relatively popular theme with Gandhāran artists, but few steles are so well preserved or depict the occasion with such animation and pathos. Buddha's companions are visibly distraught and their grief is graphically expressed by the sculptor, not only through their facial expressions but also through the gestures and postures of their bodies. One pulls his hair, another hides his head, unable to watch the scene, a third lunges dramatically to his left, while a fourth seems to shrivel at the thought of losing his master forever. Such expressive representation of emotion is characteristic of the Gandhāran school and obviously reflects artistic norms quite different from those followed in most other parts of the subcontinent, where the depiction is far more idealized, tranquil, and without the dramatic tension evident in this relief.

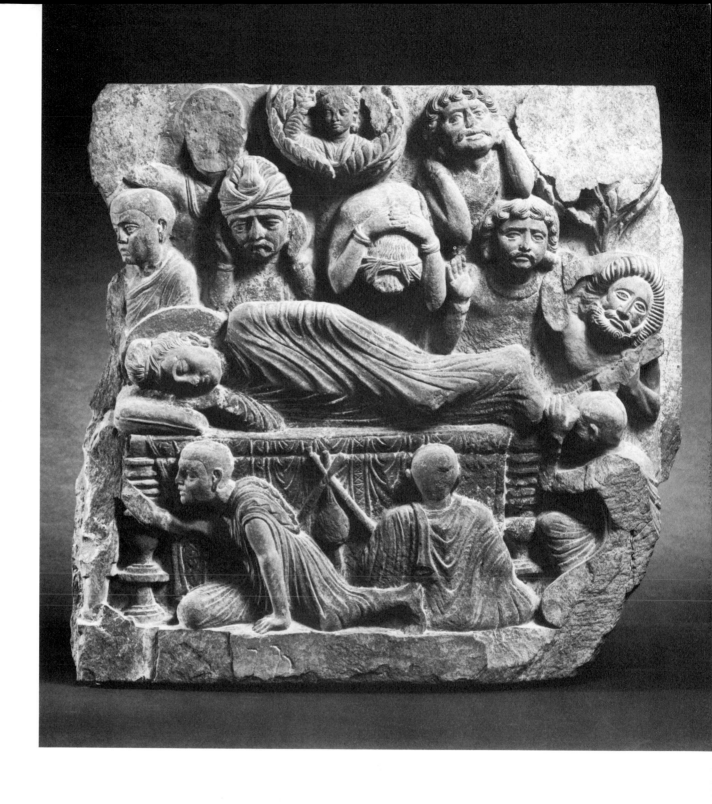

13. A Goddess

Uttar Pradesh, Mathura region
4th century
Spotted red sandstone
h: 41½ in. (105.4 cm.)

The goddess stands in the *samapada*
posture, holding the stem of a lotus in
her left hand and forming the
abhayamudrā with her right. But for
a heavy necklace, her torso is bare and
her skirtlike garment is adorned at the
hips with a chainlike girdle known in
Sanskrit as a *mekhalā*. The exact
identification of such female figures
when they are removed from their
context is difficult to determine, for
the lotus is a ubiquitous symbol and
can be held by several goddesses, such
as the Hindu Pārvatī and Śrī-Lakshmī
and the Buddhist Tārā.

A historically important sculpture, it probably belongs to the
transitional phase between the heroic,
ponderous style of the Kushān period
(A.D. 1–300) and the more graceful,
lyrical style of the Gupta period
(A.D. 300–600). The disposition of the
right hand, the heavy necklace, and
the chain girdle are seen more often in
Kushān sculpture, whereas the subtle
modeling, the fluent outline, and the
more idealized facial features are
characteristic of Gupta sculptures.

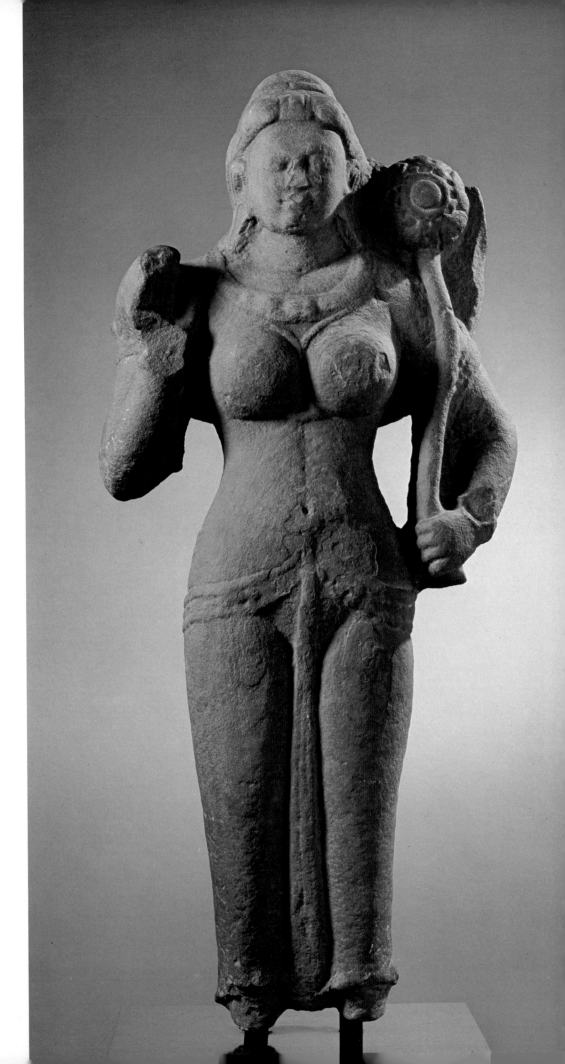

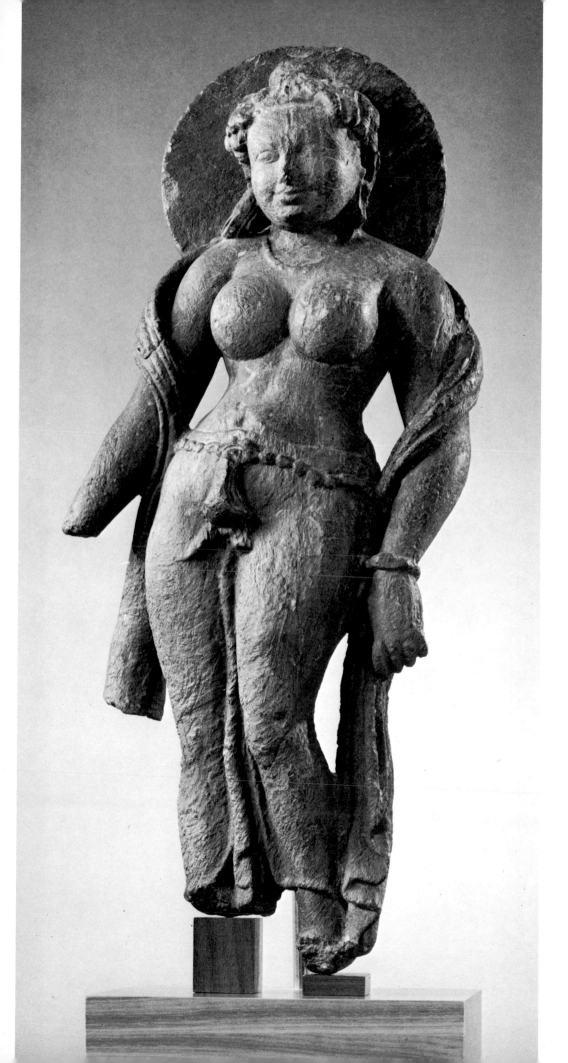

14. A Goddess

Rajasthan
Ca. 500
Gray schist
h: 24½ in. (62.2 cm.)

This nimbate goddess must once have
stood on a simple base, as do other
examples from a group of sculptures
found several years ago near the
village of Tanesara-Mahadev in
Rajasthan (see Agrawala, pl. XXII).
Most of those sculptures represent
unusual forms of mother goddesses
sporting with infants in a variety of
postures. Probably the right hand of
this figure also held a playful infant
tugging at her garment. Since the
male images found in the group
portray either Śiva or Kumāra, it is
possible that these mother and child
sculptures represent Pārvatī with the
infant Kumāra.

 The sculptures are stylistically
homogeneous and obviously were the
products of a single atelier. All are
characterized by a simple elegance and
spontaneity that certainly indicate a
date in the Gupta period. The movement of the figure is unselfconscious
and the form expresses a remarkable
natural grace. Other examples are in
the Los Angeles County Museum of
Art, the Cleveland Museum of Art, the
Allen Memorial Art Museum, and
The British Museum. For a more
recent discussion of the sculptures than
the article cited above, see Pal, 1971,
pp. 105ff.

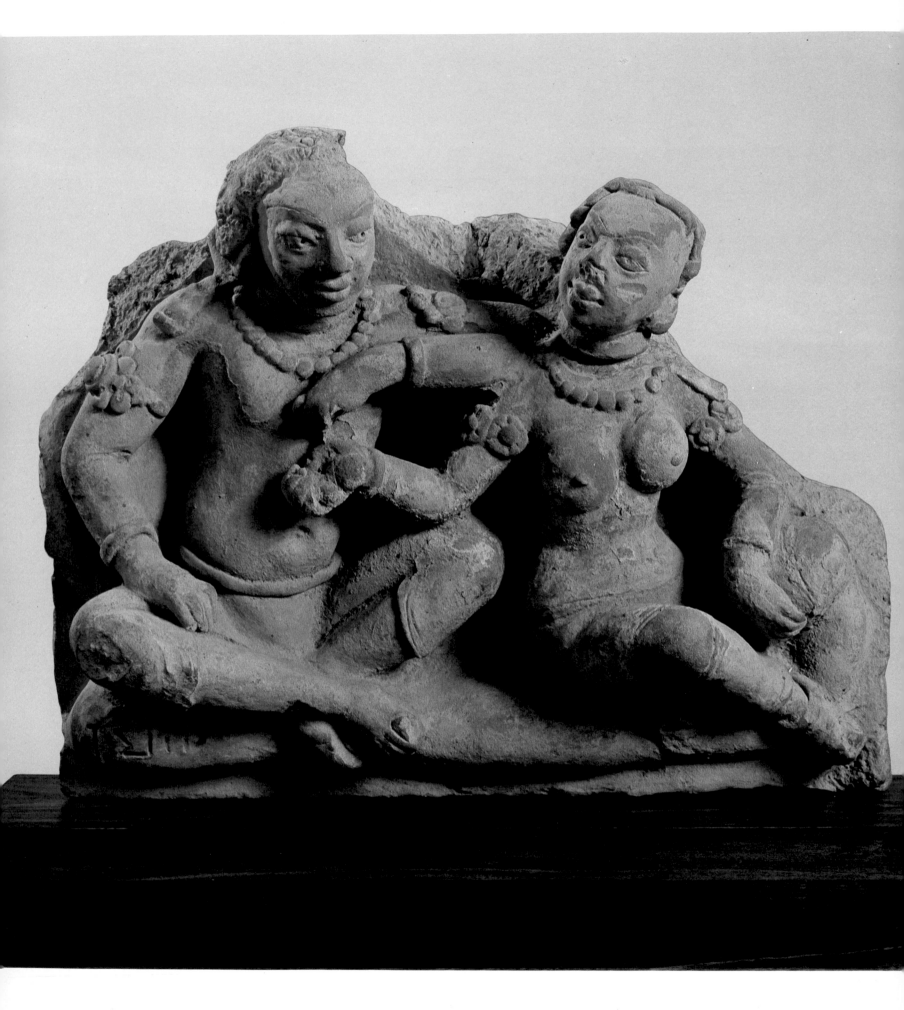

15. A Couple in Dalliance

Uttar Pradesh, Ahichchhatrā
5th century
Molded terra-cotta
h: 11⅜ in. (28.9 cm.)
w: 15 in. (38.1 cm.)

This molded terra-cotta plaque depicts a subject that has been represented in endless variations by Indian artists throughout the ages and can be considered the most popular theme in their repertoire. In this essentially human interpretation the artist shows a couple engrossed in tender intimacy. Both sit in the typical Indian fashion; the man rests his left elbow on her shoulder, while she seems to be offering him something edible, possibly a betel nut. The head of this female probably does not belong to the body.

Ahichchhatrā was a flourishing city into the early medieval period and had at least one important Saiva temple during the Gupta period; this plaque may have decorated that temple. The site was excavated in the 1940s and yielded innumerable terra-cotta sculptures and plaques which are now in the National Museum, New Delhi. The faces of the molded figures with high foreheads, wide staring eyes, and thick lips and noses are typical of Ahichchhatrā. The forms are modeled with remarkable economy, yet they are opulent and sensuous. A similar piece is in the Cleveland Museum of Art.

16. The God Sūrya

Uttar Pradesh
6th century
Buff sandstone, slightly polished
h: 45½ in. (115.5 cm.)

Although the worship of the sun god,
Sūrya, goes back to the Vedic age
(1500 B.C. and earlier), the earliest
known images of the god are only as
old as the second century B.C. The
image type represented in this
magnificent Gupta sculpture seems to
have been invented even later,
possibly no earlier than the Kushān
period (first–third century A.D.). The
god is portrayed in a strictly frontal
posture with his two hands holding
lotus flowers. He is clad in a long tunic
and his feet, now broken, once wore
shoes. This attire was borrowed from
the Scythians and other Central Asian
tribes such as the Kushāns, who had
established themselves in northwestern
India about the first century A.D.
There is a legend that a special form
of sun worship was introduced into
India at about this time by priests
immigrating from eastern Persia.
However, except for the costume, the
image shows no significant Persian
iconography. The sun god is accompanied by his two acolytes, Piṅgala and
Daṇḍi. Piṅgala, the slightly corpulent
figure on his right holding a tablet and
a writing implement, is the god's
scribe and keeps an account of man's
deeds. Daṇḍi, who holds a sword and a
shield, is the god's bodyguard.

Carved from the same stone as
the Sarasvatī (no. 17), this sculpture
is stylistically so similar to it that
clearly they once belonged to the
same temple. Despite Sūrya's hieratic
stance, his figure is as serenely elegant
as that of Sarasvatī. His acolytes are as
graceful as those in the other sculpture
and are modeled with a similar
emphasis on smooth, flowing volumes
defined by a taut outline. Especially
stylish is the manner in which the
sculptor has rendered Sūrya's scarf,
the ends merging with the nimbi to
create a gently undulating rhythmic
pattern that enhances the liveliness of
the composition.

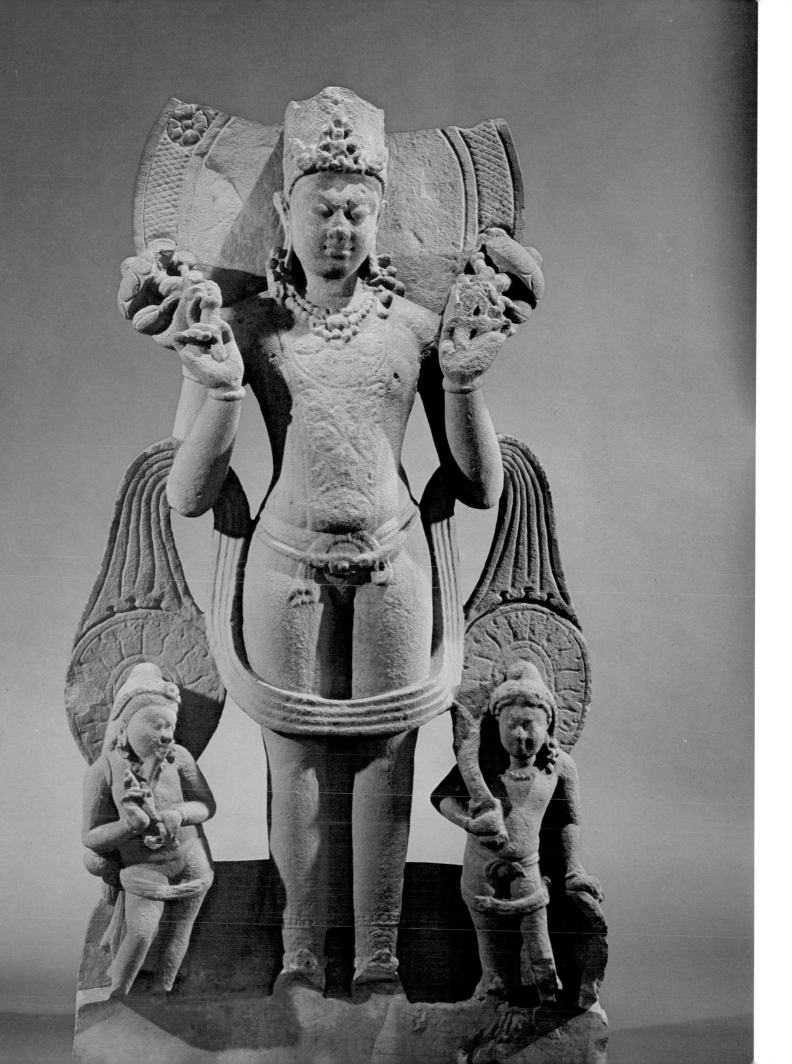

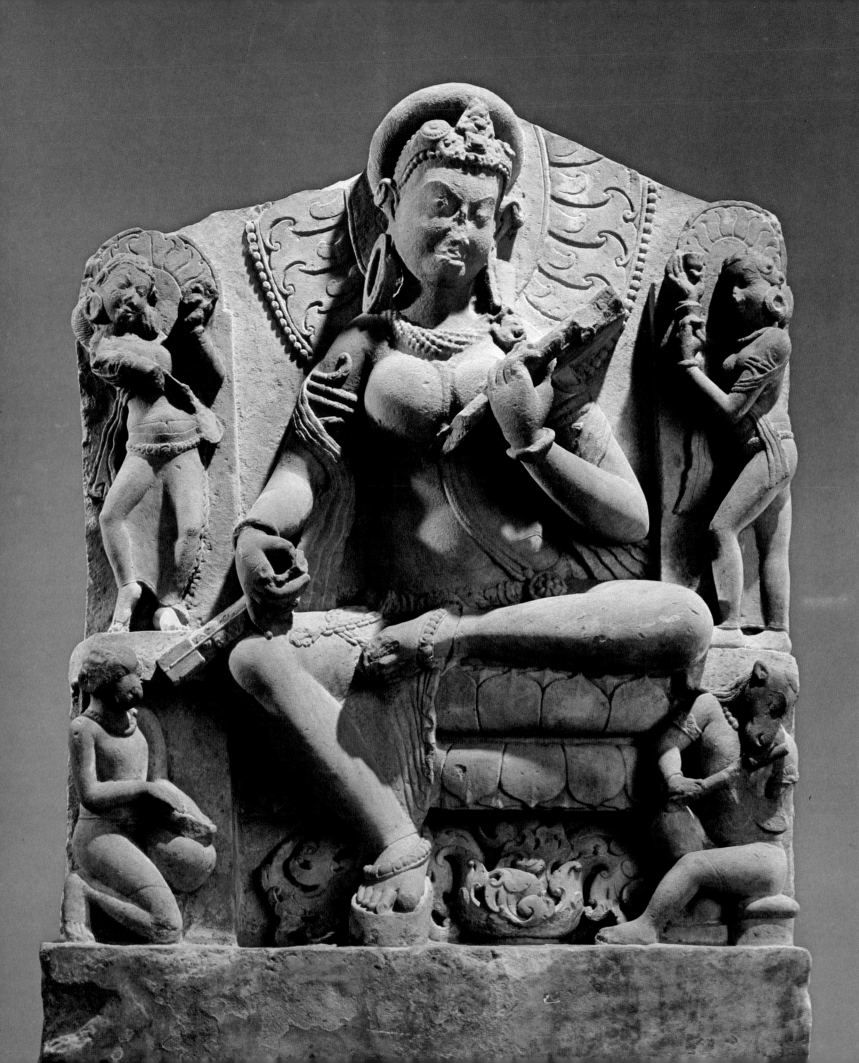

17. The Goddess Sarasvatī

Uttar Pradesh
6th century
Buff sandstone, slightly polished
h : 33 in. (83.8 cm.)

Sarasvatī is the goddess of both wisdom and music in the Hindu pantheon but is also revered by the Buddhists and the Jainas. Seated here in *lalitāsana* on a lotus, she plays the vina, accompanied by two musicians with animal heads. The one with the head of an ape is apparently playing a drum, while the figure with a horse's head plays the flute. These animal-headed musicians represent the *gandharvas*, a class of celestial beings who provide music in the realm of the gods. Above them are two females, one dancing and the other playing cymbals. The nimbi behind their heads indicate that they also are divine.

Not only is this a superb example of Gupta sculpture, but it is perhaps the finest representation of Sarasvatī known. Each figure is represented in a different posture, which makes the composition unusually lively, despite the strong emphasis on symmetry. The sculpture must have graced one of the principal subsidiary chapels of the same temple that housed the equally beautiful Sūrya (no. 16).

18. The Jaina Teacher Pārśvanātha

Uttar Pradesh
6th century
Sandstone with pink tinge
h: 44 in. (111.8 cm.)

Like Mahāvīra, Pārśvanātha was a
historical figure and is one of the most
important of the Jaina saints, known
also as Tīrthaṃkaras. He is believed to
have been born in 817 B.C. and to have
died almost a century later. Details of
his life, however, are enmeshed with
myths that are remarkably similar to
those about the Buddha Śākyamuni.
Like the latter, Pārśvanātha was a
prince, left his family and home at the
age of thirty, and became an
enlightened teacher. Images of
Pārśvanātha are distinguished by the
seven-hooded serpent that forms a
canopy above his head. In fact, he is
so closely associated with serpents that
there must be a historical basis for it,
although none is known. The story
is told that a serpent king, out of
gratitude for an earlier act of kindness,
once protected him from the sun
while the master meditated in the
kāyotsarga posture, as he does here.
The serpent king was none other than
Dharaṇa, who subsequently became
his male attendant. Here he appears
on the Tīrthaṃkara's left, fanning
him with a flywhisk. Each Jaina
Tīrthaṃkara has at least two companions, known as a *yaksha* and a
yakshiṇī. The *yakshiṇī* of Pārśvanātha
is Padmāvatī and she is the graceful
lady holding a parasol on the master's
right. The two kneeling figures presumably represent the donors of the
image.

Pārśvanātha's figure, particularly
his arms and the lower portion of his
body, is unusually elongated. The
extension of the arms is in keeping with
the description of a universal monarch,
whose arms are supposed to reach his
knees (*ājānulambita*). The treatment of
the serpent, whose coils form a cushion
behind the Tīrthaṃkara, seems unique
to this image, and the two attendants
are closely related in style to those of
Sūrya (no. 16). The face is very much
like that of a Sarnath Buddha except
for the prominently slanting eyes.

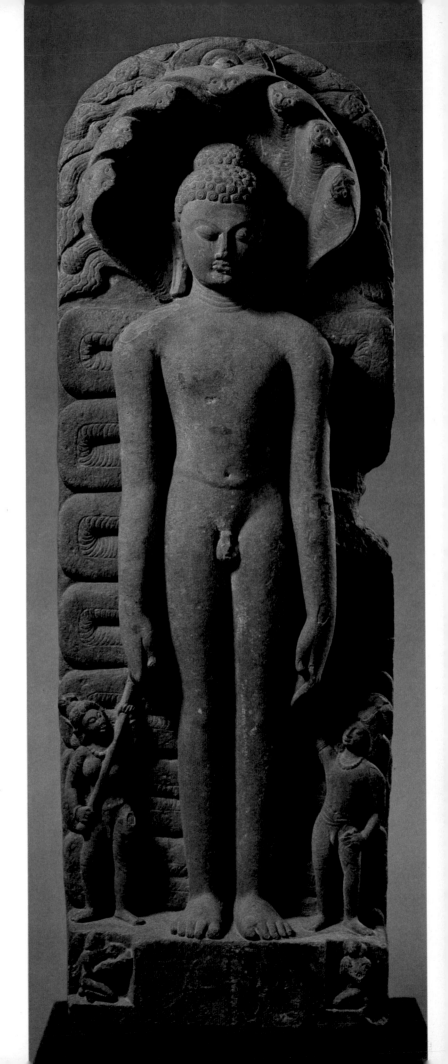

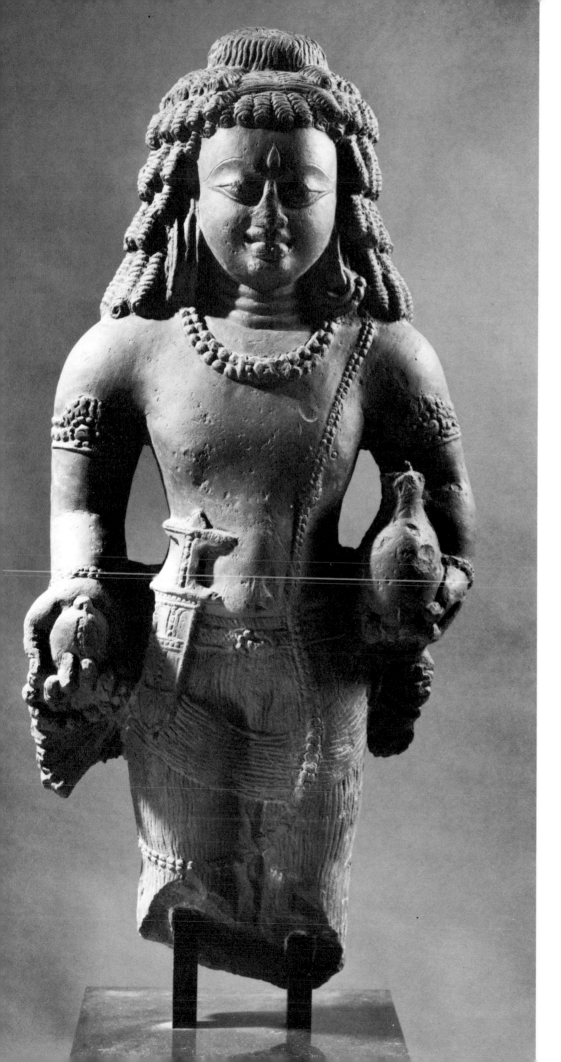

19. A Male Deity
Bihar
6th century
Black basalt
h: 30 in. (76.2 cm.)

This is possibly the most enigmatic figure in the collection. But for the emblems in his hands, he might well be an idealized portrait of a prince. He wears a dhoti, a sacred cord, and several ornaments, including two different kinds of earrings. The thin, wavy, vertical pleats of the dhoti and the sash are unusual, as is the inclusion of the dagger. The figure carries a fruit, possibly a pomegranate, and a waterpot. If the flame-shaped mark on his forehead were a third eye, he could easily be identified as Siva. The emblems are quite appropriate for the god and the dagger is given to at least one figure of Siva in The British Museum, which also has only two arms. There, however, the erect phallus and the third eye are quite clearly shown.

Even without an exact identification, this figure remains one of the most significant sculptures in the collection. It is certainly from Bihar and admirably reflects the local variation of the Gupta style. The shape and features of the face, the hair style like a judge's wig, and the sensuous though abstract modeling are typical characteristics of the Gupta tradition, but the massive shoulders, the heaviness of the form, and the disproportionately large hands seem to be local traits. The sculpture is closely comparable to the well-known Garudāsana Vishnu now in Cleveland (see Pal, 1972, pl. XXVII).

20. A Goddess, Probably Ambikā

Bihar, Sahabad district
6th century
Buff sandstone
h: 24¾ in. (62.9 cm.)

This nimbate goddess is seated in
lalitāsana on a lion. Her lower left hand
supports a male child whose head is
unfortunately lost; her upper left hand
is broken, but may originally have
held a weapon. Her lower right hand
holds a fruit, and the object in her
upper right hand appears to be a
bunch of fruit. If they are mangoes,
then the figure must be identified as
Ambikā, the Jaina *yakshī* associated
with the Tīrthaṁkara Nemiṇātha. In
that case, the weapon in the upper left
hand might have been an elephant
goad. However, the Hindu goddess
Durgā is also known as Ambikā,
especially in her maternal aspect, and
the lion is her mount as well. The
Jaina Ambikā's concept and form are
therefore closely related to those of
Durgā and Pārvatī.

Stylistically similar sculptures,
rendered in the same buff sandstone,
have been found in the Sahabad
district of Bihar and are now in the
Patna Museum and Bharat Kala
Bhavan, Banaras (see *Guide to the Patna
Museum*, Patna, 1955, p. 10 and pl. v;
A. Krishna, ed., *Chhavi*, Varanasī,
1971, fig. 343). Rendered with stylish
elegance, all these sculptures reveal
strong influences of the neighboring
Sarnath school. Despite their hierati-
cism, like most sculptures of the Gupta
period the figures seen here are endowed with consummate natural
grace, evident particularly in the
lively representation of the infant.

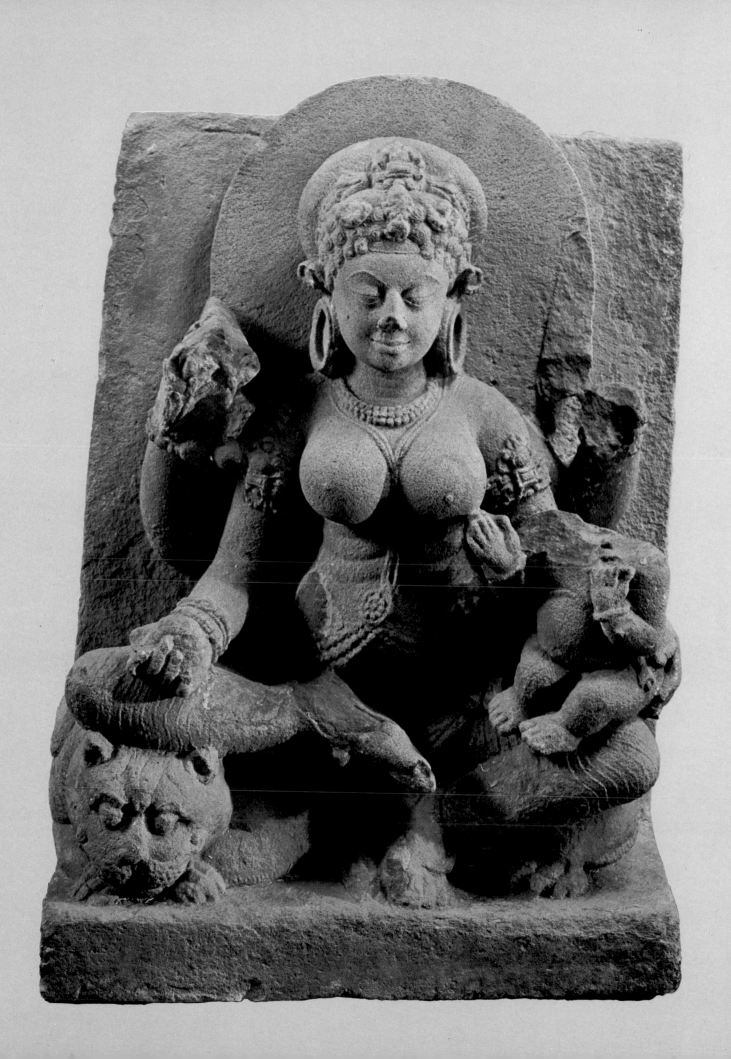

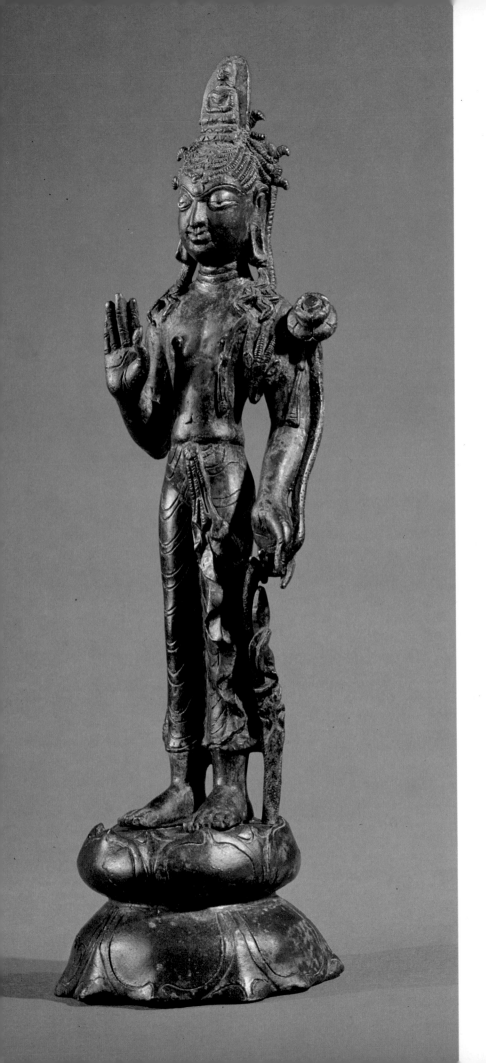

21. The Bodhisattva Padmapāṇi

Pakistan, Swat Valley (?)
6th century
Bronze with dark patina
h: 11½ in. (29.2 cm.)

The compassionate savior of the
Mahayana pantheon, Padmapāṇi
("lotus-bearer"), is represented here
in his simplest form, standing in
samapada on a lotus and grasping its
stem in his left hand. He wears a
simple dhoti, carries a buckskin over
his left shoulder, and displays the
effigy of his parental Tathāgata in
front of his tall chignon. The buckskin
and the chignon cast him in the role
of an ascetic like the Hindu gods
Brahma and Siva.

   Although the facial features are
related to both Kashmiri and Swat
Valley bronzes of the seventh and
eighth centuries, the metal is more
akin to bronzes of the Swat Valley
only. The proportions and modeling
of the figure, as well as the treatment
of the lotus, however, have very little
in common with bronzes from either
region. As I have suggested elsewhere
(see below), the paleographic peculiarities of the dedication inscribed on
the lotus base suggest a date in the
sixth or early seventh century. In my
opinion, the bronze was an attempt by
an artist of the Swat Valley to copy a
Gupta model from the Sarnath area.
The slim proportions and the soft,
almost abstract quality of the modeling, the treatment of the lotus, and the
pleats of the dhoti have their parallels
in fifth-century Sarnath sculptures
rather than in later sculptures.

Published: Pal, *Bronzes of Kashmir*,
1975, pp. 210–11.

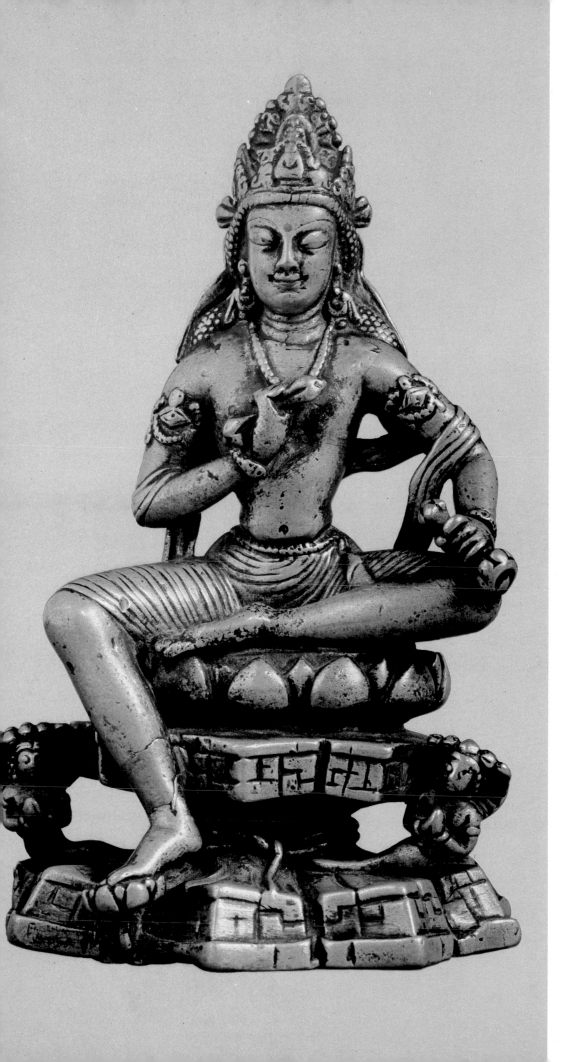

22. The God Vajrasattva

Kashmir
8th century
Brass with silver inlay
h: 6⅝ in. (16.9 cm.)

This elegantly crowned and coiffured Vajrasattva, one of the most important divinities of the Vajrayana Buddhist pantheon, is seated in *lalitāsana* on a lotus supported by a lively mountain-shaped pedestal. A pair of *nāgas* are engaged in adoring Vajrasattva, their serpentine tails squeezing the rock formations into a narrow stem. The mountains represent Mt. Sumeru, the home of Vajrasattva. Since Sumeru is also considered to be the *axis mundi* in Indian cosmogony, we can surmise how eminent a deity Vajrasattva is; his importance is further emphasized by the inclusion of all five Tathāgatas in his crown. His emblems are the thunderbolt and the bell, which are two of the most essential implements in Vajrayana ritual.

Intricately designed bronzes were also made in other parts of India, for instance in Kerala (see no. 89) after the fifteenth century, but nowhere with as much finesse and subtlety of imagination as in medieval Kashmir. This serenely majestic figure of Vajrasattva contrasts with the jagged and contorted rocks below him, providing a superb example of both the inventiveness and the technical virtuosity of the unknown Kashmiri sculptors.

Published: Chow, no. 2; Pal, *Bronzes of Kashmir*, 1975, pp. 162–63.

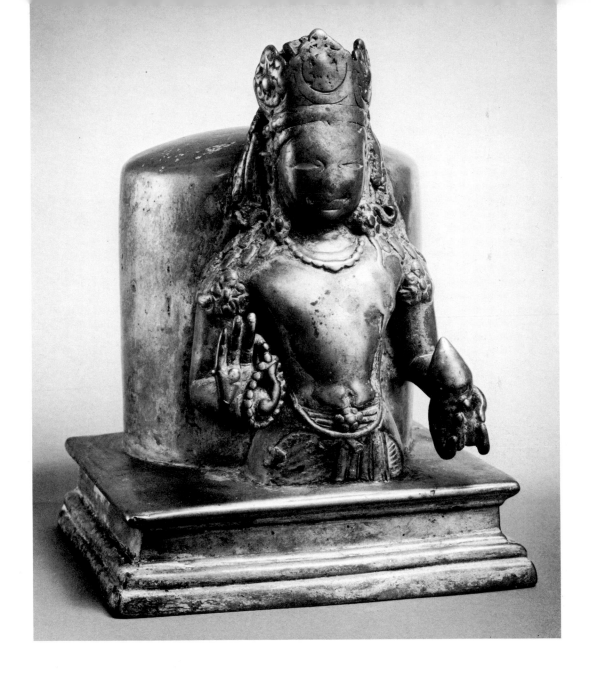

23. Ekamukhaliṅga (Phallus with One Face)

Kashmir
8th–9th century
Brass with silver and copper inlay
h: 13½ in. (34.3 cm.)

The phallic emblem of Siva is known as a *linga* and those with faces or busts attached to them are called *mukhaliṅga*. Although the linga is the most popular votive object of the Saivas, examples in metal are not very common. Rising from a simple rectangular base, this linga is shaped more like a pillar than a naturalistic phallus. The bust representing Siva has impressive proportions and majestic bearing. A tigerskin is draped over his dhoti and snakes adorn his locks, which fall in curled ringlets down both shoulders, a hair style that was popular in the earlier Gupta period. His right hand holds a rosary as it forms the *vyākhyāṇamudrā*, and his left a citrus fruit that symbolizes the seeds of the universe. The latter is a symbol of fertility, the former of asceticism.

Apart from their dull golden color, Kashmiri bronzes are also distinguished by frequent use of silver inlays in the eyes and copper inlays in the lips and garments. Siva's eyes here are inlaid with silver, while faint traces of copper still remain on the lips.

Published: Pal, *Bronzes of Kashmir*, 1975, pp. 58–59.

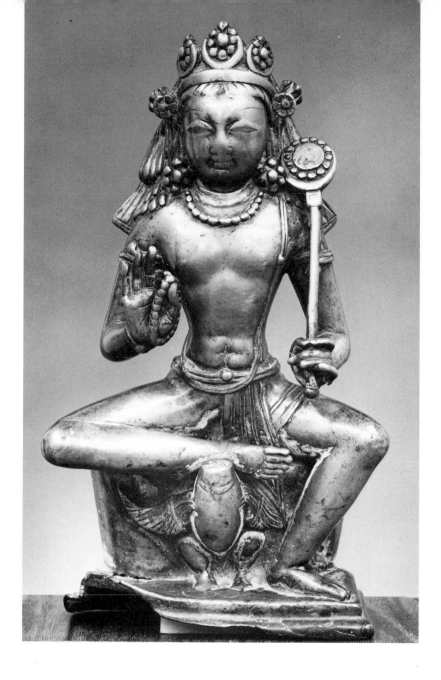

4. Kumāra, the Hindu War God

Kashmir
9th century
Brass with silver inlay
h: 10⅝ in. (27.0 cm.)

The son of Śiva and Pārvatī, Kumāra (the young prince) is also known by other names such as Skanda and Kārttikeya. He seems originally to have been a protector of children, but became the divine commander after his adoption into the Hindu pantheon. His martial aspect is emphasized by the spear, which is given a rather unusual form in this bronze. Instead of the usual pointed tip, the stem is surmounted by a motif that seems to combine both the solar and the lunar symbols, which are usually held by his father in certain Kashmiri (see no. 30) and Central Asian images. Also like his father (see no. 23), Kumāra holds the rosary in his right hand as it forms the *vyākhyāṇamudrā*. Although unusual, this is not inconsistent with Kumāra's multifarious aspects, for in later Hindu mythology he came to be regarded as the great teacher of the scriptures as well. He is seated here in *lalitāsana* and against the plain seat is the effigy of his mount, the peacock, whose head is unfortunately broken.

Stylistically, the bronze is remarkably close to the Ekamukhaliṅga (no. 23) in modeling as well as in salient details. The hair style, the pleats of the dhoti, the treatment of the right hand, and the shape and features of the face are so similar that the two bronzes must be regarded as works of the same atelier, if not of the same artist. The eyes here also are inlaid with silver.

Published: Chow, no. 4; Pal, *Bronzes of Kashmir*, 1975, pp. 84–85.

25. The God Vāsudeva

Kashmir
9th century
Brass with silver inlay
h: 11⅜ in. (29.0 cm.)

Vishnu is known as Vāsudeva when he is depicted as the supreme (*para*) deity, as in this bronze, which represents a classic image of the god that was very popular in medieval Kashmir. He is appropriately attired and ornamented, with a garland of wild flowers (*vanamālā*) that stretches almost down to his ankles. Apart from the emblems in his hands, Vishnu can be recognized by this garland as well as by the diamond-shaped symbol on his chest. This symbol, known as *śrīvatsa*, indicates the constant presence of his consort Śrī on his person. One of his right hands still holds a lotus stem, and his corresponding left hand supports a conch shell. His other two hands rest on the nimbi of his attendants. The female, known as Gadānārī, is the personification of the mace (*gadā*), and the male, known as Chakrapurusha, is the personification of the wheel (*chakra*). Gadānārī holds the mace in her right hand, while her left hand touches her face; Chakrapurusha fans Vishnu with a flywhisk, and his left hand is placed against his thigh. Both look up at Vishnu, as does the earth goddess between his feet. The spout on the rectangular pedestal of this bronze was used to drain liquids that were poured over the image when it was ceremonially bathed during worship.

Kashmir was one of the few medieval schools of art that continued to represent Vishnu's attributes in personified forms, a practice that had been more common during the earlier Gupta period. Curiously, the Pan-Asian collection includes a rare Vishnu from Bihar (no. 51), in which we also see Gadānārī and Chakrapurusha, though their positions are reversed.

Published: Chow, no. 6; Pal, *Bronzes of Kashmir*, 1975, pp. 68–69.

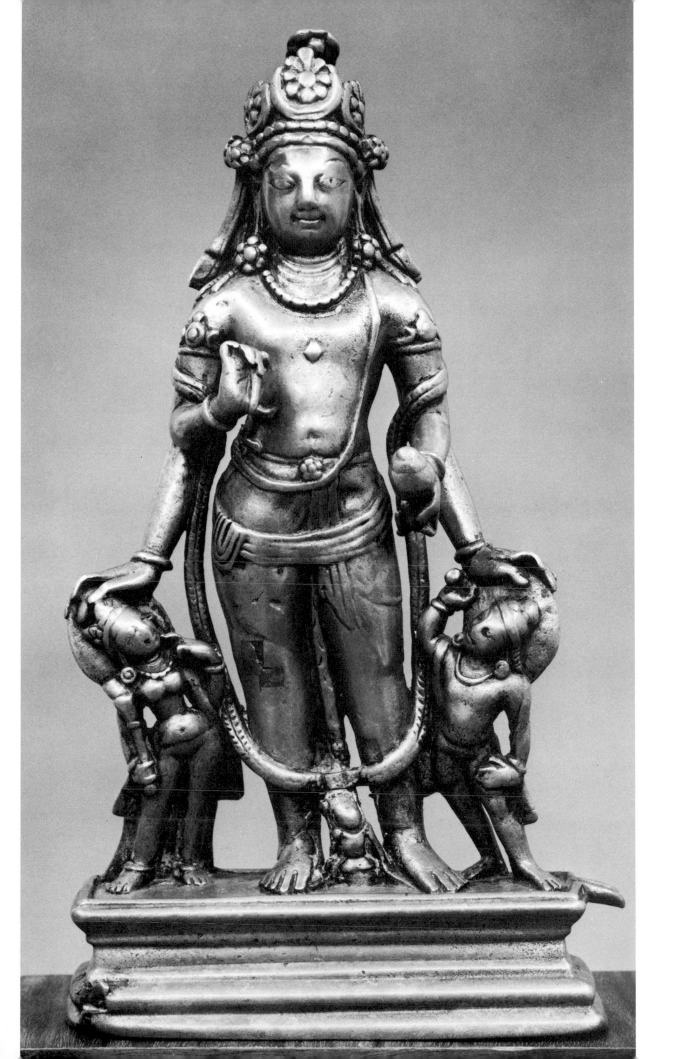

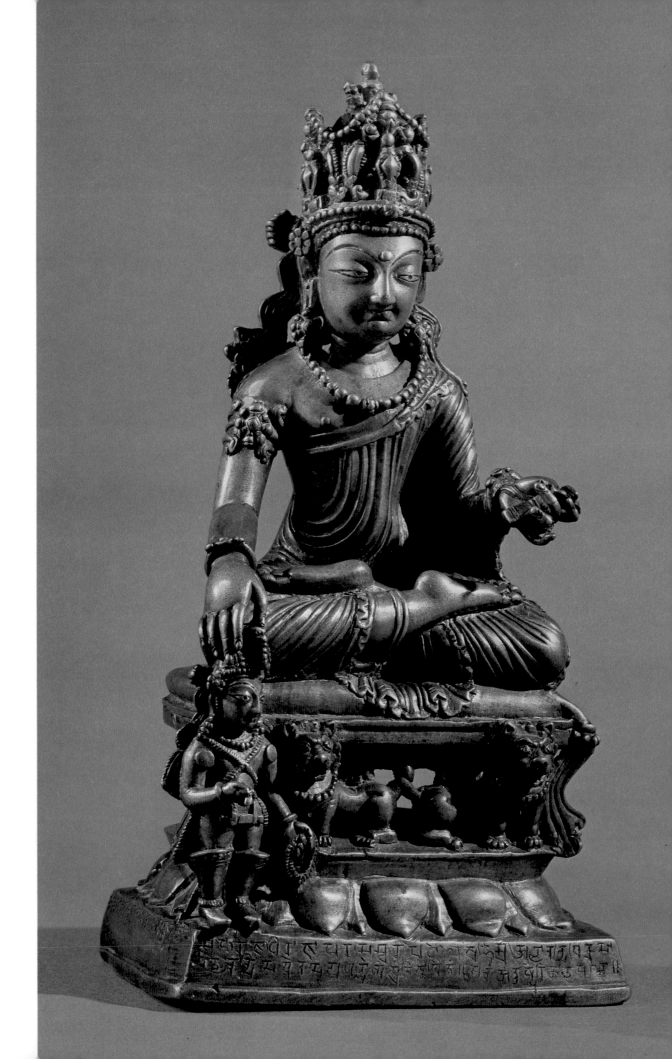

26. Buddha Śākyamuni

Kashmir
9th century
Brass with silver inlay
h: 11⅜ in. (29.9 cm.)

But for his monk's robes, one would be hard pressed to identify this figure as that of Buddha Śākyamuni. The elaborate crown and ornaments are intended to proclaim his spiritual majesty, for as he himself once declared: "A king am I, Sella, the king of righteousness." He is seated in the yogic posture on a throne composed of rather whimsical lions, each shown part frontally and part in profile, with their tails interlocked. Śākyamuni's left hand holds a manuscript as it gathers up the end of his robe; his right is placed on the head of a princely figure, presumably the donor of the bronze.

According to the inscription on the base, the bronze was dedicated in the year six of an unspecified era by Nandi Vikramāditya, who is styled as the king of kings (*mahārājādhirāja*) and as *parameśvara*, a term generally used by monarchs devoted to Siva. At any rate, the standing figure must represent King Nandi Vikramāditya, although no king by that name is known in Kashmiri history, which is fairly well documented. He might have belonged to the family of Surendra Vikramāditya, who is known to have ruled in the Gilgit area, now part of Pakistan. Nandi Vikramāditya is dressed in the Scythian mode, which was favored by the Shāhis and other rulers of Central Asian origin. His crown displays a lion disgorging pearls, and his left hand holds a wreath of a kind seen frequently in the hands of Sassanian monarchs of Persia.

Published: Pal, *Bronzes of Kashmir*, 1975, pp. 108–9.

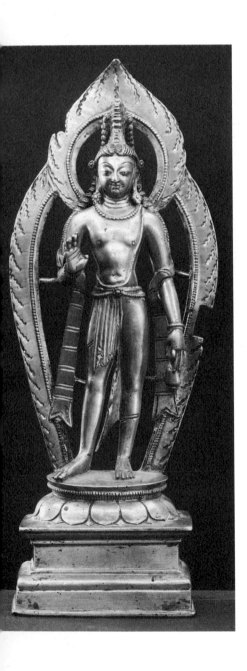

27. The Bodhisattva Maitreya
Kashmir
10th century
Brass
h: 15 in. (38.1 cm.)

Beautifully framed by a flaming nimbus and aureole, Maitreya stands gracefully on a lotus-topped pedestal. Clad in a dhoti, he is elegantly adorned with strings of pearls. His hair is arranged in a tall chignon crowned by a tiny stupa, which is his distinctive emblem. A scarf drapes his shoulders and hangs down both legs. His right hand is raised in *abhaya-mudrā*, his left carries a pot containing the elixir of immortality. It is predicted that Maitreya, the future Buddha, will be born in a brahman family, hence the sacred cord around his chest.

All the typical characteristics of Kashmiri sculpture appear in this elegantly simple bronze. The plain artichoke-shaped lotus petals and the oval aureole decorated with pearl and flame motifs are quite distinctive of Kashmiri bronzes. Also characteristic are the shape and features of the face, as well as the subtle though fleshy modeling with some attempt made to indicate the muscles of the body.

Published: Munsterberg, 1972, p. 30; Pal, *Bronzes of Kashmir*, 1975, pp. 128–29.

28. Siva and Pārvatī
Kashmir
11th century
Dark gray schist
h: 21¼ in. (54.0 cm.)

This composition showing Pārvatī and a three-headed Siva standing side by side in a single stele was a favorite with Kashmiri artists. Both stand in slight *tribhaṅga*, accompanied by their two sons, Gaṇeśa and Kārttikeya, and by Siva's bull, Nandi, whose head is carved near his master's right thigh. A tigerskin is wrapped around Siva's thighs and his erect phallus is decorously covered by his dhoti. Each of his three faces is different, but all have the third eye. The central face is placid, that on the right is awesome, and the one on the left is female. Thus, in the same image both his creative and destructive aspects are emphasized. He carries his emblems—the trident, the lemon, and the waterpot—and one of his right hands forms the *varadamudrā* with the palm facing the body, a mode that is typical of Kashmiri sculptures. Pārvatī's right hand forms the same gesture and her left hand holds a mirror. More interesting is her costume, consisting of a tight-fitting jacket and a long skirt that overflows her feet. This Central Asian mode of dress was popular in Kashmir and the northwest and is a peculiarity of Kashmiri goddess images.

It is interesting to note that the sculptor has not distinguished the two deities in terms of their size and proportions; generally, the female is much smaller than the male. Also, the figures are somewhat squat, as sculptures of the tenth century or later often are.

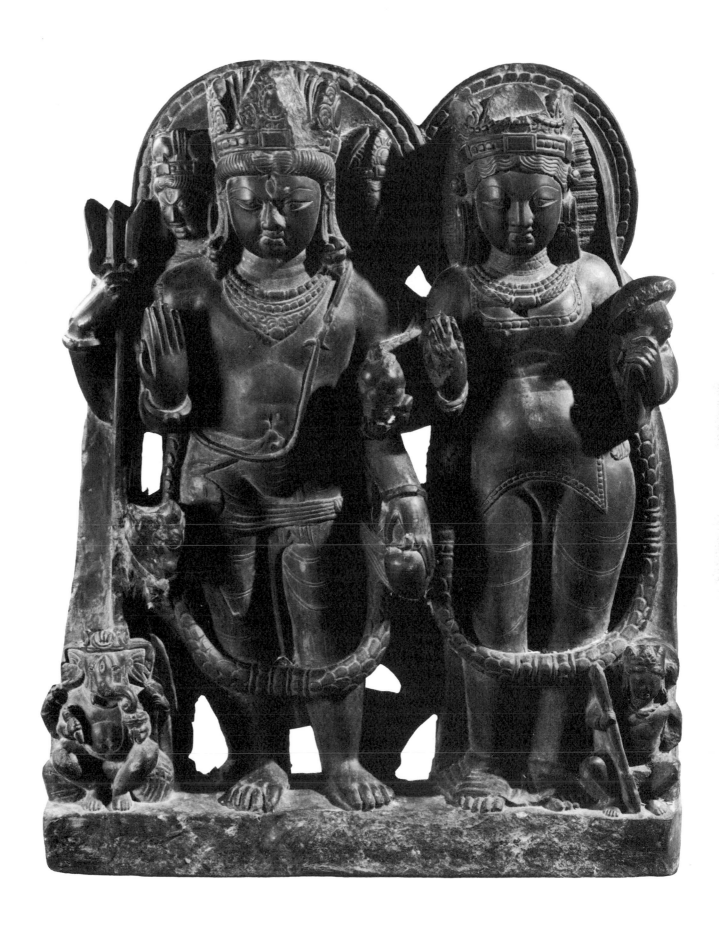

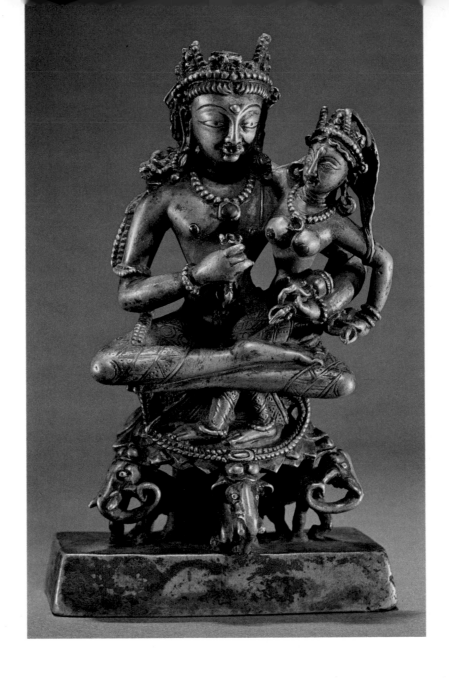

29. Vajrasattva and Consort

Kashmir
11th century
Brass with silver and semiprecious stone inlay
h: 5⅝ in. (14.3 cm.)

In this sculpture Vajrasattva is seated in the yogic posture on a multi-tiered lotus supported by three elephants. His damaged crown is embellished with effigies of all five Tathāgatas and his ornaments are mostly of pearls, although the pendant of his necklace is inset with a semiprecious stone. His right hand holds a thunderbolt against his chest and his left both grasps a bell and supports his consort. Perched on his left thigh, she holds the same emblems as Vajrasattva and is similarly crowned and ornamented, although he has an additional garland and she is given a scarf that forms a nimbus behind her head. The textile designs are vividly rendered in both figures.

It is noteworthy that no mountains have been delineated here (see no. 22), although the elephants may be intended to symbolize the cardinal directions and thereby emphasize the god's omnipresence. Rather unusual is the position of the goddess's legs, circled by those of her consort. Her form is particularly related to goddesses seen in paintings from western Tibet, where much of the art was influenced by the Kashmiri tradition.

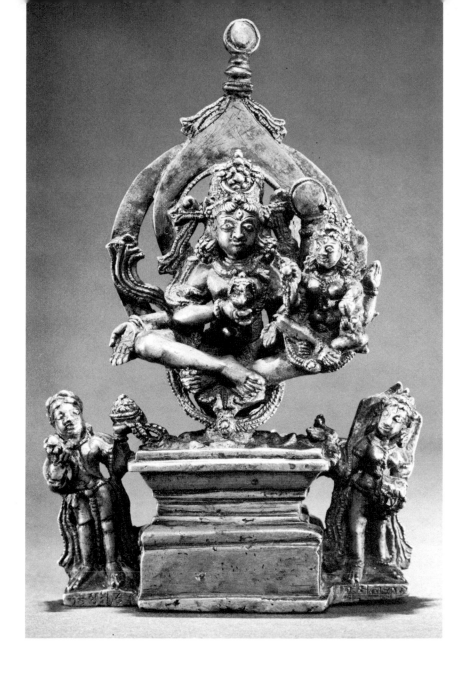

Umā-Maheśvara
Kashmiri style
11th century
Bronze with silver inlay
h : 6⅜ in. (16.2 cm.)

A comparison with several other Umā-Maheśvara images (see nos. 83, 100) reveals how the same basic theme was distinctly represented in different regions of the subcontinent. These differences are not merely limited to style, but also affected iconography. In this bronze, although Umā is in her traditional position on her husband's left thigh, both are seated rather unusually with their legs crossed at the ankles. Śiva's right hands form the *varadamudrā* and hold a pot, while one of his left hands prominently displays a disc that is probably a solar symbol. His second left hand supports his wife, who also is given four arms, two forming the *varadamudrā* and the *abhayamudrā*, the others holding a lotus and a pot. The fact that both figures hold waterpots and sit with their legs crossed indicates that they are engaged in some yogic ritual, and Śiva may here be portrayed as Kumbheśvara, or Lord of the Waterpot.

Equally interesting are the two figures who stand on either side of the high pedestal. They have brought food and floral offerings to the deities and must represent the donors. Their names are not clearly discernible in the inscription, but their clothing indicates that they must portray a Shāhi chief and his consort. The bronze may therefore have been made in one of the Hindu Shāhi kingdoms, either in Panjab or Afghanistan, but its style is unmistakably Kashmiri.

Published : Pal, *Bronzes of Kashmir*, 1975, pp. 60–61.

31. The Goddess Destroying Mahishāsura

Himachal Pradesh
9th–10th century
Gray schist
h : 30 in. (76.2 cm.)

The story goes that after Mahishāsura, the chief of the *asuras* ("anti-heroes"), had vanquished the gods, they created a goddess out of their combined energy and equipped her with all their weapons to destroy the *asuras*. This goddess was called Chaṇḍikā or Ambikā and after a prolonged battle she killed Mahishāsura and came to be known as Mahishāsuramardinī. Also known as Durgā, she is worshiped all over India, with the most celebrated festival in her honor held in Bengal each fall.

In this unusually animated sculpture, modeled almost in the round, we see the radiantly youthful goddess plunging a dagger into the belly of Mahishāsura, who is emerging from a decapitated buffalo (*mahisha*). Toward the end of the battle, the *asura* had desperately disguised himself as a buffalo in order to mislead the goddess, who saw through his trick. Her left leg holds the buffalo in place as her left hand seems to drag Mahishāsura out. The goddess's two normal arms are intact, but her other arms are broken, as are her right leg, part of her left foot, and the entire lower portion of the sculpture. Her face is severely mutilated and Mahishāsura's is completely destroyed. Perhaps because we see only two arms the struggle appears to be between two equals and this human scale imparts dramatic intensity to the entire composition. While the expression of physical energy is restrained, as is always the case with Indian sculpture, we are nonetheless made aware of a condensed vitality, not only in the complex intertwining of the figures, but also in the overall rhythmic pattern of the composition.

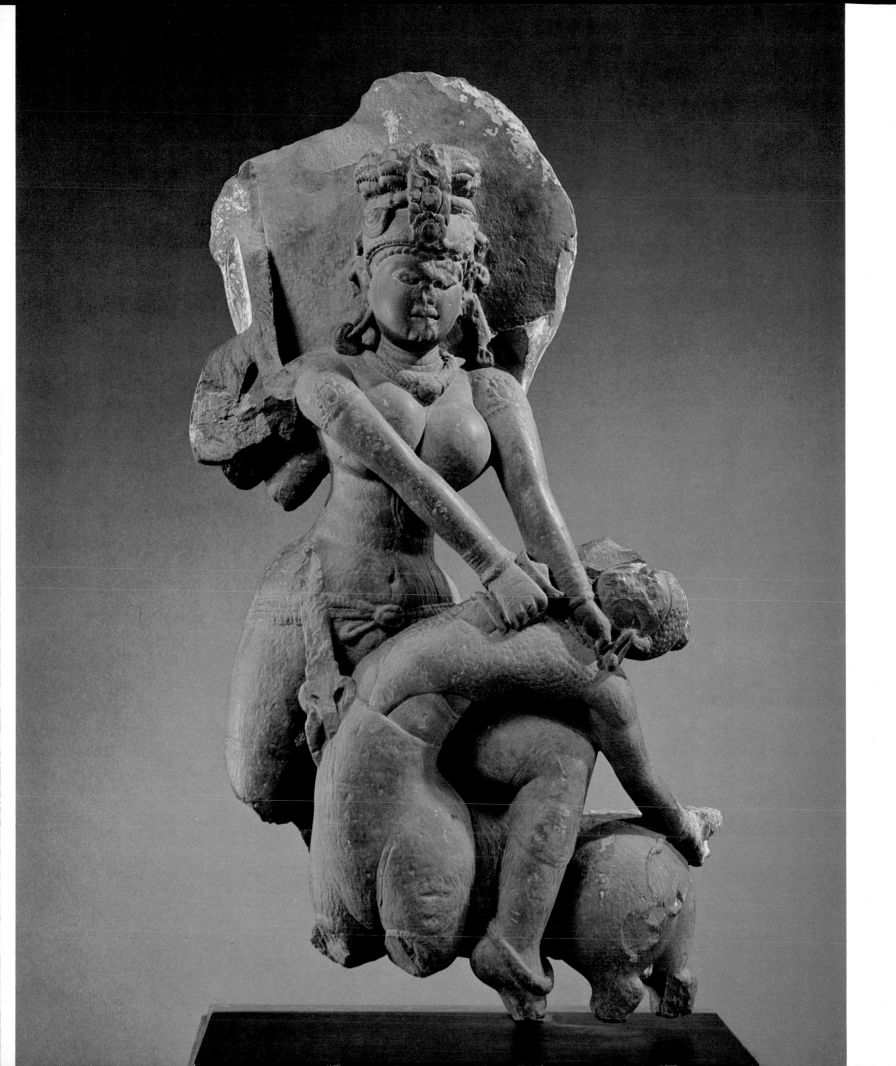

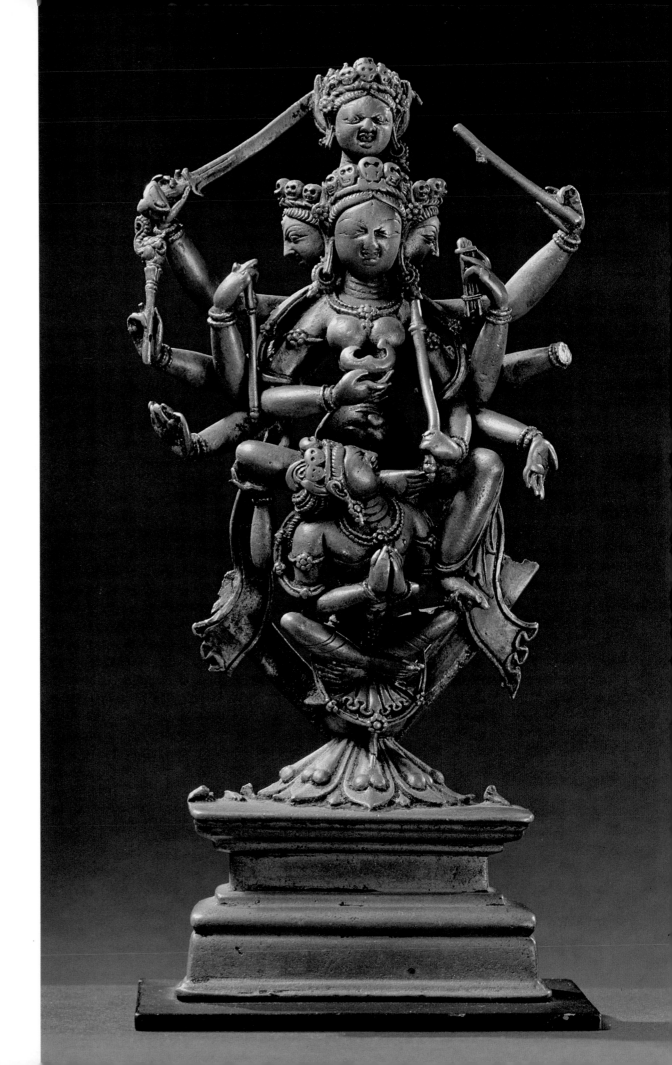

32. The Goddess Mahābhairavī

Panjab or Himachal Pradesh
11th century
Brass
h: 8¾ in. (22.2 cm.)

A goddess with ten arms and four
heads is seated on a male with four
arms, who sits with his legs crossed
at the ankles on a lotus. Like those of
the goddess, his head is adorned with
a tiara of skulls. His face is turned
toward the goddess and his forehead
bears the third eye. Two of his hands
form the *añjalīmudrā* and the other two
support the goddess. One of her four
faces is awesome, but the others are
benign and attractive. Her emblems
include a sword, a battle-ax, a skull
cup held below her breasts, and a
manuscript. Some of her other
weapons are unfortunately broken,
and only the feet of two attendant
figures remain attached to the top of
the rectangular pedestal.

As I have discussed elsewhere (see
below), this goddess represents one of
the eight forms of Mahābhairavī,
who are manifestations of Durgā and
consorts of the corresponding eight
Bhairavas, the angry aspects of Siva.
What is curious, however, is that here
one of the Bhairavas acts as a mount
for the goddess, thereby clearly
indicating her superiority. A similar
but more ornate bronze representing
the same goddess is in the National
Museum, New Delhi, also discussed
in the reference cited below. The
National Museum bronze was
recovered from the Kangra Valley in
the Panjab Himalayas and it may
have been crafted locally or in the
neighboring region of Chamba, which
has an ancient tradition of bronze
casting. The present example may also
be a product of a Chamba atelier.

Published: Pal, *Bronzes of Kashmir*,
1975, pp. 226–27.

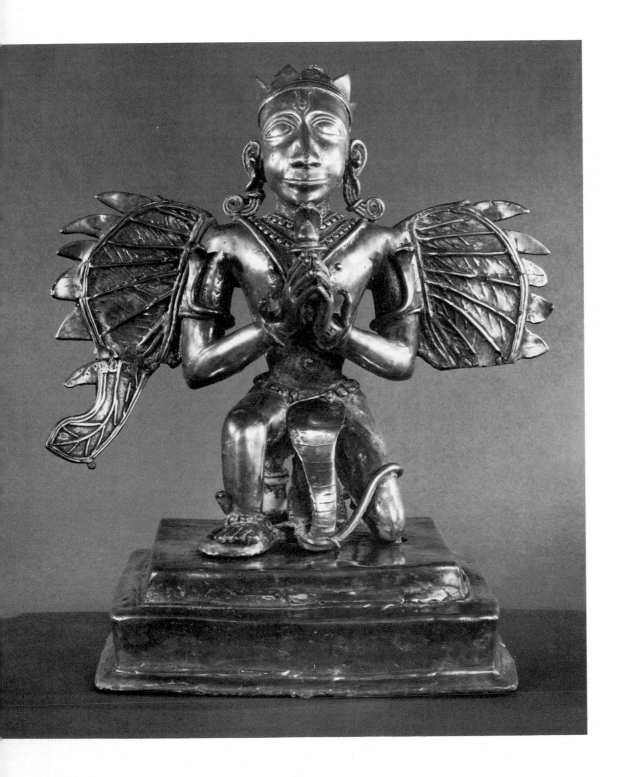

3. Garuḍa
Himachal Pradesh
16th–17th century
Brass
h: 21½ in. (54.6 cm.)

The mythical bird Garuḍa has a long
ancestry in Indian mythology and was
originally conceived as a sun bird.
Because of Vishnu's early career as a
solar deity in Vedic mythology, he
came to inherit Garuḍa as his mount.
Garuḍa is also an avowed enemy of
snakes—trampling some here and
wearing others as ornaments. Because
he is a creature of fantasy, Garuḍa had
particular appeal for the artists in all
of Indian Asia (see nos. 104, 152) and
the countless varieties of his images
reflect the unlimited possibilities of the
human imagination.

In this impressively large sculpture, Garuḍa kneels triumphantly
over a cobra that raises its hood
menacingly. At the same time, his
posture and the gesture of his hands
announce his humility and devotion to
his master, whose image he must
originally have faced. Unusually, he
holds the aniconic emblem of Vishnu
(śālagrāma), which is sheltered by
another serpent. Except for the wings
attached to his arms, Garuḍa here has
been conceived essentially as a human
being. The bronze is probably from
the Chamba region, which continued
to be an important center for bronze
casting during this period.

4. Simha-vyāla
Uttar Pradesh
8th century or earlier
Beige sandstone
h: 29½ in. (74.9 cm.)

In Sanskrit, *vyāla* is a generic term
meaning a beast of prey or vicious
animal. In reference to Indian art, the
word is applied to a leonine animal
that is usually shown rampant and
may have the head of a lion (*simha*), as
here, or of any other animal, bird, or
fish. Although a recurrent motif in
Indian art—it frequently appears on
the sides of a throne (see nos. 52, 53)—
the symbolic significance of the *vyāla*
remains unexplained. Sometimes a
simha-vyāla may attack an elephant
or trample a warrior, but at other
times it is attacked by a man with a
sword, as in the present example. The
animal seems to completely dwarf the
man as it turns violently to shake him
off. Worked almost in the round, this
sculpture achieves a harmonious
balance between supple form and
linear rhythm.

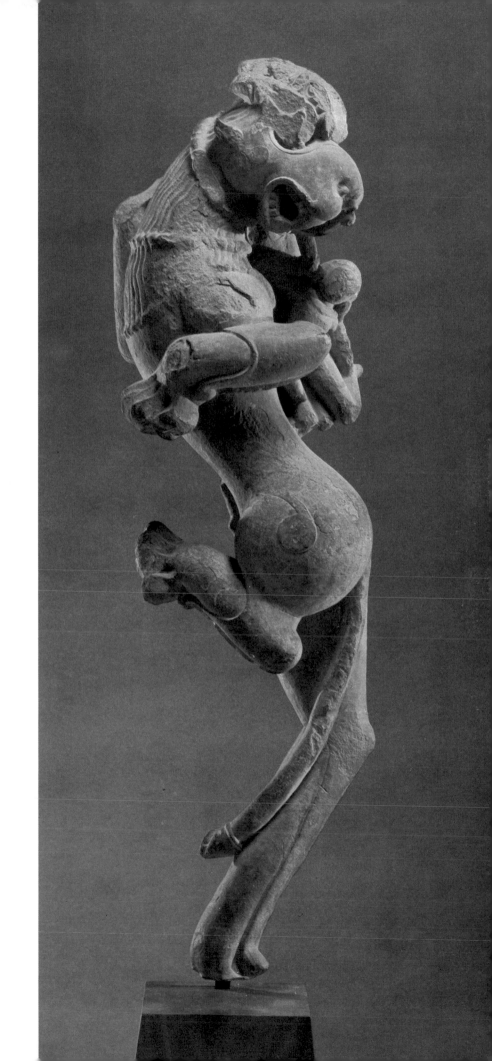

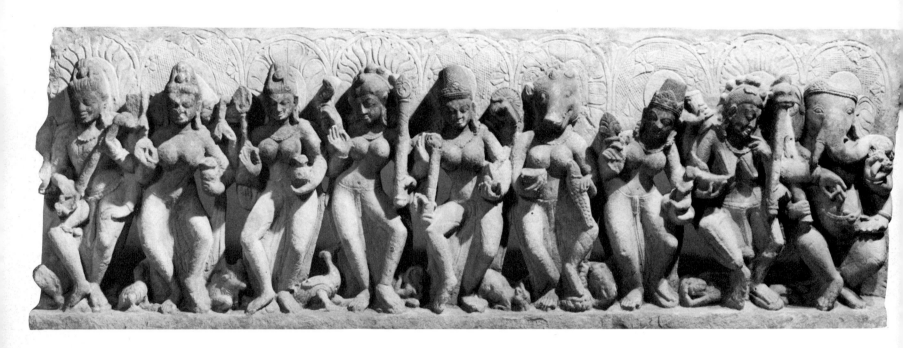

35. The Seven Mothers with Vīrabhadra and Gaṇeśa
Uttar Pradesh
8th century
Buff sandstone
h: 20 in. (50.8 cm.)
w: 53 in. (134.6 cm.)

The seven mother goddesses (Mātrikā) are represented here with Vīrabhadra and Gaṇeśa. Vīrabhadra, a mani- festation of Siva, plays the vina as he leads the group (see no. 67). He is followed by Brahmāṇī, Māheśvarī, Kaumārī, Vaishṇavī, Vārāhī, Indrāṇī, Chāmuṇḍā, and Gaṇeśa. As their names indicate, each of the first six mothers represents the energy inherent in the god of the same name, and they were created by Durgā during her struggle with Mahishāsura (see no. 31). The emaciated Chāmuṇḍā is a separate entity, although she too was created during the same struggle (see no. 48). All the figures are dancing, and the maternal aspect of the goddesses is emphasized only by Indrāṇī, who carries an infant.

Such reliefs of mother goddesses can be found in most Hindu temples, usually as lintels over a minor shrine or doorway. The goddesses are frequently shown dancing and in this particular relief, which is remarkably well preserved, they form an unusually lively group. The sculptor seems to have made a special effort to vary their postures and consequently the com- position is more than usually exciting and compelling. A fragment of a similar relief is in the Allahabad Museum (see P. Chandra, 1970, pl. CXXXVI, 415).

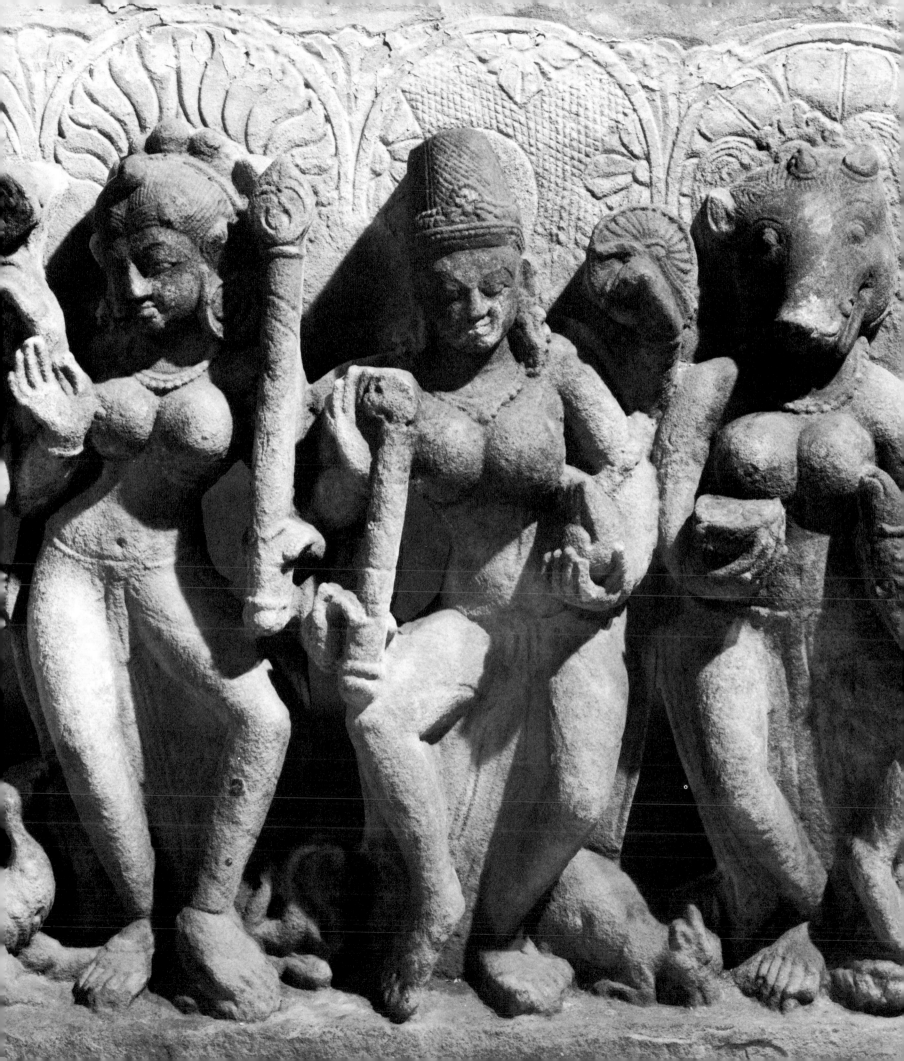

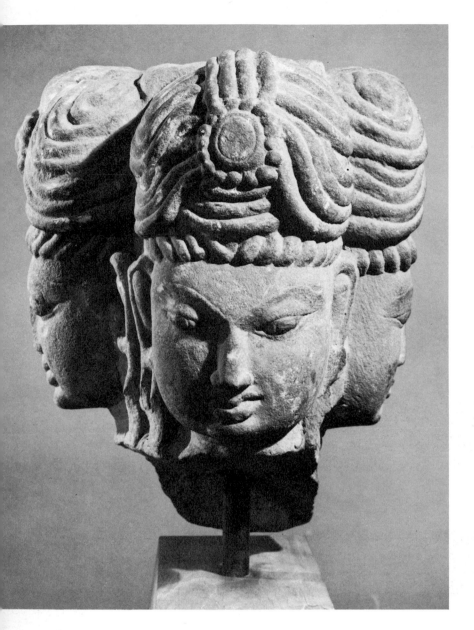

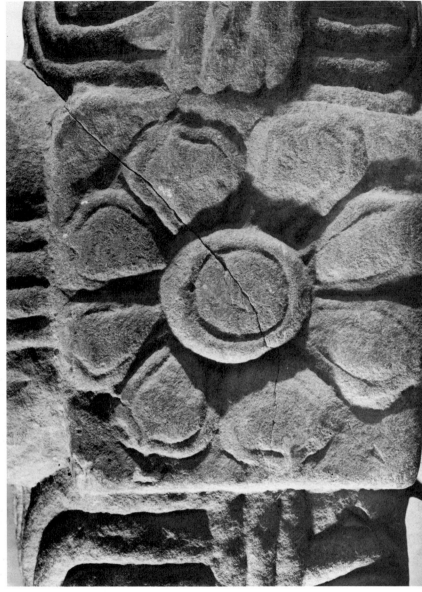

36. The God Brahma

Uttar Pradesh
8th–9th century
Buff sandstone
h: 17 in. (43.2 cm.)

Only the four heads of what must once have been a handsome full-length sculpture of Brahma remain. Each head, with matted hair held by a simple tiara, represents an ascetic. The elongated earlobes are one of the signs that Indian sculptors used to distinguish a god from a mortal. The top of the four heads join in a lotus. Along with Vishnu and Siva, Brahma constitutes part of the Hindu trinity and is responsible for all creation. In mythology he also plays the role of counselor and teacher to the gods, and his four heads symbolize the four Vedas, which are the oldest Hindu scriptures. The idealized features, as well as the elegant chignon, are rendered with a simplicity and sensitivity reminiscent of Gupta sculpture (cf. the similar heads of the Cambodian Brahma, no. 142).

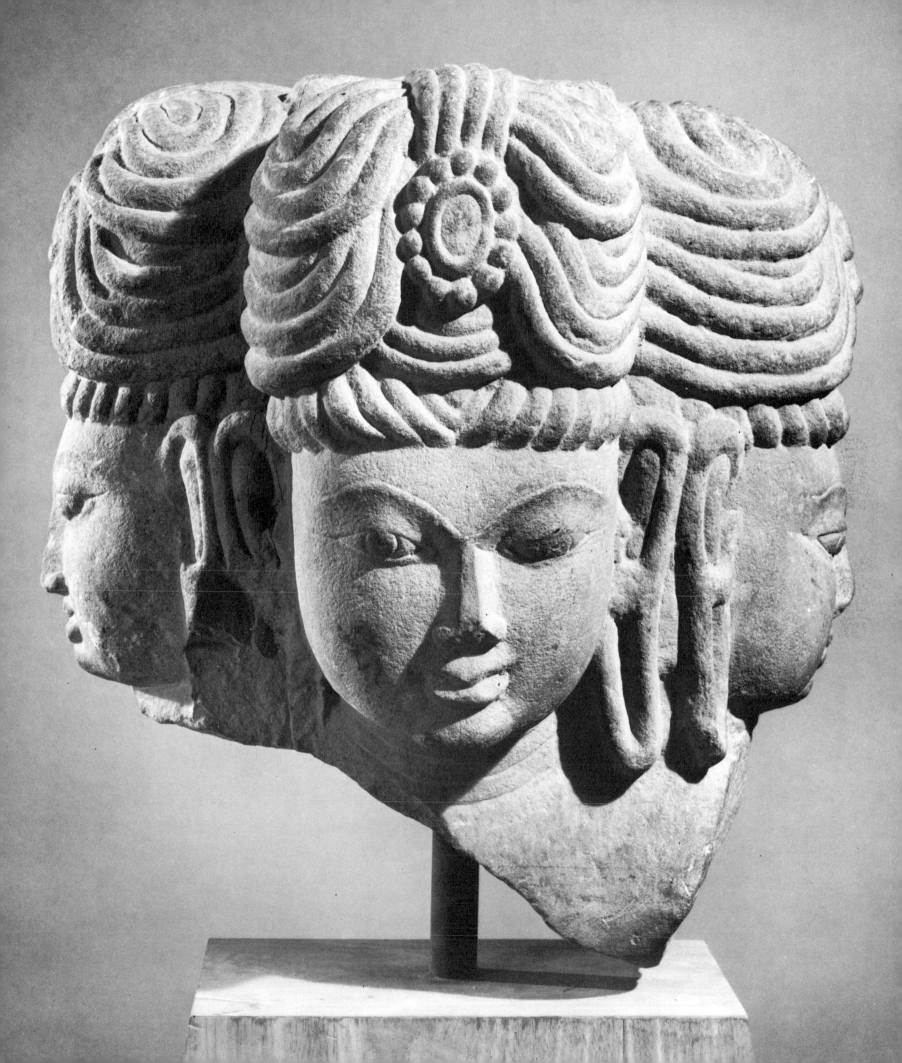

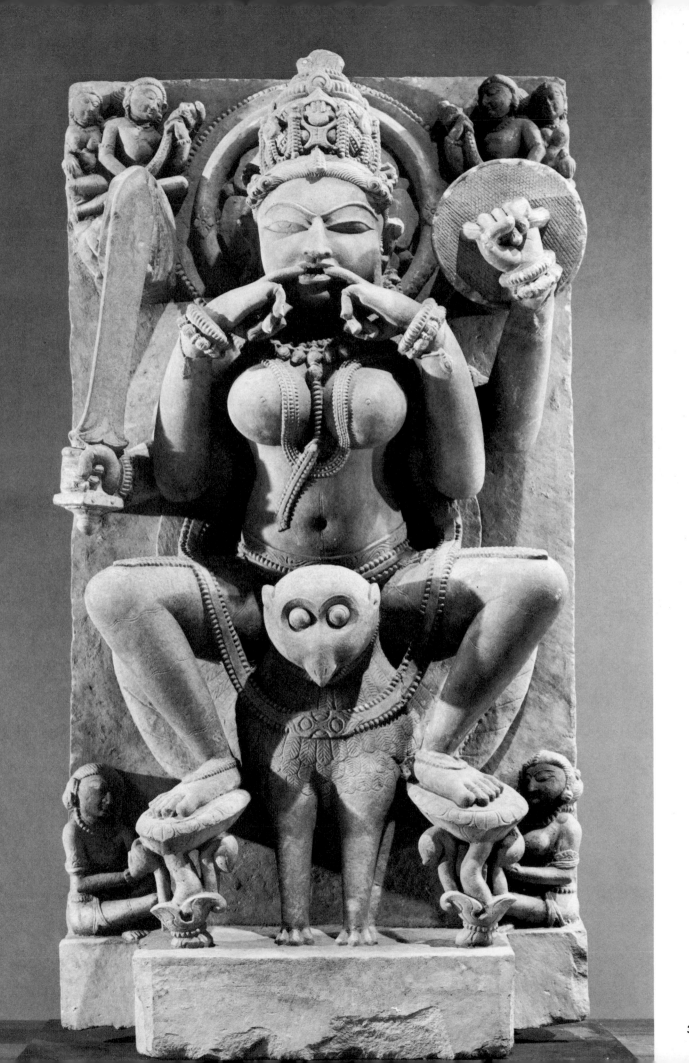

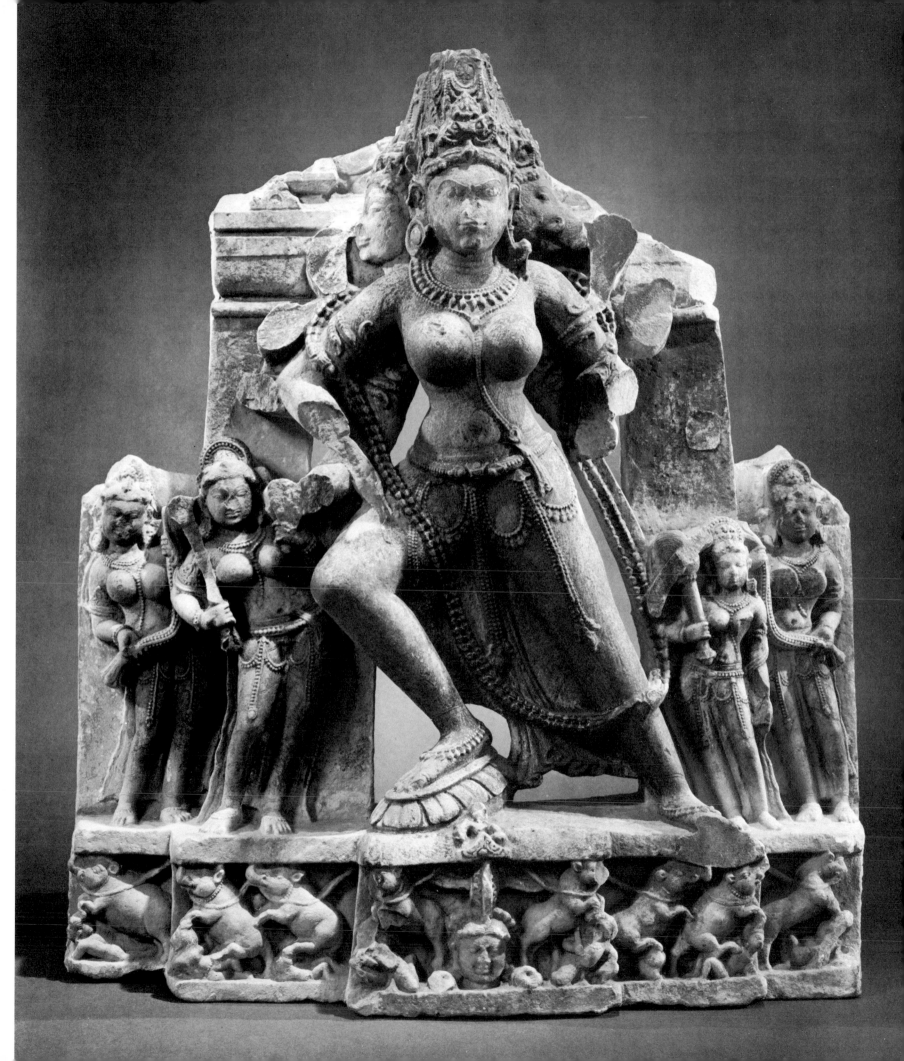

37. A Yogini

Uttar Pradesh or Madhya Pradesh
10th century
Buff sandstone
h: 33 in. (83.8 cm.)

This four-armed goddess sits astride a bird, her feet supported by two lotus leaves with tendrils. She is beautifully formed and ornamented and only her attributes emphasize her awesomeness. With her two principal hands she seems to be expanding her mouth; the other two hands hold a sword and a shield. Her bird mount is very likely an owl, which is normally the vehicle of Śrī-Lakshmī but is sometimes also ridden by terrifying mother goddesses such as Chāmuṇḍā (*chāmuṇḍā ulugavāhinī*).

Indeed, this goddess may well be a manifestation of Chāmuṇḍā (see no. 48), since she is included in the pantheon of the sixty-four Yoginis. A yogini normally is the feminine counterpart of a yogi, but the word is also employed to designate sixty-four goddesses, usually of terrifying nature, who are collectively worshiped by the Saktas. Originally they were probably goddesses individually worshiped in different localities and, once accepted within the fold of the Sanskritic religious tradition, they came to be regarded as manifestations of the great mother.

For a more elaborate sculpture representing the same goddess, see Davidson, p. 42, no. 55.

38. The Goddess Mārīchi

Uttar Pradesh
11th century
Buff sandstone
h: 37½ in. (95.2 cm.)

The name Mārīchi is derived from the word *marichi*, meaning "rays of the sun." Hence Mārīchi is regarded by the Buddhists as the goddess of the dawn or the queen of the heavens. Like the Hindu sun god she travels through the sky, but in a chariot pulled by pigs rather than horses. One of her three heads is that of a sow, and her charioteer is Rāhu, the bodiless demon who devours the sun and the moon, thereby causing eclipses. That she was conceived as a solar goddess thus seems clear, but some of the other iconography is difficult to explain.

In this impressive sculpture the goddess strikes an aggressive posture, towering above her companions like an amazon. All of her ten arms are broken, but this seems to be aesthetically advantageous, for one senses better the plasticity of her form, which has been modeled almost in the round. Along the base is a lively frieze of seven rampant pigs and one lion (?) crushing eight dwarfish figures that must represent the demons of darkness, who are also encountered in images of Sūrya. The naked demons are almost cherubic in appearance and are depicted in a wide variety of postures. In the middle of the frieze is the head of the charioteer Rāhu, while on either side of Mārīchi stand four female attendants bearing flywhisks and garlands. According to the texts, her principal face displays passionate love; the sow's face, wrath; and the remaining face, serenity.

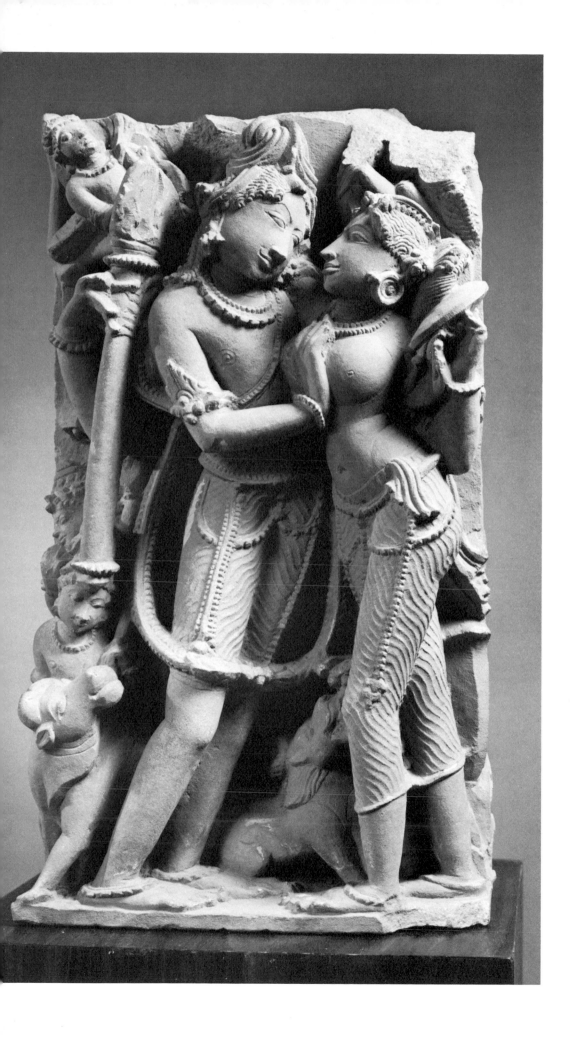

39. Siva and Pārvatī

Uttar Pradesh
11th century
Beige sandstone
h: 14½ in. (37.8 cm.)

This charming relief shows Siva and
Pārvatī in a particularly intimate pose.
The four-armed Siva holds a trident
in one hand and possibly a snake in
another. His two normal hands are
engaged in caressing the goddess, who
has one of her hands around his neck
and holds a mirror in the other. Both
their animals, the bull and the lion,
look up at them like devoted pets. Siva
is provided with two male attendants,
and two celestial beings, one now
effaced, hover above the divine
couple's heads.

    The conjugal relationship be-
tween Siva and Pārvatī has remained
one of the most popular themes in
Indian art. Their love for one another
is expressed in this sculpture with
particular tenderness and delicacy.
Typical of the Indian aesthetic tradition, this is done not merely by the
disposition of their faces with their
eyes interlocked, but also by their
postures and by the gestures of their
hands. Even the animals are involved
with the intimacy of the pair's fond
embrace, and, as we watch, we can
only say with the poet Bhagīratha that
the eyes of the divine couple are
"sweet, loving, innocent and motion-
less with love" (Ingalls, p. 89).

40. The God Balarāma

Uttar Pradesh or Madhya Pradesh
11th century
Red sandstone
h: 56 in. (142.2 cm.)

Balarāma, the foster brother of Krishna, is regarded as the eighth avatar
of Vishnu. His most distinctive attributes are the plowshare, which he holds
with his upper left hand, and the snake
hoods that form a canopy above his
head. His lower left hand holds a cup,
for Balarāma is very fond of drinking.
Unfortunately, the two right hands are
broken, but one of them must have
held a pestle, part of which seems to
be attached to the upper right arm,
which was once raised in the gesture
of authority assumed by universal
monarchs. Stylized *makaras* and *vyālas*
decorate the side of the stele, and a
thick floral garland forms a cushion
between the head and the nimbus.
Despite the worn face, the sculpture
is a rare and impressive image of
Balarāma from the medieval period
and very likely was the principal icon
of a temple dedicated to the god.

Such imperious and heroic
representations of Balarāma are
characteristic of the much earlier
Kushān period from which a number
of fragmentary, though monumental,
examples have survived. Few later
sculptures of Balarāma, however,
repeated the Kushān formula as
faithfully as the present image. The
asymmetrical disposition of the raised
right arm and the imposing snake
hoods impart astonishing vitality and
compelling rhythmic force to the
representation. The attenuated figure
of the god and the abundance of
jewelry reflect a rococo tendency that
is characteristic of much medieval
Indian sculpture, but in no way do
they detract from the dramatic
assertiveness of the form.

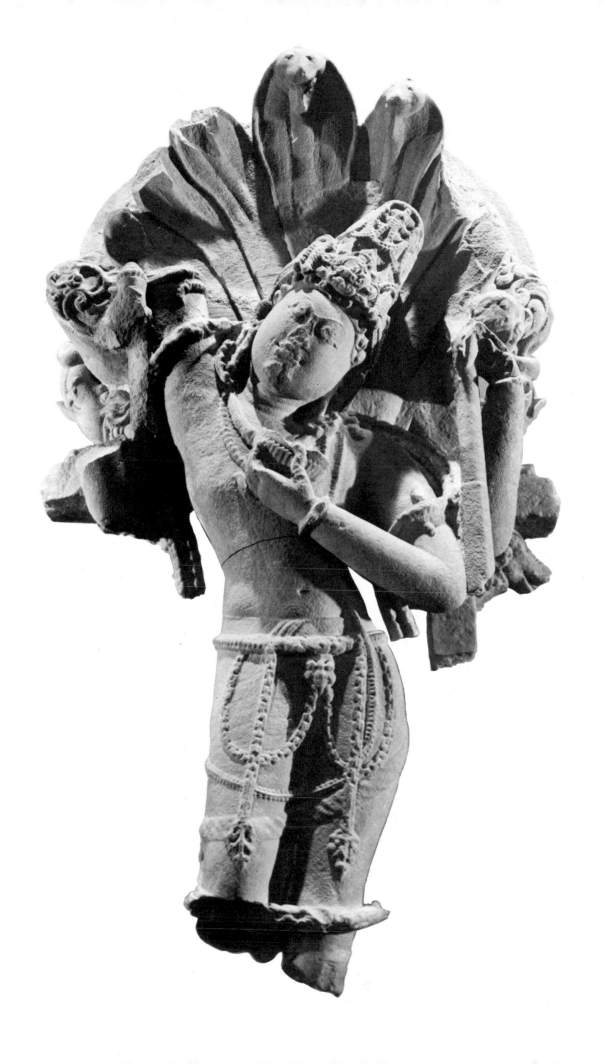

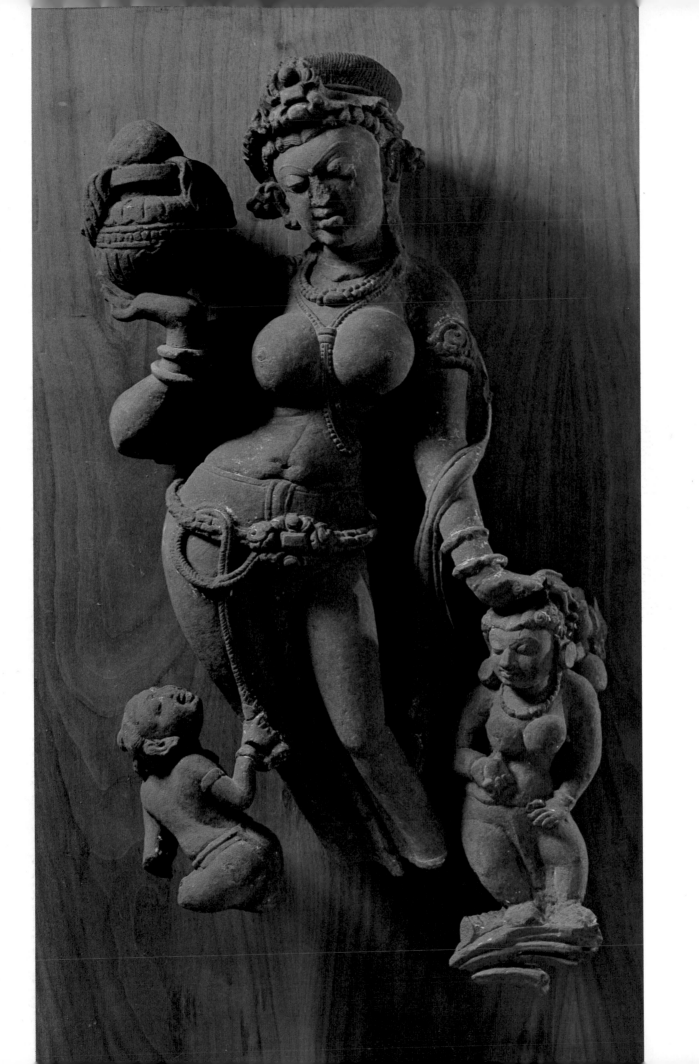

41. A River Goddess

Madhya Pradesh
7th–8th century
Pink sandstone
h: 27½ in. (69.8 cm.)

Only three partially preserved figures remain from what must once have been a crowded relief. The large figure in the middle, striking a provocative pose, holds a waterpot with a plant in her right hand; her left hand rests on the head of a dwarf female attendant. The waterpot suggests that she represents either Gaṅgā or Yamunā, the two river goddesses whose images flank the entrances of many Indian temples. A second dwarfish and grotesque male seems to be pulling the chain belt that forms a loop on her right thigh.

The classic simplicity of the Gupta period (see nos. 17, 20) here becomes baroque, both in the luxurious expansion of the volumes and in the exaggerated sway of the posture. The goddess seems almost unable to support the burden of her ample bosom and hips, while the playful grotesque dwarf strikes an impossibly contorted posture. Such grotesques are often associated with beautiful women, both in the literary and the visual arts, and, apart from the fact that they add a touch of humor by their comical behavior, they also serve to emphasize by contrast the beauty of their mistresses. Two other stylistically similar sculptures are now in the Heeramaneck collection in the Los Angeles County Museum of Art, and probably all three belonged to the same temple.

42. Lakulīśa (Lord of the Staff)

Madhya Pradesh
8th century
Pink sandstone
h: 31 in. (78.7 cm.)

Lakulīśa was a great Śaiva teacher who may have lived in western India during the first century A.D. He may have been responsible for reorganizing the Pāśupata sect of Śivaism and certainly came to enjoy a position of pre-eminence in the later Śaiva pantheon. The fact that he is shown with four arms announces his divine status and his identification with Śiva. Indeed, the Śaivas regard him as an avatar of Śiva.

He is represented here as a yogi seated with his legs crossed at the ankles and held in position by a *yoga-paṭṭa*. The lotus base rises from the water symbolized by two *nāgas*. His hair is arranged in an elegant chignon and, like Śiva's, his phallus is erect. His two principal hands form the *dharmachakrapravartanamudrā*, which is used more commonly by the Buddhists. Since Lakulīśa was also a great teacher, artists obviously felt it was appropriate to give him this gesture. His upper right hand holds the rosary and the corresponding left hand holds the snake-entwined staff (*laguḍa* or *lakuṭa*) that is his distinctive emblem. He is accompanied by four smaller figures who must represent his four principal disciples—Kuśika, Mitra, Garga, and Kaurushya—traditionally regarded as the founders of the four subsects of the Pāśupata system.

In the simplicity of its composition and the abstract though sensuous modeling of the figures, the sculpture echoes the chaste elegance of the Gupta aesthetic. It is closely related in style to another sculpture in the collection (no. 43) and both are probably from the same region.

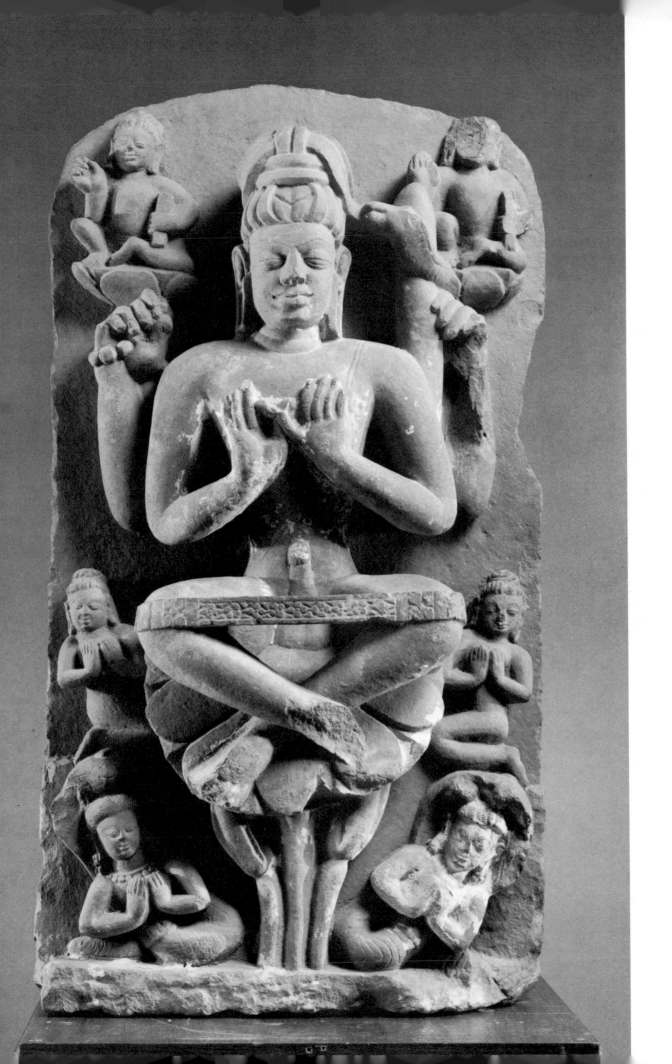

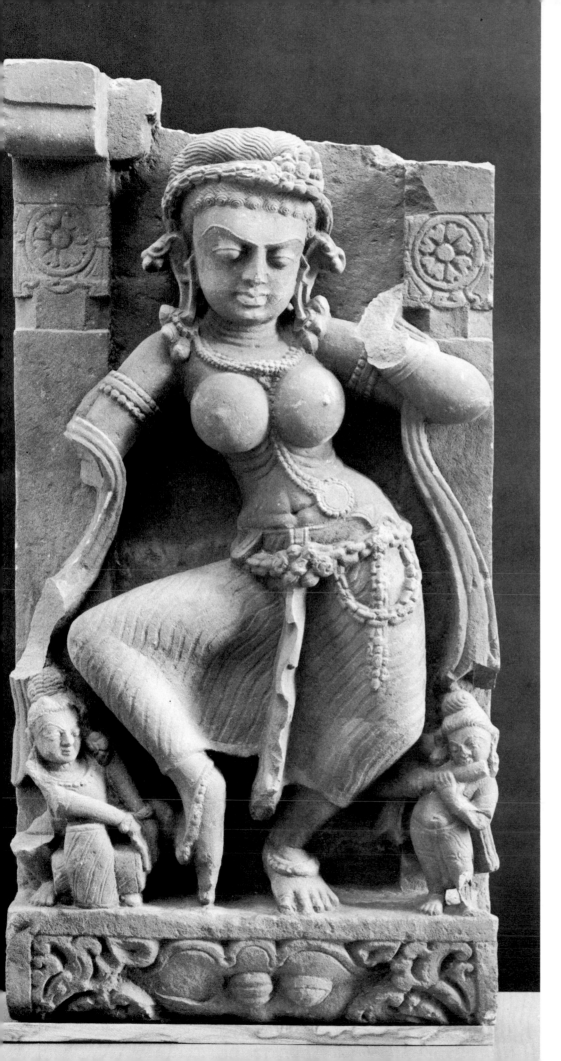

43. A Celestial Nymph
Madhya Pradesh
8th–9th century
Pink sandstone
h: 26½ in. (67.3 cm.)

Framed by two square columns, a
celestial nymph is seen dancing to the
music provided by a drummer and a
flutist. The skillful use of the archi-
tectural setting and the shadows
produced by the deep relief create such
an illusion of depth that the figure
seems to come forward as if on a stage.
Moreover, the severe vertical upright
of the columns helps to accentuate the
curves of her body. She dances
voluptuously on a platform whose
front is decorated with foliage and a
partially seen *kīrttimukha*, which
associate the nymph with fecundity
and water cosmology. Despite the
opulence of her form, she appears as a
nimble-footed dancer, and it is
obvious that the sculptor was well
acquainted with the dancer's repertoire, as most contemporary aesthetic
manuals instructed him to be. The
sculpture is stylistically related to the
splendid Lakuliśa also in this
collection (no. 42).

44. The Boar Incarnation of Vishnu

Madhya Pradesh
9th–10th century
Cream sandstone
h: 55 in. (139.7 cm.)

In his Varāha, or boar, incarnation, Vishnu rescued the earth from under the waters. According to some versions, the earth was sinking because it was unable to bear the weight of the population growth and the consequent increase in grain production; according to others, a demon called Hiraṇyāksha had seized the earth and fled to the bottom of the ocean. Whatever the reason, the gods appealed to Vishnu, who assumed the form of a boar and dove into the waters to rescue the earth. There seems good reason to believe that such legends are only later attempts to explain away the primeval worship of the boar as a fertilizing divinity.

In contrast to the diminutive figure of the earth goddess, Vishnu is a colossus dominated by a massive boar's head. His dynamic posture conveys a sense of tremendous energy, while the earth goddess's helplessness and gratitude are communicated with subtle and quiet charm. One of the god's right hands rests against his thigh immediately below a dagger, the other holds the mace. One of his left hands supports the demure earth goddess and holds a wheel against his chest. The thrust of this elbow further emphasizes the energetic diagonals of the form. The conch is held by his remaining left hand, and a lotus leaf serves as a parasol above the god's head. Noteworthy are the streaming strands of hair, which are not usually encountered in such images. The ornaments are crisply delineated and the figure is attached to a remarkably plain stele. That the sculpture is from Madhya Pradesh seems certain, but whether it is from the Rewa or Chhatarpur districts is more difficult to determine. For comparable though later examples from these two districts, see P. Chandra, pls. CXXXIX, p. 421; CXLI, p. 425; CXLIII, p. 433.

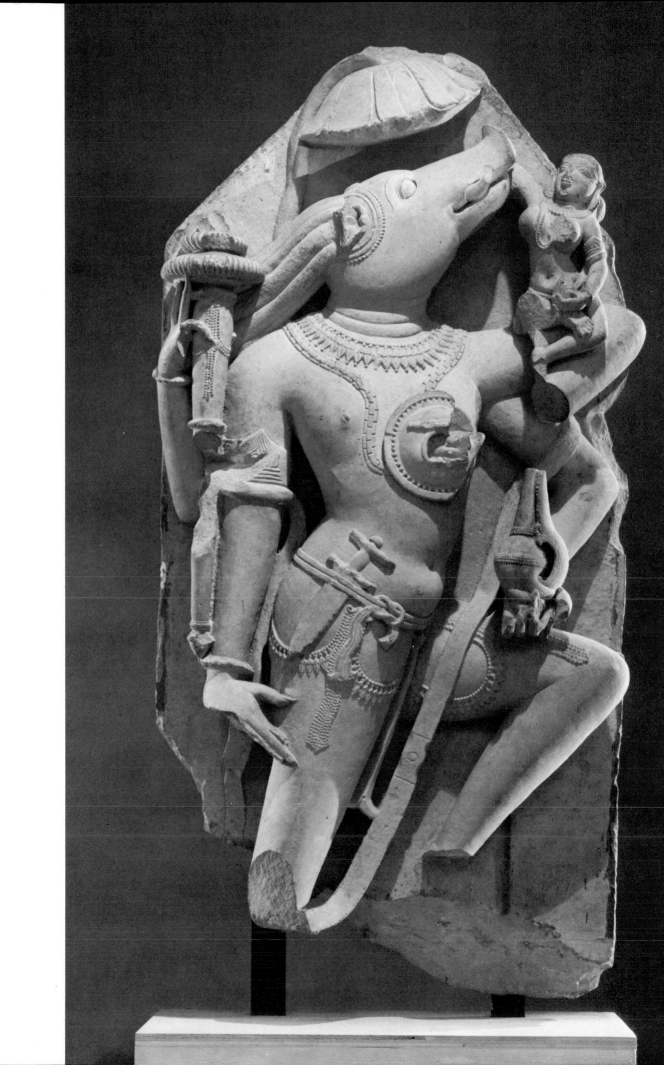

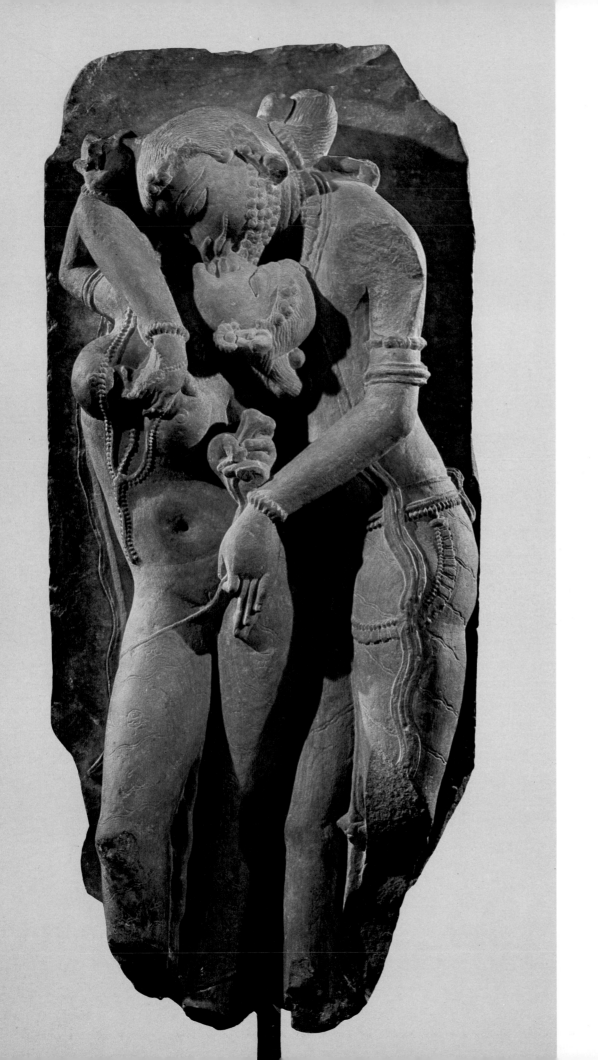

5. Lovers (Mithuna)
Madhya Pradesh
11th century
Rust-colored sandstone
h: 29⅛ in. (74.0 cm.)

A loving couple, or *mithuna*, is one of
the most popular and ancient themes
in Indian art. Symbolizing the close
correspondence between agriculture
and the sexual act, it is probably a
substitute for the ritual intercourse
performed in the fields during neolithic times to enhance the fertility of
the soil. Later, the motif of a couple,
often engaged in an overt sexual act,
was employed freely on the external
walls of a temple and is still regarded
as an auspicious symbol.

In this relief a princely man, his
masculinity emphasized by his beard
and his long hair gathered in an
elegant bun, is about to disrobe his
voluptuous partner. She is not yet
prepared to submit totally, for she
holds on to her garment with her left
hand. Each appears totally engrossed
in the other and while he is gentle, she
is more passionate, though coquettish.
Although the two figures are separate
entities, their forms seem to flow into
one another with effortless ease. The
composition is handled with exquisitely
understated eroticism, and the
entwining figures display a rhythmic
ecstasy that is at once joyful and
decorous.

6. A Celestial Female
Madhya Pradesh
11th–12th century
Pink sandstone
h: 33⅛ in. (84.4 cm.)

Sculptures representing celestial
females, who are known generally as
apsarā or *apsaras*, were used prolifically
by medieval Indian artists to decorate
the external walls of temples. Although
meant to depict divine rather than
human creatures, they always look
eminently desirable. Most are
engaged in mundane activities; this
lady, for example, was very likely
gazing into a mirror as she fixed her
hair ornament with her right hand.
She gracefully leans against the trunk
of a tree and above her head are
curving tendrils that emphasize her
own sinuous form. Obviously she is a
symbol of fertility and abundance and
thereby embodies a concept that had
its roots in the civilization's neolithic
past.

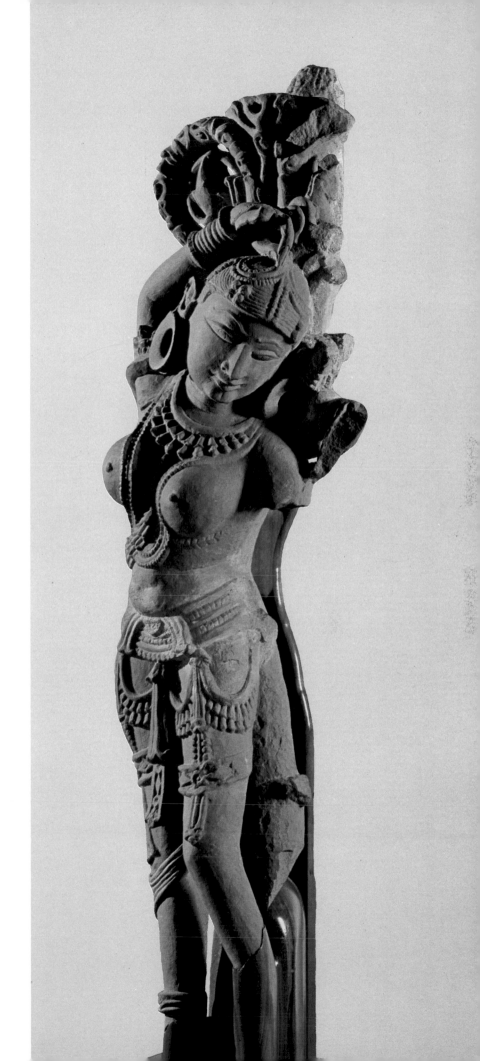

47. Bhairava Head (?)
Madhya Pradesh or Rajasthan
10th century
Buff sandstone
h: 13½ in. (34.2 cm.)

The awesome expression of this handsome head is due especially to the
bulging, rolling eyes and the gaping
mouth with protruding fangs. It is also
given a beard and a moustache, and
hair that is rolled forward on the head,
looking almost like a Phrygian cap. A
decorated band separates the plain
bun from the curlicued locks that form
a fringe along the temples. The head
may have belonged to an impressive
image of Bhairava or to an angry Saiva
attendant. A similar facial type, with
the same beard and moustache but
with a benign expression, was used
frequently in medieval Indian sculpture in both Madhya Pradesh and
Rajasthan. A comparable beard and
hairdo, though with the bun hanging
loosely on the neck, can be seen in the
male lover in no. 45.

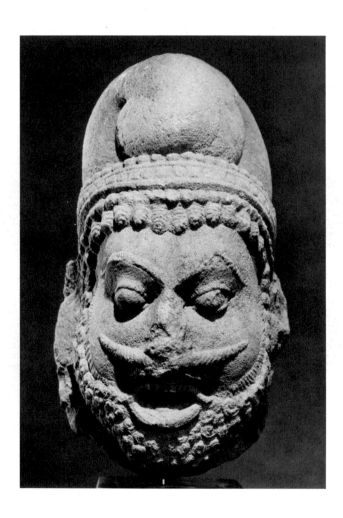

48. The Goddess Chāmuṇḍā
Rajasthan, Dungarpur region
10th century
Gray schist
h: 23½ in. (59.7 cm.)

Also known as Kālī, Chāmuṇḍā is one
of the mother goddesses (see no. 35)
and an emanation of the great goddess
Durgā, or Mahishāsuramardinī (see
no. 31). During her battle with the
asuras, Durgā created a terrifying and
emaciated goddess who destroyed,
among others, the brothers Chaṇḍa
and Muṇḍa. Thereafter, she became
known as Chāmuṇḍā, "the destroyer
of Chaṇḍa and Muṇḍa." This explan-
ation of her name seems rather tenden-
tious; more likely the word is of non-
Sanskritic origin, and she may have
been a tribal goddess who was later
adopted into the Hindu pantheon.

With a grinning, awesome face,
the emaciated goddess sits in *lalitāsana*
on a man with long, flowing hair. She
is four-armed and wears a garland of
severed heads, arms, snakes, and a skull
that emphasizes her macabre character. In her hands she holds a severed
head, a dagger, and a skull cup from
which she drinks the blood of her
victims. Her remaining left hand is
raised to her gaping mouth, her little
finger touching one of her fangs. In
addition, she has a trident and a
staff bearing a grinning skull. It is
interesting to note that the head she
holds with her right hand has long
hair, as does the man who serves as her
seat. It is possible, therefore, that the
prostrate figure represents one of the
asura brothers, while the decapitated
head belonged to the other.

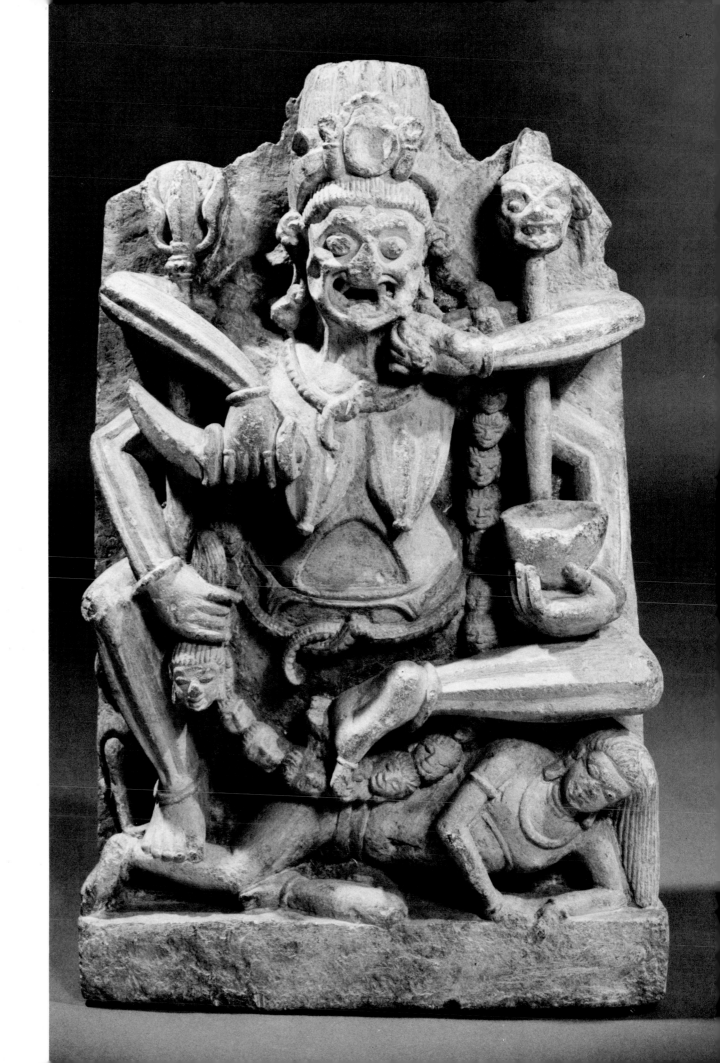

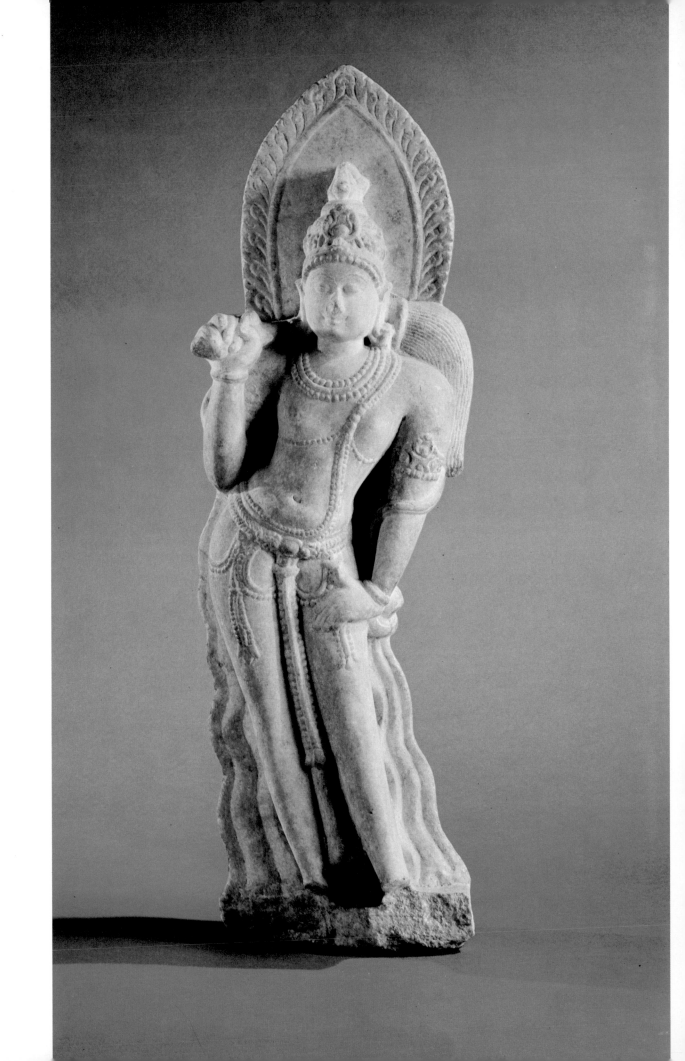

49. A Flywhisk Bearer

Rajasthan, Mt. Abu region
10th–11th century
Marble
h: 26 in. (66.0 cm.)

This handsome figure stands gracefully in *tribhaṅga* with his left hand resting on his thigh and his right holding a flywhisk that goes around his shoulder and falls behind his left arm. His bejeweled and crowned head is set off against a pointed, flaming nimbus, which unquestionably establishes his divine status. At the same time, however, he was probably an attendant *yaksha* who stood behind the figure of a Jaina Tīrthaṁkara (see no. 50). Radiantly youthful and ideally proportioned, the figure is modeled with almost feline suppleness. Marble is the principal sculptural medium in the Mt. Abu region of Rajasthan and hence it is easy to identify the provenance of this sculpture.

50. A Jaina Tīrthaṁkara
Bihar
7th century
Gilt copper
h: 13 in. (33.0 cm.)

The majestic figure of this Tīrthaṁkara is seated like a perfect yogi on a lotus raised on a stepped pedestal. He is completely naked, with his hair drawn back and four symmetrical strands falling down his shoulders. His hands are placed in his lap in *dhyānamudrā*. Two *yaksha* attendants stand on either side, each bearing a flywhisk. The seat is provided with a back, thereby making it a throne, and on the top of it balances a circular flaming nimbus supported by two beautifully rendered geese. The nimbus is surmounted by three umbrellas with festoons. On the base of the pedestal is an animal relief, which is unfortunately much too worn for a positive identification. If it is an antelope, then the Tīrthaṁkara can be identified as Śāntinātha, but if it is a goat, then the figure may represent Kuṇṭhunātha. The former identification seems the more likely one.

The closest stylistic parallel for the Tīrthaṁkara's figure can be seen in a stone Vishnu in a Hindu monastery at Bodhgaya, generally dated to the seventh century (see Pal, 1972, pl. XXVIIIA). Especially noteworthy is the similar modeling and the close resemblance of the shape and features of the two faces. Like the Vishnu, the Tīrthaṁkara has a commanding presence and an inner vitality that echo qualities seen in earlier Gupta sculptures. Compare also a bronze Śiva from Bengal (Saraswati, 1962, pl. II, fig. 6) for which a seventh-century date has been suggested.

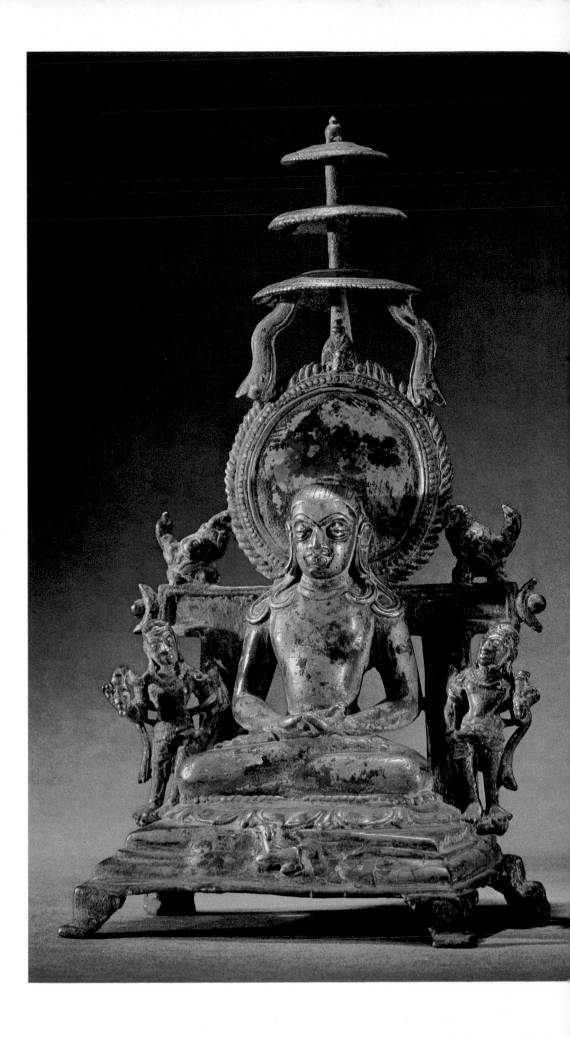

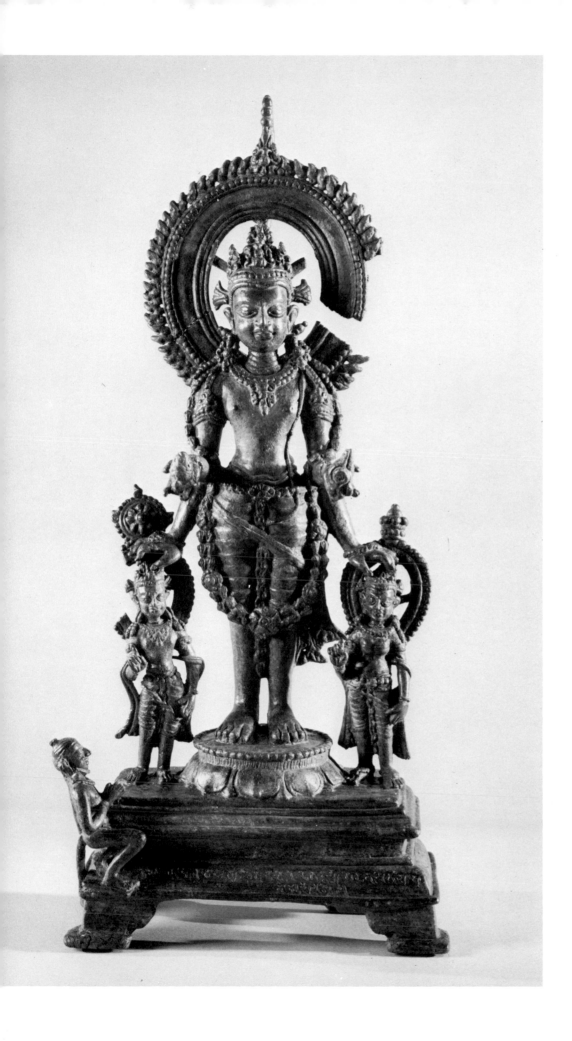

51. The God Vishnu

Bihar
Ca. 800
Bronze with traces of green patina
h: 20¾ in. (52.7 cm.)

Represented here in one of his princi-pal emanations (*vyūha*), Vishnu stands as firm as a pillar on a lotus-topped pedestal. Crowned and ornamented, he is also given a garland of flowers (*vanamālā*). A circular nimbus decorated with pearl and flame motifs sets off his head. Two of his hands carry a conch shell and a round object symbolizing a lotus seed. His two additional hands rest on the heads of his personified attributes, the wheel and the mace, which have parts of their emblems depicted above their nimbi. An ascetic-looking donor kneels above the right foot of the pedestal with his hands in the *añjalīmudrā*.

Few scholars would disagree that this bronze is earlier than the well-known Balarāma bronze from Kurki-har, which was dedicated in the ninth regnal year of Devapāla, who is said to have ascended the throne in about 810 (see Pal, 1972, pl. xxvIIIb). A close stylistic parallel for this bronze can be seen in another bronze Vishnu, also with personified attributes, dis-covered in the Rajshahi district of Bangladesh (see R. C. Majumdar, ed., *History of Bengal*, Dacca, 1963, I, pl. LIX, p. 146). The Rajshahi bronze is generally dated to the eighth century and hence the suggested date of this Vishnu, which seems to be confirmed by the paleography of the inscription.

The inscription is as follows: *u namo kapilavāstavyasya prajñākara devadharmmoya datayitam māpṛto ātmanaścha*. Written in rather corrupt Sanskrit, it tells us that the image was dedicated by Prajñākara, a resident of Kapilavāstu, for the welfare of his parents and himself. The inscription, therefore, has considerable signifi-cance since the wording suggests that either Prajñākara himself was a Buddhist from Kapilavāstu or that the scribe was a Buddhist who employed the usual Buddhist formula in the text.

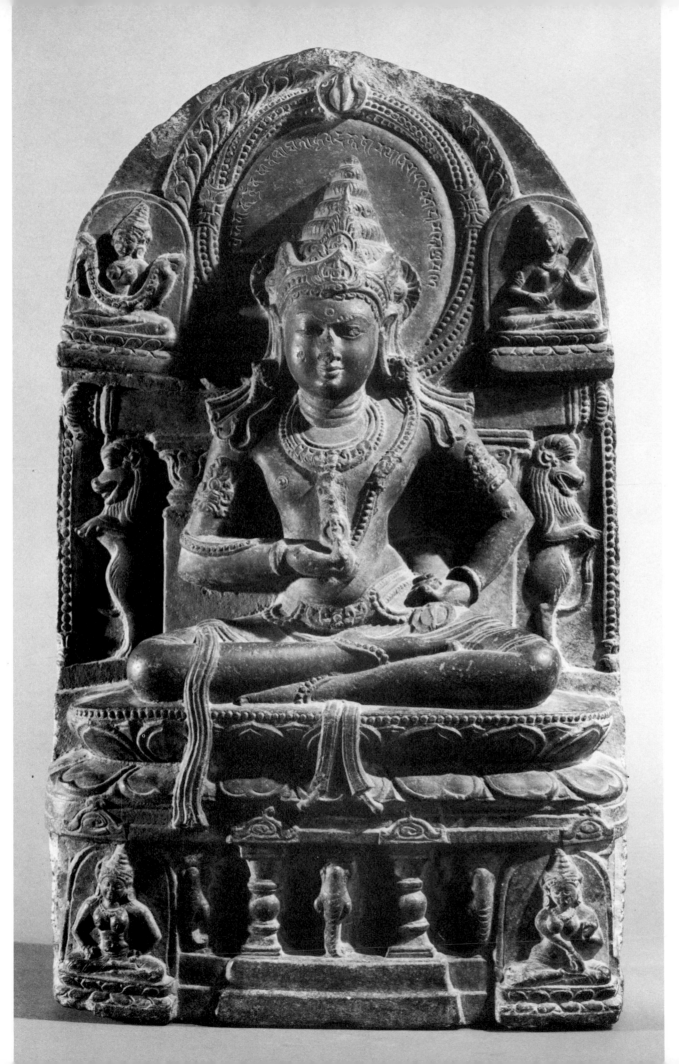

52. The God Vajrasattva

Bihar
10th century
Black schist
h: 29 in. (73.6 cm.)

Although Vajrasattva is a widely revered deity of the Vajrayana pantheon, there is some ambiguity about his importance and nature. Some texts consider him to be the sixth Tathāgata, but he is invariably represented as a bodhisattva, elaborately crowned and bejeweled. Moreover, four of the five Tathāgatas are usually portrayed in his crown, as in this image, an indication that he does not belong to any particular family. His exalted position is symbolized here by the thunderbolt adorning the apex of the image.

Vajrasattva is generally supposed to sit on the summit of Mt. Sumeru (see no. 22), but here he is seated on a lotus throne supported by three elephants and framed by two rampant lions. The base of the throne consists of pillars and a molding decorated with the *chaitya* window motif. Also unusual is the presence of four goddesses; two of them hold a garland and a musical instrument, a third seems to be dancing even while she is seated, and a fourth holds two objects that are too indistinct to be identified. They may represent the four dancing goddesses known as Lāsyā, Nrityā, Mālyā, and Gītā. The Buddhist creed is inscribed on the flaming nimbus, as it is in the image of Tārā (no. 53). The two sculptures are closely related stylistically and may be the products of the same atelier.

53. The Goddess Tārā

Bihar
10th century
Black schist
h: 30½ in. (77.5 cm.)

The Buddhist savior Tārā is seated in
lalitāsana on an elaborate and richly
decorated lion throne. Her right foot is
supported by a lotus flanked by two
adoring devotees. The goddess is
sumptuously ornamented and a gos-
samer scarf is hardly sufficient to
contain her well-formed breasts. Her
right hand forms the *varadamudrā* and
is marked with a floral motif; her left
hand holds the stem of a *nīlotpala*
("blue lotus"). The base of the throne
is supported by lions and elephants,
and two more rampant lions disgorging pearls decorate the sides. At the
base of the flaming nimbus are two
kinnaras playing the drum and cymbals. The surface of the nimbus is
inscribed with the Buddhist creed, and
the apex is crowned with a *kīrttimukha*.

Typical of the finest Pāla sculptures, the modeling is taut yet delicate,
an embodiment of grace and serene
elegance. The compassion that is Tārā's
principal virtue is well expressed by
her contemplative countenance with
its particularly sweet expression and
by the gesture of her right hand.

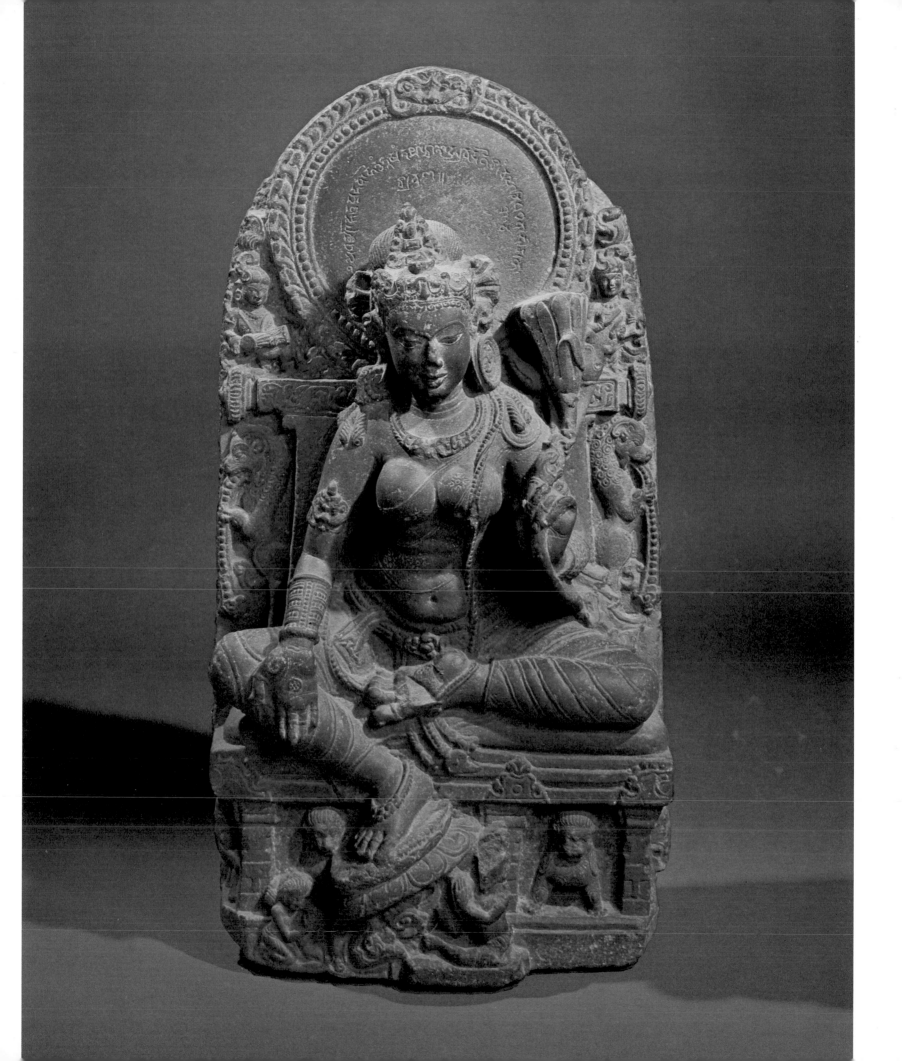

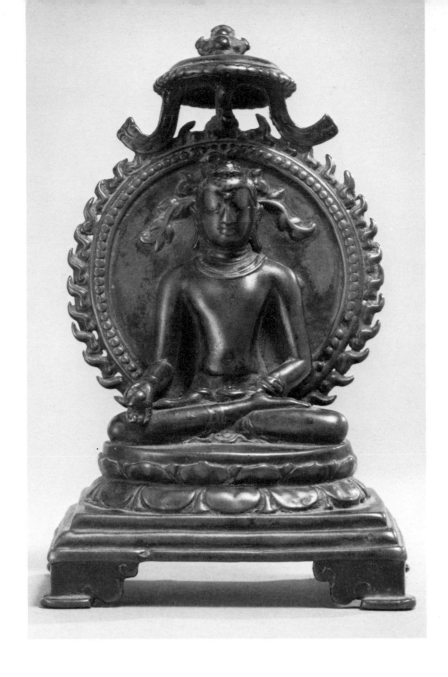

54. A Tathāgata
Bihar, Kurkihar style
10th century
Bronze with dark patina
h: 5½ in. (14.0 cm.)

That this meditating figure represents a Buddha or a Tathāgata is not in doubt. However, whether it is an image of the Buddha Śākyamuni or of Ratnasambhava, a member of the Vajrayana pentad, is more difficult to determine. The *varadamudrā* formed by the right hand is common to both, but if the object held by the hand is a jewel, then the figure must represent Ratnasambhava ("the jewel-born"). If, however, the tree behind his head is a pipal, then the figure can be identified as the Buddha Śākyamuni. It must be stressed though that the leaves do not look like those of a pipal and that usually when Śākyamuni is portrayed below this tree, his right hand forms the *bhūmisparśamudrā*. Thus, the figure is probably meant to depict Ratnasambhava. The flaming nimbus is surmounted by a parasol with fluttering festoons.

Kurkihar is a village only seventeen miles from Gaya, where the Buddha attained enlightenment. In 1920 a chance excavation for the foundations of a new building there brought to light a hoard of 233 bronzes, which are now in the Patna Museum. Apparently there was once an important monastery at Kurkihar, which was probably destroyed by the Muslims sometime in the twelfth century, when the bronzes were no doubt hidden underground by the monks. Although related to the bronzes created in the neighboring, and better-known, monastic establishment of Nalanda, Kurkihar bronzes have peculiarities that clearly distinguish them from those of the Nalanda school. This bronze Tathāgata is a fine example of the Kurkihar style and may have been taken by a pilgrim to Tibet. The Buddhist creed is inscribed on the plate underneath the image.

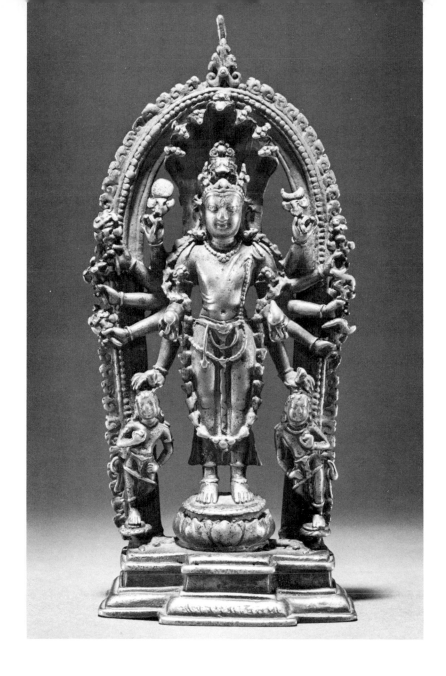

55. The God Siva-Balarāma (?)
Bihar, Kurkihar style
10th century
Brass with silver inlay
h: 7½ in. (19.2 cm.)

A twelve-armed male deity, his head sheltered by a seven-hooded serpent, stands in *samapada* on a lotus. Accompanying him on two smaller lotuses are two male attendants who stand rather precariously with one foot behind the other. All three figures are framed by an oval aureole decorated with flames and pearl motifs. The deity wears a crown embellished with a lion's head, various ornaments, the sacred cord, and a long garland. His forehead seems to be marked with a third eye, all three eyes being inlaid with silver. All his emblems cannot be easily recognized, but the conch shell, the solar and lunar symbols, and the lotus are clearly discernible. Others seem to include a mace, a plowshare, a *khaṭvāṅga*, and an animal that may be an antelope. Two of his hands grasp two objects resembling lotus buds that emerge from the heads of his empty-handed attendants.

At first glance it is tempting to identify this figure as Balarāma, the foster brother of Krishna, who is also worshiped as one of the avatars of Vishnu. The snake hood, the conch shell, the lotus, the garland, and the lion crown would certainly identify the figure as partly Vaishnava. And if two of the attributes are indeed the plowshare and the mace, Balarāma would be a logical choice. However, the presence of the third eye on the forehead would be inconsistent with such an identification, for it is unquestionably a mark of Siva. Moreover, the sun and the moon, the antelope, and the *khaṭvāṅga*-like object are other attributes of Siva. Therefore, this is either a little-known cosmic representation of Balarāma or a syncretic icon combining the forms of Balarāma and Siva.

Stylistically the bronze is closely related to a conventional Balarāma image from Kurkihar that is datable to the ninth century (see Pal, 1972, XXIIIb). The dedicatory inscription on the pedestal is too faint to be legible.

56. Dancing Gaṇeśa

Bengal
10th–11th century
Black basalt
h: 37½ in. (95.2 cm.)

Gaṇeśa, the elephant-headed son of
Śiva and Pārvatī (see no. 39), is
represented here dancing like his
father (see no. 77). Three of his eight
arms are broken, but his surviving
hands hold a battle-ax, a rosary, a
flower with leaves, a snake, and a bowl
of sweets which he is eating. The two
raised hands probably formed
gestures of the dance. Two musicians
playing drums and cymbals provide
the necessary rhythm, while a rat looks
up at his master in admiration. The
donor of the sculpture kneels in front
of the animal and holds up a garland as
an offering.

   Images of dancing Gaṇeśa became popular in Bengal during the
Pāla period. What is remarkable in
these sculptures is how deftly the
sculptor has depicted such a bulky
figure as a nimble-footed dancer.
Despite his elephantine form, Gaṇeśa
dances gracefully and effortlessly,
springing up "lightly from the earth
that trembles at the stamping of his
feet..." (Ingalls, p. 89).

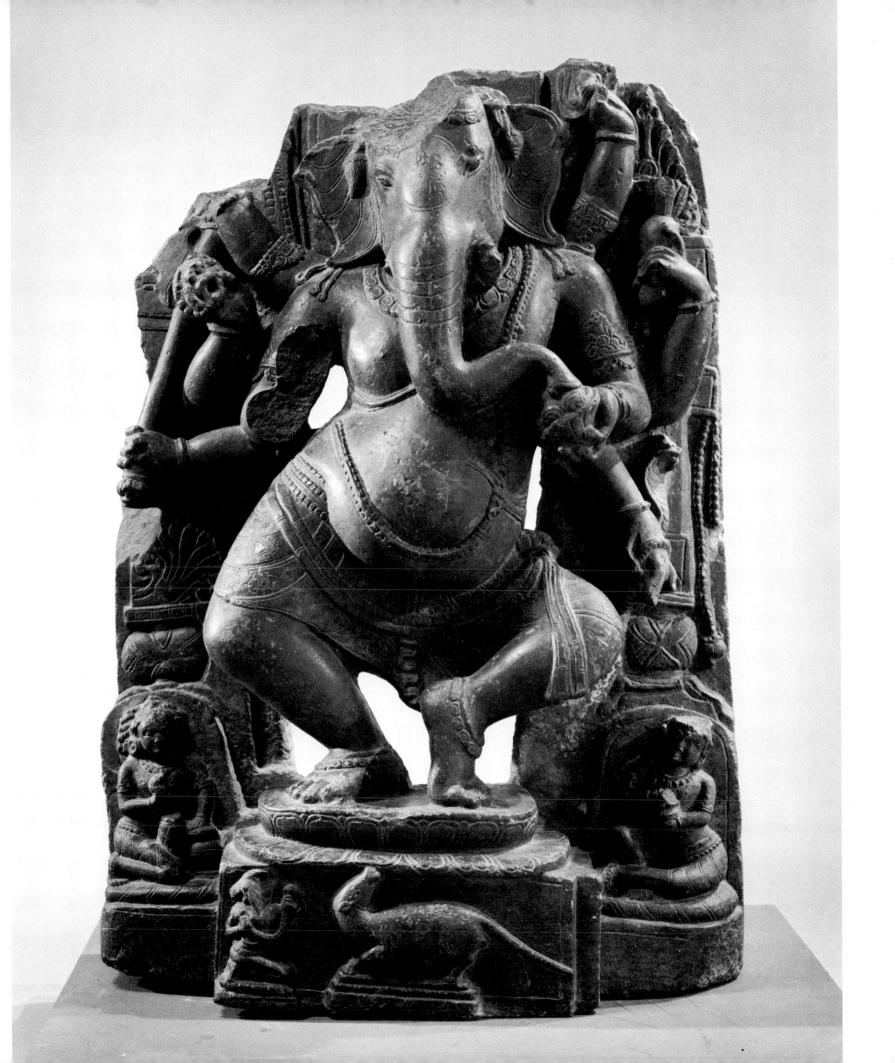

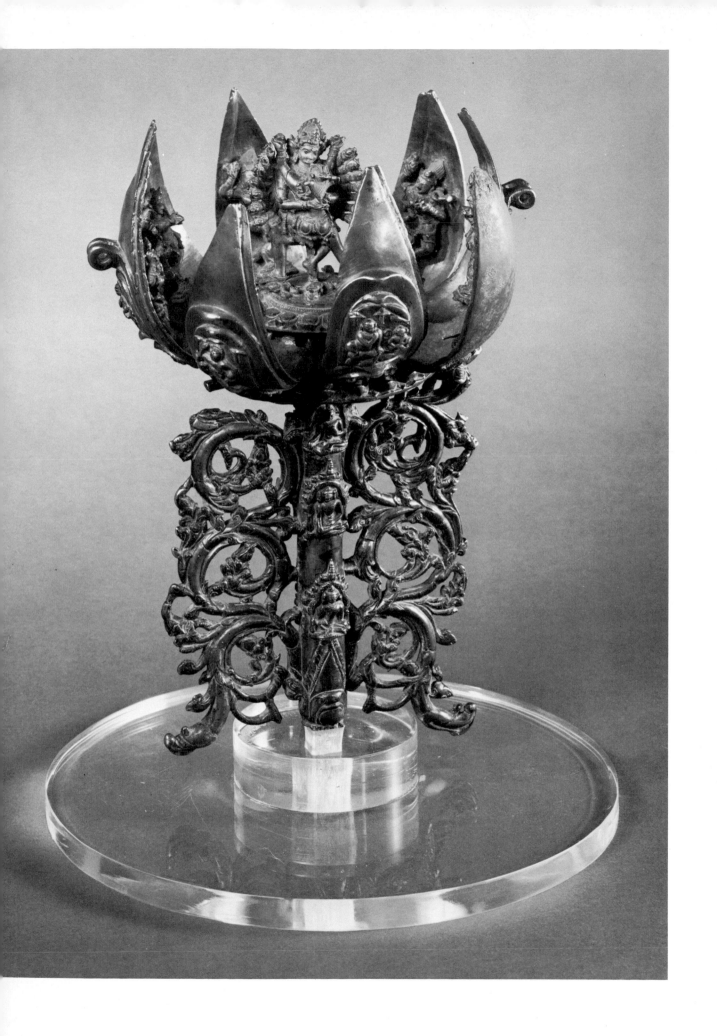

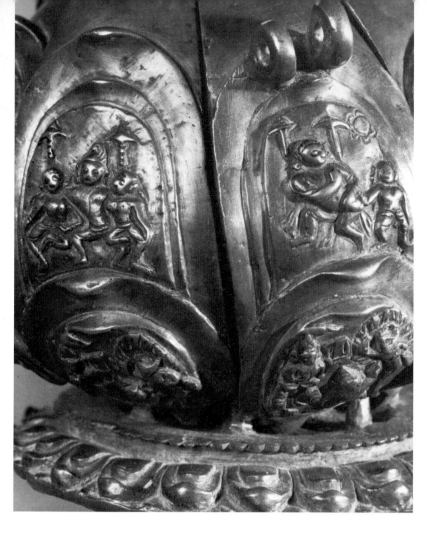

57. A Lotus Mandala

Bengal
11th century
Brass with paint
h: 12½ in. (31.7 cm.)

This elaborate sculpture, made in
several parts and skillfully joined,
represents a mandala in the form of a
lotus. At the center of the lotus stand
the embracing figures of Hevajra, one
of the most important Vajrayana
Buddhist gods, and his consort,
Nairātmyā. Eight goddesses, known
as Ḍākinīs, dance around them, each
against a petal of the lotus (one, however, is missing). We are told in the
texts that Hevajra is "Joy Innate" and
in a state of bliss; with their songs the
goddesses urge him to awaken.

The outside of each lotus petal is
embellished with two tiers of reliefs.
On the lower register of each petal an
identical scene appears with a snake,
a stupa, a fire, a tree, and two figures,
one of whom is dancing. Each scene
probably represents a cemetery,
eight of which usually surround a
mandala. The upper tiers each show
two figures, either seated or dancing;
these may represent some of the
Mahāsiddhas, or "perfected beings,"
a few of whom were historical figures
who played a prominent role in
spreading the cult of Hevajra and
other exotic cults of later Buddhism.
The lotus is supported by a stem from
which stylized rhizomes, equally well
finished at the front and back, branch
out on either side. Four Tathāgatas
and two bodhisattvas, each within a
shrine, are depicted on both sides of
the stem. The execution of these
figures, as well as of the scenes on the
petal exterior, is not as refined as that
of the principal figures or the rhizomes. Nonetheless, this lotus mandala
is a technical tour de force and is perhaps the most elaborate of all known
examples.

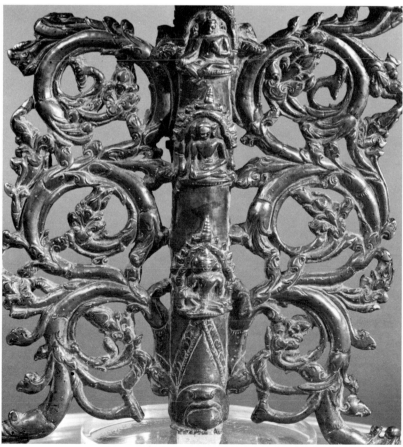

58. The God Vishnu

Bengal
11th century
Brass
h: 14½ in. (36.9 cm.)

This bronze is a typical Bengali Vishnu
image of the type that apparently came
into vogue during the late Pāla period
(10th–11th century) and has remained
popular with Vaishnavas ever since.
The shrine has an elaborate pedestal of
the type known as *pañcharatha*, and a
tall aureole, fringed with prominent
flame motifs and ending in a pointed
arch that was probably once surmounted by a parasol. Vishnu is, of
course, the largest figure and stands in
the middle, rigidly upright. He holds
his attributes the mace and the wheel
in his upper hands and the lotus seed
and the conch shell, now missing, in his
lower hands. Flanking him are his two
consorts Śrī-Lakshmī and Sarasvatī.
The former, the goddess of wealth,
holds a flywhisk and a lotus; the latter,
the goddess of wisdom and music,
plays the vina. That the donor of this
image was a woman is indicated by the
worshiping figure on the pedestal.

For comparable shrines, see R. C.
Majumdar, ed., *History of Bengal*,
Dacca, 1963, 1, pls. LXXI, p. 172;
LXXIII, p. 176; LXXIV, p. 177.

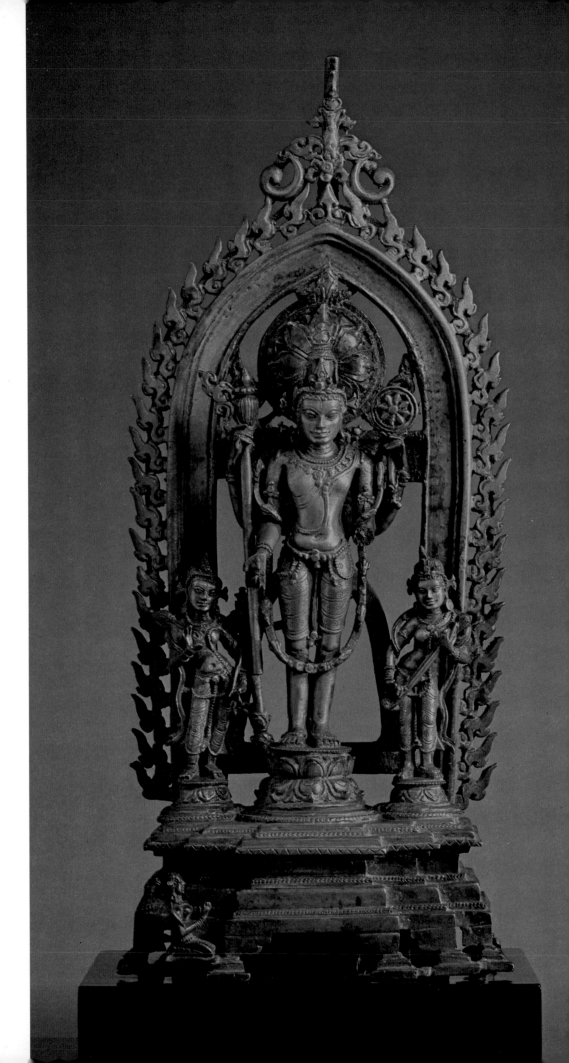

The Bodhisattva Maitreya
Bengal
12th century
Silver, inlaid with semiprecious
stones, copper, and gold; gilt-bronze
lotus
h: 12¾ in. (32.4 cm.)

The future Buddha, Maitreya, is represented here as a bodhisattva. Although
his hair is arranged in an ascetic's
chignon, he is sumptuously ornamented. A tiny stupa is lodged in his matted
hair, and a waterpot is attached to the
lotus whose sinuous stem he holds in his
left hand. His right hand forms the
abhayamudrā. The exposed edge at the
bottom of the lotus base indicates that
it must once have been inserted into a
pedestal, as the Vishnu bronze was
(no. 58).

Silver sculptures of this size are
extremely rare and few Bengal metal
images are so richly inlaid with both
metal and stone. To my knowledge
none reveals so engagingly busy a surface. The chasing of the exuberant
ornaments and the inlay work are
executed with a jeweler's finesse. The
gilt-bronze lotus on which the figure
stands is curious and may be a later
replacement. That the sculpture
found its way into Tibet is evident
from the traces of cold gold around the
face and from the blue paint on the
hair, for the Tibetans frequently
applied such paint to their figures.

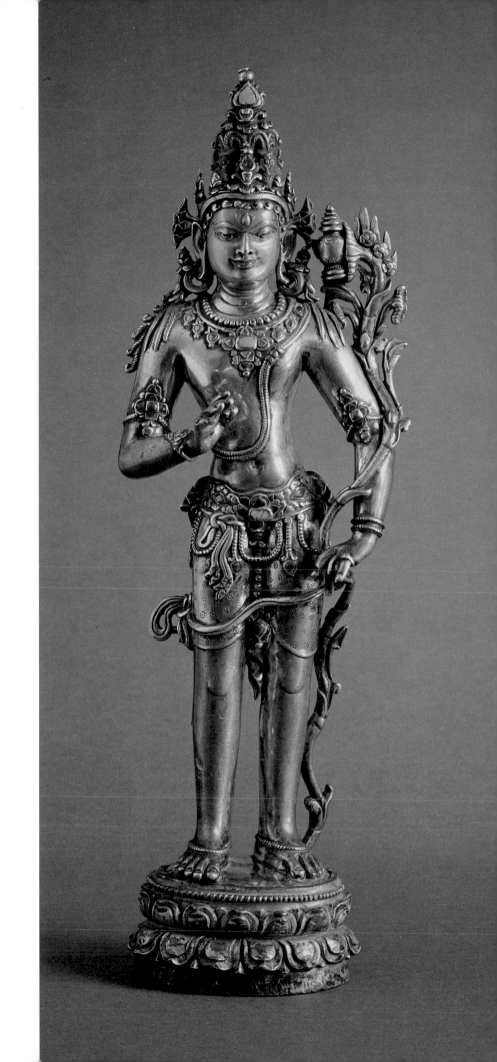

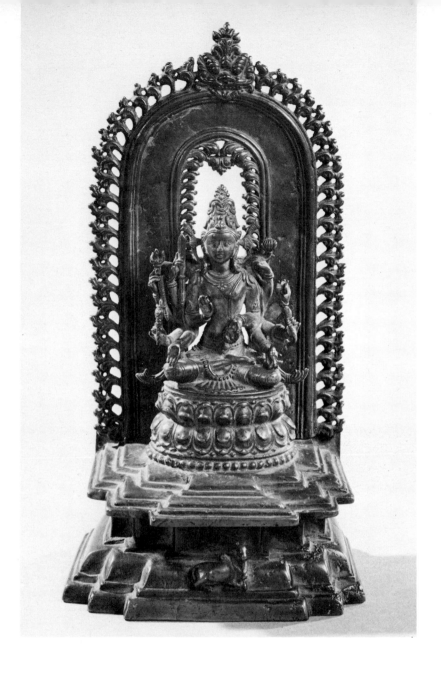

60. Sadāśiva

Orissa

11th century

Copper

h: 9½ in. (24.1 cm.)

Sadāśiva is the supreme form of Śiva, representing the quintessence of the entire philosophy of the Śuddha-Śaiva school of Śivaism. He really is formless, but since the ordinary mortal could not easily comprehend his subtle, luminous, and all-pervading nature, it was necessary to devise a tangible form. According to the texts, Sadāśiva can be represented with five heads or one, but he must have ten arms, which should display: on the right, a spear, a trident, a *khaṭṭvāṅga*, the *varadamudrā*, and the *abhayamudrā*, and on the left, a blue lotus, a kettle-drum, a snake, a rosary, and a citrus fruit. The present figure fits this description in every detail. His image is framed by a tall aureole, crowned by a *kīrttimukha* and fringed with the flame motif, representing his efful-gence. A tiny but remarkably natural-istic representation of the bull is attached to the front of the pedestal.

Metal images of Sadāśiva are rare enough, but rarer still is this Orissan example. Although Orissa is known to have produced stone sculp-tures with astonishing profusion during the medieval period, few bronzes of the period have yet come to light. Among the few known examples, this one is particularly handsome and finely crafted.

61. Embracing Couple (Mithuna)

Orissa, Bhuvanesvar (?)

11th–12th century

Grayish brown schist

h: 33 in. (83.8 cm.)

This sculpture once embellished the external wall of a temple and hence its narrow, bracketlike shape. Such unabashed *mithunas* were among the most popular subjects with Orissan sculptors. Generally the *mithuna*, although not always as bold as this, is regarded as an auspicious symbol and forms an integral part of the iconographic program of an Indian temple, whether Hindu, Buddhist, or Jaina. The man represented here has a shaved head and a beard, which his

partner is playfully pulling. He may represent an ascetic figure, but his smile leaves no doubt as to his evident pleasure. Although the legs seem somewhat stiff and columnar, the composition as a whole is imbued with organic rhythm, and the bodies are as pliant and sinuous as the lush plants below and above them. The right hand of the woman appears to clutch a branch, emphasizing the close relationship between woman and nature.

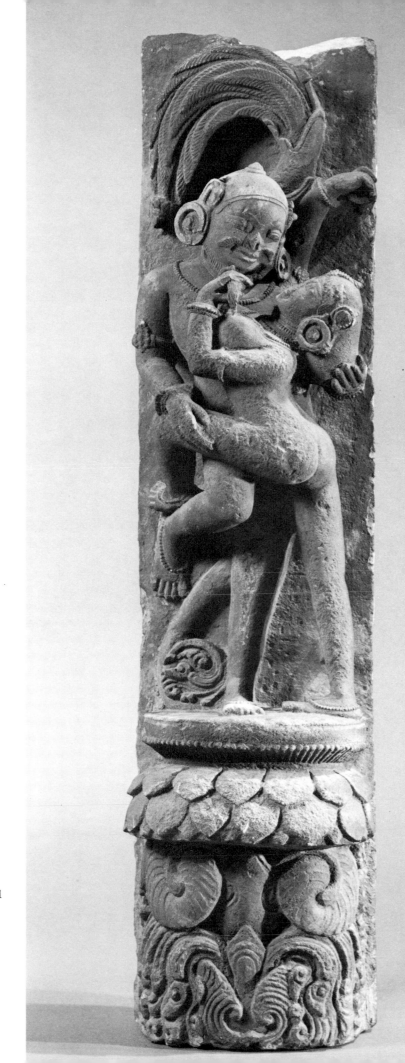

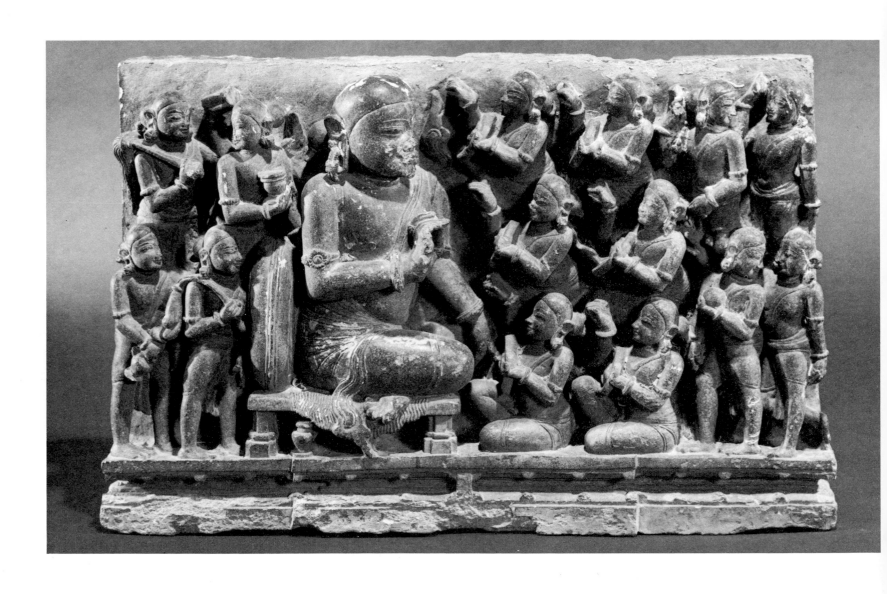

62. A Scene of Discourse

Orissa
13th century
Reddish black basalt
h: 13 in. (33.0 cm.)

A Vaishnava saint, distinguished by his disproportionately large size, is seated on a stool preaching to devotees. He is represented in a three-quarter view, facing a group of seated and standing figures, who in turn are oriented toward him. This arrange-ment is an unusual departure from most such scenes where the partici-pants face the viewer. That the saint is engaged in a discourse is evident from the gesture of his right hand. Some figures in the lively audience in front of him are engrossed in the discourse and appear to carry either manuscripts or writing implements as if they were taking notes. Others stand at the far end with offerings and seem to engage in conversation. Four figures approach the saint from the back of the throne, carrying various articles such as a sack, a flywhisk, and pots. Despite the hieratic arrangement of the figures in formal registers, the relief is an animated depiction of a theme seldom encountered in Indian sculpture.

Such scenes from life appear to have been popular with the Orissan artists in the thirteenth century and several others are now in the National Museum, New Delhi (see *Bulletin National Museum*, no. 1, New Delhi, 1969, pl. 31). The present relief is executed in the same basic style as those in the National Museum and all the examples may have belonged to the same monument. At any rate, they certainly seem to be the works of a single atelier or family of sculptors.

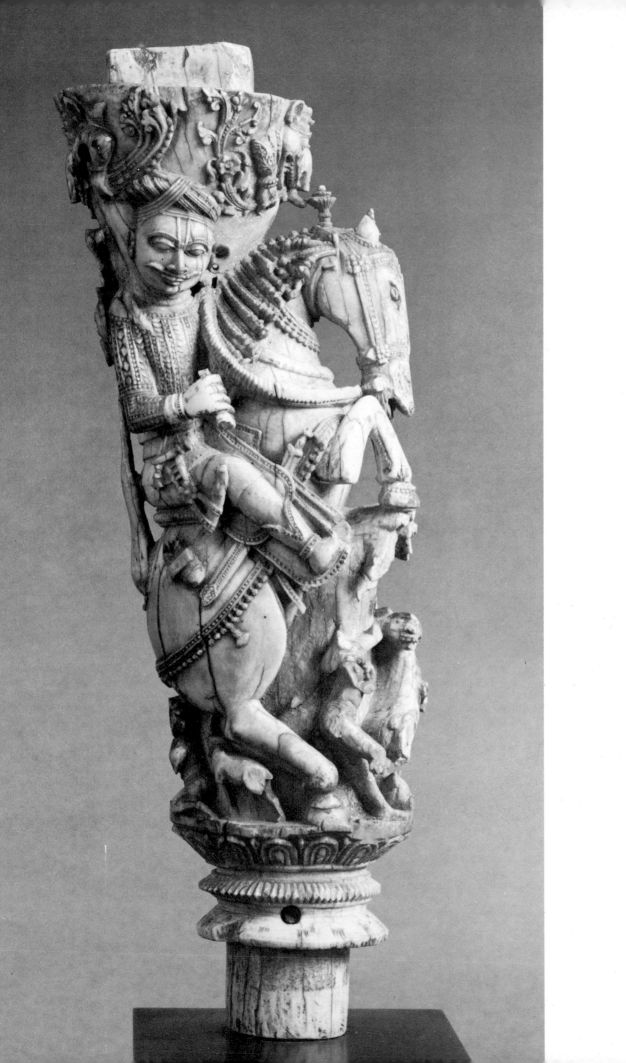

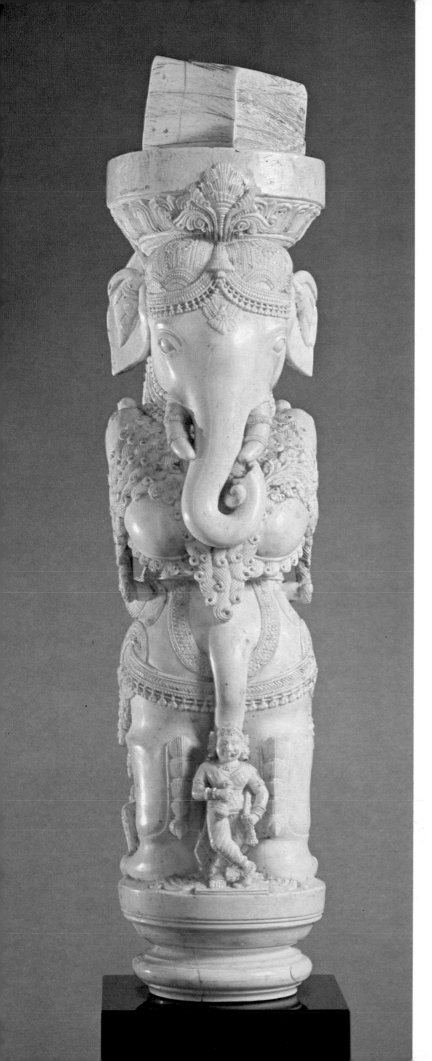

63. Throne Legs

Orissa
(a) 15th century
Patinated ivory
h: 11¾ in. (29.8 cm.)
(b) 17th century
Ivory
h: 15½ in. (39.3 cm.)

Ivory has been a favorite sculptural medium in India since very early times and has been used for both secular and religious purposes. Thrones of both rulers and deities were often made from ivory. Orissa has had a long-standing tradition of ivory carving and continues even today to produce finely carved decorative objects. These two richly carved legs probably belonged to royal rather than divine thrones since both are adorned with scenes of hunting. Indeed, hunting scenes predominate in most ivory throne legs that have so far come to light. Usually animal motifs, such as the horse in the earlier example (a) and the combined *gajasimha* ("elephant-lion") in the later (b), occupy much of the composition, following the natural shape of the tusk.

In the earlier leg a turbaned and armored rider attempts to control his spirited horse as several smaller hunters crowd two lionesses who are so intertwined that they appear to be locked in combat. A couple of deer watch the scene from rock caves, as do two fallen hunters. Interestingly, the forehead of the noble rider is marked with the sectarian sign of a Vaishnava. Two stylized lion heads are carved on either side at the top, and the bottom is carved into a lotus. In the second leg the body of the composite animal is mostly that of a lion, with an additional elephant head carved in the front (not visible in this view). Below the hind parts of the lion is a tiny figure of a female attendant holding a wine jug with her right hand. On the reverse two horsemen attack a boar below a stylized flowering tree in which sit two parrots. The carving of both legs is particularly delicate, and the two different designs reveal the Orissan carvers' imagination and technical skill.

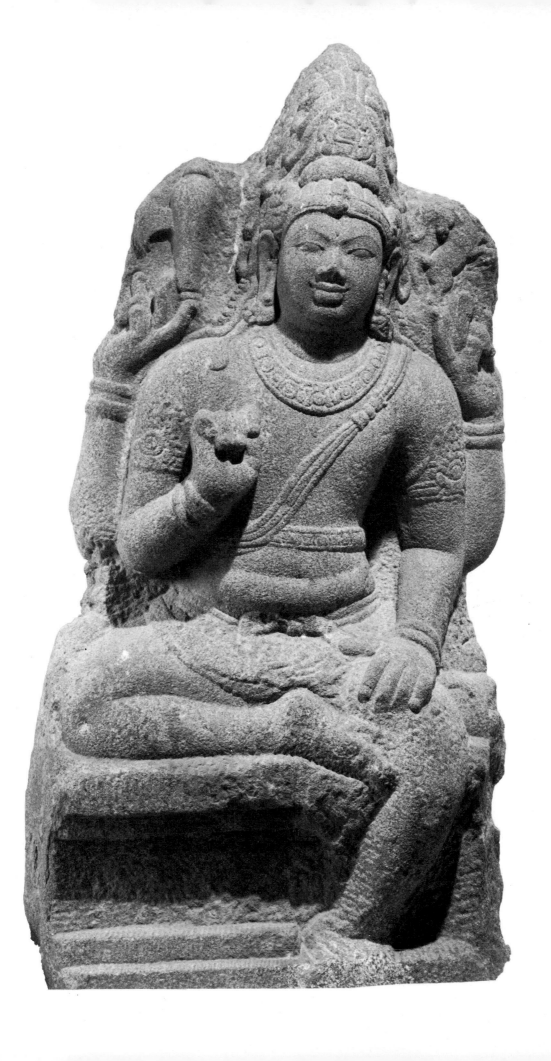

64. The God Siva

South India, Pāṇḍyan style
8th–9th century
Beige granite
h: 57½ in. (146.0 cm.)

This imposing sculpture represents a classic image type of Siva in the South Indian sculptural tradition. Generally referred to as *sukhāsanamūrti* ("image of the relaxed posture"), the form is employed with minor variations for all peaceful images of the god. Normally when Siva is seated in this posture his right leg is pendant, as in the Somāskanda image (no. 68), but some texts, such as the *Pūrva-Karaṇāgama*, give instructions for the left leg to be pendant, as it is here. With his two upper hands Siva holds the battle-ax and the deer; his normal left hand is placed on his left thigh and the corresponding right forms, somewhat tentatively, the gesture known as *siṁhakarṇamudrā*. His ascetic grandeur is reflected by the beautifully rendered crown of matted locks and his face has an unusually serene expression.

Very likely this sculpture was once attached to a rock-cut sanctuary like those abounding in the regions of Tamilnadu and Kerala that were within the Pāṇḍyan kingdom during the eighth and ninth centuries. The sculpture is rendered in the same basic style as the monumental figure of Pārvatī in the Rockefeller collection (see Lee, 1970, I, fig. 11 and p. 31). The Pāṇḍyas were a powerful dynasty that rivaled the Cholas but they are not as well known and the history of their sculpture has yet to be written. However, the few examples that have received recent attention reflect a vigorous style with a distinctly local expression that distinguishes them from both Pallava and early Chola sculptures.

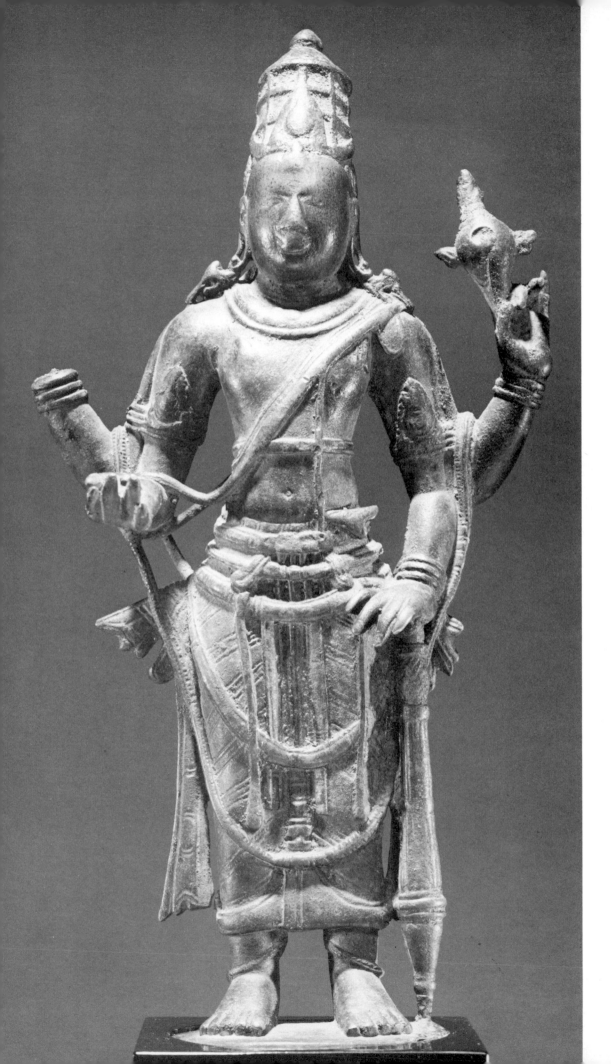

65. The God Vishnu

(a) Tamilnadu
8th–9th century
Bronze
h: 11 in. (28.0 cm.)
(b) Kerala (?)
9th century
Bronze with green patina
h: 7⅝ in. (19.4 cm.)

(a) Represented in his supreme, or *para*, aspect, Vishnu stands here in strict symmetry, as firm as a pillar. His majesty is proclaimed by his distinctive cylindrical crown (*kīriṭamukuṭa*) and by the mace in his lower left hand. His upper right hand, now broken, once held the wheel, in opposition to the conch shell displayed prominently by his corresponding left hand. His lower right hand is disposed in a gesture that seems to beckon the devotee.

Scholars are strongly divided in their opinions about the provenance of bronzes in this style. Most are agreed that they cannot be dated later than the ninth century, but the question seems to be whether they should be characterized as Pallava (seventh–ninth century) or as Chola, the dynasty that succeeded the Pallavas in this region. Curiously, most of these bronzes portray Vishnu and are rather diminutive in size. Apparently they were intended for domestic altars rather than for temples, as is also indicated by the well-rubbed faces, worn by the constant application of unguents.

(b) On a fully blown lotus, placed upon a pedestal decorated with simple moldings and pilasters, Vishnu is seated in *lalitāsana*. He wears a tall, cylindrical crown and a dhoti that is held at the waist with a sash sporting a simple *kīrttimukha* clasp. The jewelry is simple, as it is in (a), but here the sacred thread does not go over Vishnu's right arm and he is also given a garland that just overhangs the lotus. His upper right hand holds the wheel, but the conch shell in the corresponding left hand is broken. His lower right hand grasps a lotus, his lower left holds a mace. His right foot rests on a cushion placed on an extended petal of the lotus. The back of the figure is well finished and the hair falls in two rows of spiral curls on the shoulder. A *śiraśchakra* ("nimbus") with tassels is attached to the back of the crown. On either side of the base are two small armlike extensions where the god's two consorts once sat. The uprights at the back supported the aureole, which is now missing.

The two most unusual features of this bronze are the lotus in the right hand and the horizontal disposition of the mace, which is usually held upright. The lotus, of course, is one of Vishnu's most distinctive attributes, but it is rarely seen in his hand in either Chola or the so-called Pallava bronzes. The narrow face, as well as the slim, elongated torso, distinguishes it from other such early bronzes and brings to mind the Nallur Naṭarāja (see Barrett, 1965, pl. 61), which is generally regarded as a work of the end of the ninth century. However, the bronze is probably from Kerala.

Published: (a) *Indische Kunst*, no. 98, pl. 35.

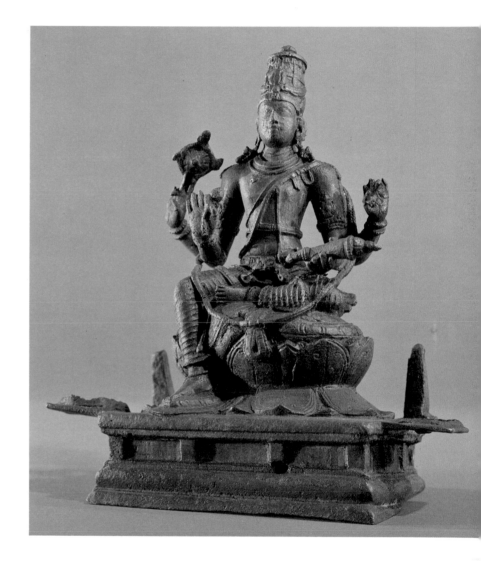

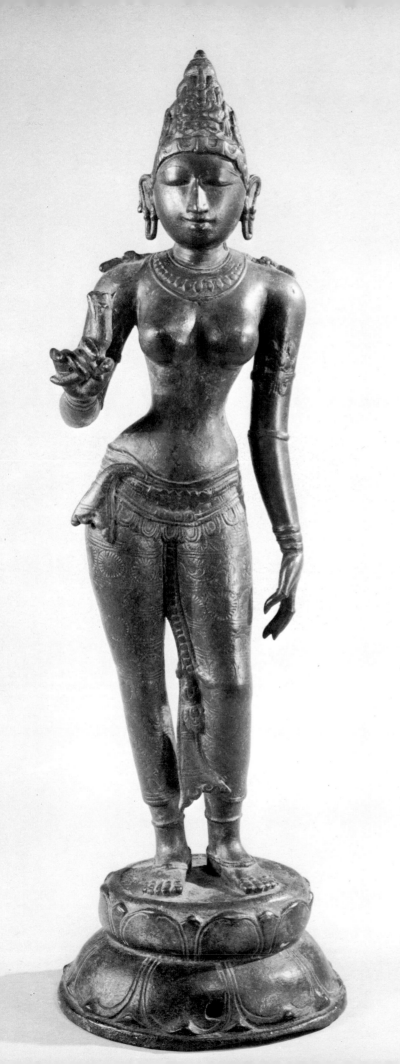
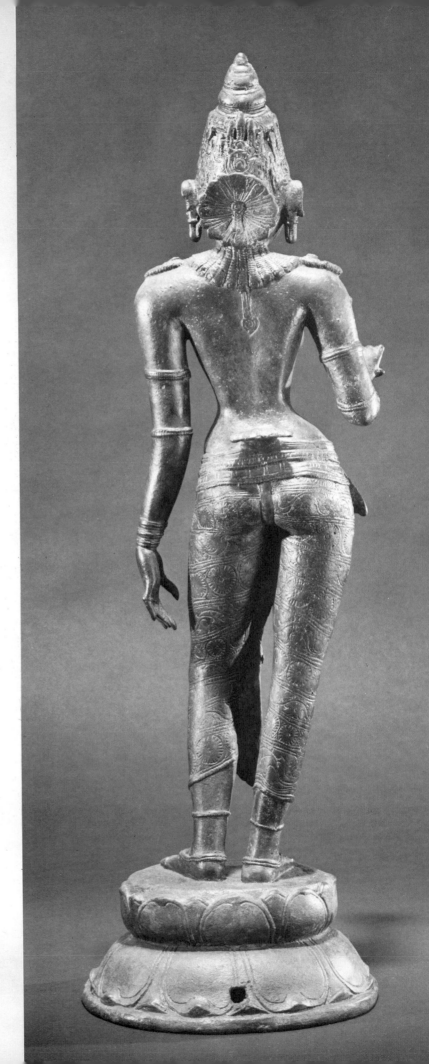

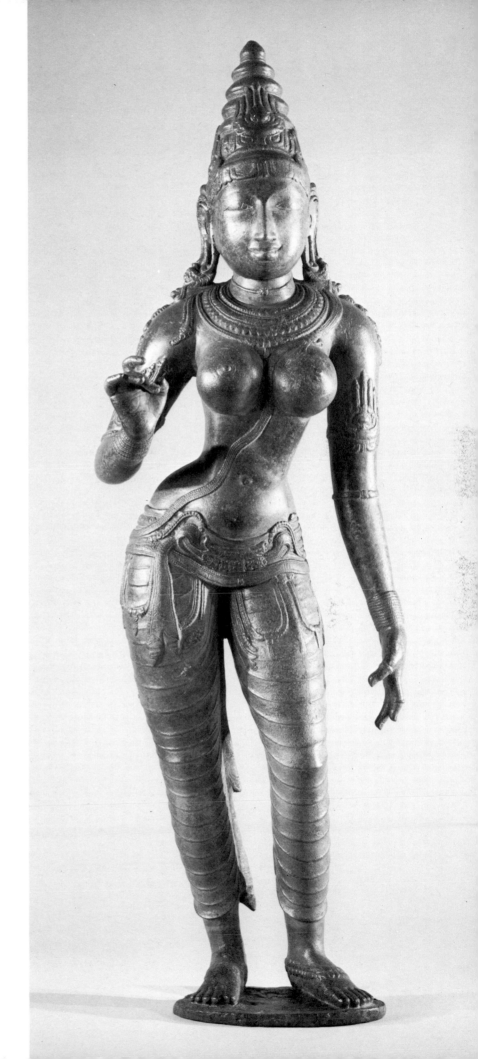

66a

66b

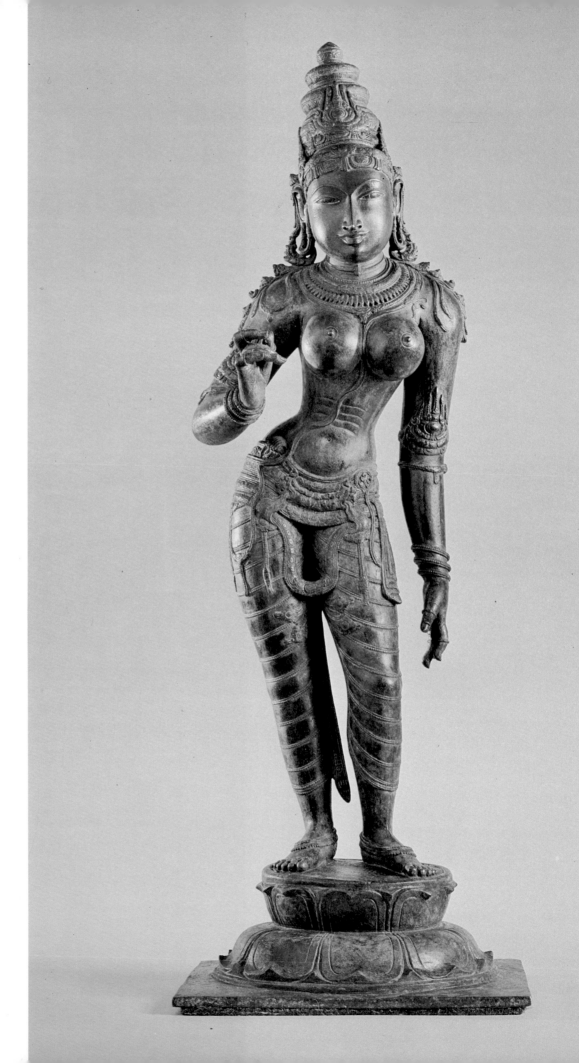

66. A Goddess

Tamilnadu
(a) 10th century
Bronze with dark patina
h: 25¼ in. (64.2 cm.)
(b) 11th century
Bronze with green patina
h: 29 in. (73.6 cm.)
(c) 13th century
Bronze with green patina
h: 31¾ in. (80.7 cm.)

These three bronzes represent a classic
figure type that Chola artists used with
only minor variations for the consorts
of several gods. Generally, however,
they can be said to portray Siva's wife
Pārvatī, although the earliest figure
(a) was identified as Bhū-devī, one of
Vishnu's consorts, in an earlier
publication (see below). This under-
scores the difficulty in identifying such
figures when they are separated from
their male partners. In all three
examples the goddess stands gracefully
on a lotus, her legs draped with a
clinging garment and her torso bare.
Each has her head crowned, the
crowns varying in shape and design.
The left hand extends along the left
thigh in *lolahasta* and the right hand
holds a lotus flower or bud, which is
missing in two of the bronzes.

Each bronze is a superb example
of its period and admirably displays
the stylistic peculiarities of its age. The
earliest figure (a) is characterized by
greater simplicity in ornamentation,
the naturalistic shape of the breasts,
the fluent outline of the slim body,
and the gentle sensuousness of the
modeling. By the eleventh century
(b) a number of changes have
occurred, most notably in the broader
shape of the face, the slightly heavier
proportions, the higher waistline,
the more rotund breasts, and the
somewhat richer jewelry. By the
thirteenth century (c) the soft pliancy
of the mass, still apparent in the
eleventh century, has given way to a
more mannered elegance. The breasts
have grown in substance but are not
as shapely, the hip is thrust out
further, but with less grace, the nose
has become more prominent and the
features more sharply defined, the
folds of the belly are clearly marked,
and the opulent form is further
embellished with a rich array of
jewelry.

Published: (a) *Masterpieces of Asian Art
in American Collections*, New York, 1970,
II, pp. 44–45, no. 11.

66c

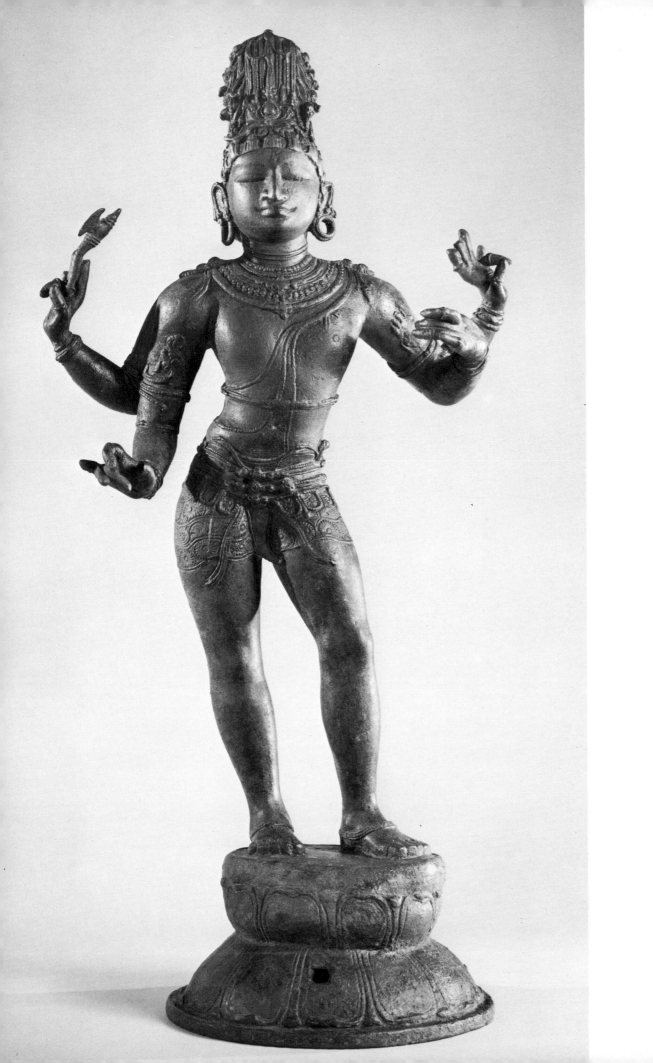

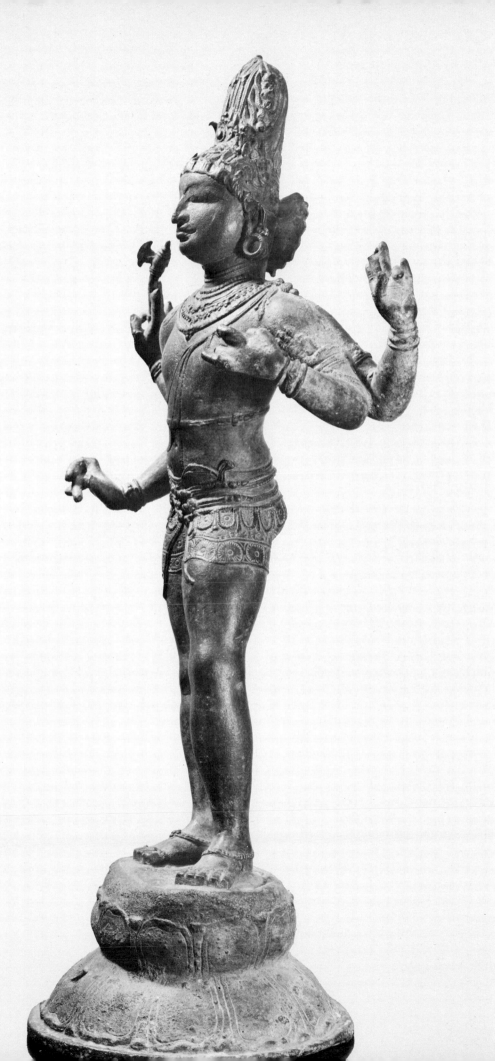

67. Siva as the Lord of Music

Tamilnadu
Ca. 1000
Dark bronze
h: 22¼ in. (56.5 cm.)

Siva is regarded as the original teacher
of both dance and music. Just as a
special form was conceived to represent
him as the Lord of the Dance, so a
particular type was invented to
portray him as the Lord of Music. In
iconographic terminology, this image
type is known as *vīṇādhara
dakshiṇāmūrti*, meaning "the image of
grace bearing the vina."

This unusually boyish Siva
strikes a graceful posture as he stands
on a lotus base. Richly ornamented,
he wears a short, printed dhoti and a
tall, elegant chignon. The crescent
moon and a serpent adorn his hair and
the third eye is etched on his forehead.
The dhoti is held together by a sash
with a richly detailed clasp showing
the *kīrttimukha* motif. The upper right
hand holds the battle-ax; the deer,
once held by the corresponding left
hand, is now missing. The two
principal hands once held the vina,
which may have been separately
attached. The bronze is superbly
modeled both front and rear.

Published: *Indische Kunst*, no. 103,
pl. 38.

68. Somāskanda

Tamilnadu
Ca. 1000
Copper
h: 21½ in. (54.6 cm.)

In this family group, we see Siva and Umā (or Pārvatī) seated with their son Skanda, or Kumāra, standing between them. The pedestal supporting the figures is decorated with simple moldings and pilasters; the separate *prabhā*, or aureole, that was once attached to the back is now missing. The four rings at the sides were used to anchor the sculpture to the wall. This image type is peculiar to South India and was very popular with the artists of the Chola period. This particular example is one of the finest bronze representations of the subject.

Although both are portrayed frontally, Umā's is the slightly more relaxed figure, possibly because of the disposition of her right leg. It is noteworthy that in such images Umā's left leg generally dangles and her right leg is folded, but here the reverse is true. The smooth, supple bodies of both deities are adorned with restrained elegance and their faces are radiant with extraordinary serenity. Siva's upper hands hold the battle-ax and the deer, the latter symbolizing his intimate association with animals. His lower right hand forms the *abhayamudrā* and in the palm of his left hand rests a fruitlike object which may be a citrus fruit symbolizing his creative aspect. Umā holds a water lily in her right hand, a symbol of grace and beauty. Skanda stands gracefully, slightly behind his parents, naked except for his ornaments. Like his mother he holds a flower, this time a lotus bud, in his right hand.

Published: *Indische Kunst*, no. 102, pl. 39; Munsterberg, 1970, pp. 132–33.

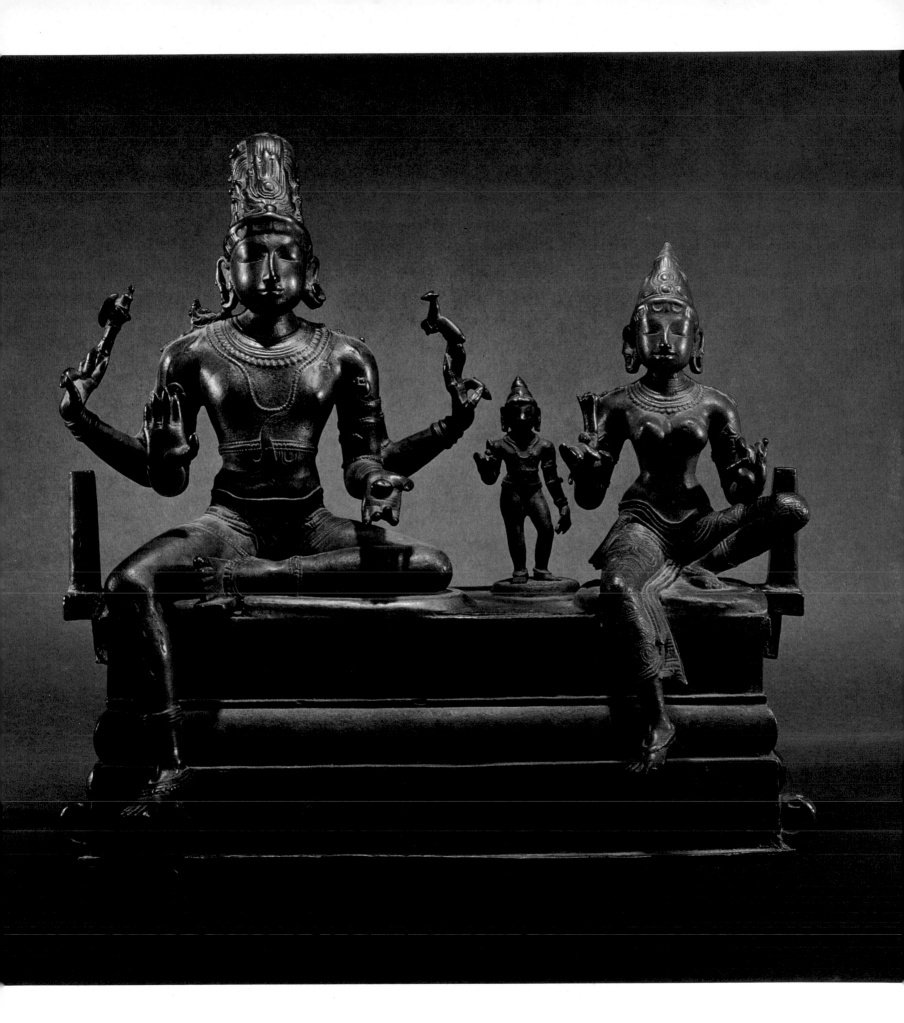

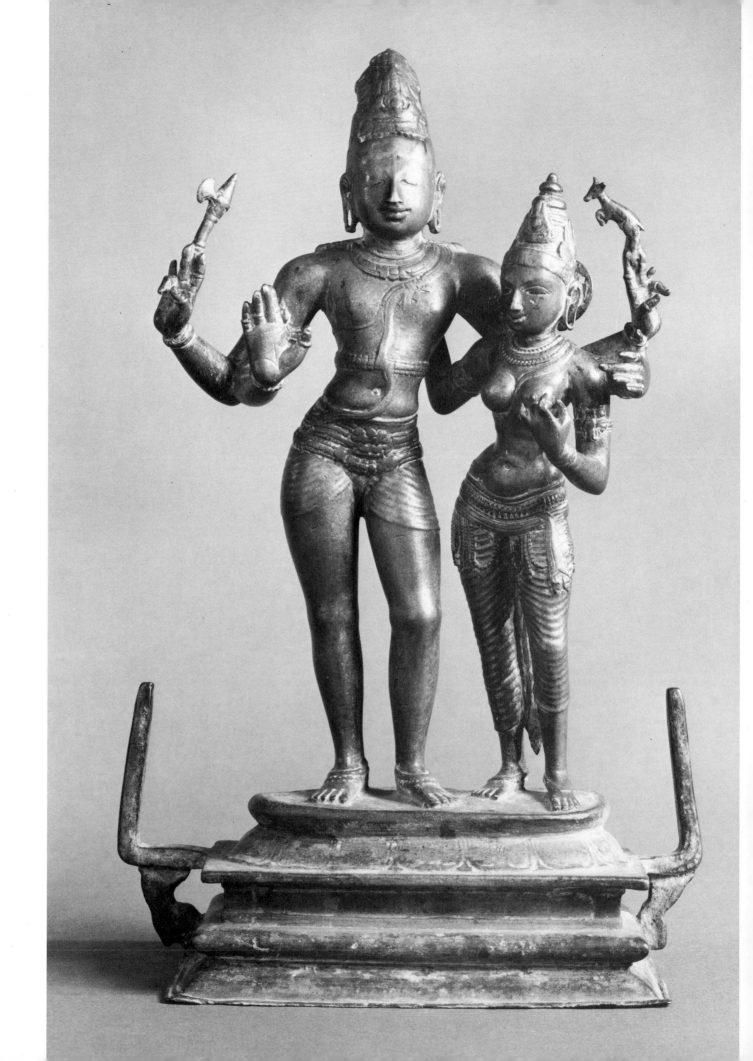

69. Siva and Pārvatī

Tamilnadu, Tanjore district
11th century
Copper with green patina
h : 14 in. (35.5 cm.)

Siva and Pārvatī stand gracefully on a lotus placed upon a pedestal. One of Siva's left arms encircles her while her right hand fondly touches his shoulder at the back. Siva's form is basically the same as that encountered in Somāskanda images (see no. 68), and while his divinity is emphasized by his two additional arms, Pārvatī, as usual, is essentially human. Siva's nimbus is missing as is Pārvatī's emblem, which may have been a mirror or a lotus.

Such images of the loving couple standing with their arms around each other are known as *pradoshamūrti* or *āliṅganamūrti*. The intimacy between the two is conveyed not only by subtle gestures, but also by the total composition. Even though Siva's arm does not touch Pārvatī, it seems to envelop her with tenderness. The bodies of both are elegantly modeled and a rhythmic sense of movement flows gently from one to the other. Compare this sculpture with the North Indian representation of the same theme (no. 39).

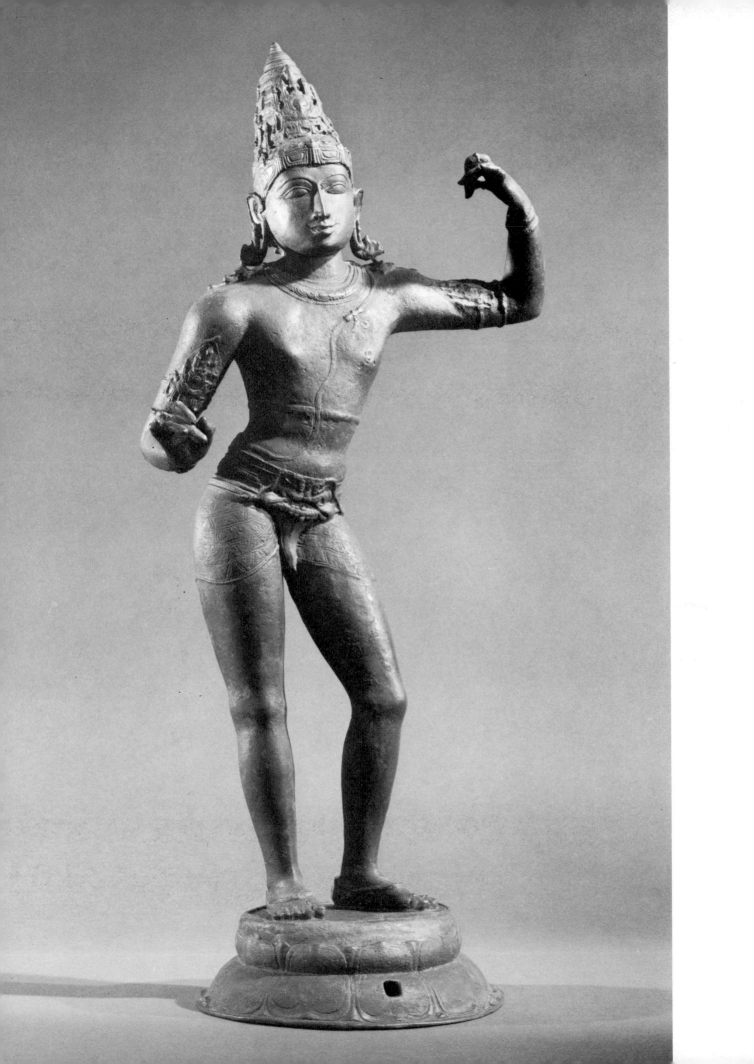

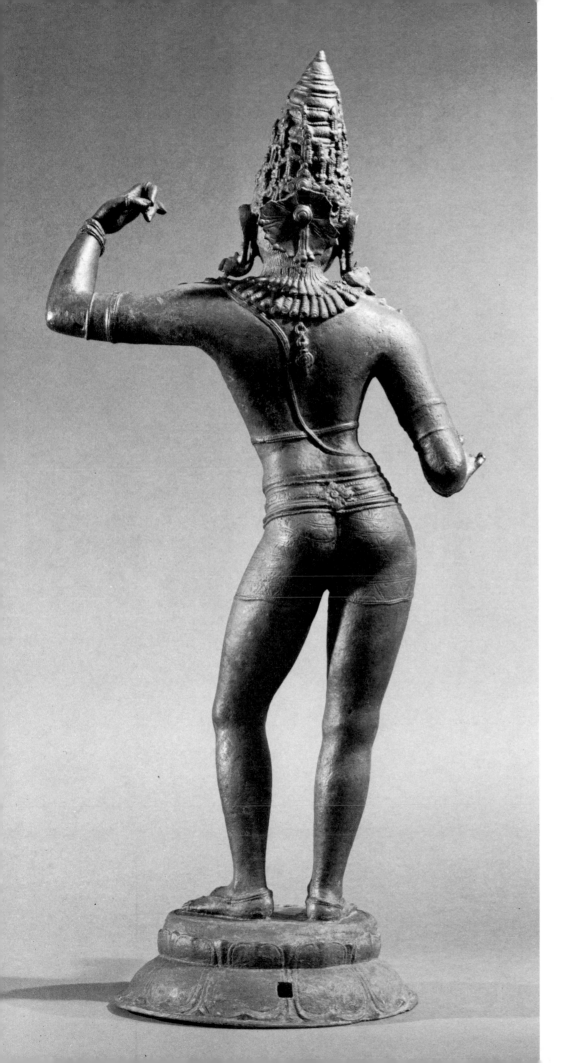

70. The God Rāma

Tamilnadu
11th century
Bronze
h: 31⅞ in. (81.0 cm.)

Rāma, the hero of the Hindu epic
Rāmāyaṇa, was a king of Ayodhya and
is regarded as an ideal ruler and a
paragon of virtue. Whether or not he
was a historical figure, he so captured
the Hindu imagination that in the
course of time he came to be regarded
as one of the incarnations of Vishnu.
He is, therefore, still worshiped as a
god all over India, and some of his
finest bronze images were created by
unknown Chola artists.

Although apotheosized, Rāma is
never given the multiple arms of a god.
Rather, he appears as an ideal human
figure standing gracefully, his majesty
indicated by his elegant crown, as in
this impressive realization. His raised
left arm once held a bow and his right
hand an arrow, thereby emphasizing
his martial nature, for in the *Rāmāyaṇa*
he is both a righteous king and a heroic
warrior. This bronze is superbly
modeled, the round, firm flesh
contained by an outline of extraordinary fluidity.

71. Hanumān

Tamilnadu
11th century
Bronze
h: 25⅜ in. (64.5 cm.)

A species of large monkeys with black
faces is known in India as *hanumān*.
According to the epic *Rāmāyaṇa*, Rāma
was living as an exile in a forest with
his brother and his wife, Sita, when
she was abducted by Rāvaṇa, the
king of Laṅkā. In his efforts to rescue
his wife, Rāma was aided by the
monkeys, one of whom, called
Hanumān, became his special devotee
and was later deified and venerated
by the Vaishnavas. Thus he is almost
always represented with Rāma, just as
Garuḍa is with Vishnu and Nandi is
with Siva.

This bronze figure of Hanumān is
the finest known example among
Chola representations. Except for the
face and the tail, he is essentially a
human figure and similar to that of his
master (no. 70). He too stands
gracefully on a lotus, wears a dhoti,
and is elegantly crowned and
ornamented. Like Rāma, he is even
provided with the sacred cord worn
only by brahmans and *kshatriyas*, the
two highest castes. This image must
originally have formed part of a group,
although not the same group to which
the Rāma belonged. The slight
forward tilt of the body indicates his
subservience, while the remarkably
expressive and elegant gestures of his
hands suggest that he was engaged in
animated conversation, presumably
with his master.

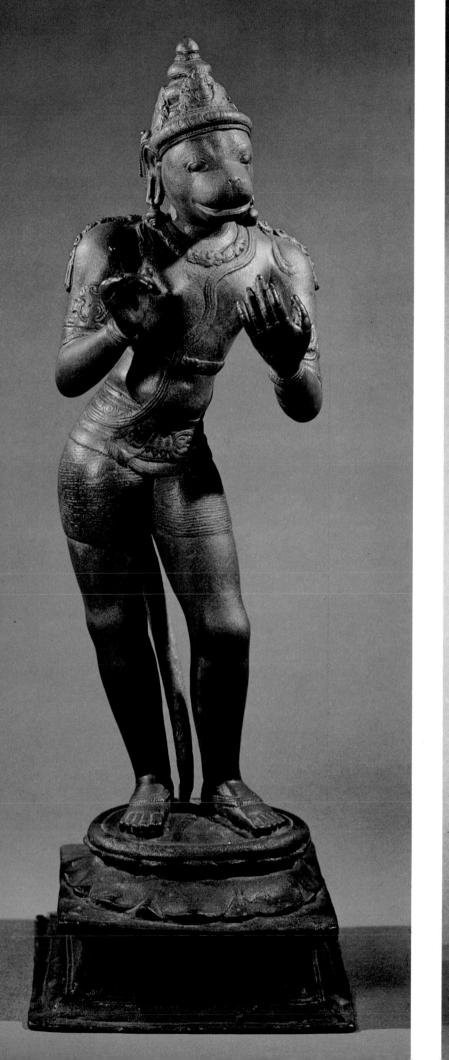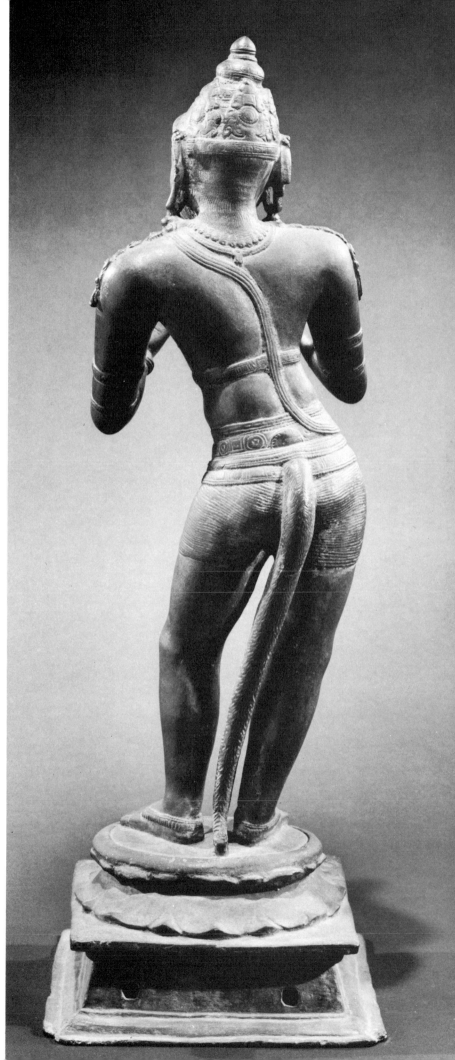

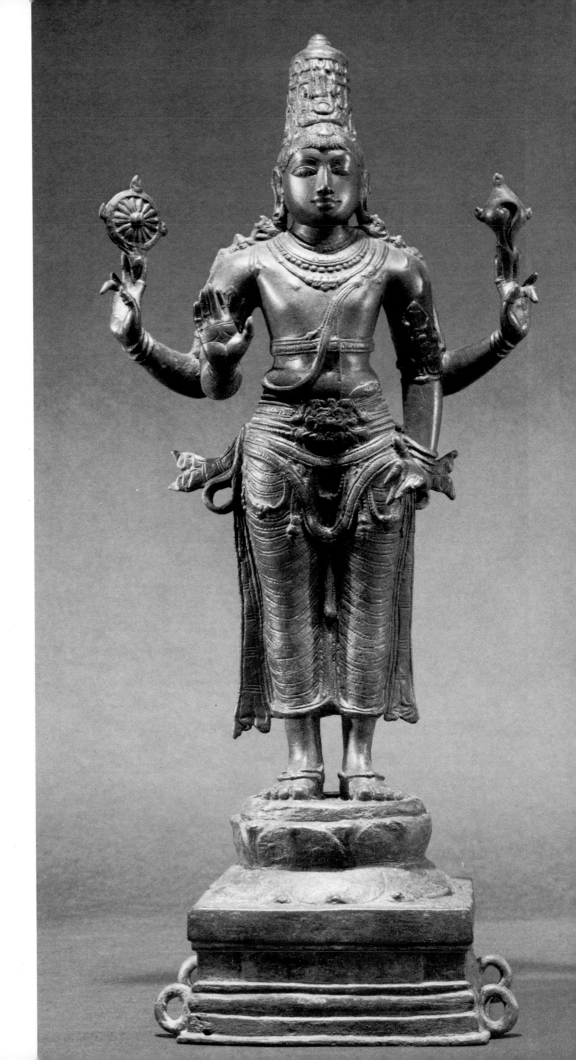

72. The God Vishnu

Tamilnadu
11th century
Dark bronze
h: 25½ in. (64.7 cm.)

This handsome bronze is a fine
example of a typical Chola Vishnu and
was probably once flanked by two
other figures representing his two
wives. A cursory comparison with the
two earlier bronzes (no. 65) will make
it apparent that while the style has
changed considerably, the iconography has not. More often than not,
in the alleged Pallava bronzes (see
no. 65), Vishnu's lower right hand
forms the *varadamudrā* somewhat
tentatively, and the sacred thread
goes over the right arm. In typically
Chola Vishnu images, such as this
example, the lower right hand
invariably is in *abhayamudrā* and the
sacred thread remains attached to the
body. Among other differences, the
crown in a Chola bronze is slightly
more tapered, the ornaments are more
richly designed, the dhoti is treated
quite differently and is always held
together by the *kīrttimukha* clasp,
a feature never present in the earlier
group of bronzes.

Published: *Indische Kunst*, no. 106.

73. A Saiva Devotee

Tamilnadu, Madurai district
11th century
Dark bronze
h: 22½ in. (57.2 cm.)

The cult of saints is as strong in Hinduism as it is in Roman Catholicism. Bronze images of saints and extraordinary devotees are essential parts of temple iconography, particularly in South India where Saiva saints are known as *nayanārs* and Vaishnava saints as *ālvars*. There is no formal ceremony of canonization in India, but once a devotee or teacher becomes well known for his spiritual qualities, he begins to be worshiped by his followers, even while alive. The tradition is an ancient one and two of the most celebrated of such teachers are, of course, the Buddha Śākyamuni and the Tīrthaṁkara Mahāvīra. Some of these saints are easily recognizable, but others are not, as is the case with this figure.

Standing gracefully on a lotus, the saint joins his hands in front of his chest in *añjalīmudrā*. As in images of Siva, his hair is arranged in a tall chignon, indicating his ascetic nature, and yet he is quite elaborately adorned with various ornaments. Rather unusual is the spread of his sash in front of the dhoti. If there were a battle-ax in the crook of his left arm, the figure could be identified as Chaṇḍikeśvara, but his matted hair does indicate that he is a Saiva rather than a Vaishnava saint or devotee.

Although a product of the Chola tradition, the bronze differs somewhat in general style as well as in details of garments and ornaments from contemporary Chola works created around Tanjore. It is possible that the bronze is from Madurai, which was the capital of the Pāṇḍyan kingdom and must also have been a center of artistic activity.

Published: *Indische Kunst*, no. 113.

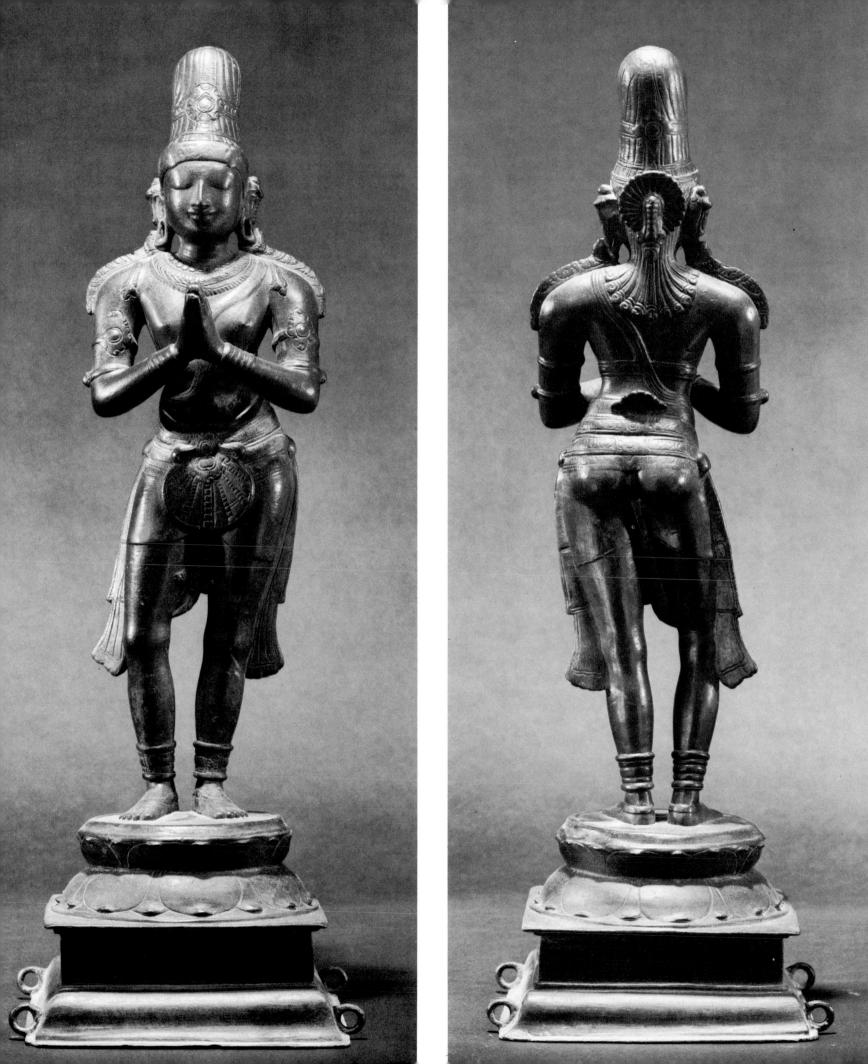

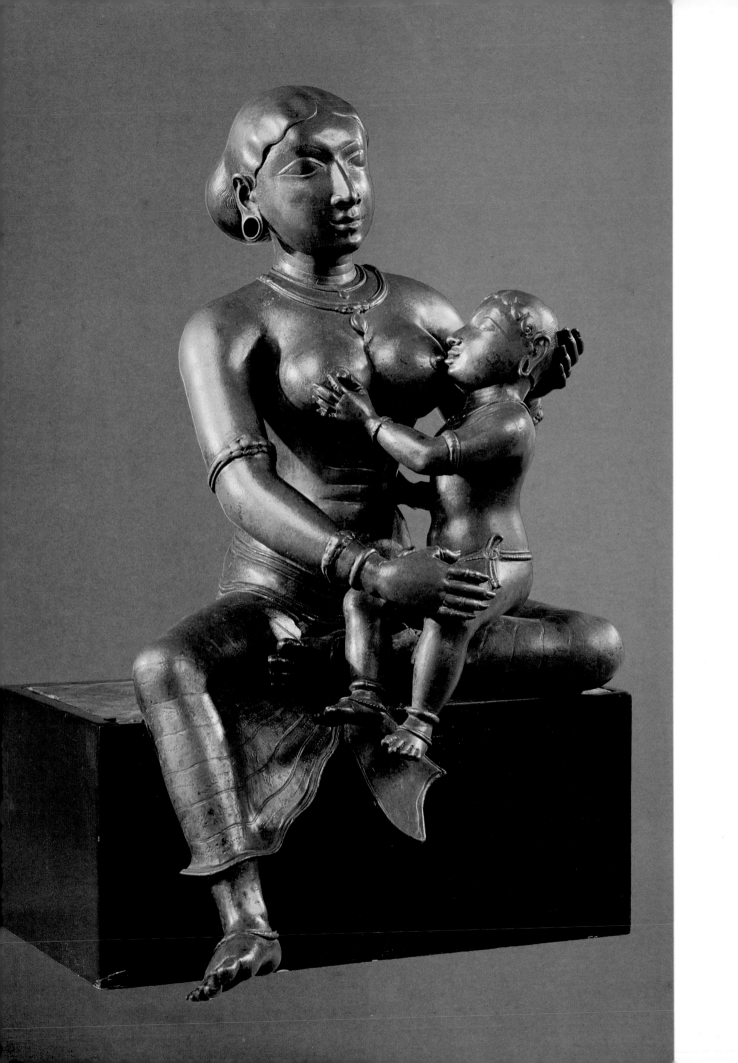

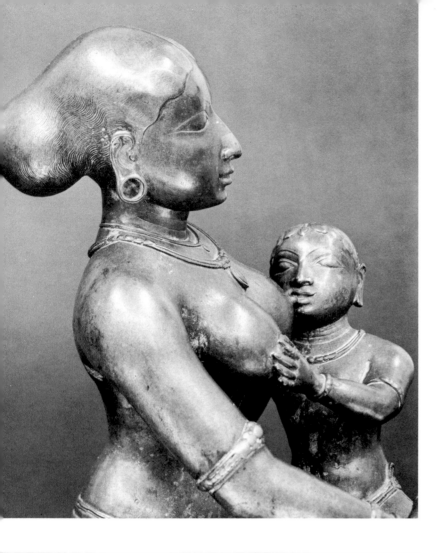

74. Yaśodā and Krishna

Tamilnadu
11th–12th century
Copper
h: 13⅛ in. (33.3 cm.)

Representations of the infant Krishna
and his foster mother Yaśodā are quite
rare in Chola art, and apart from this
outstanding example, only two or three
other bronzes are known. Not only is
this bronze much larger than the
others, but it is unsurpassed for its
restrained elegance and tender expression. With remarkable perception and
candor, the sculptor has shown the
infant playing with one of his mother's
nipples while he sucks the other. Such
a sensitive interpretation of the intimacy between a nursing mother and
her baby is altogether unusual for
South Indian sculpture. With the
utmost economy and subtlety in modeling, the sculptor has given us a remarkably naturalistic and animated
representation. Yaśodā was the wife
of a cowherd and is appropriately
portrayed as a robust young peasant.
Her ornaments are unostentatious, her
hair is gathered at the back in a simple
though elegant bun, and her left nostril
is provided with a tiny hole to which a
separate nose ring was once attached.
Few superfluous details are allowed to
detract from our enjoyment of the pure
form, and the essential humanism of
the theme makes the work universally
appealing.

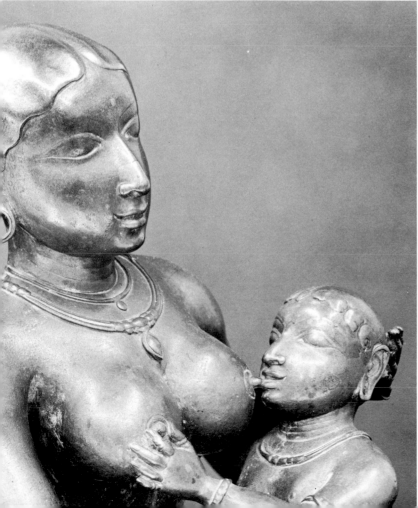

129

75. The God Gaṇeśa

Tamilnadu
12th century
Bronze with traces of green patina
h: 25⅛ in. (64.0 cm.)

Universally venerated in India, Gaṇeśa is the benevolent god who removes obstacles and bestows success on all endeavors. In Hindu mythology, he is the older son of Siva and Pārvāti and is said to have been born from the dirt on Pārvāti's body while she was taking a bath. There are many other stories about his origin, however, and what does seem clear is that in all probability he was a tribal god assimilated into the Hindu pantheon around the beginning of the Christian era. His elephant head is possibly a survival from his totemistic past.

His short, plump legs are those of a healthy child and his belly is bloated with the sweets he loves to eat. Indeed, his left hand holds a sweet that is about to disappear into his trunk. He stands in *tribhaṅga* on a lotus placed upon a pedestal etched with beautiful floral designs. His dhoti is so short that it is hardly visible and his hair is arranged into a tall chignon as his father's usually is (see nos. 67, 68). His second left hand holds a lasso and his two right hands carry a battle-ax and one of his own tusks. The tusk probably doubles as a cornucopia, for Gaṇeśa is also the god of abundance.

When first published (see below), this superb bronze was dated to the fourteenth century, which seems much too late. Both in the subtlety of its naturalistic modeling and the finesse of its details, the bronze is an excellent example of Chola craftsmanship of the twelfth century.

Published: *Indische Kunst*, no. 114, pl. 43.

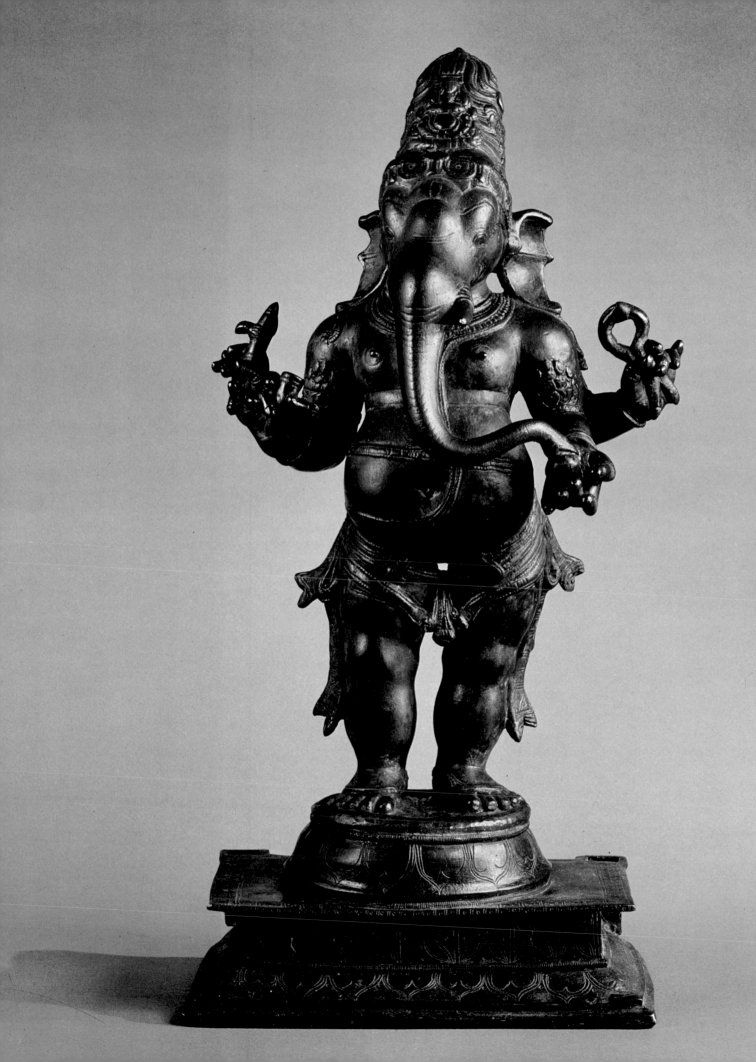

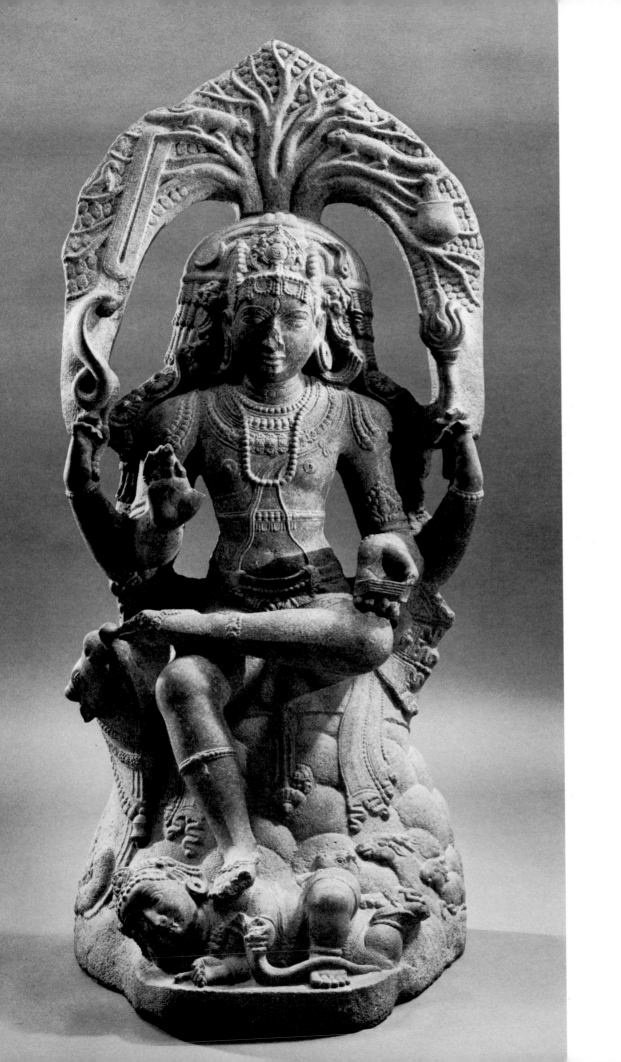

76. Siva as the Supreme Teacher
Tamilnadu, Tanjore region
(a) 12th century
Buff granite
h: 58 in. (147.3 cm.)
(b) 13th century
Copper with traces of green patina
h: 7 in. (17.8 cm.)

This image type, generally enshrined on the southern wall of a typical South Indian temple, is known as *jñāna-dakshiṇāmūrti*. The word *jñāna* means "wisdom" or "knowledge" and *dakshiṇa* means "grace." We are told

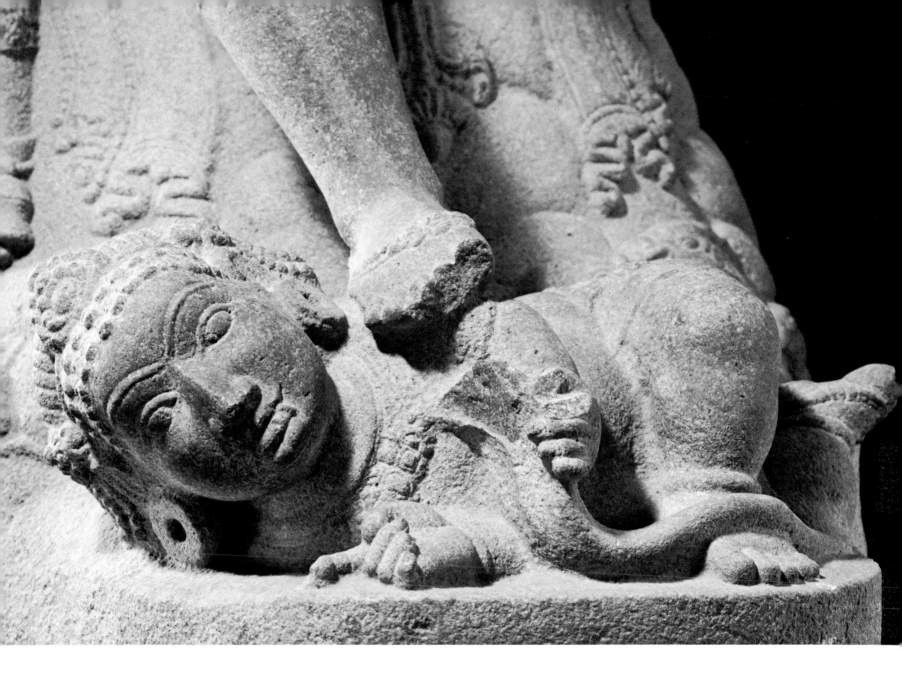

in the *Dakshiṇāmūrti Upanishad* that only through Siva's infinite wisdom and grace can one attain supreme knowledge of the self (*ātma-vidyā*) and be redeemed from the bondage of the phenomenal world. That an entire text is devoted to this concept indicates its importance in Saiva thought and art, particularly in South India.

(a) In ancient India the forest was considered the most appropriate place for gaining insight into the meaning of existence. In this sculpture the artist has indicated the locale by the banyan tree, inhabited by squirrels and birds, and the rocky base where deer and tigers peacefully coexist. Siva

sits on the back of his favorite bull, Nandi, whose tongue adoringly licks his master's foot. The god's right leg crushes a dwarf who symbolizes ignorance and who plays with a snake. Siva also holds a snake in one of his right hands, while yet another snake, along with a crescent moon, embellishes his elaborate hairdo of matted locks. His second right hand, when undamaged, must have formed the *jñānamudrā*, as we see in the bronze (b). The two left hands hold a manuscript and a flaming torch, both symbolizing knowledge. Even though Siva is an ascetic, the sculptor has lavishly adorned him with various kinds of

ornaments. His matted hair, also enriched with jewelry, emphasizes his ascetic nature, as do the waterpot and the band suspended from the tree (the use of the band is demonstrated in the bronze [b]).

(b) In some ways this diminutive representation, intended once for a domestic altar, is even more elaborate than the stone sculpture. Four images of ascetics are added on the rectangular base and the bronze is also finished at the back. Indeed, one must study the back to clearly apprehend the form of the tree, which is skillfully integrated with the matted locks to form a single appendage that also serves as a nimbus.

Siva seems to be sitting directly on a mound incised with a stylized rock design. The dwarf beneath his foot looks more like a child playing with a toy snake than a personification of ignorance. Siva's upper right hand here holds a rosary instead of a snake and his lower left arm rests on his knee, the hand extended gracefully. The two ascetics in front are bearded and pot-bellied, while the two at the back are young and handsome; all except one seems to carry a manuscript in his left hand. There are minor differences in their postures and gestures, but their right hands all display either the *jñānamudrā* or the *abhayamudrā*.

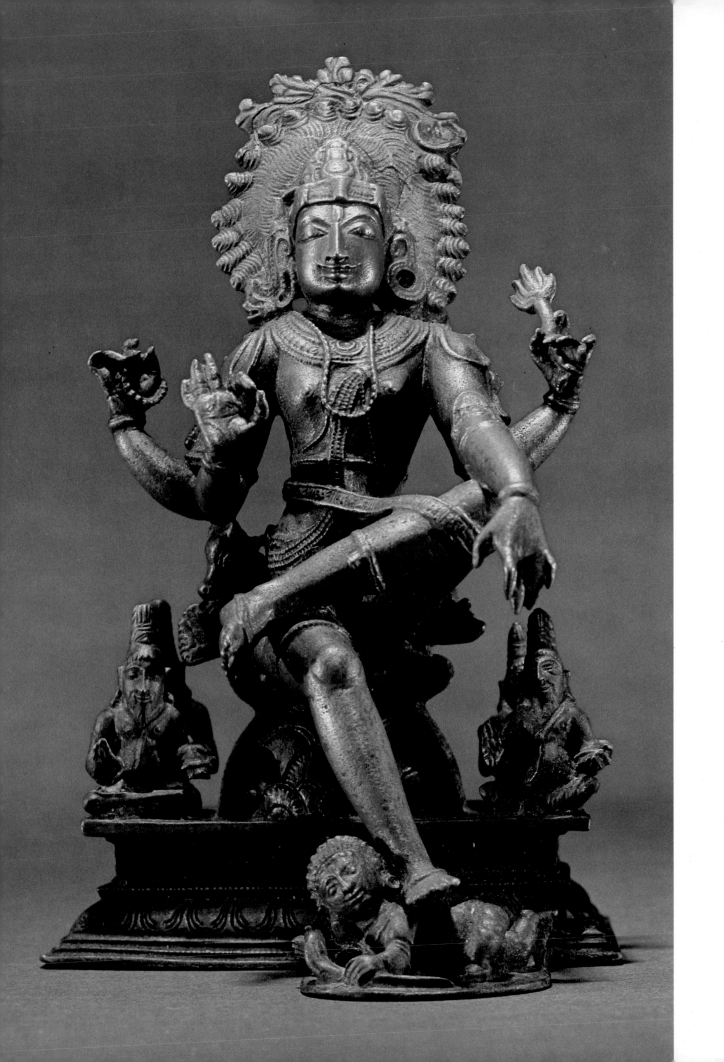

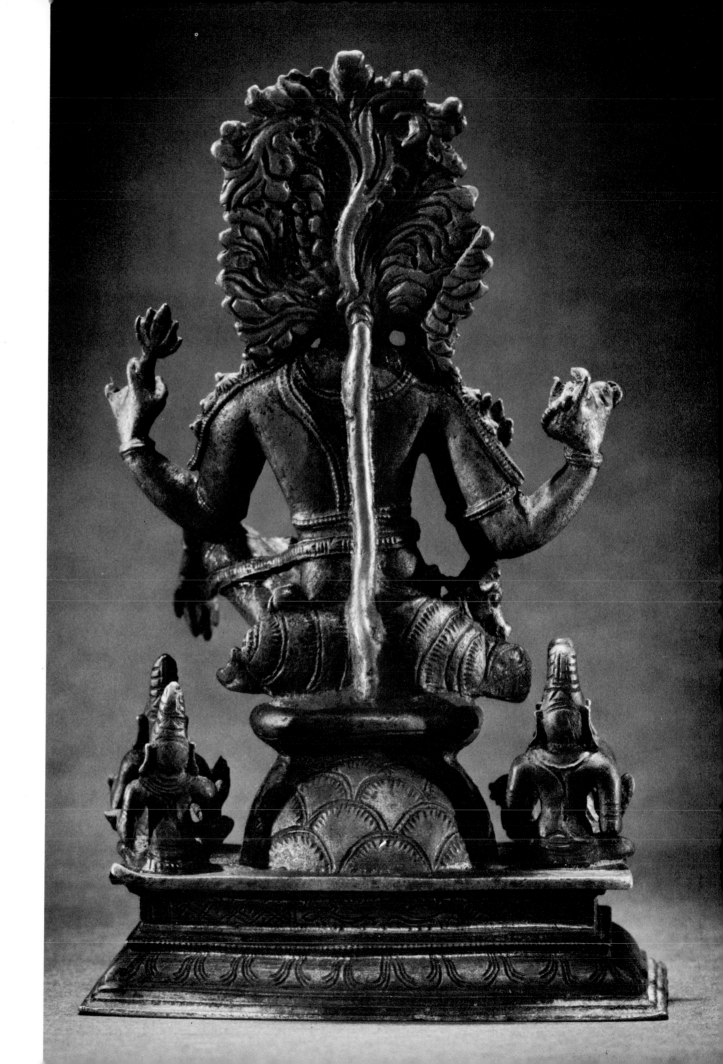

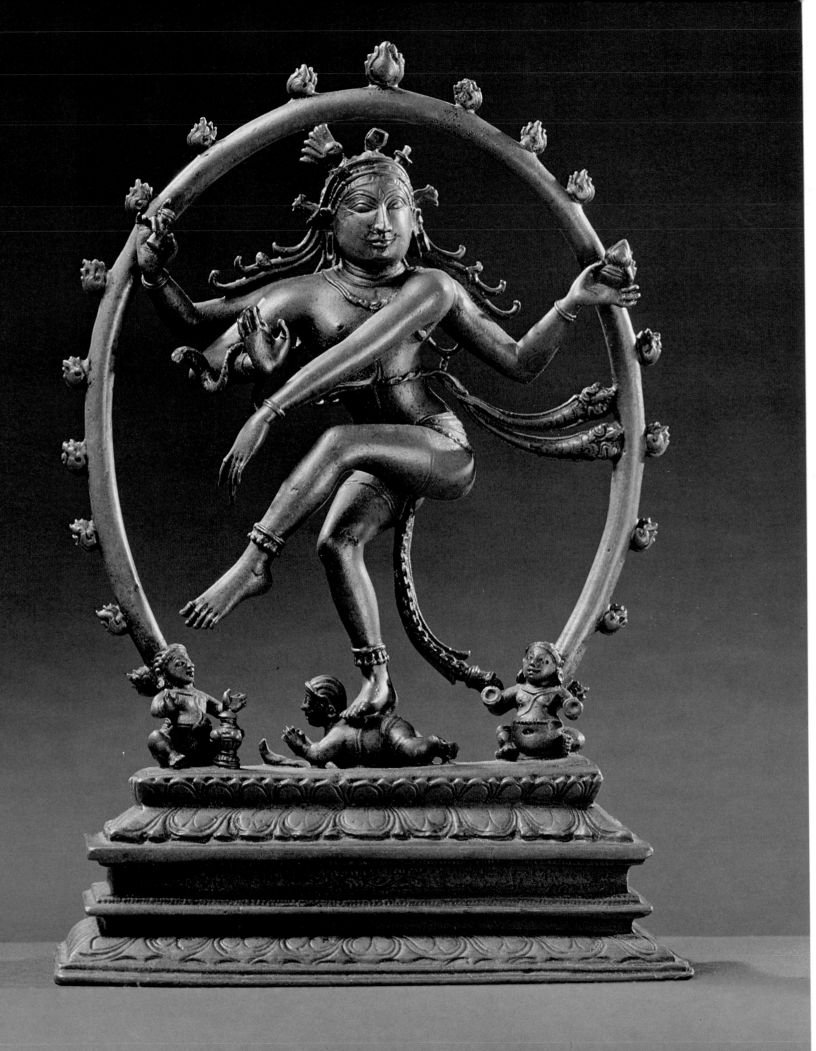

77. Naṭarāja (Lord of the Dance)
Tamilnadu, Tanjore district
13th century
Copper
h : 8¾ in. (22.2 cm.)

Framed by a flaming aureole symbolizing either nature or the human heart burning with desire, Siva dances with his right foot resting on a dwarf and his left foot thrown across his body. The hapless dwarf, playing with a serpent, symbolizes ignorance, which Siva removes with his wisdom. Two other cherubic dwarfs sit at either end of the lotus base and provide their master with music. One beats a drum that looks like a jar, and the other plays the cymbals. One of Siva's left arms stretches across his body, parallel to his left leg, and points to his left foot, where the devotee can find refuge. The corresponding right hand, the forearm entwined by a snake, forms the *abhayamudrā*. With his upper right hand he plays the drum, signifying time, and with the corresponding left hand he holds the flame, symbolizing knowledge or wisdom.

Although diminutive, this bronze is a fine example of Naṭarāja sculptures, both in the harmoniously balanced composition and the serenely elegant expression. It is amazing how the right leg alone provides stability for so animated a figure, whose every detail, whether arms, ornaments, hair, or sash, expresses ceaseless, rhythmic movement. An almost identical bronze, with two similar musicians, is in the Madras Museum (Sivaramamurti, pl. 28b). However, the Madras bronze is about four times as large and very likely was the model for this image, which must have been intended for a domestic shrine. The bronze is stylistically comparable with the *Dakshiṇāmūrti* in the present collection (no. 76b).

78. The Goddess Kālī or Bhairavī

Tamilnadu
12th–13th century
Bronze with green patina
h: 30⅛ in. (76.5 cm.)

Although this iconic type is encountered frequently in South India, her exact identification remains undefined. She is generally identified as Kālī, the dreadful goddess who appeared from the forehead of Durgā during her battle with Mahishāsura and destroyed the *asuras* Chaṇḍa and Muṇḍa (see no. 48). However, in the text where this legend is recounted, Kālī is described as an emaciated figure, whereas in all such South Indian images she is invariably fleshly and voluptuous. Only her face and hair are indicative of her ferocious nature. Two of the emblems seen here, the elephant goad and the noose, are more commonly associated with Bhairavī, but the trident and the cup used for drinking her victim's blood are appropriate attributes for Kālī. It is interesting that this goddess is almost an exact female counterpart of the Bhairava images of South India (see no. 86). At any rate, whether she is Kālī or Bhairavī, she is ultimately a manifestation of the great mother. This particular form may have been adopted from the tribal or non-literate tradition and identified later as an awesome emanation of Durgā.

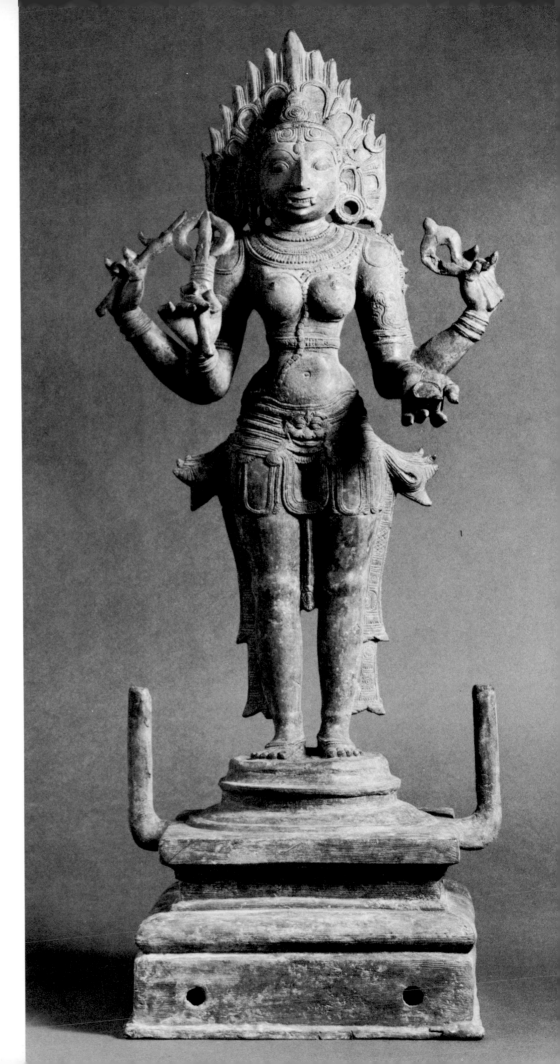

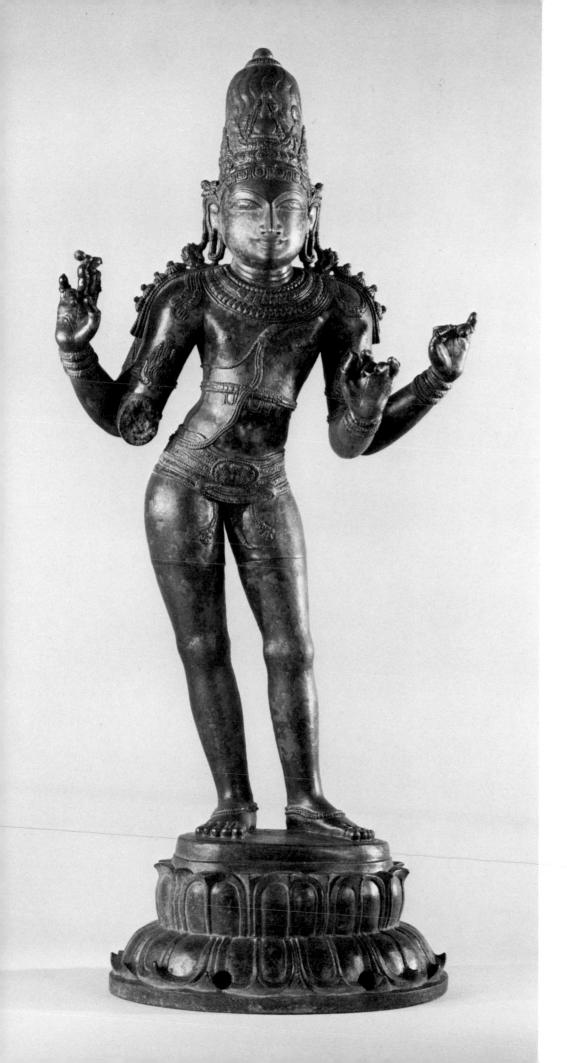

79. The Bodhisattva Maitreya

Tamilnadu, Nagapattinam area
12th–13th century
Bronze
h: 30½ in. (77.5 cm.)

Four-armed images of Maitreya are
extremely rare, as are any representations of the bodhisattva Maitreya
from South India. This figure, but for
the stupa in his chignon, might easily
be mistaken for Siva (see no. 69). The
lower right hand is unfortunately
broken, and the upper right hand
once held a rosary, only parts of which
are still attached to the fingers. When
it was last published (see below), the
rosary was still intact. The upper left
hand probably held a *nāgekeśara*
flower, now lost, while the remaining
left hand forms the *siṁhakarṇamudrā*.

Nagapattinam, in the Tanjore
district of Tamilnadu, was one of the
last strongholds of Buddhism in India
and the monasteries there remained in
close touch with Buddhist countries
such as Java and Sri Lanka. Not only
does the bronze closely imitate Chola
images of Siva, but it is also rendered in
the same basic style as Chola bronzes.
The only significant difference
between this and a Chola bronze can
be observed in the lotus base, which is
treated in a style distinctive of
Nagapattinam sculptures.

Published: *Indische Kunst*, no. 112,
pl. 43.

80. Dancing Krishna

Tamilnadu, Pāṇḍyan style (?)
13th century
Bronze
h: 18½ in. (47.5 cm.)

The image of dancing Krishna was almost as popular in South India as Siva Naṭarāja (see no. 77). But whereas Siva's dance is that of an adult and has cosmic significance, Krishna is always a boy when he dances. Sometimes he dances victoriously on the hood of Kāliya (see no. 81), but mostly his dance is an expression of joy after he has successfully raided his mother's larder.

In all such images, Krishna strikes the same characteristic pose, and yet each representation has its own flavor. Here he is completely naked except for his sumptuous ornaments; the artist's ideal was obviously a pampered royal child, for as the son of a cowherd in Vrindavan, Krishna would hardly have worn such jewels. What is remarkable about such sculptures is that the god is represented essentially as a winsome baby boy, plump and slightly mischievous. This particular example reveals certain interesting features both in its proportions and facial characteristics that distinguish it from more typical Chola and early Vjayanagar representations. It may, therefore, be a rare example of a Pāṇḍyan-style bronze.

81. Destruction of Kāliya (Kāliyadamana)

Tamilnadu
14th–15th century
Copper
h: 32 in. (81.2 cm.)

The story goes that when Krishna was a child, a giant serpent named Kāliya lived in the river Yamunā near Vrindavan and was a constant threat to the cows tended by Krishna and his companions. Deciding to rid the waters of this evil, Krishna fought and killed Kāliya. The story is obviously an allegory of the struggle for supremacy between the serpent worshipers and the devotees of Krishna around the Mathura region. Even today in some parts of India, for instance in Mathura and Benares, the entire incident is reenacted with a boy playing the role of Krishna, who is lowered from a tree onto the hood of an artificial serpent.

During the medieval period the sculptors of Tamilnadu depicted this theme with effective brevity by showing the child dancing jubilantly on the head of Kāliya. In such bronzes, as in the present example, the composition is determined more by hieratic needs than dramatic intent. By destroying Kāliya, Krishna gives him perpetual release from the chain of rebirth and hence the act is one of grace rather than of malice or revenge. Thus the artist made no attempt to display agony or tension, and the unconcerned child dances merrily on the serpent hood, his extended left arm grasping the tail, his right hand reassuring the faithful, including Kāliya, who remains calm and apparently grateful for his release.

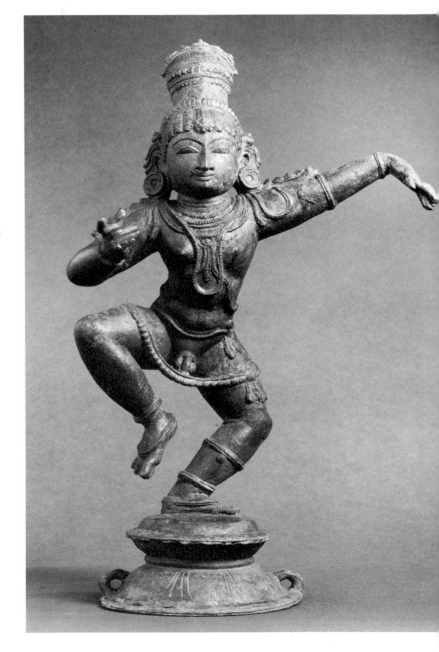

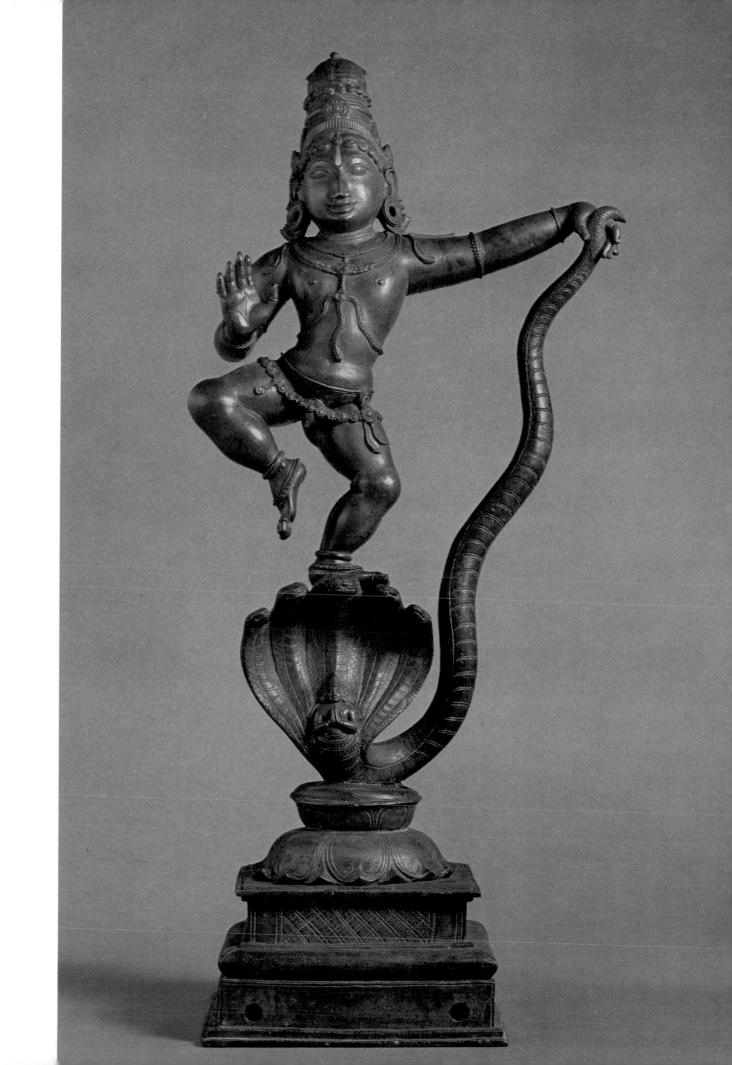

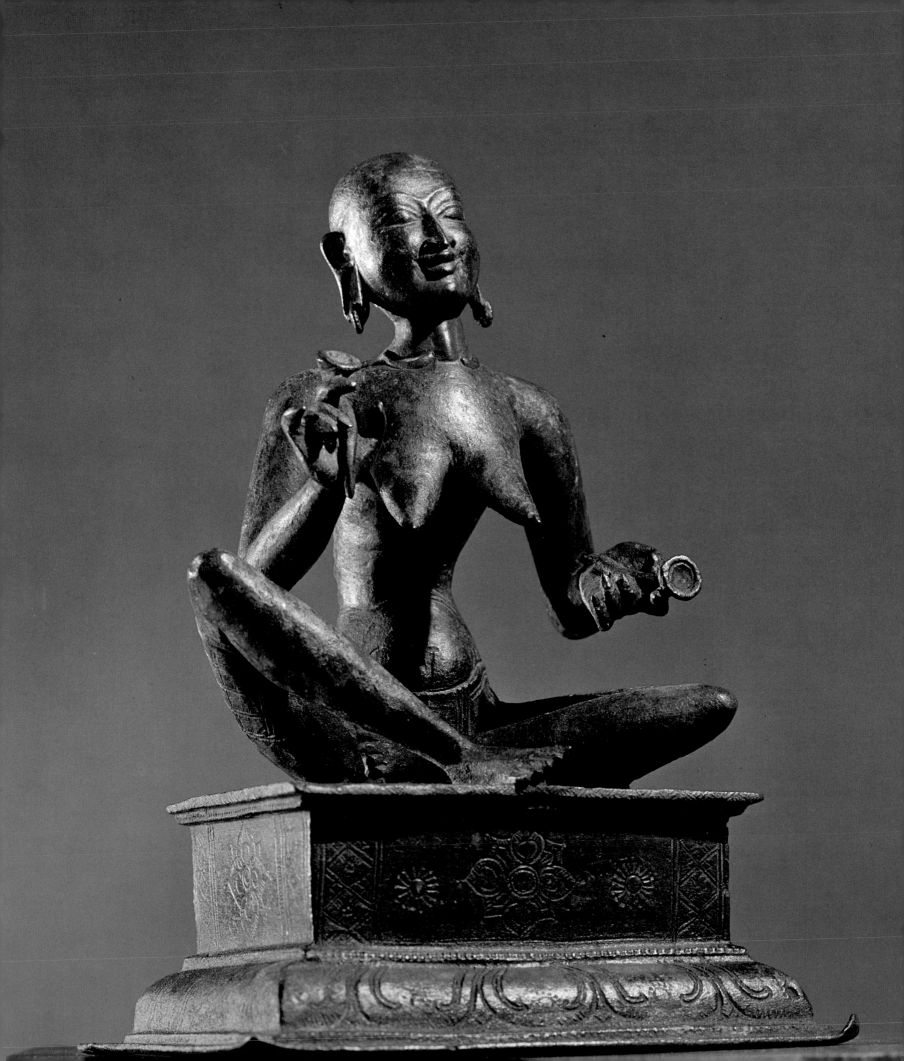

82. Karaikkalammaiyar, a Saiva Saint

Tamilnadu
15th century
Bronze with green patina
h: 9⅛ in. (23.2 cm.)

Karaikkalammaiyar was a great devotee of Siva who lived in a village named Karaikkal. She belonged to the vaisya caste, but this did not prevent her from being elevated to sainthood. She was well known for performing severe austerities and hence she is often portrayed with an emaciated body. Her body here is extremely attenuated, with a humped back and clearly visible ribs. The concavity of her stomach is further emphasized by the pointed conical breasts that protrude from her body like spears. Her head is tonsured, except for a few strands at the back, and her smiling face vividly expresses her inner serenity. Karaikkalammaiyar loved to sing in order to see visions of Siva dancing, and hence she holds a pair of cymbals with her hands. She was obviously the Saiva counterpart of Meerabai, the Rajasthani mystic who similarly invoked Vishnu through her songs.

Few bronzes of this female saint have been published, the best known being that in Kansas City (Kramrisch, 1965, fig. 150). There, however, she has been represented almost as a fearsome being, complete with fangs. It would appear that the sculptor responsible for the Kansas example was identifying Karaikkalammaiyar with Kālī, who also is regarded as the consort of Siva. In this bronze, however, her human characteristics predominate.

83. Umā-Maheśvara
Karnataka
11th century
Bronze with dark green patina
h: 10½ in. (26.7 cm.)

Images like this of Śiva and Pārvatī, also known as Maheśvara and Umā, respectively, sitting in intimacy, are known as Umāsahitamūrti or Umā-Maheśvaramūrti. In this bronze, the divine couple is beautifully framed by an elegantly ornate aureole or *toraṇa*. Seated in *sukhāsana*, Śiva takes up much of the lotus base and Umā is delicately perched on his left thigh. Śiva's right hands hold the trident and the citrus fruit; one of his left hands supports Umā and the other holds a simple ring that may represent a noose. His head is set off against a nimbus decorated with an unusual rope motif. With her hair gathered in a large doughnut-shaped bun known as a *dhammila*, Umā displays coquettish elegance as she places her right arm around her husband's waist. Her left hand, unfortunately broken, may once have held a lotus or a mirror. The couple is flanked by much smaller images of their two sons: Kārttikeya, riding a peacock, and Gaṇeśa, seated on a lotus. In front of the elaborate four-footed pedestal is the figure of Nandi, Śiva's bull.

This bronze, along with others in a group found in the Tandantottam village in the Tanjore district, was first published (see below) as a work of the early Chola period, possibly from the second half of the ninth century. Despite the fact that the bronze was discovered in Tamilnadu, it is certainly not of local workmanship. The composition of the central couple, the style of the figures, the presence of a nimbus behind Śiva's head instead of the *śiraśchakra*, Umā's hair style and posture, and the design of the pedestal as well as of the floriated aureole are seldom encountered in Chola bronzes. They are more characteristic of western Chālukyan works of the tenth–eleventh century, which is a far better date for this bronze than the suggested ninth. A Jaina Ambikā in the Los Angeles County Museum of Art (Rosenfield et al., 1966, p. 92, no. 101) and a Jaina Yaksha in the Seattle Art Museum (Trubner et al., p. 102, fig. 24), both of which are assigned to the Deccan, are the closest stylistic parallels to this charming Umā-Maheśvara. Two other bronzes, a Śiva Tripurāntaka and an Aiyanār triad from the same hoard, are now in the Norton Simon Museum of Art, Pasadena.

Published: Nagaswamy, pl. XXVIII, fig. II.

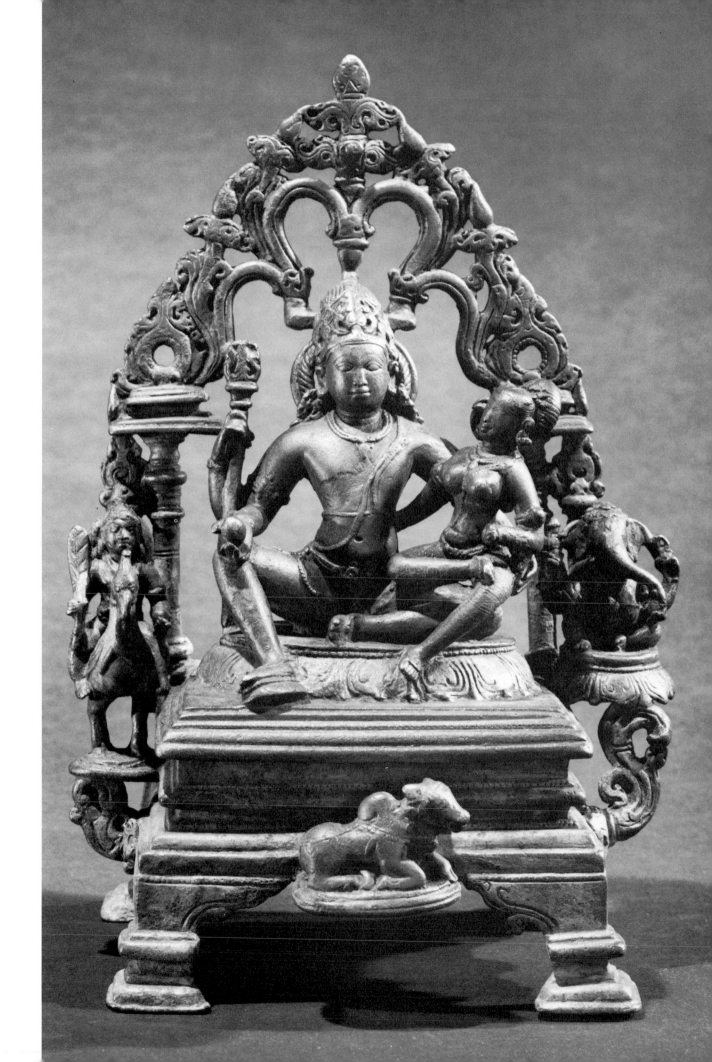

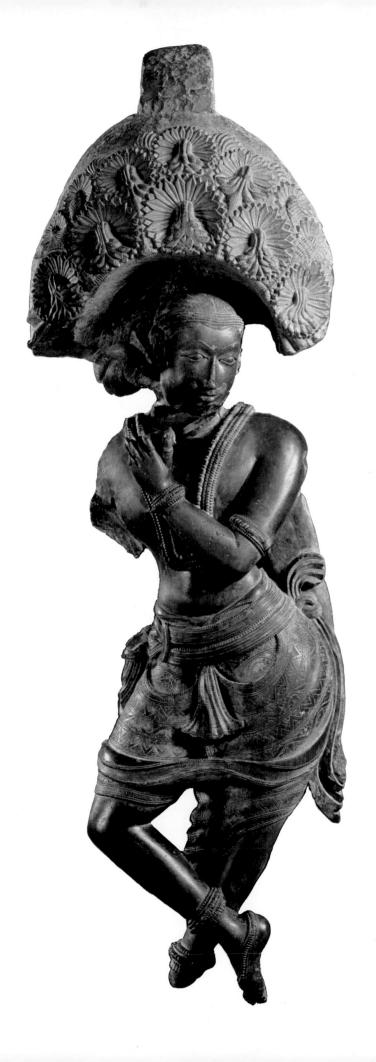

4. A Celestial Flutist

Karnataka
11th century
Brown slate, with traces of paint
h: 40¾ in. (103.5 cm.)

Below a stylized flowering tree, an
elegant figure stands playing a flute,
only parts of which are still attached to
his graceful fingers. He sports a
moustache and his hair is gathered in
a stylish bun. His ornaments and sashes
are rendered with great finesse and
the incised textile pattern of his dhoti is
richly detailed. Once again we note
the subtle, organic interrelationship
between the figure and the flowering
plant above. The supple figure has a
sinuosity that captures both the rhythm
and the vitality of plants. The rich
brown stone, unusually well polished,
has an appealingly tactile quality.

Although it is tempting to
identify this figure as the god Krishna,
who enchants the cowherdesses of
Vrindavan with the sweet sound of his
flute, we have refrained from doing so
because there is no symbol, such as a
nimbus, to establish the figure's
divinity. Certainly the pose is typical
of Krishna, but if the sculpture had
been used only as a bracket figure,
then it may simply represent a celestial
flutist. Most probably the sculpture is
from the Dharwar district of the
Deccan, which in the eleventh century
formed part of the western Chālukyan
kingdom. A companion piece depicting a celestial female musician is in the
Heeramaneck collection at the Los
Angeles County Museum of Art (see
Pal, 1976, pp. 52–53, figs. 23, 24).

85. Head of Hanumān

South India, Karnataka (?)
11th century
Gray schist
h: 20 in. (50.8 cm.)

This impressive head must once have
belonged to a nearly life-size sculpture
of Hanumān. Fragments of his right
hand are still attached to the crown as
if he was originally saluting someone, a
gesture indicating that Hanumān is
here portrayed as a heroic figure rather
than the subservient devotee seen in
the bronze statue (no. 71). In all probability this image once served as the
principal icon in a temple devoted to
Hanumān.

The exact provenance of the
figure is difficult to establish. Similar
schist is used in a large part of the
Deccan, particularly in the Karnataka
region. That it belongs to South rather
than North India seems evident from
the design of the crown. Compare with
the nearly contemporary guardian
Hanumān from Cambodia (no. 138).

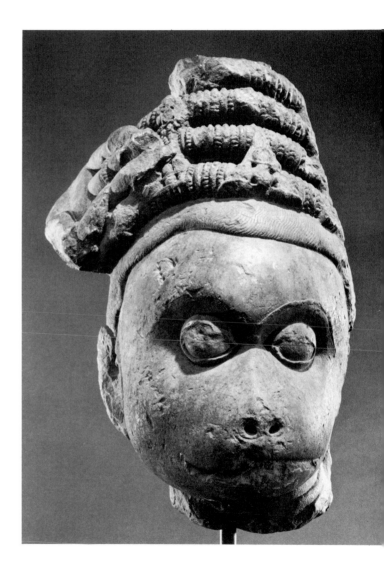

86. Siva as Bhairava

Karnataka
12th century
Dark schist
h: 38 in. (96.5 cm.)

Siva is shown here in his ferocious or angry manifestation known commonly as Bhairava. Both his staring eyes and protruding fangs emphasize his anger, while the upheld sword symbolizes his militancy. Obviously he has just decapitated two demons, and one's severed head is displayed as a trophy in his lower left hand. The blood dripping from the suspended head is eagerly consumed by a dog (in his Bhairava aspect Siva is associated with a dog rather than with his bull). Additional heads of other destroyed demons are strung together in a garland around his waist. The macabre scene is enlivened by the four emaciated attendants who are obviously in a festive mood. Except for his sumptuous ornaments and crown and his pair of wooden slippers, Siva is completely naked, like a true ascetic. In addition to the sword and the severed head, he carries a shallow dish, a trident, and a rattle drum. The arch above his head is embellished with a *kīrttimukha* from whose mouth spring two rhizomes.

A similar Bhairava in the Prince of Wales Museum in Bombay is said to be from Karnataka (see M. Chandra, fig. 144). This sculpture also seems to belong to that region and can be regarded as an example of the twelfth-century western Chālukyan style, although it does have some features in common with the Hoyśala style of that period.

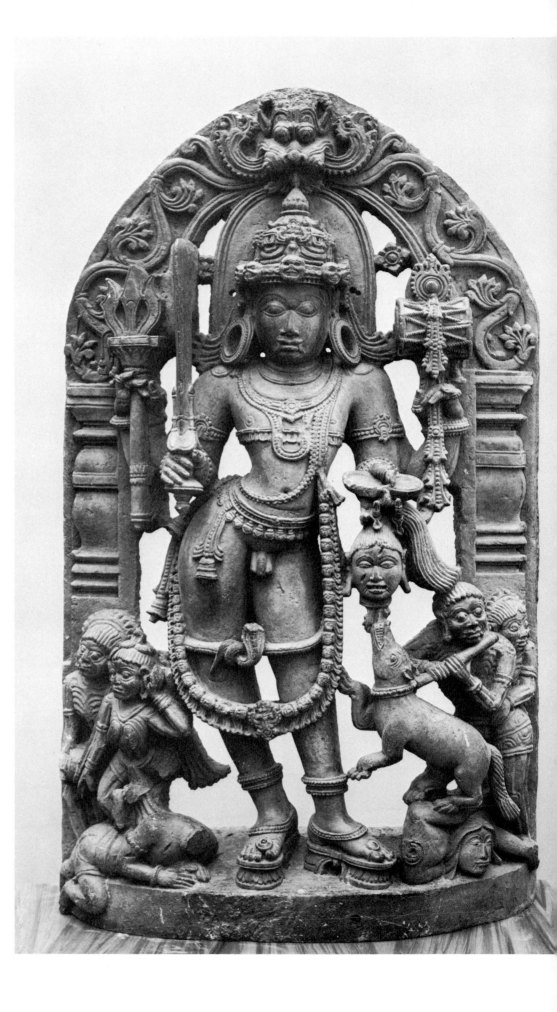

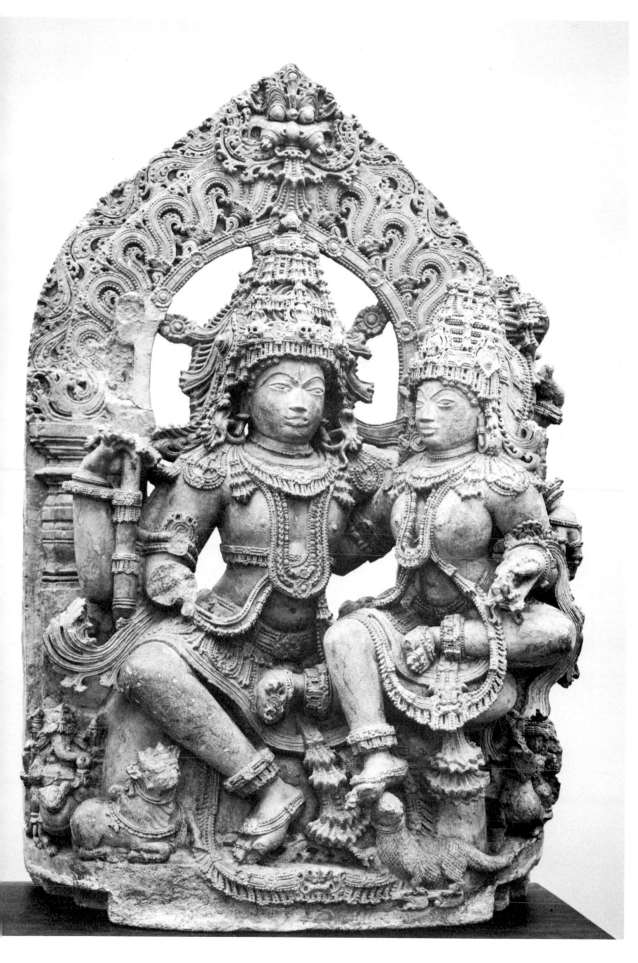

87. Umā-Maheśvara

Karnataka, Halebid region (?)
12th–13th century
Chloritic schist
h: 39 in. (99.1 cm.)

Basically this image is a more elaborate
version of the earlier bronze representing the same theme (no. 83). Śiva's
upper left hand here holds the drum
and Umā's right foot rests on an animal
that is supposed to represent an iguana
(*godhā*). Generally the lion is her
mount but in certain forms, such as
Gaurī, she is given the iguana.

The sculpture probably once
graced a niche on an exterior wall of a
Śaiva temple in the Halebid region of
Karnataka (known once as Mysore).
During the twelfth and thirteenth
centuries, this area was ruled by the
Hoyśala dynasty, who were munifi-
cent patrons of art. It is obvious that
they delighted in luxuriantly decorated surfaces, as we see in this overly
ornate sculpture. Indeed, had the
sculptor not left space around the
principal figures, they would scarcely
be visible through the forest of ornamental motifs. It is this passion for
exuberant and intricate ornamentation that distinguishes the Hoyśala
sculptures from all other schools and
makes them easily recognizable.

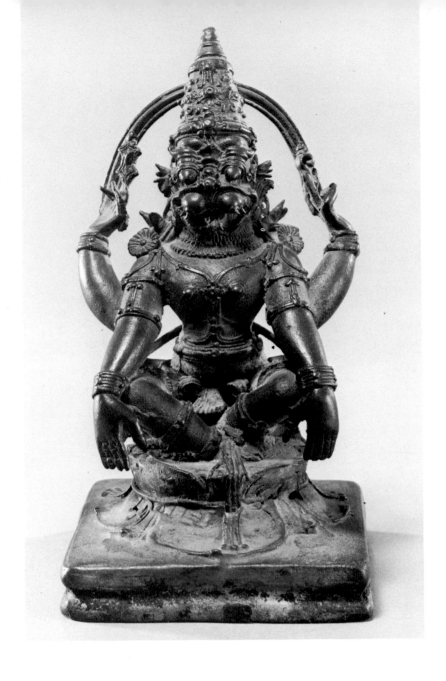

88. Yoganarasiṁha
Karnataka or Kerala
15th–16th century
Bronze
h: 8½ in. (21.5 cm.)

This bronze represents one of the principal avatars of Vishnu. Once upon a time King Hiraṇyakaśipu had a son named Prahlāda, who was a devout follower of Vishnu. The arrogant Hiraṇyakaśipu, a devotee of Siva, tried vainly to discourage his son from worshiping the god and one day asked his son where Vishnu was. Prahlāda replied that Vishnu was everywhere, even in the pillar beside them. The enraged Hiraṇyakaśipu kicked the pillar, whereupon the pillar shattered and Vishnu appeared in his man-lion incarnation and destroyed the unbelieving king. Hence, in images representing this avatar, Vishnu is always portrayed with a lion's head and is known as Narasiṁha ("man-lion").

This hieratic bronze was meant for worship and hence no narrative elements were included. The god is seated with his knees raised and his legs crossed at the ankles in the yogic posture known as *utkuṭikāsana*. The two normal arms overhang the knees, a position also associated with meditation. Hence, in this particular form, the image is known as *Yoganarasiṁha*.

His upper hands hold a thunderbolt and a conch shell. Usually the right hand holds the wheel, but certain texts also recommend the thunderbolt as one of his weapons (Smith, p. 141). The two upper hands are connected by a simple arch that forms a halo.

The design of the crown suggests that this bronze may be from either Karnataka or Kerala, but admittedly it is nowhere near as ornate as are the other bronzes from these regions and from this period (see no. 89).

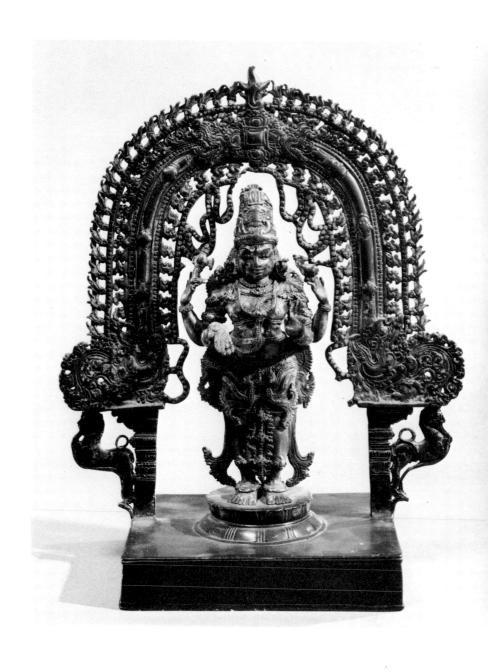

89. Siva as Chandraśekhara
Kerala
16th century
Bronze
h : 14¾ in. (37.5 cm.)

This is the same image type, known generically as Chandraśekhara ("adorned with the moon"), that we have already encountered in Chola and Pāṇḍyan sculptures (nos. 64, 69). The basic iconographic features have not changed, but the style has. Most noteworthy are the emphatically different proportions used by the Kerala artists of this period and their inordinate love of ornateness. Siva's figure, slim and elegant in Chola or Vijaynagar bronzes, has here become considerably more plump and squat.

The penchant for exuberant ornamentation is not merely confined to the sumptuously designed aureole, but is also apparent in the figure of Siva which is swathed in masses of ornaments and frilled sashes. The Kerala artists obviously continued the ornate style developed by their predecessors during the Hoyśala dynasty (nos. 86, 87).

90. A Celestial Nymph

Andhra Pradesh, Warangal district
Early 13th century
Grayish slate
h: 39 in. (99.0 cm.)

This sculpture depicts in high relief a celestial nymph striking a dance posture. It was probably used to embellish the external wall of a temple and may have formed part of a frieze depicting similar dancing figures. Although her legs and arms are broken, much of her body fortunately remains intact. There is an elegance about her movement as she thrusts her breasts forward and her hips sideways.

Stylistically comparable pieces can be seen in the great Rudreśvara temple at Palampet in the Warangal district of Andhra Pradesh (see S. G. Murthy, *The Sculpture of the Kākatiyas*, Hyderabad, 1964, figs. 19–22). Built in 1213, this temple is one of the finest examples of Kākatiya architecture. The Kākatiya-period sculptures are not very well represented outside India, and this is one of the few known examples.

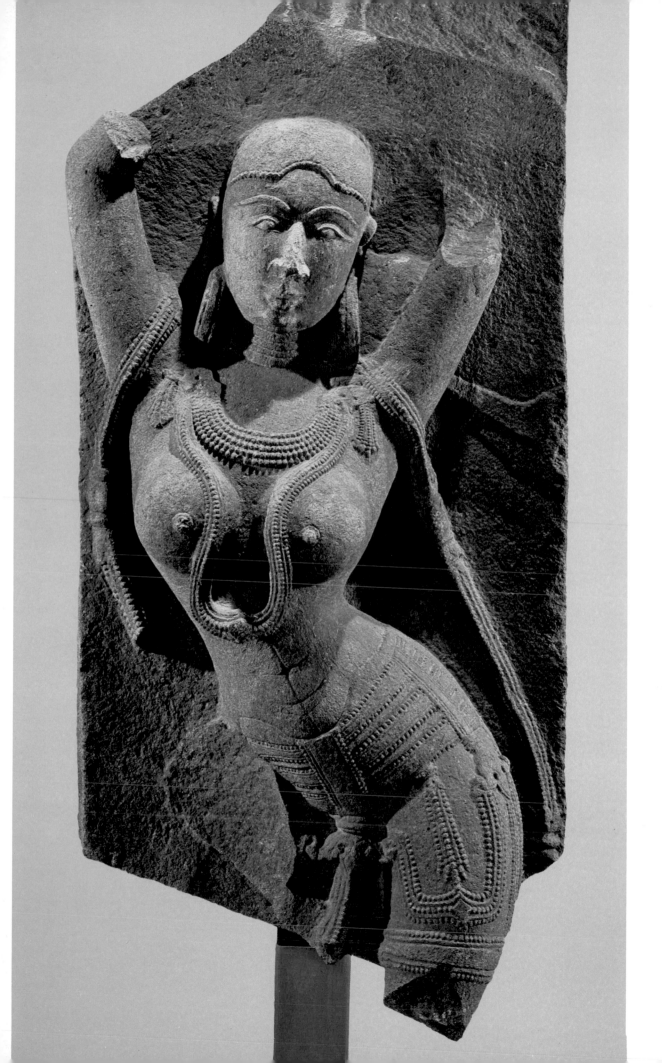

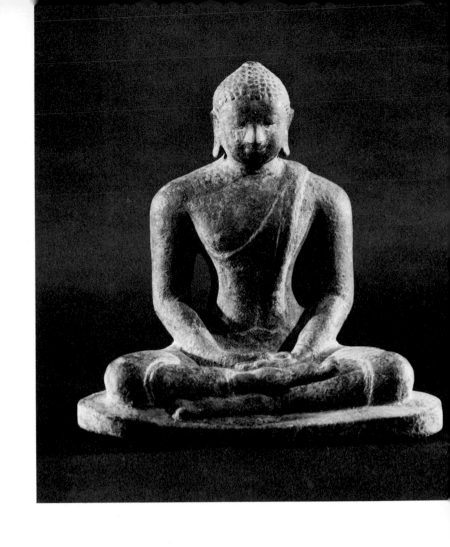

91. Buddha Śākyamuni

   (a) Sri Lanka, Anuradhapura
   8th–9th century
   Copper with green patina
   h: 5¼ in. (13.3 cm.)
   (b) Sri Lanka, Polonnaruva region
   11th century
   Copper with traces of gilt and paint
   h: 8½ in. (21.0 cm.)
   (c) Sri Lanka, Kandy region
   17th–18th century
   Gilt bronze
   h: 6 in. (15.2 cm.)

All three images represent a classic type of figure that has remained a favorite of Sri Lanka artists from early times. Śākyamuni meditates in the typical yogic posture, with his hands in the gesture of meditation placed gently in his lap. Since the *ushnīsha* in the Anuradhapura bronze (a) is damaged, we cannot be certain whether or not it originally had the flame, as do the two later Buddhas (b and c). The flame symbolizes knowledge or wisdom and appears in certain Buddha images in India and Sri Lanka almost simultaneously after the tenth century.

In both the Anuradhapura (a) and Polonnaruva (b) figures, we note the same volumetric treatment of the torso, with the wide shoulders and strong arms exuding a sense of both stability and grandeur. Their impassive monumentality and overbearing solemnity justify Coomaraswamy's characterization of such Sri Lanka Buddhas as "primitives." There is little stylistic difference between these two figures except in their physiognomic variations and in the contrast of the somewhat squarer frame of the Polonnaruva figure with the rounder shoulders and more fluent outline of the Anuradhapura figure.

The tremendous conservatism of the sculptural tradition in Sri Lanka can be observed by comparing this Kandyan image (c) with the two earlier figures (a and b). We notice the same predilection for wide shoulders, strong limbs, and rigid frontality, but

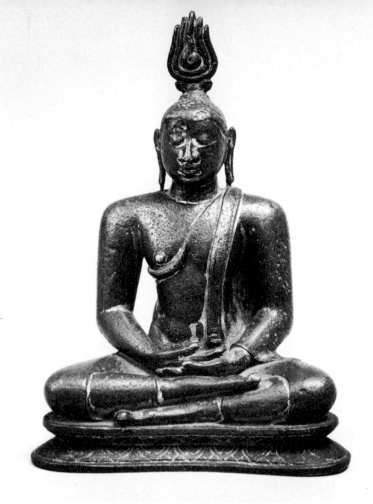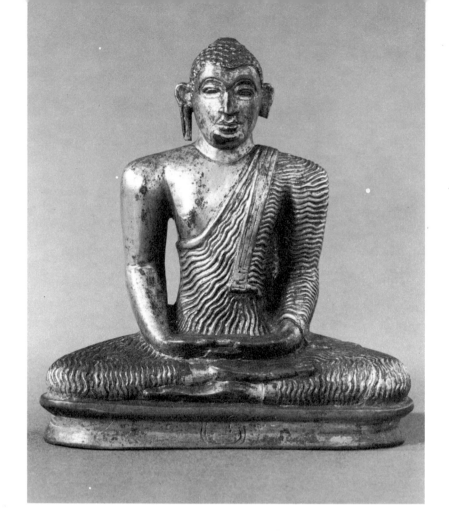

the modeling is less subtle. This is particularly evident in the delineation of the feet and hands, which look like inert masses compared to the lively and sensitively rendered limbs of the earlier figures. The most notable differences, however, appear in the shape and features of the face, as well as in the treatment of the drapery. The face is no longer classically "Aryan" but reflects strong local ethnic features. The rippling garment with its water-like effect is perhaps the most distinc- tive characteristic of the Buddha images of Kandy during this period and adds a pleasantly decorative touch to the figure. The flame above the head and part of the left ear are broken, but the *urṇā* still appears as a lightly incised spiral on the forehead. Curiously, only the front of the image has been gilded, obviously to econo- mize on the use of gold, since the statue would be viewed only from the front.

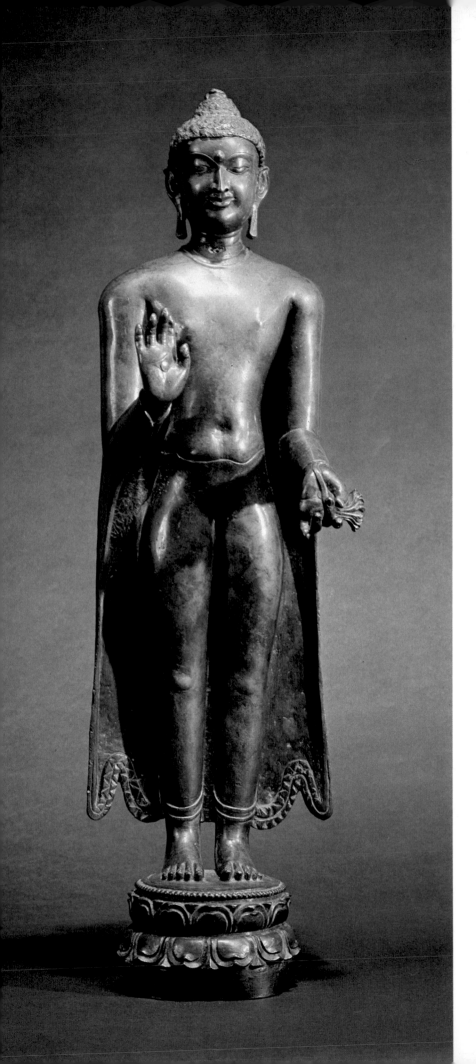

92. Buddha Śākyamuni

Burma, Pagan (?)
(a) 12th century
Copper
h: 24 in. (61.0 cm.)
(b) 18th century
Brass
h: 17¾ in. (45.1 cm.)

In the larger of the two images (a),
Buddha Śākyamuni stands in the
samapada posture on a lotus. His right
hand forms the *abhayamudrā* and his
left hand delicately grasps the pleated
end of the drapery. In keeping with his
superhuman character, his earlobes
are extraordinarily elongated, his
urṇā is a prominent spiral knob, and his
ushṇīsha may once have had a flame
appendage.

The broad shoulders, strong face,
and columnar body, which looks
almost naked beneath the transparent
garment, impart to this impressively
large bronze figure an unusual hieratic
grandeur. There can be little doubt
that the bronze was modeled after a
similar Indian bronze Buddha of the
Pāla period, such as those discovered at
Kurkihar. At the same time, however, the summary delineation of the
lower ends of the robe, as well as the
greater tendency to stylization, are
elements encountered in numerous
Burmese statues of the Buddha during
this period (see Luce, *Old Burma,
Early Pagan*, III, pls. 431–32). Like the
Buddhas published by Luce, the back

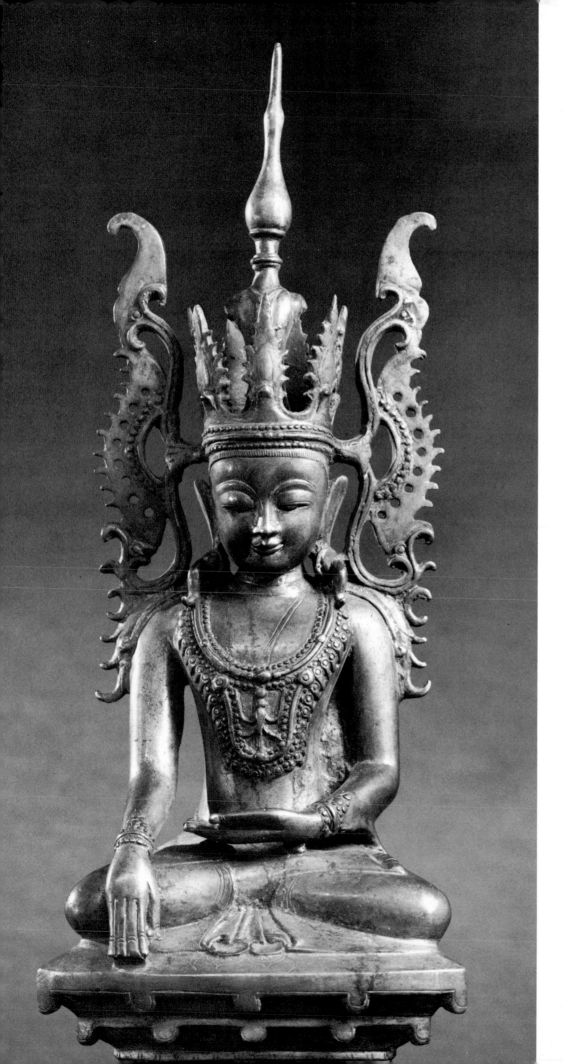

of this bronze is somewhat unfinished.

In the eighteenth-century bronze (b) we encounter a crowned Buddha Śākyamuni of a type that became particularly popular in Burma during this period. Although the basic iconography of the figure conforms to that employed much earlier in India and Thailand to represent the enlightenment of Śākyamuni, both the style and meaning of these late Burmese images are different. According to local legend, the image portrays Śākyamuni as the subduer of King Jambhupati, who had threatened to annex the kingdom of Bimbisāra of Rājagaha. Bimbisāra appealed to Śākyamuni, who miraculously built a magnificent palace and was sitting on a jeweled throne when his messenger brought Jambhupati before him. Overwhelmed at the splendid sight, Jambhupati instantly became a convert. Such crowned figures are simply called Jambhupati in Burma.

Apart from this change in meaning, stylistically too this bronze is notably different from the earlier example. The shape and features of the face are now much more Burmese in appearance and there is far greater concern with rich ornamentation than with simple form. Especially note-worthy are the elongated *ushnīsha* crowned with a finial and the decorative appendage attached to the head and the shoulders, which possibly served as a nimbus.

Nepal and Tibet are northern neighbors of India, from which they both borrowed basic religious and artistic ideas. But they are also each other's neighbors, and culturally as well as commercially the two countries have interacted from very early times. Both Hinduism and Buddhism flourish in Nepal, although Hinduism is far more prevalent there, while Tibet has remained predominantly Buddhist.

Both geographically and culturally Nepal is closer to India than is Tibet. It is also a much smaller country and all the Nepali bronzes included here were created in the Kathmandu Valley by a people called the Newars. The Newars also played an important role in the artistic production of Tibet and at times the stylistic similarities between the bronzes of the two regions are so strong that it is impossible to determine whether a particular work was made in Nepal or in Tibet. Although the artistic styles and norms in Nepal were imported from India, no single Indian school predominates. In Tibet, however, we can broadly differentiate among three separate schools or traditions. The western Tibetan tradition was inspired first by the art of Kashmir (from about the eighth through the twelfth century) and thereafter by that of Nepal. Central Tibet, where by far the largest and most important cities and monasteries are located, produced art that reveals strong influences both of Indian schools, particularly of Bihar and Bengal (eighth through twelfth century), and those of Nepal, with a good measure of Chinese influence as well. Not too much is known of artistic activity in eastern Tibet, an area closer to mainland China. The majority of Tibetan bronzes in this collection are presumably from central Tibet, although there is no certainty as to their exact provenance. Bronzes with their faces painted in cold gold were certainly worshiped in Tibet, but one cannot state definitely that they were always made there.

93. The Bodhisattva Vajrapāṇi

Nepal
8th century
Copper with traces of gilt
h: 7 in. (17.8 cm.)

Two figures stand gracefully on distinct though connected lotuses. The larger figure represents the bodhisattva Vajrapāṇi, his right hand holding a boss against his chest. His left hand grasps the prongs of a thunderbolt that emerges from the head of the dwarf, who is the personification of Vajrapāṇi's emblem and is known as Vajrapurusha. An animated snake serves as his sash, and his arms are crossed in front of his chest in the attitude of reverence signifying humility.

This is one of the earliest Nepali bronzes known, and both figures display the abstract, though sensuous, modeling characteristic of Gupta sculpture. The elegantly coifed hair of the bodhisattva is also encountered in Gupta art as is the convention of anthropomorphizing the emblem. Typical of Nepali sculpture are the linear pliancy and the soft, gentle facial expressions.

Published: Pal, *The Arts of Nepal*, 1974, I, fig. 203; Pal, *Buddhist Art in Licchavi Nepal*, 1974, fig. 77; Pal, "Bronzes of Nepal," 1974, p. 34, fig. 6; Pal, *Nepal/Where the Gods Are Young*, 1975, p. 65, fig. 23.

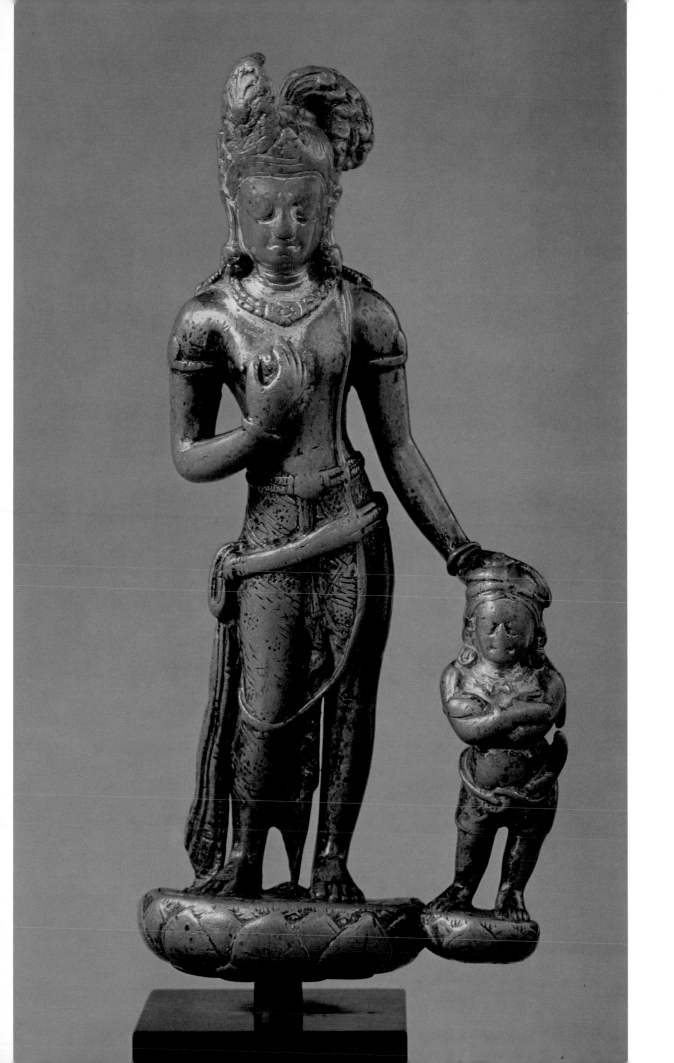

94. The Bodhisattva Padmapāṇi
Nepal
(a) 9th century
Copper
h: 13¼ in. (33.6 cm.)
(b) 11th–12th century
Gilt copper
h: 23½ in. (59.7 cm.)

Both figures represent Padmapāṇi, or
Avalokiteśvara, who is the most
important bodhisattva in the Buddhist
pantheon. The embodiment of
compassion and grace, he is continuously engaged in helping humanity
toward the path of enlightenment. He
is portrayed here in his simplest form,
although there are minor icono-
graphical differences between the two
figures. The lotus pedestal and the
flaming nimbus are missing in the
larger bronze, while the lotus emblem
is lost in the smaller bronze. The right
hand of the larger figure (b) is
extended in *varadamudrā*, but that of
the smaller figure (a) is raised in the
vyākhyāṇamudrā. The smaller figure has
a pearl necklace and two floral ear-
studs; the larger one has armlets and
bracelets as well as ornaments and
ribbons behind the ears.
    A comparison of the two bronzes
reveals not only their remarkable
similarities but also differences that

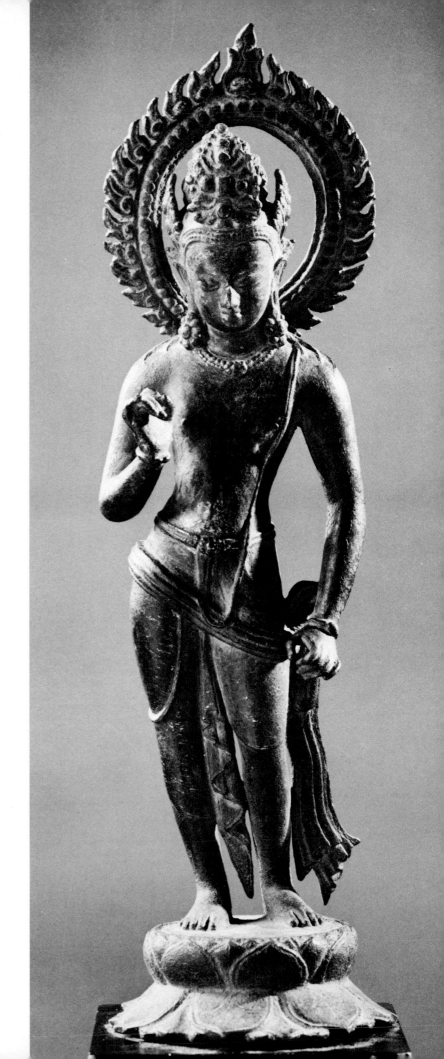

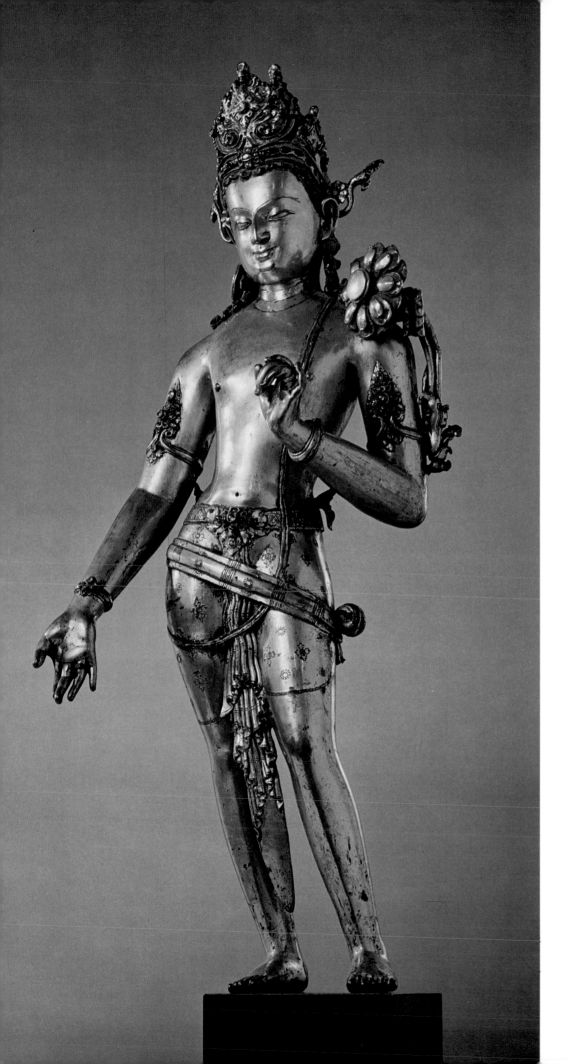

help us to determine their relative chronological positions. The modeling of both figures reflects a similar penchant for supple, fleshy volumes and smooth, subtle surfaces. However, the flowing pleats of the garments between the legs and the ends of the sash fall far more naturally in the small figure, comparable with those of the eighth-century Vajrapāṇi (no. 93). With their half-shut eyes and down-ward glances, the faces of the Vajrapāṇi and the small Padmapāṇi are much more reminiscent of Gupta figures than is the larger Padmapāṇi, which has quite different facial features and expression. It also reveals a greater concern for ornamentation and a more mannered treatment of the pleats of the dhoti. Moreover, the mode in which the lotus stem is attached to the left arm became fashionable only after the tenth century. Both bronzes are attractive for different reasons: the smaller figure expresses better the compassionate nature of the bodhi-sattva; the larger bronze is a strong sculptural statement that impresses the viewer with its majestic bearing.

Published: (a) Chow, p. 7; (b) Pal, *Nepal/Where the Gods Are Young*, 1975, p. 74 and fig. 15.

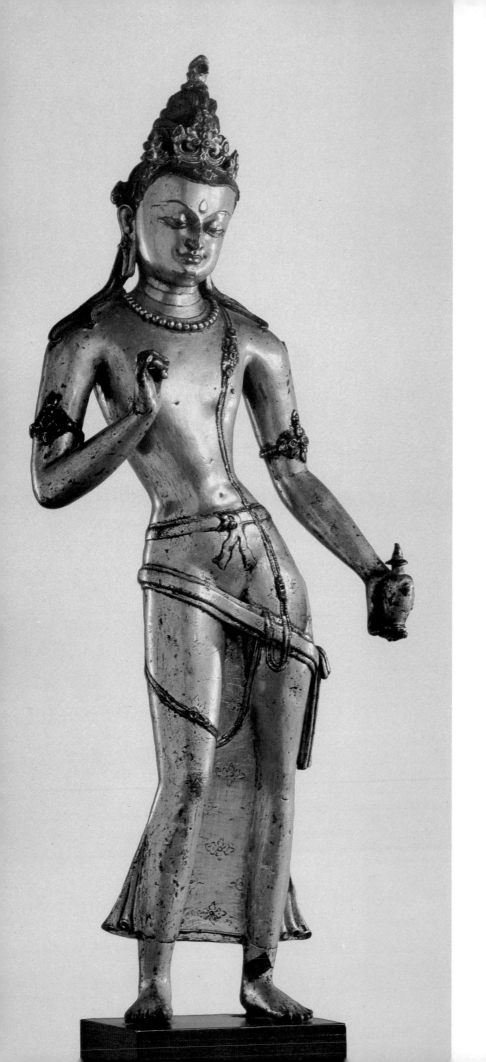

95. The Bodhisattva Maitreya
Nepal
(a) 9th century
Gilt copper with paint
h: 26 in. (66.0 cm.)
(b) 9th–11th century
Gilt copper with paint
h: 10½ in. (26.7 cm.)

Both these extraordinarily radiant
bronzes depict Maitreya, the future
Buddha. In one (a) he stands in
tribhaṅga, in the other (b) he is seated
in *lalitāsana* on a large lotus, his left

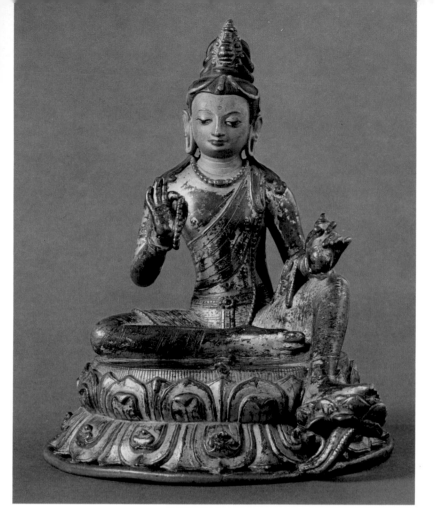

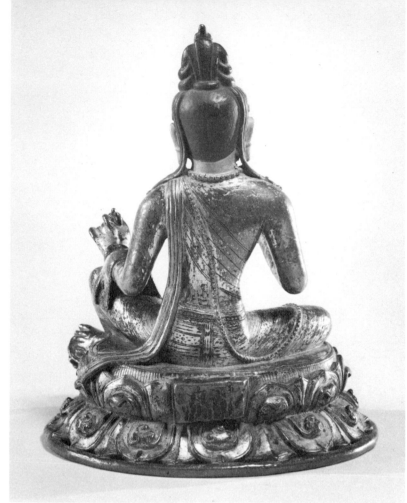

foot supported by a smaller lotus. The left hand of each figure holds a pot, although in different ways. The right hand of the standing Maitreya is now empty but very likely it once held a rosary, as does that of the seated figure. A stupa embellishes the tiara of the seated figure, which also has an antelope skin thrown across the left forearm. The seated Maitreya's torso is draped with a light shawl and he wears a dhoti of printed material; the standing figure has no upper garment and his plain dhoti drapes the lower portion of his body like a skirt. The hair and eyes of both figures are painted and the entire face of the seated Maitreya is painted in cold gold, which in no way detracts from the precise definition of the features.

The standing figure is a remarkably close copy of a model that must have belonged to the Sarnath school of the Gupta period. This is particularly evident from the shape and features of the face, as well as the treatment of the dhoti. Details such as the delicately rendered fingers and the simple pearl necklace also continue the Gupta tradition. The seated figure reflects a similarly simple elegance and spiritual presence, particularly in the beatific expression of the face, but it is much more a Nepali opus. Both bronzes are modeled in the round, but the back of the standing figure is more summarily delineated than that of the seated Maitreya. Each bronze is charming in its own way and shows with graphic clarity how different artists could work with the same basic iconographic formula yet create such divergently expressive forms. While the standing figure with its strong linearity is eloquently mannered, the seated bronze shows the balance between line and modeling that is always a hallmark of the finest Nepali bronzes. Both figures are equally effective in communicating the compassion that is the essence of Maitreya.

Published: (a) Pal, *Buddhist Art in Licchavi Nepal*, 1974, fig. 71; Pal, "Bronzes of Nepal," 1974, p. 85, fig. 7; Pal, *Nepal/Where the Gods Are Young*, 1975, frontispiece and p. 74.

96. The Goddess Umā

Nepal
9th–10th century
Copper with traces of gilt and semiprecious stones
h : 12 in. (30.5 cm.)

Very likely this goddess once sat beside
her husband Siva in what must have
formed an exceptionally imposing and
attractive Umā-Maheśvara group
(see no. 100). Isolated as she now is,
however, she appears as a gracefully
regal lady with an almost arrogant tilt
of the head. She sits languidly,
balancing her posture with her right
hand, which may originally have
rested on Siva's thigh. The fingers of
her left hand, which probably once
held a lotus, are particularly delicate
and expressive. Although idealized,
her form is modeled with subtle
naturalism both front and back. Such
naturalistic expression is unusual for
Nepali sculpture and it would seem as
if the sculptor had modeled her from
life. An embodiment of luscious
opulence and vivacious charm, this is
perhaps the finest realization of the
female form in Nepali bronzes. The
gilding has worn off a large part of the
body, which has acquired a rich,
warm, reddish tone that enhances her
tactile appeal.

Published : Pal, *Nepal/Where the Gods
Are Young*, 1975, p. 119, fig. 69.

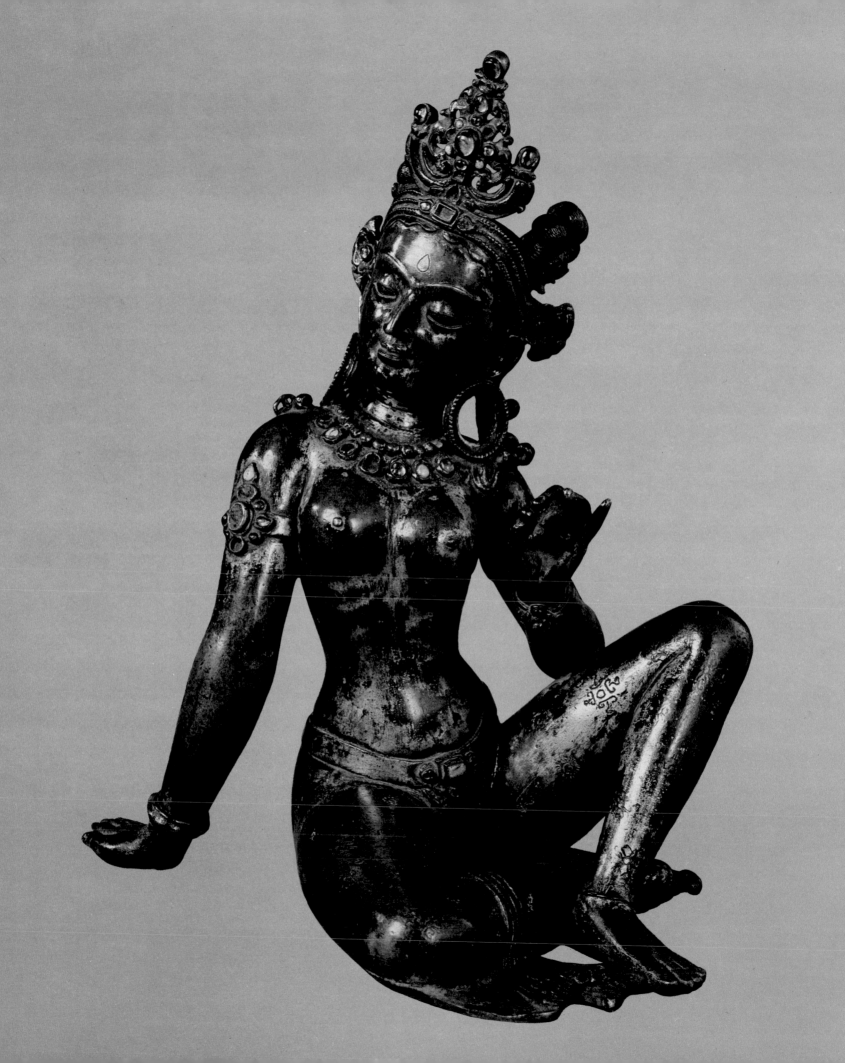

97. An Angry Form of Mañjuśrī

Nepal
10th century
Gilt copper with paint
h: 15 in. (38.1 cm.)

The figure strides aggressively to the left in a militant posture known as *āliḍha*. His bellicose attitude is underscored by the gesture of admonition formed by his left hand, by the sword (only the hilt now remains) held in his right hand, and by his fierce mien. There seems little doubt that he is an angry manifestation of Mañjuśrī. In addition to the sword, which is one of the most important of his emblems, the distinctive tiger-claw necklace and the peculiarly braided hair style (*triśikha*) are typical of this bodhisattva. Mañjuśrī is frequently described as a young prince and this necklace and hair style were typical affectations of young boys in ancient India.

The painted face and hair indicate that the image was once worshiped in Tibet. However, its Nepali origin is unquestionable and stylistically it is closely related to an image of Mañjuśrī still worshiped in a temple in Kathmandu (see Pal, *The Arts of Nepal*, 1974, I, fig. 33). Not only is this figure iconographically unique, it is also one of the earliest known representations of Mañjuśrī. A well-proportioned and animated figure, the modeling is both strong and subtle.

Published: Pal, *Nepal/Where the Gods Are Young*, 1975, fig. 35, pp. 79–80.

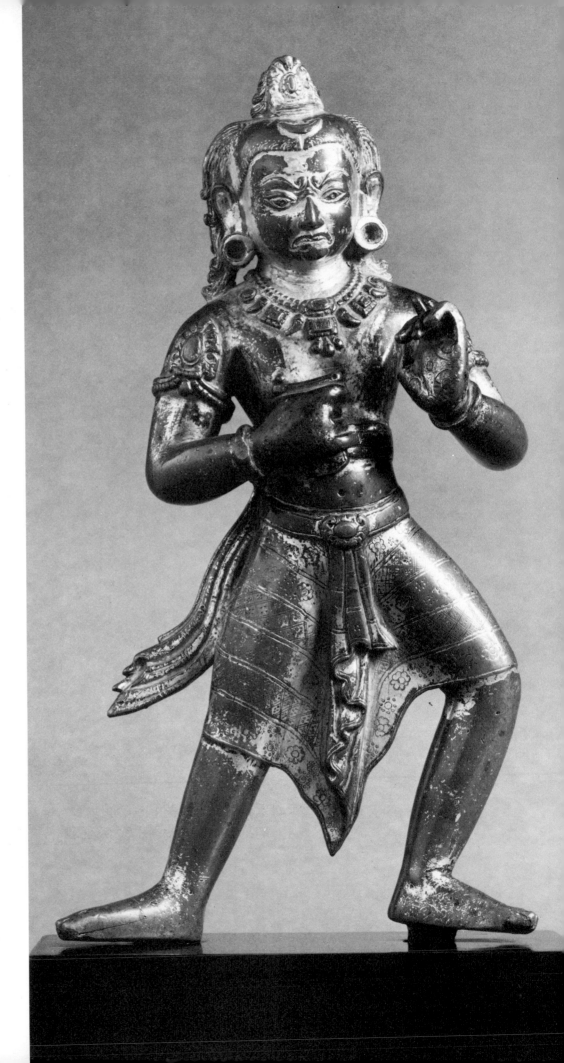

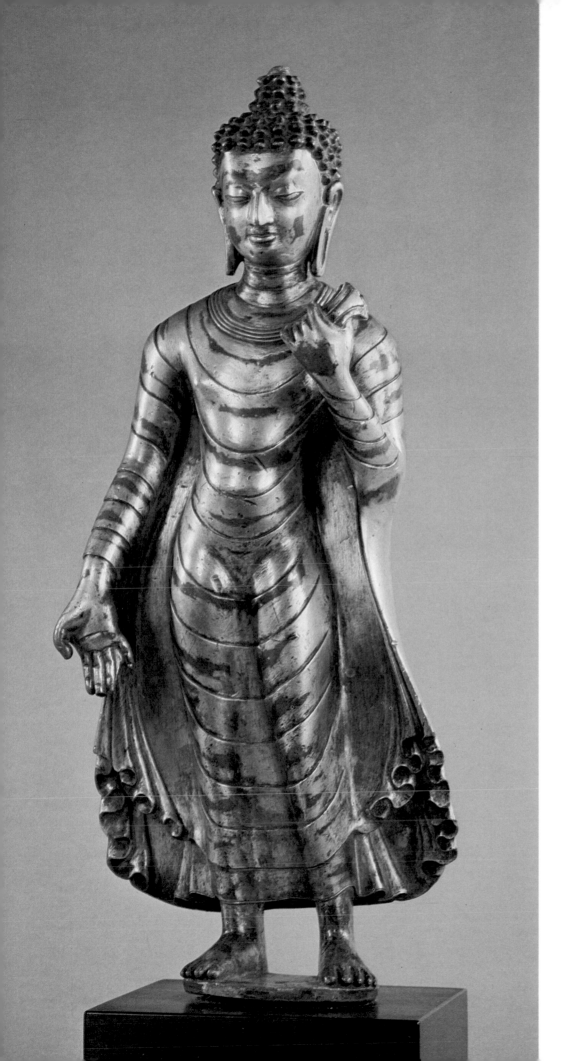

98. Buddha Śākyamuni

Nepal
10th century
Gilt bronze with painted hair
h: 11 in. (27.9 cm.)

On a narrow base that must once have been attached to a lotus, the Buddha Śākyamuni stands in a gentle *tribhaṅga* posture. Signs of his greatness are elongated earlobes, a cranial bump (*ushṇīsha*) signifying extraordinary intellect, and webbed fingers. The indigo paint on the hair indicates that the bronze was once worshiped in Tibet. His right hand is extended in the *varadamudrā* and his left hand holds the end of the shawllike *saṅghāti* near his shoulder. The face is a perfect oval, the nose is prominent, and the eyes are half-shut.

The figure clearly demonstrates the remarkable persistence of the Gupta tradition in Nepal. The mode of indicating the *saṅghāti* in uniform semicircular striations continues a stylization affected by the Mathura sculptors of the Gupta period. The exuberant treatment of the rippling ends of the *saṅghāti*, however, is typically Nepali and considerably enhances the effect of movement.

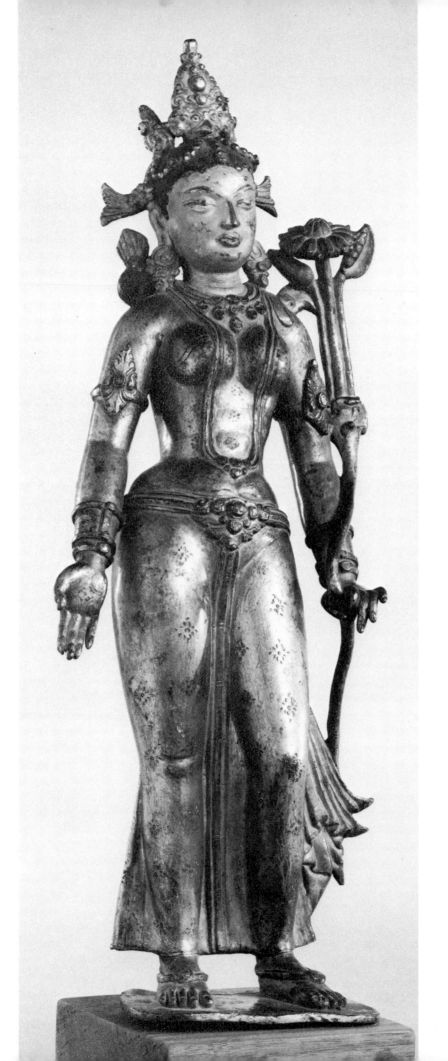

99. The Goddess Tārā

Nepal
11th–12th century
Gilt bronze with paint
h: 16½ in. (42.0 cm.)

Depending on the context, a lotus-bearing lady may represent almost any goddess. The fact that the face of this divine figure is painted in cold gold indicates that the image has been worshiped in Tibet, a Buddhist country, and hence she must be Tārā. Tārā is the great savior and goddess of mercy in the Mahayana pantheon and is thus the feminine counterpart of Padmapāṇi. Like him, she holds her principal attribute, the lotus, in her left hand and extends her right in *varadamudrā*. Also like him she is more often than not represented with grace and simplicity, expressing both compassion and radiance. Here she stands in the *tribhaṅga* posture, with her pelvis gently thrust forward in a languorous movement. Her limbs are firm but supple, and the sinuous stalk of the lotus, as well as the flowing ends of her upper garment, emphasizes the organic rhythm of the form.

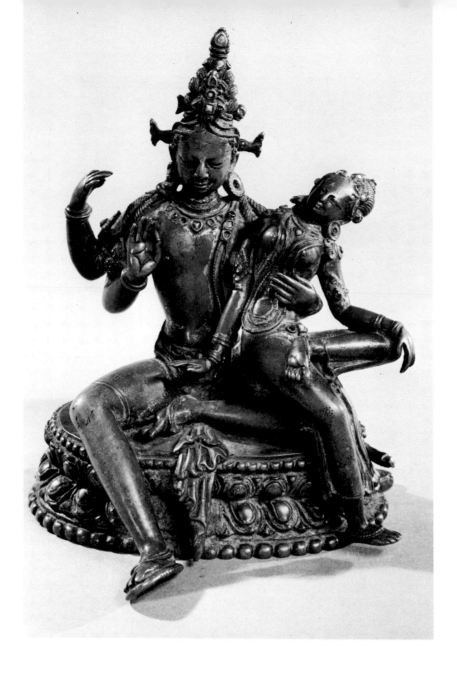

100. Umā-Maheśvara
Nepal
14th century
Copper with traces of gilding and
inlaid with semiprecious stones
h: 7 in. (17.8 cm.)

Of all the Śaiva themes rendered in
Nepali sculpture that of Umā-
Maheśvara is certainly the most
popular. That this charming bronze

has been worshiped in a domestic
shrine for ages is indicated by the worn
foreheads and the still-adhering
vermilion. It is a common practice in
Nepal, as in India, to anoint the
images daily with vermilion, which
probably serves as a substitute for
sacrificial blood.

Here, as in a Deccani bronze of
the same subject (no. 83), Śiva
occupies much of the lotus as he sits in
lalitāsana, the pleats of his dhoti

draping over the base. Except for his
hairdo, adorned with the crescent and
the skull, and the snake serving as his
right ear ornament, which are the only
signs of his ascetic nature, he is
portrayed as a princely figure. His two
upper hands, now empty, may once
have carried a trident and a rosary.
His normal right hand forms the
vyākhyānamudrā and the corresponding
left hand supports the separately cast
figure of Umā.

Ornamented like her husband,
but without the skull and crescent,
Umā sits on his left thigh with her right
leg pendant and her left folded across
her right thigh. Her left hand idly rests
on her thigh, and she seems relaxed
and at ease, her head cocked to one
side as if to look at Śiva. Despite the
divinity of the subjects, the theme is
essentially human and is always
delineated by Nepali sculptors with
loving intimacy, as in this bronze.

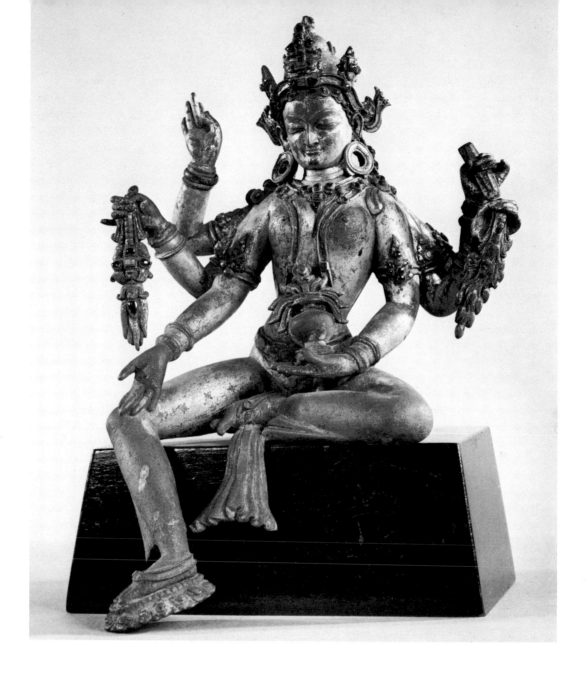

101. The Goddess Vasudhārā

Nepal

14th century

Gilt copper with painted hair and inlaid with semiprecious stones

h: 11 in. (28.0 cm.)

Vasudhārā ("stream of gems") is the goddess of wealth and fortune in the Mahayana Buddhist pantheon. As such, her popularity among Nepali Buddhists is understandable and the artists of that country have consistently created beautiful images of this goddess, both in bronze and in painting (she is rarely, if ever, represented in stone). Her images have generally graced domestic altars, as images of Lakshmī do in Hindu households. Curiously, she does not enjoy the same popularity in neighboring Tibet, a predominantly Buddhist country, as she does in Nepal.

The six-armed goddess is here seated in *lalitāsana*, her pendant right leg supported by a small lotus. Her full and fleshy figure bends gently to one side, thereby intensifying the effect of animation. Her arms are so symmetrically arranged that they almost describe a mandala. Beginning with the lower right hand and moving clockwise, her attributes are: *varada-mudrā*, a spray of gems, *tathāgatavanda-nāmudrā*, a manuscript, a sheaf of grain, and a potted plant. She is, therefore, not merely the goddess of wealth and plenitude, but also of wisdom, which is symbolized by the manuscript.

102. The God Indra

Nepal
15th century
Gilt copper inlaid with semiprecious
stones
h: 9½ in. (24.1 cm.)

Indra, a powerful deity in the Vedic
pantheon, was reduced to the titular
position of head of the gods and regent
of the eastern quarter in later Indian
mythology. In Nepal a special festival
in his honor is still observed annually,
and on that occasion innumerable
images of the god are carried in
procession. The present sculpture, like
most others known outside the
country, is probably such a proces-
sional image and depicts Indra in a
manner quite typical of Nepal.

The youthful god, resplendent in
his sumptuously decorated crown and
ornaments, sits relaxed in the posture
known as *mahārājalīlā*, which obviously derives its name from the way
that Indian princes sat on their
thrones. Apart from his distinctive
crown, the king of the gods is also
distinguished by the third eye
marked horizontally across his forehead. As a cosmic god, Indra is
described in the Vedas as thousand-
eyed (*sahasrāksha*) and the third eye
here is obviously symbolic of the
thousand. His right arm rests languidly on his right knee; his left hand,
which helps to balance the posture,
holds the stem of a lotus, which supports a thunderbolt. Both the third eye
and the thunderbolt are legacies of his
Vedic past, when he was an eminent
god of thunder and rain. This
particular form of Indra appears to
have been a Nepali invention, for no
Indian prototype is known.

103. The Goddess Durgā

Nepal
15th century
Gilt copper inlaid with semiprecious
stones
h: 8¼ in. (21.0 cm.)

This goddess, provided with eighteen
arms, is represented in a militant
posture. Her principal hands probably
held two snakes, as we know from
similar Nepali images, and the other
hands hold various weapons, some of
which are now missing. Two quivers
are attached to her shoulders, but
otherwise the back is rather summarily modeled. Her forehead is
marked with the third eye, and she is
sumptuously adorned with ornaments
richly encrusted with semiprecious
stones. Even in battle the goddess is
serene, unruffled by human emotions.

The beautifully arrayed multiple
arms, enclosing the elegant torso like a
mandorla, provide a harmonious
visual pattern enriched by the
dazzling gilded surface and sparkling
gems. A work of rather appealing
ostentation, the bronze radiates the
brilliance and boldness of design for
which Nepali artists are justly famous.

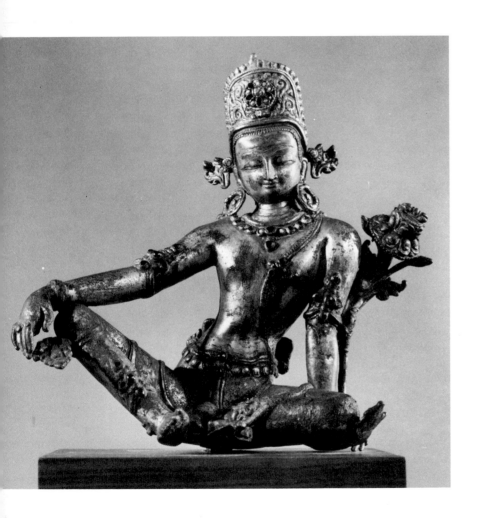

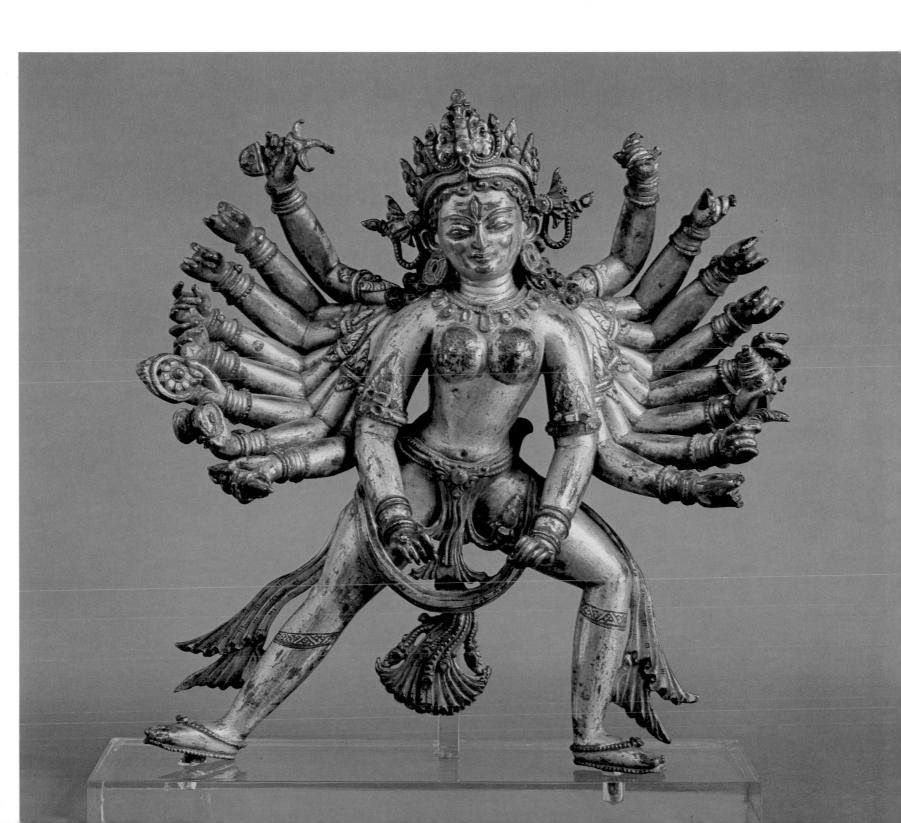

104. Garuḍa Finial

Nepal
15th–16th century
Gilt bronze, inlaid with turquoise and
partially painted
h: 4⅜ in. (11.1 cm.)

This striking sculpture probably
served as a finial at the apex of an
elaborate shrine. It shows the mythical
sun bird Garuḍa with outstretched
arms and wings, ready to take off.
Half-avian and half-human, he has the
face, hindquarters, and talons of a
bird, but the torso of a man. A snake
serves as his necklace, and his tail
feathers, of an elegant floriated
design, form a decorative nimbus
behind his head.

   Nepali sculptors were apparently
very fond of this hybrid creature and
used him over the centuries in a
variety of delightfully inventive
forms. Even though Garuḍa is primarily the mount of the Hindu god
Vishnu, he frequently appears as the
crowning motif in Nepali shrines and
tympana, particularly in Buddhist art.
This particularly animated example
exhibits the continued vitality and
virtuosity of the Nepali sculptors long
after the sculptural tradition in India
itself had lost its creative force.

105. Samvara and Nairātmyā

Nepal or Tibet
16th century
Gilt copper, inlaid with semiprecious
stones and partially polychromed
h: 12½ in. (31.7 cm.)

With his feet firmly planted on the
chests of the two prostrate figures of
Bhairava and Kālarātri, the
Buddhist god Samvara is engaged in a
sexual embrace with the goddess
Nairātmyā. His two hands form the
vajrahuṁkāramudrā as they hold a
thunderbolt and a bell. The goddess's
arms are flung around Samvara's
neck, one holding a skull cup, the
other brandishing a chopper.

   The faces of the figures are
painted in cold gold, their eyes and
eyebrows outlined in black, white, and
red. We can be certain, therefore, that
the bronze was worshiped in Tibet, but
if made there it must have been the
handiwork of a Nepali artist. The
alternative is that it was cast in Nepal
and then taken into Tibet. Whatever
its exact provenance, the bronze is a
beautiful realization of joyous and
rhythmic movement. The blissful and
serene faces have a stillness about them
that belies the overt passion in their
loving embrace. The sense of movement is enhanced further by the
swirling masses of drapery and floriated
scrollwork very similar to that seen in
the Garuḍa finial (no. 104).

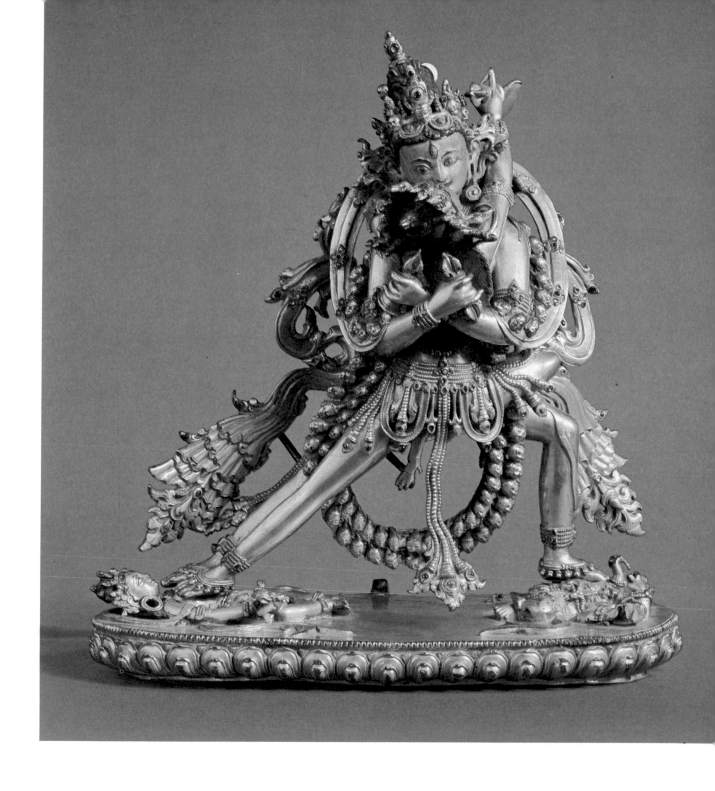

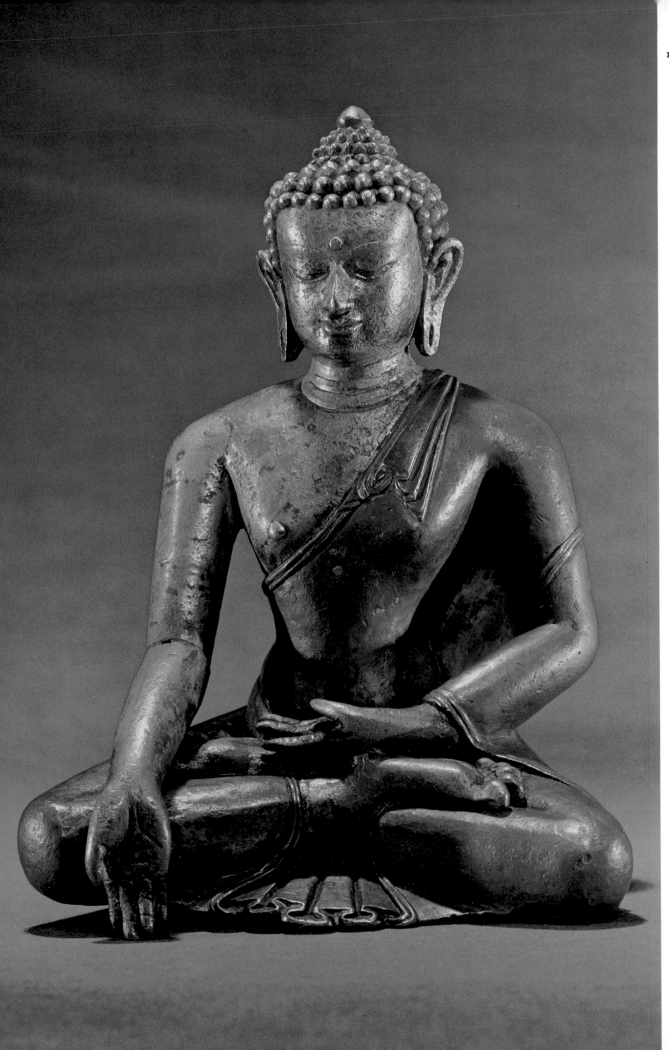

106. Buddha Śākyamuni

Tibet (?)
12th–13th century
Gilt copper
h: 7 in. (17.8 cm.)

The Buddha Śākyamuni is seated in
meditation, his right hand extended in
varadamudrā and his left resting in his
lap. His earlobes are elongated, an
applied dot serves as the *urṇā*, and the
ushṇīsha is surmounted by a slightly
pointed ball. The face is somewhat
square and the nose unusually aqui-
line. What is even more unusual is
the application of a red slip, probably
of copper, to distinguish the garment.

Although the figure is identified
as the Buddha Śākyamuni, the
gesture of the right hand might
indicate that it represents instead the
Tathāgata Ratnasambhava. The
practice of variegating the surface of
the same bronze with two different
metals was more common in Tibet and
Burma, but stylistically the bronze is
much closer to Nepali than to Burmese
bronzes (see no. 92). The facial
features, the treatment of the hair, the
folds of the garment, and the sensitive
rendering of the hands definitely point
to Nepali workmanship. The colored
robe, however, is unusual for Nepal
and the bronze may have been cast in
Tibet following a Burmese model.

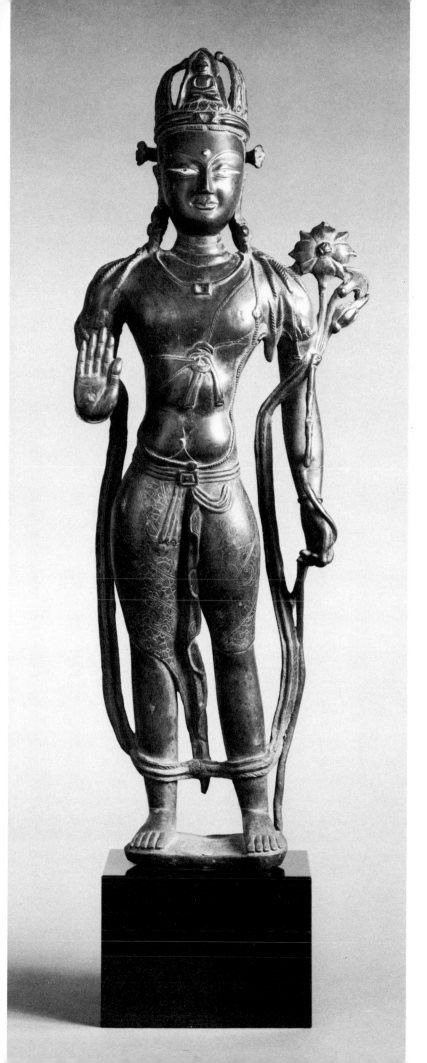

107. The Bodhisattva Padmapāṇi

Western Tibet
13th century
Copper with silver inlay
h: 22¼ in. (56.5 cm.)

The bodhisattva Padmapāṇi holds the sinuous stem of a lotus with his left hand; his right hand forms the *abhayamudrā*. A deerskin, indicative of his ascetic nature, is thrown around his left shoulder and tied in the middle of his torso. His parental Tathāgata, Amitābha, is represented in the crown and his eyes and *urṇā* are inlaid with silver.

The bronze is an impressive example of western Tibetan sculpture, reflecting strong influences of the Kashmiri style. The modeling of the figure reveals the same penchant for emphasizing abdominal and other muscles of the body that one finds in Kashmiri sculptures, although the calves have been rendered with a total lack of modeling. Obviously the artist employed an altogether different set of proportions, for the figure is far more elongated than those seen in the average Kashmiri bronze. The design and treatment of the drapery are also different and, while the face is still strongly Kashmiri, the somewhat narrow eyes and the high cheekbones reveal ethnic features that can be regarded as Tibetan. Characteristic also of Tibetan craftsmanship is the more summary treatment of the back.

108. The Bodhisattva Mañjuśrī

Western Tibet
13th–14th century
Brass, painted and inlaid with
turquoise, opal, and silver
h: 7 in. (17.8 cm.)

This elaborately crowned and ornamented figure is seated in meditation.
A sash crosses his torso diagonally and
his elegantly braided locks fall down
both shoulders. His face was once painted with cold gold, his eyes are inlaid
with silver, and the pupils are indicated
with black paint. Although the figure
might be confused with the Tathāgata
Amitābha, his flowing braids and tiger-
claw necklace definitely identify him as
the bodhisattva Mañjuśrī, who, in this
particular form, is known as *Dharma-
śaṅkhasamādhi*. The majestic bearing of
the figure is also suitable for Mañjuśrī,
who is generally described as a prince.

The bronze is interesting as a
synthesis of both the Kashmiri and
Nepali styles. The face has the plump-
ness of Kashmiri examples, which are
also commonly inlaid in silver; however, the attenuated and almost
abstract modeling of the body, as well
as the design of the crown and armlets,
is more commonly found in Nepali
figures. Such a synthesis could only
have occurred in western Tibet or the
Ladakh area, and that the bronze was
certainly in use there is evident from
the paint applied to face and hair.

109. The Goddess Vajravārāhī

Tibet
14th–15th century
Gilt bronze
h: 14 in. (36.0 cm.)

The completely naked figure of the
goddess Vajravārāhī is shown dancing
with her left leg bent in the posture
known as *ardhaparyaṅka*. Her right
hand brandishes a chopper with
which she destroys the forces of evil
and all non-believers, and her left hand
holds a skull cup from which she drinks
her victim's blood. The sow's head
protruding from above her right ear is
her most distinctive attribute and
justifies part of her name, for the word
vārāhī means "sow." Except for this
element, she is no different iconographically from Nairātmyā (no. 105),
and one is really a manifestation of
the other.

A very important goddess in
esoteric Buddhism, Vajravārāhī is
especially venerated in Tibet. It may
be recalled that there is an important
Hindu mother goddess known as
Vārāhī, and that she too frequently is
shown dancing (see no. 35). Since of
all the mother goddesses only Vārāhī
inspired an individual cult, particularly in Orissa, it is possible that she
served as some sort of prototype for the
Buddhist Vajravārāhī. Orissa, along
with Bengal and Bihar, was a strong-
hold of Vajrayana Buddhism during
the medieval period. Although the
bronze is here attributed to Tibet, it
may have been cast in Nepal, or more
likely, in Tibet by a Nepali artist.

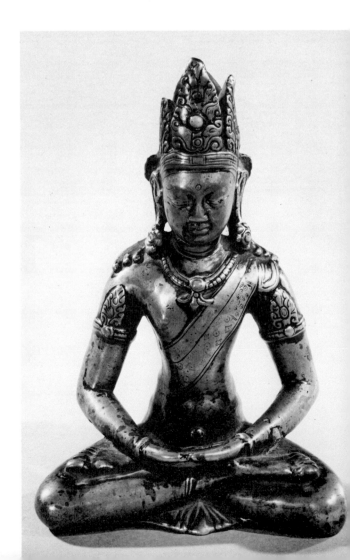

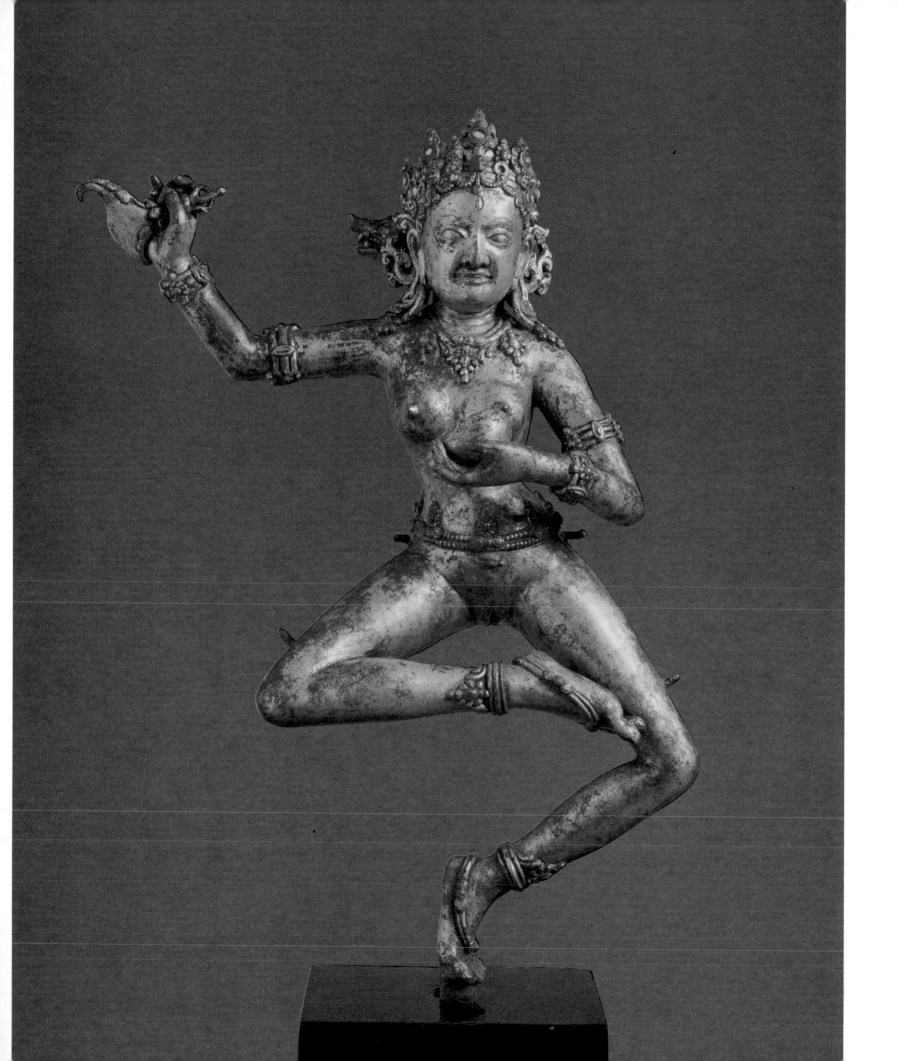

110. An Esoteric Form of Mañjuśrī

Tibet
15th–16th century
Gilt copper, inlaid with turquoise and
polychromed
h: 9⅞ in. (25.1 cm.)

This three-headed, six-armed god is
seated in *lalitāsana* on a lotus, locked in
a sexual embrace (*yab-yum*) with a
goddess. The lotus is placed on the
back of a lion that seems to snarl at the
two deities. The faces of the couple
express both passion and anger and
each forehead is marked with the third
eye. The matted hair of each is
encircled by a snake and embellished
with the *viśvavajra* symbol. The
principal arms of the god encircle the
female as his hands form the
vajrahuṁkāramudrā and hold a bell and
a thunderbolt. Two other hands hold a
bow and arrow; his third right hand
touches his partner's breast; and the
remaining left hand holds a skull cup
full of blood. The goddess's arms and
feet are flung around her partner and
her hands also hold a thunderbolt and
a bell.

Several Buddhist deities, including the bodhisattva Mañjuśrī, have the
lion as their mount. However, the bow
and arrow are important emblems of
Mañjuśrī, and the *vajrahuṁkāramudrā* is
commonly given to many of his esoteric
(*gūhya*) forms, such as Gūhyasādhana,
Gūhyamañjuvajra, etc. Whether or
not the figure is Mañjuśrī, the bronze
illustrates the Tibetan artists' innate
love of splendor and sumptuousness.
The brightly gilt surface is further
enriched with numerous turquoise
inlays, while blue, green, and black
paints add to its colorfulness. The lion
with its green mane and tail is a
delightfully whimsical creature that
adds a comical touch to an otherwise
profoundly mystical subject.

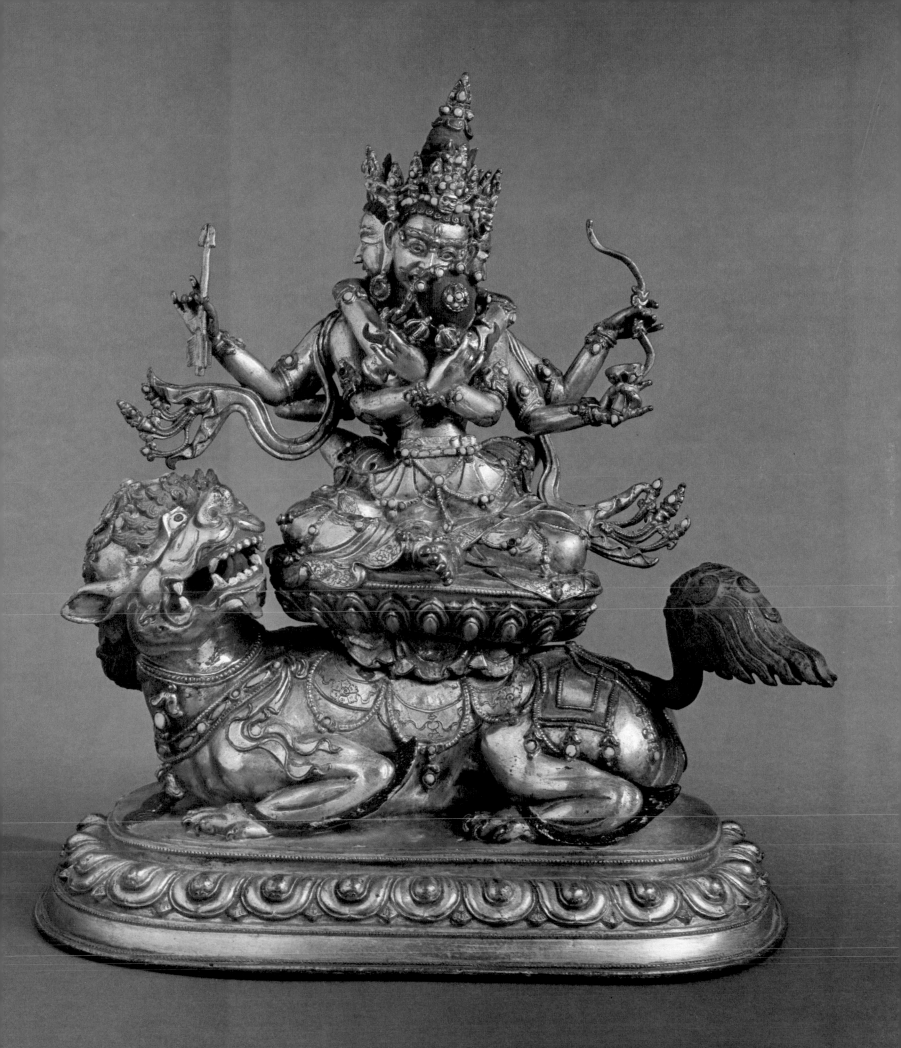

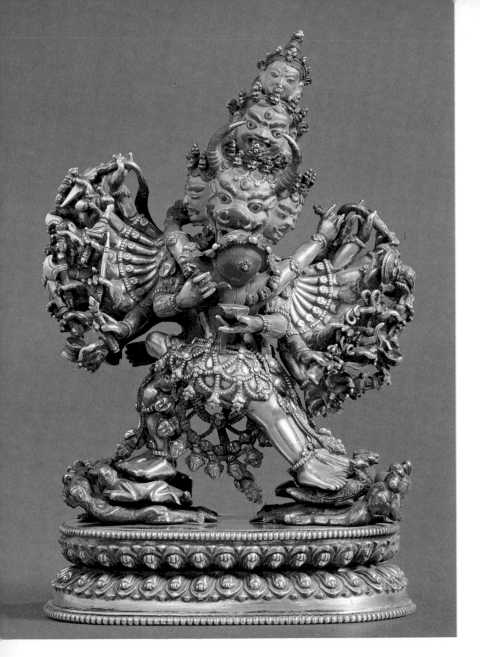

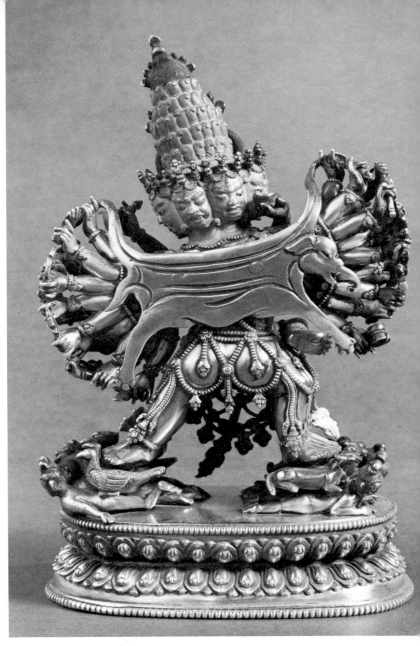

111. Vajrabhairava and Partner

Central Tibet

(a) 15th century
Silver and polychrome
h : 9¼ in. (23.5 cm.)

(b) 16th century
Bronze and polychrome
h : 15⅜ in. (39.0 cm.)

One of the most powerful of the wrathful divinities in the Vajrayana

pantheon, Vajrabhairava is an angry manifestation of the bodhisattva Mañjuśrī, the god of wisdom. His principal head is that of a buffalo and he is provided with multiple arms and legs. The symbolism of his form is best explained by Tsongkha-pa, the founder of the Geluk-pa sect of Buddhism in Tibet. Vajrabhairava's "nine faces point to the ninefold classification of the scriptures; his two

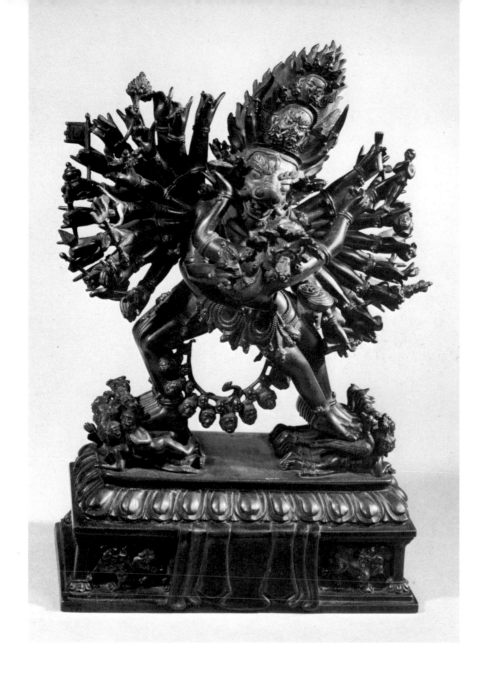

horns to the two truths [conventional and ultimate]; his thirty-four arms together with his spirituality, communication and embodiment in tangible form to the thirty-seven facts of enlightenment; his sixteen legs to sixteen kinds of no-thing-ness; the human being and the other mammals on which he stands to the eight attainments; the eagle and the other birds on which he tramples to the eight surpassing strengths; his nakedness to his being undefiled by emotional upsets and by intellectual fogs...." (H. V. Guenther, *Tibetan Buddhism without Mystification*, Leiden, 1966, pp. 38–39.)

Both sculptures reveal the extraordinary expressive power of Tibetan imagery, as well as the finesse with which such complex metaphysical ideas were transformed into easily apprehensible form. The Tibetans were remarkably adroit in sublimating the grotesque and in creating compelling and harmonious compositions, as seen in these two examples. The silver sculpture, perhaps the slightly earlier of the two, is possibly the finest known Tibetan work in this medium—a tour de force in both its astonishingly detailed and rich craftsmanship as well as its dynamic expression. By contrast, the larger bronze with its reddish metal stresses more the wrathful character of the god and the passionate nature of the divine embrace. One must emphasize here that such images were not intended for public worship but were used exclusively in esoteric rituals.

Published: (a) *Artis* (Das Aktuelle Kunstmagazin), 12 December 1973, cover.

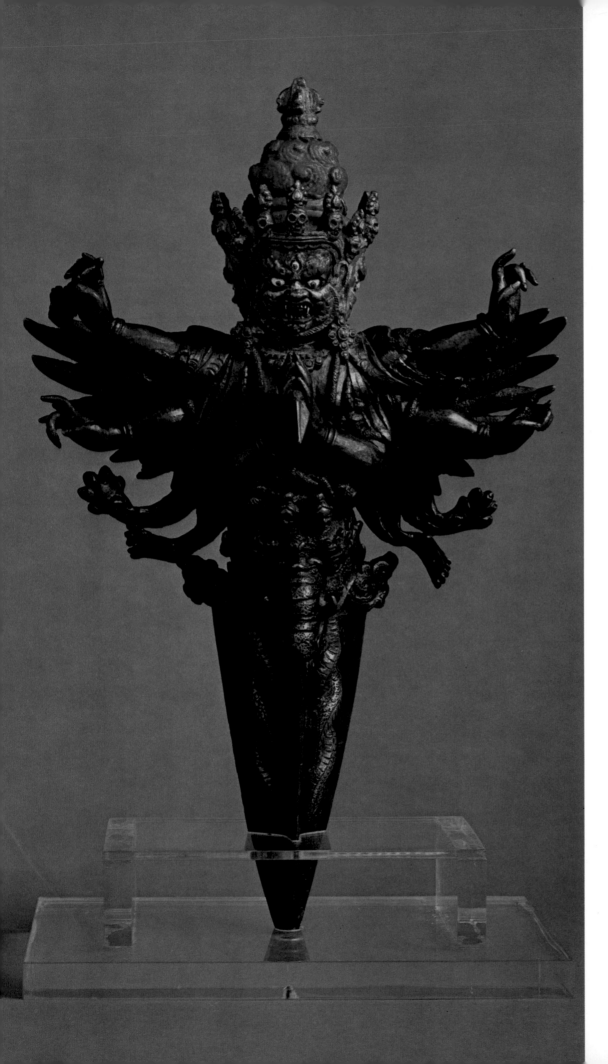

112. A Ritual Dagger (Phur-pa)

Tibet
16th century
Polychromed bronze
h: 12 in. (30.5 cm.)

This is perhaps the finest known example of a *phur-pa*, a dagger with a three-sided blade commonly called a *magic dagger* or a *magic dart*. It is used in rites of exorcism and in the ritual destruction of the enemies of the faith, both human and divine. It may also be employed symbolically to destroy the "demon of the self." Although the Tibetan Buddhists claim an Indian origin for the *phur-pa*, nothing similar is known among Indian ritual implements. More likely the implement is of Tibetan origin and may have been used in pre-Buddhist days by local shamans.

Of the numerous varieties of *phur-pa*, this particular type with the handle rendered in the form of a deity is rather rare. The three-headed winged god, holding a *phur-pa* with his principal hands as if about to plunge it into his victim, is probably the personification of the implement itself and is regarded as a tutelary divinity of the Ningma-pa sect of Tibetan Buddhism. The representation of the deity is unusually sculpturesque for a ritual implement of this type. The three blades of the *phur-pa*, superimposed with the combined motif of serpent and *makara*, are said to symbolize the three virtues of charity, chastity, and patience.

Published: Fisher, p. 29 and fig. 29.

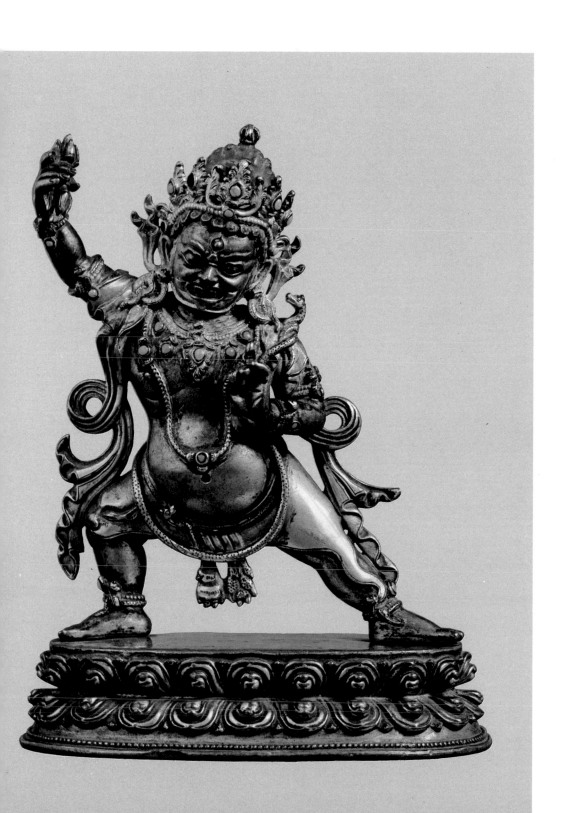

113. The Buddhist God Hayagrīva

Tibet
17th century
Gilt bronze and silver, inlaid with turquoise and painted
h: 5⅝ in. (14.3 cm.)

Hayagrīva's name literally means "one with a horse's head" and in the Hindu pantheon he is an incarnation of Vishnu; usually his image does have the head of a horse instead of that of a human. However, the Buddhist Hayagrīva, as in this bronze, is altogether a different deity and has nothing to do with his Hindu counterpart. Rather, he shares features more in common with the Bhairava aspect of Siva, such as the angry face, the third eye, the snake ornaments, and the animal skin. To justify his name, however, a tiny effigy of a horse's head is attached to his hair; in this instance it can be seen behind the crown. In the Tibetan pantheon Hayagrīva is an important deity, worshiped especially by people who earn their livelihood with horses.

In this instance he is an angry pot-bellied figure who stands in a militant posture, brandishing a thunderbolt with his right hand. His left hand, raised in *tarjanīmudrā*, once held a lasso. What is remarkable about this image is the use of various materials in its construction, which gives it a fascinatingly variegated surface. The figure itself is cast in silver, the lotus base in gilt copper, but far more exciting is the use of selective gilding for all ornaments, the crown, the scarf, the animal skin, and the beard. Moreover, the statue is richly encrusted with turquoise and the chignon is painted red, for all wrathful deities have flaming hair.

Indonesia

Sumatra and Java are the two largest of the thousands of islands that comprise Indonesia. Of the two, Java is by far the more significant, for not only was it the main stage where the principal dynasties played out their historical roles, but virtually all the great Indonesian religious monuments are located in this luxuriantly verdant tropical island. Most of the Indonesian sculptures depicting both Hindu and Buddhist divinities in the Pan-Asian collection were very likely created in central Java during the ninth and tenth centuries under the Śailendra dynasty. It must be remembered that no thorough study of the chronology of Javanese bronzes has yet been made and hence these attributions should be regarded as tentative.

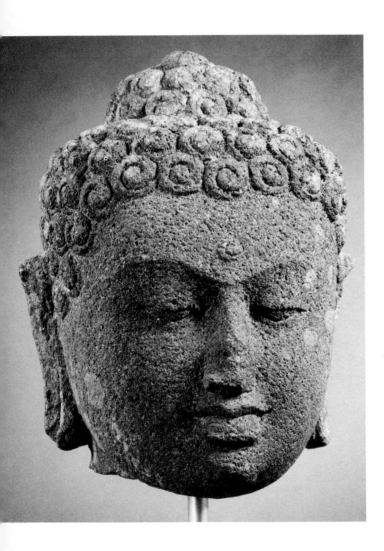

114. Head of a Tathāgata

Central Java, Borobudur style
Ca. 800
Gray volcanic stone
h: 13⅜ in. (34.0 cm.)

This head once belonged to a seated
Tathāgata figure such as that
illustrated in no. 115. Typical of the
head of a Tathāgata or Buddha, the
hair is arranged in short circular locks
curled to the right, the *urṇā* is a prominent dot in the middle of the forehead,
and the earlobes are elongated. The
gentle and serene visage is rendered
according to the texts that say the face
of the Buddha "should be made
squarish in form, sharply delineated,
beautifully full and endowed with
brilliant and pleasing marks."

Several similar heads are in
Western collections and they are
usually characterized as "Borobudur"
heads. Certainly the head is stylistically analogous to those still attached
to the seated images of Tathāgatas on
the several terraces of the great stupa
at Borobudur. However, it could have
belonged to other such Buddha images
found in both the Prambanam and
Kedu regions.

115. A Preaching Tathāgata

Central Java, from Chandi Sewu (?)
9th century
Gray volcanic stone
h: 27¾ in. (70.5 cm.)

Despite its missing head, this larger
than life-size figure of a Tathāgata
is impressive for both its austere
simplicity and sheer physical presence.
The gesture of the hands indicates
that he is engaged in teaching as
he sits in the classic posture of meditation. Although similar images of
preaching Tathāgatas are placed
within the latticed stupas on the top
terraces of Borobudur, their hands are
placed further from the body and
hardly touch one another as they form
the gesture (see Bernet Kempers,
pl. 96). On the other hand, the
formation of the gesture in this image
is very similar to that seen in Tathāgata
figures from Chandi Sewu (ibid., pl.
128). Moreover, this figure, like the
Chandi Sewu Tathāgatas, is broader
and considerably heavier than the
Buddhas from Borobudur.

Unquestionably, the prototypes
for such images must have been
bronzes brought from Gupta India.
While it is tempting to relate them to
Sarnath Buddhas, primarily because
of the plain and transparent treatment
of the drapery, the impassive grandeur
of the figure and the emphasis on
ponderous volume remind one of the
equally monumental Buddha images
in the excavated temples at Ajanta or
the colossal Buddhas of Anuradhapura
in Sri Lanka. The solid mass of such
Buddha figures appropriately conveys
the idea behind certain similes used
constantly in literature to describe the
Buddha. He is often characterized as a
bull among men whose image should
be *nyāgrodhaparimaṇḍala*. The
nyāgrodha is the famous banyan tree
which is regarded both as well proportioned and noble, characteristics
that are essential for a Buddha image.

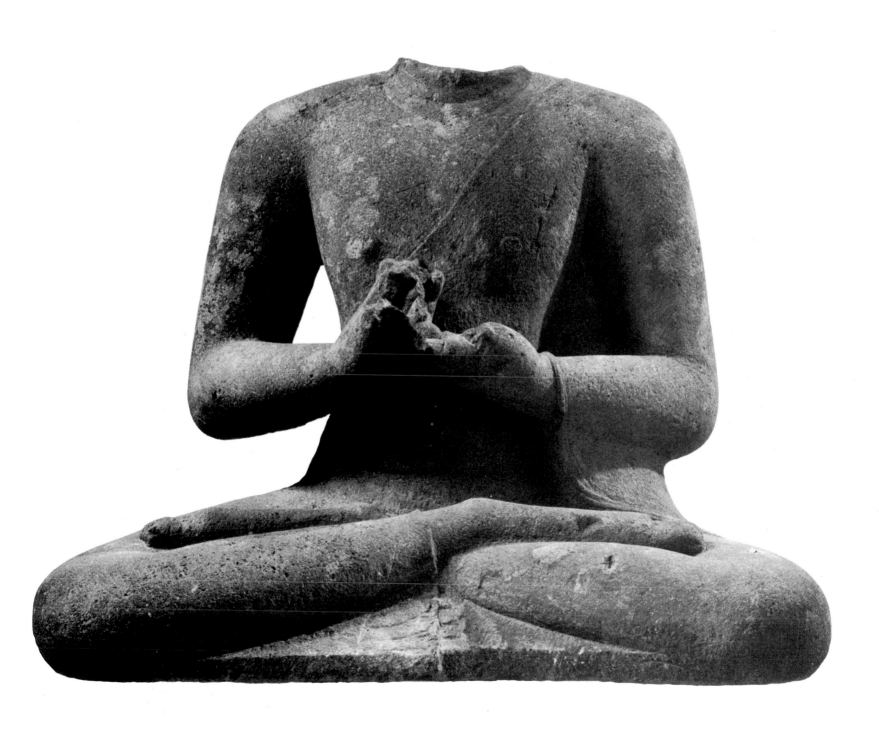

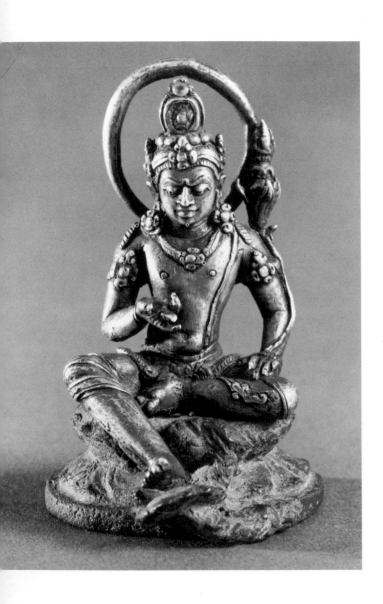

116. The Bodhisattva Vajrapāṇi

Central Java
9th–10th century
Silver inlaid with ruby (figure) and
bronze with green patina (base)
h: 3¼ in. (8.2 cm.)

The bodhisattva sits gracefully on a
lotus with a smaller lotus projecting
in front to support his pendant right
foot. However, the foot does not touch
the lotus and the fact that the figure
is silver and the base is bronze may
indicate that they do not belong
together. The bodhisattva's right
hand forms a gesture that may denote
charity. His left hand holds the stem of
a lotus on which is placed his distinctive attribute, the thunderbolt. His
head is haloed by a simple ring and his
oval chignon is inset with a ruby; such
an inlay is unusual for Javanese
bronzes.

 The figure is stylistically similar
to a bronze bodhisattva in the
Museum Pusat in Jakarta (see
Fontein et al., no. 40, p. 77). However, rather unusual is the frowning
expression on the face of this silver
figure, emphasized by raised, wavy
eyebrows.

117. A Goddess

Central Java
9th century
Bronze with green patina
h: 8⅜ in. (22.2 cm.)

A goddess stands in *samapada* position
on a lotus placed upon a square
pedestal. Bejeweled and crowned, her
hair is gathered into a topknot like
that of an ascetic. Her lower right hand
forms the *varadamudrā*, and her upper
right holds a truncated sword. Her
upper left hand grasps a manuscript;
the object in her lower left hand may
be a waterpot or a severed human
head. If the latter, then the presence of
the sword would help to identify the
figure as a form of Durgā.

 Both in its shape and features, the
face bears a strong similarity to some
of the Buddha heads from Borobudur
(see no. 114). She is imbued with a
sense of stately elegance, and her well-
endowed form is especially attractive
because of the slight elongation of the
lower portion. The balance between
modeling and line and the feeling of
quiet sensuousness are reminiscent of
seventh- and eighth-century Indian
sculptures from such sites as
Muṇḍeśvari in Bihar and Sirpur in
Madhya Pradesh.

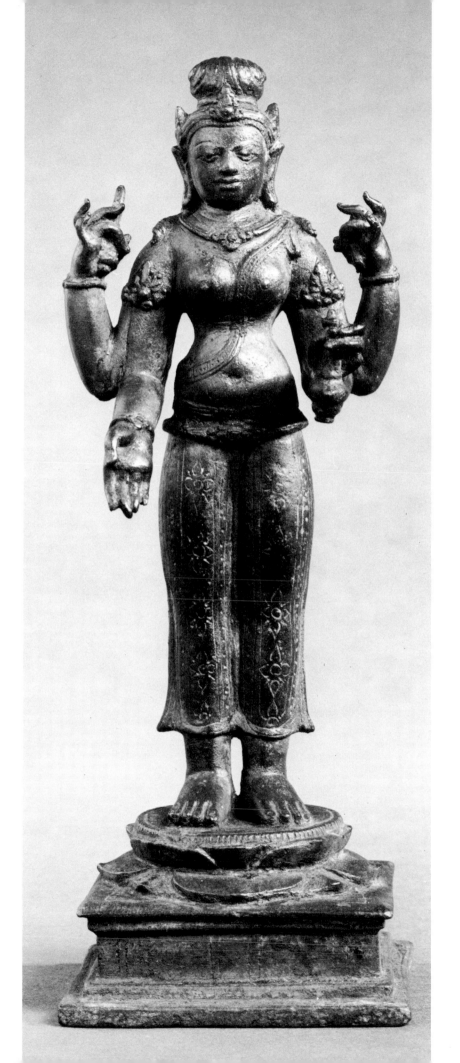

118. A Goddess

Central Java (?)
9th–10th century
Beige stone
h: 26½ in. (67.3 cm.)

This nimbate goddess is seated in *lalitāsana* on a substantial cushion. Her left hand is placed on the cushion and provides her with additional support; her right hand simply rests on her thigh. The prominent curves of both her hips and stomach make her form seem as volumetric as the cushion on which she sits. Very likely she represents Tārā, the Buddhist goddess of mercy.

The color of the stone suggests that the sculpture may have come from the Prambanam Valley. A close stylistic parallel can be seen in the figure of Hārīti on the stair riser of the Mendut temple, which is also conceived essentially in simple, convex volumes and with the same bouffant hairstyle as this goddess. The shape and form of the cushions on which the two goddesses sit are almost identical. Javanese sculpture of this period is said to be heavily influenced by Pāla sculptures of Bihar, but a stylistic comparison of this figure with contemporary Orissan sculptures would perhaps be more appropriate.

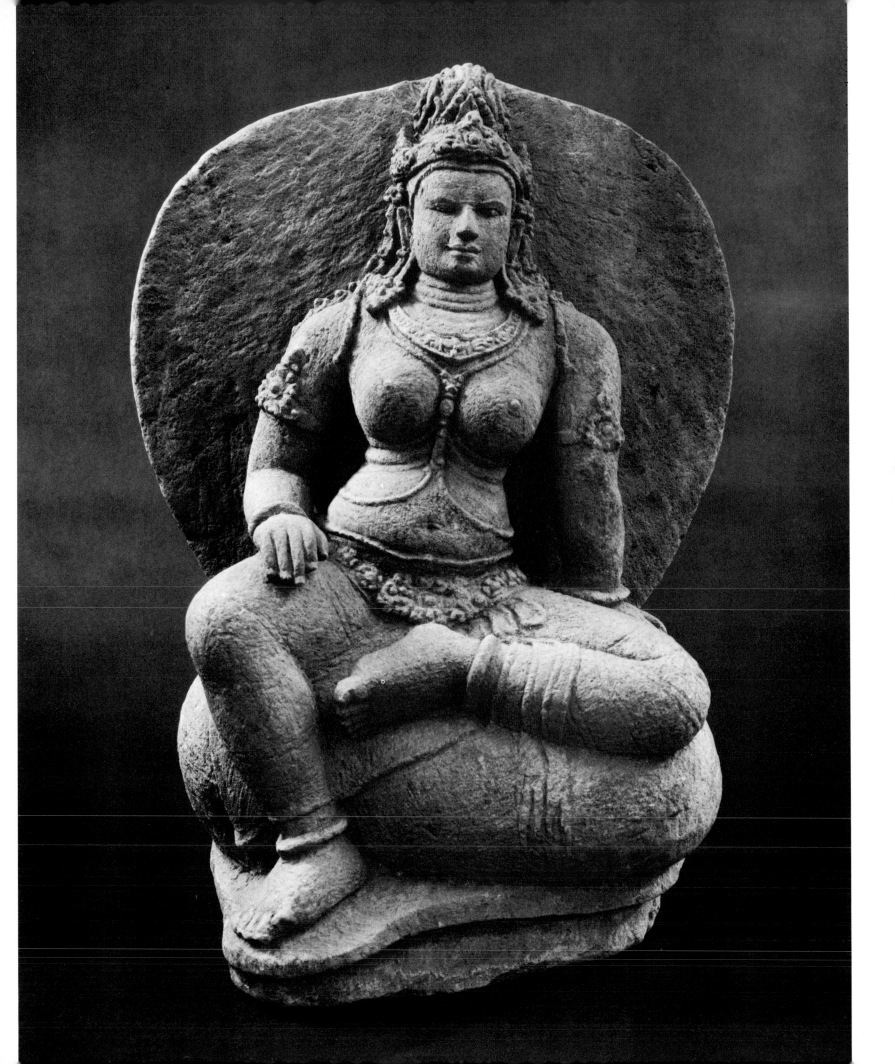

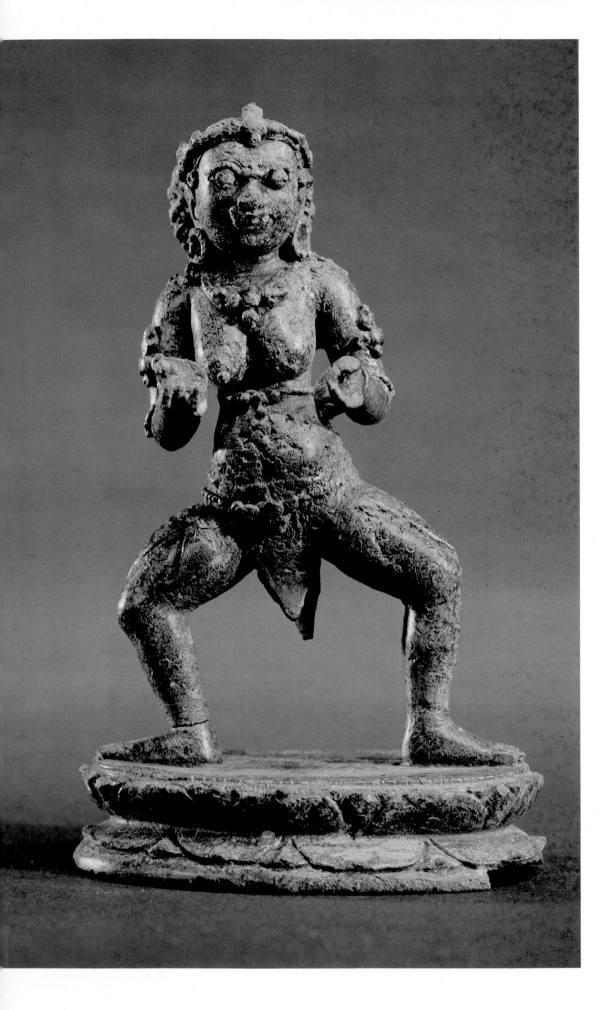

119. A Semi-Divine Ogress

Central Java
10th century
Bronze with green patina
h: 4½ in. (11.4 cm.)

This intriguing little bronze represents a grotesque lady standing with her legs well apart, probably in a dancing posture. Her hands are empty. She seems to wear a garment of leaves held around her loins by a chain. The fangs protruding from her mouth, her round rolling eyes, and her pendulous breasts give her a forbidding appearance.

The fact that she stands on a lotus indicates her divine status, but it is difficult to tell whether she is a ḍākinī of the Buddhist pantheon or a *rākshasī*, a class of malevolent semi-divine ogresses that play an important role in Hindu mythology. Male counterparts of such figures, carved in stone, serve as guardians outside most temples in Java, but females are less common. To my knowledge, this is the only known bronze representation of such a figure, and despite her grotesque appearance, she is a delightful product of an unknown master's fantasy.

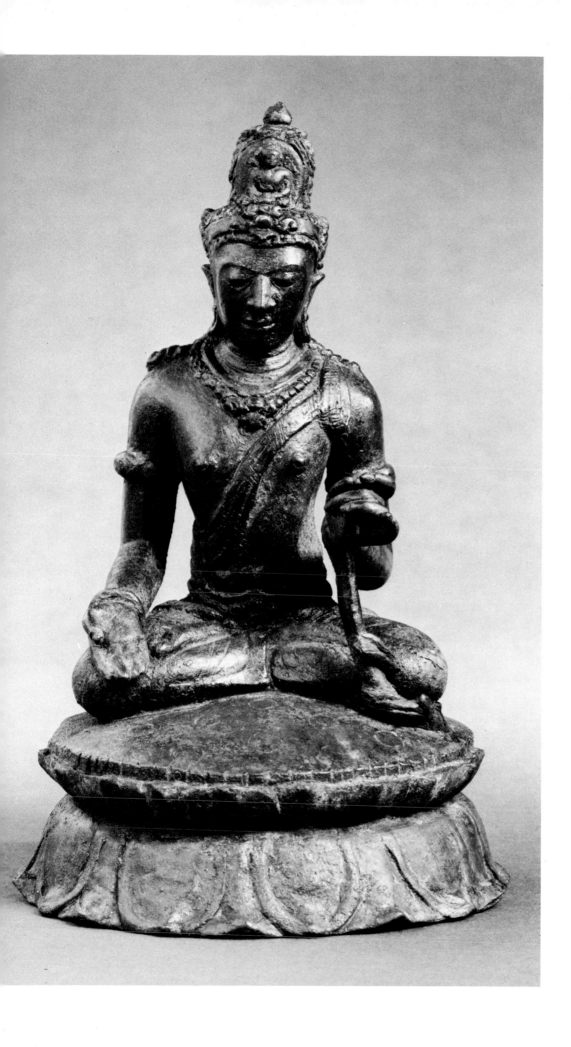

120. The Bodhisattva Padmapāṇi

Java
10th century
Bronze with green patina
h : 8½ in. (21.5 cm.)

Padmapāṇi, the Buddhist god of compassion, is seated like a yogi on a lotus. His right hand forms the *varadamudrā* and his left holds the broken stem of what must have been a lotus. The effigy of Amitābha, his parental Tathāgata, embellishes his chignon. A simple oval nimbus was once attached to his shoulders.

The study of Javanese sculpture, particularly of bronzes, is still in a nascent stage, and hence it is extremely difficult to determine either the provenance or the date of such sculptures. The task is all the more formidable when one is confronted with a bronze such as this which shows some unusual features, such as the pronounced elongation of the face with pointed chin and the slender proportions of the torso that at the same time seems strong and assertive. For somewhat similar figures, see Fontein et al., figs. 40 and 44, and Le Bonheur, p. 155, no. 3630.

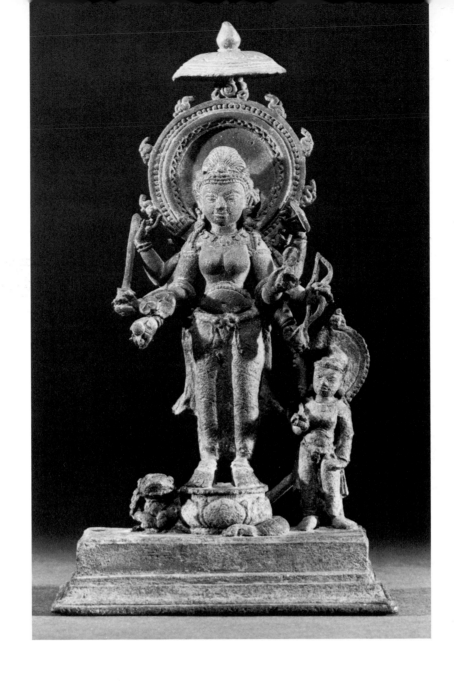

121. The Goddess Durgā

Central Java
10th century
Bronze with green patina
h: 9¼ in. (23.5 cm.)

In this rare and interesting bronze, Durgā is represented with eight arms and accompanied by a female attendant. The Hindu goddess stands in *samapada* on a lotus placed on the back of the lion, who appears to be crushed by it. He nevertheless seems happy to carry his burden, for he raises his forepaws like an affectionate puppy. This is the only known example of so peculiar a disposition of the animal. One of the goddess's hands is delicately extracting an arrow from a quiver; the others hold a sword, a boss, a flower, a trident, a conch, a bow, and a shield. She is provided with a nimbus and a parasol and her female attendant, also nimbate, holds a flywhisk.

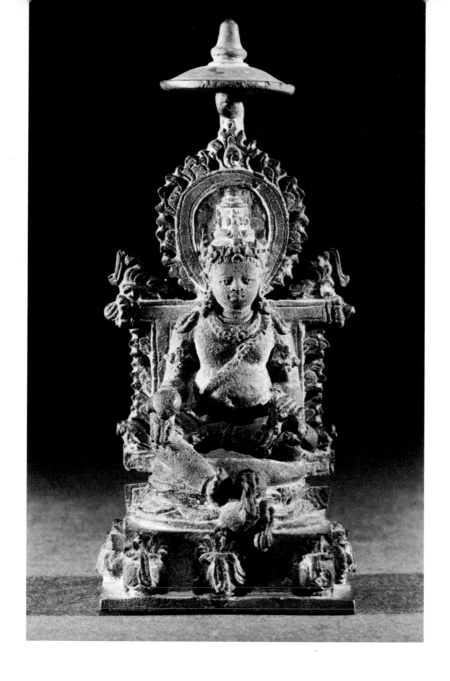

122. Kubera, the God of Wealth

Central Java
10th century
Bronze
h: 5½ in. (14.0 cm.)

Appropriately pot-bellied and ornamented, Kubera, the god of wealth, sits in *lalitāsana* on a lotus upon a throne. His right foot rests on an overturned vase full of jewels and five additional vases are depicted along the base of the throne. A citrus fruit is attached to the palm of his right hand, which forms the *varadamudrā*. His left hand squeezes the neck of a mongoose, which disgorges a stream of jewels. The throne is surmounted by a flame nimbus to which is affixed a parasol.

Since he is the god of wealth, Kubera is worshiped with equal reverence by the Hindus and the Buddhists. In Java, too, during the Hindu-Buddhist period, such small images of Kubera must have graced many domestic altars. In the form seen here, he differs in no significant way from his images in India. He is portly but regal, for he is regarded in Hindu mythology as the king of the *yakshas*.

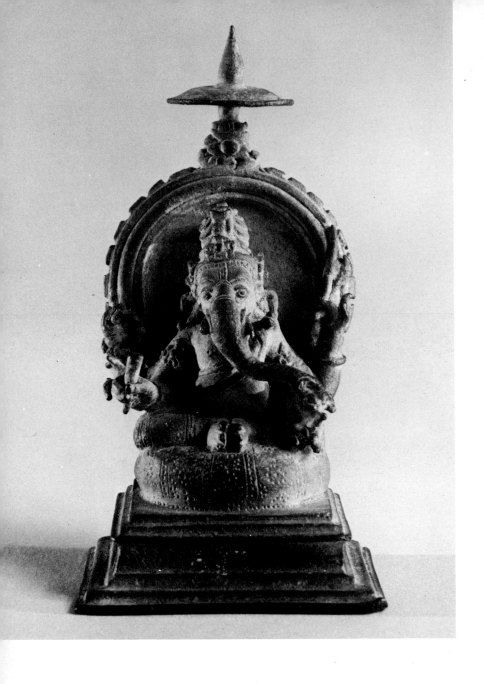

123. The God Gaṇeśa

(a) Central Java
10th century
Bronze with green patina
h: 4⅝ in. (11.7 cm.)
(b) East Java
12th century
Gray volcanic stone
h: 23 in. (58.4 cm.)

Gaṇeśa, the Hindu god of auspiciousness and success, was naturally popular in Java. In the bronze he is seated on a cushion and in the stone sculpture on a lotus, but in both the soles of his feet join each other. A snake is coiled around his sacred cord and he is given the third eye. In addition, his close association with his father, Śiva, is emphasized by the crescent moon and the skull adorning his crown. His upper right hand holds a rosary and the corresponding left hand a battle-ax. His lower left hand holds a cup containing sweets which he is devouring. His broken lower left hand in the stone image very likely held part of his tusk, as it does in the bronze.

The most distinctive feature of Javanese representations of Gaṇeśa is the manner in which he sits. This particular posture, unknown in India, was in all probability a local invention, although it is also encountered in Cambodia.

Diminutive as it is, the delightfully charming bronze is certainly the earlier of the two representations and is remarkably well modeled. The date of the stone sculpture is suggested by a comparison with two others, the Chandi Banon Gaṇeśa from central Java (see Bernet Kempers, pl. 39), which cannot be dated later than the tenth century, and the Gaṇeśa of Bara, dated 1239 (ibid., pls. 212–13). The Pan-Asian Gaṇeśa reveals nothing of the exuberant ornamentation that characterizes the Bara Gaṇeśa and it is also free from the more macabre elements that seem to have become a commonplace of post-twelfth-century east Javanese Gaṇeśa images.

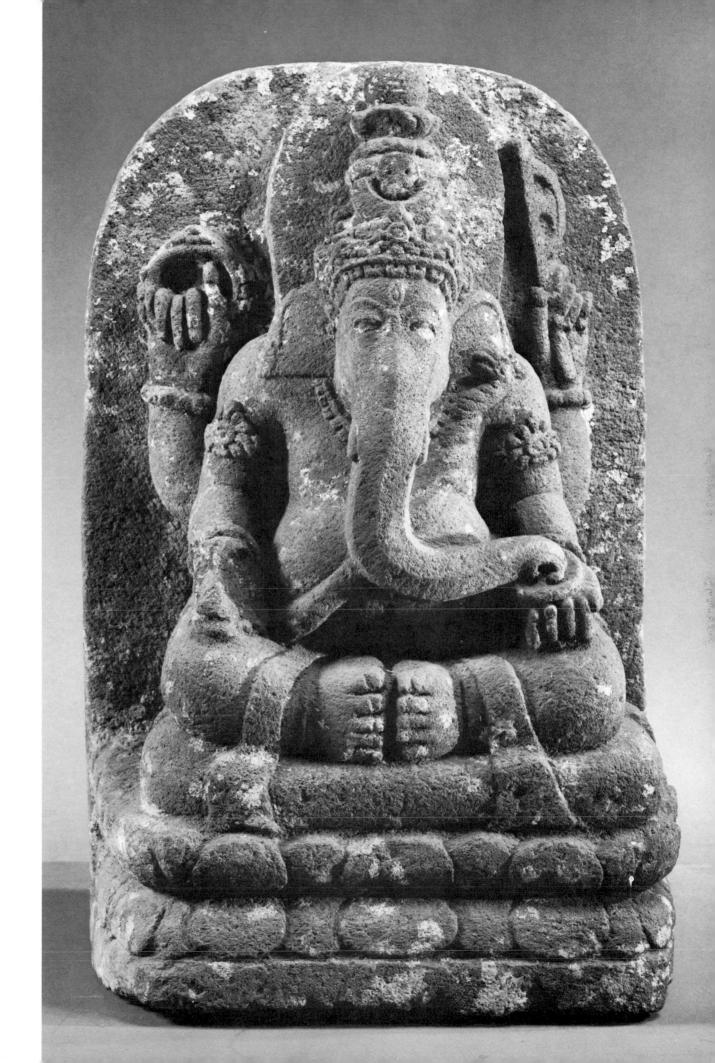

124. The God Brahma
Central Java
10th century
Bronze
h: 5½ in. (14.0 cm.)

The god Brahma, the creative member
of the Hindu trinity, is represented
here with four heads symbolizing the
four Vedas, the most ancient sacred
texts of the Hindus (see nos. 36, 142).
The hair from all four heads is combined into a single crownlike chignon.
Wearing a dhoti, the sacred cord of
the brahman, and appropriate
ornaments, Brahma stands in the
samapada posture on a lotus. His four
hands hold the rosary (now missing),
an ascetic's staff, a waterpot, and a
manuscript. Except for the remarkable
attenuation of the figure, the bronze
reflects all the stylistic characteristics
of central Javanese art of the period.
Usually most central Javanese
bronzes have somewhat fleshier bodies
(see no. 117). Note the unusual
elongation of the fingers, particularly
of the tips, which appear almost
needlelike in their sharpness. This is a
stylized affectation peculiar only to
Javanese bronzes. The closest
stylistic parallel for this figure can be
seen in a bronze Vishnu in the Musée
Guimet (see Le Bonheur, p. 215,
no. 2328).

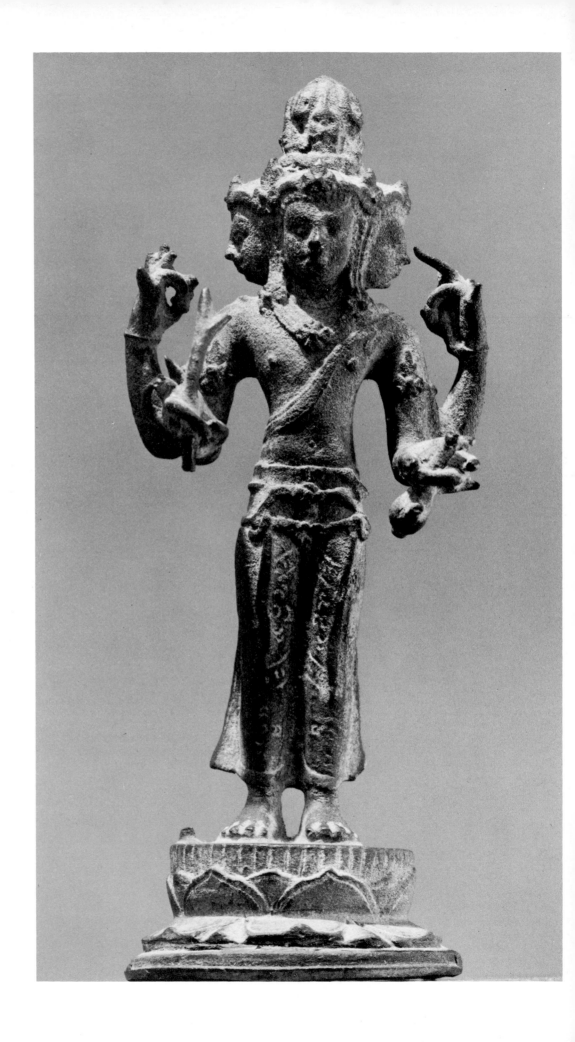

5. A Bird

East Java
13th–14th century
Bronze with green patina
h: 4 in. (10.1 cm.)

Very little is known about such bronze birds and only a few have been published so far. We are therefore unable to suggest their exact function, but they probably served as some sort of finial. Delightfully decorative, the birds are sometimes rendered realistically, but most often their forms are an imaginative combination of several species. While the origin of such forms goes back to Gupta India, they were frequently employed in central Javanese architecture both for their ornamental and symbolic functions. Since nothing much is known about such bronze birds, it is extremely difficult to suggest a precise date for this one. The date recommended here is based on a comparison with similar birds that fill the medallions on the walls of the main temple at Chandi Panataran, built in 1347 (see Bernet Kempers, pls. 280–82).

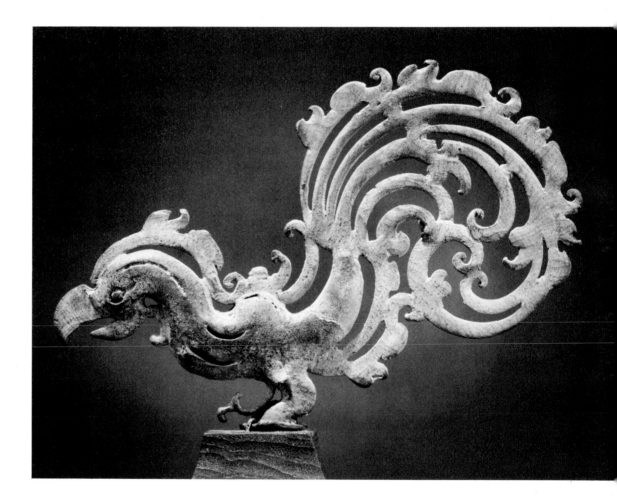

Thailand

In attributing the Thai sculptures I
have generally followed the classification system outlined by J. Boisselier
and J. Beurdeley in *The Heritage of
Thai Sculpture*. They divide the history
of Thai sculpture into several schools,
each with its distinctive stylistic
characteristics. The schools are
usually named after the various kingdoms that flourished in different
regions of Thailand during different
periods. Thus, the school of Dvāravatī
is named after the kingdom of the
same name, which flourished in
southern Thailand between the sixth
and eleventh centuries. However, the
attribution of isolated sculptures whose
provenance is not known precisely
is always difficult. It must also be
pointed out that these various schools,
particularly those that existed simultaneously, frequently interacted with
each other, and hence one cannot
always strictly define their stylistic
characteristics. Moreover, during
certain periods of Khmer domination
in parts of Thailand the influences of
Cambodian artistic styles were so
strongly felt that often Thai and
Cambodian works are as difficult to
distinguish as many Nepali and
Tibetan bronzes. Although much
work has been done on the sculptures
of central and southern Thailand, the
art of northern and northeastern
Thailand has been only sparingly
explored. For example, there are
hundreds of temples in northeastern Thailand that seem to have
been rendered in a predominantly
Khmer style, and some of the sculptures that have appeared recently and
are labeled as Cambodian may in fact
be from northeastern Thailand.

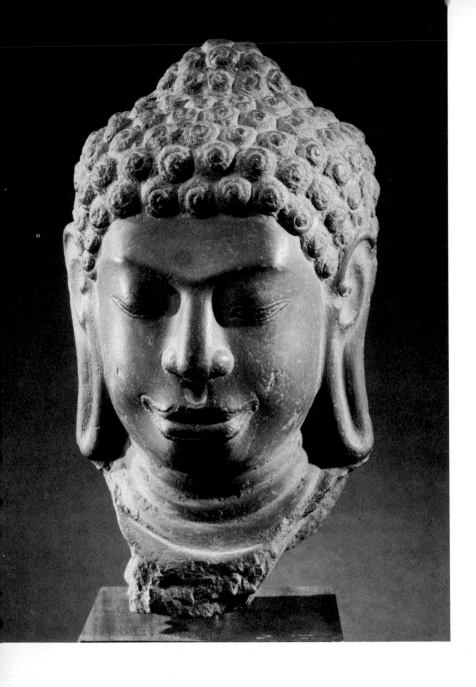

126. Buddha Śākyamuni
Dvāravatī style
7th–8th century
(a) Dark gray schist
h: 13 in. (33.0 cm.)
(b) Gray schist
h: 32⅛ in. (81.6 cm.)

These two sculptures, one only a head (a) and the other without its feet (b), portray the Buddha Śākyamuni in a classic form that was the hallmark of the Dvāravatī school. The finest sculptures of this school appear to have been created between the seventh and eighth centuries, when the prevailing form of Buddhism was that known as Hinayana. Its pantheon was largely confined to images of the historical Buddha, as it also was in Sri Lanka (see no. 91). The majority of Dvāravatī images discovered are of the type represented here, although recently smaller statues of bodhisattvas have also come to light, thereby indicating that the Mahayana form of Buddhism was not altogether unknown in Dvāravatī.

Although it is readily admitted that these Buddha images of Dvāravatī reflect the general influences of the Gupta tradition, it is difficult to point to any one school as the predominant stylistic source. The treatment of the body and the diaphanous garment undoubtedly betray an awareness of Sarnath sculptures, but those of Ajanta might have been equally influential. On the other hand, neither at Sarnath nor at Ajanta do we encounter Buddhas in such a strictly frontal stance with both arms raised and extended in so symmetrical a fashion. More easily perceptible differences are evident in the facial features, which reflect a racial type totally different from the classical Indian face.

The beautifully proportioned and polished head (a) is probably the earlier of the two sculptures. Bearing the slightest trace of a smile, the face has a noble and compassionate expression, while the half-shut eyes, focused on the tip of the nose, convey a sense of introspective calm. If this head conforms to the classical Dvāravatī Buddha images, that of the other (b), with a wider crown, higher cheekbones, and narrower eyes, appears to

be more individualistic. The modeling
of the more complete figure is not quite
as subtle as that of the head but is nonetheless rendered with considerable
finesse. It is difficult to determine
whether such differences have any
chronological significance or are simply
expressions of individual ateliers. They
do demonstrate, however, that even
within this rigid tradition each image
is a slightly different statement, just as
the same melody varies subtly when
played by different musicians. For a
head similar to that of (b) see d'Argencé
and Tse, pp. 84–85, no. 37.

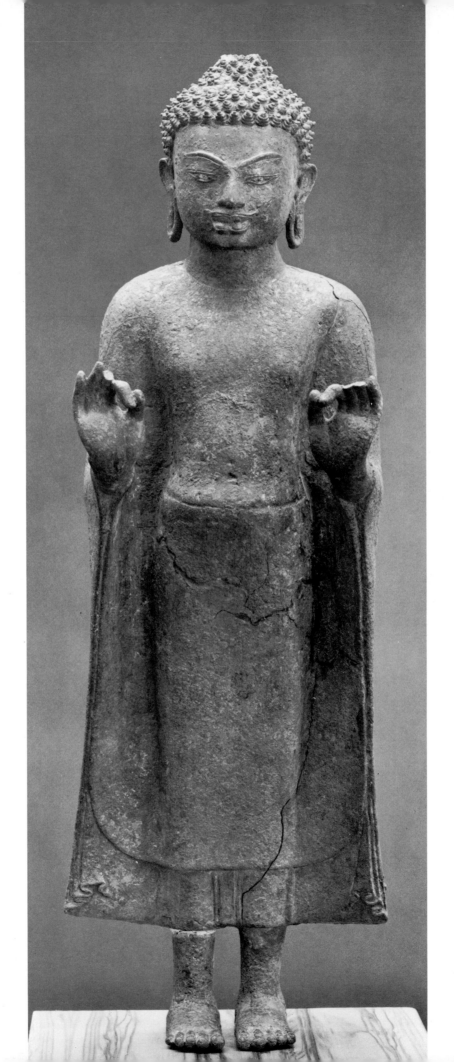

127. Buddha Śākyamuni

Buriram province, Prakon Chai
8th century
Bronze
h: 33 in. (83.8 cm.)

In 1964 a hoard of bronzes was accidentally discovered in an underground burial chamber within a neglected temple precinct at the village of Prakon Chai. The hoard contained a large number of Buddhist bronzes, most of which are now dispersed in European and American collections. Other well-known examples are in the Brundage, Rockefeller, and Kimbell Foundation collections (see below). Of the Buddha images in the group, this example is the largest and the most impressive. A comparison of this bronze with the Dvāravatī-style figure (no. 126b) reveals both their similarities and differences. The iconographic type, with both hands raised symmetrically and emphasizing a rigidly rectangular frame, is obviously derived from Dvāravatī. The form of this Buddha is more flatly modeled than in the Dvāravatī figure where the thighs are more prominently outlined. The sensitive delineation of the hands and treatment of the folds along the garment's lower edge are particularly reminiscent of Dvāravatī Buddhas. The face, however, with its broad shape, open eyes, slightly thinner lips, and moustache, is distinctly modeled after Pre-Angkor sculptures of Cambodia.

Published: Bunker, fig. 20.

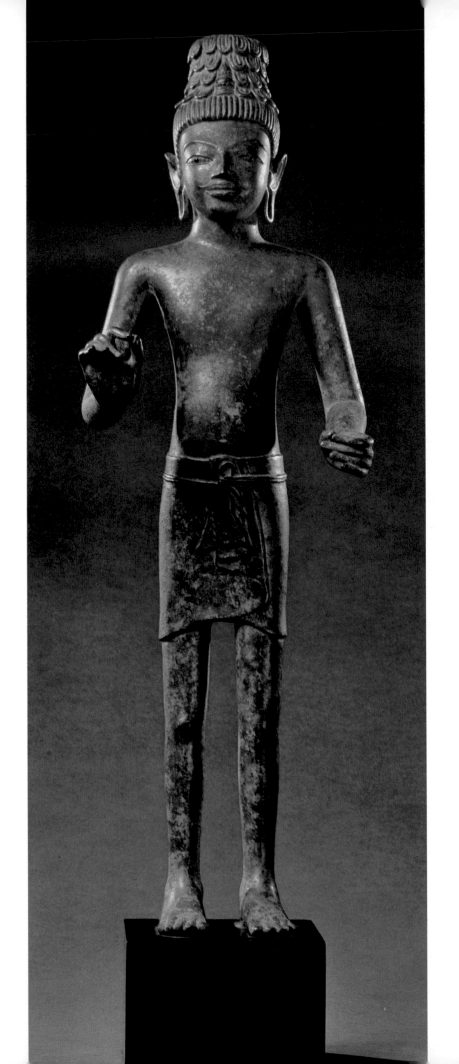

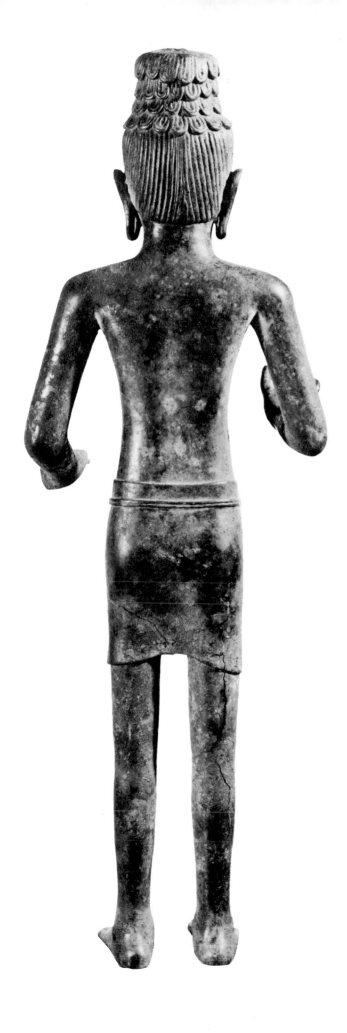

128. The Bodhisattva Maitreya

Buriram province, Prakon Chai
8th–9th century
Bronze with inlaid eyes
h: 21⅝ in. (52.5 cm.)

More typical of the Prakon Chai hoard
of bronzes than is the Buddha
Śākyamuni (no. 127), this elegant
bronze represents Maitreya, the future
Buddha. His right hand forms the
gesture of teaching and his left hand
may have once held a pot. The stupa
in his crown of matted hair identifies
him without question. The hair style is
quite typical of these and other
bronzes discovered in the Korat
plateau.

  Although several other Prakon
Chai bronzes are of more impressive
proportions, this Maitreya is one of the
finest of the group. A sculpture of dis-
arming simplicity, it is an astonishingly
graceful figure, despite its frontal posture. The hands are rendered with
particular sensitivity and the artist's
consummate sense of restrained elegance is evident not only in the subtle
modeling, but also in the delicate treatment of the chignon and the folds of
the short garment (*sampot*). Although
only a few bronzes of this style have
been found in Cambodia (see Dupont,
1955, pls. xxix, xxx), the Prakon Chai
bronzes relate generally to sculptures
of the Kompong Prei style. The extraordinary elongation of the figures with
tubular legs seems to be a particular
hallmark of Prakon Chai bronzes.

Published: Bunker, fig. 24;
Munsterberg, 1970, p. 232.

129. A Buddhist Saint (?)

Prakon Chai style (?)
9th century
Bronze
h: 5 in. (12.7 cm.)

An enigmatic bronze, both in style and iconography, this sculpture is here attributed to Thailand because of its stylistic closeness to the Prakon Chai bronzes (nos. 127, 128). A similar seated figure, though without a beard, is also in the Pan-Asian collection (Bunker, fig. 27), and other closely related figures of bearded ascetics can be seen among the ruins of Prasat Thna Dap in Cambodia (Boisselier, 1966, pl. XXXIII, p. 3). The metal with its silver sheen is of the same variety as that observed in most Prakon Chai bronzes.

If it is difficult to suggest an exact provenance for this intriguing bronze, it is equally problematic to identify the subject. The meditating posture, the beard, and the chignon would suggest that the figure is that of an ascetic, while the tiny effigy of a Buddha attached to the hair indicates a Buddhist affiliation. Although the cult of saints is popular in Mahayana Buddhism, particularly in Tibet, no other such bearded figure is known in the Buddhist art of Southeast Asia. Possibly the figure represents a local Buddhist luminary who was apotheosized and worshiped. That this was the custom in Cambodia is evident from inscriptions.

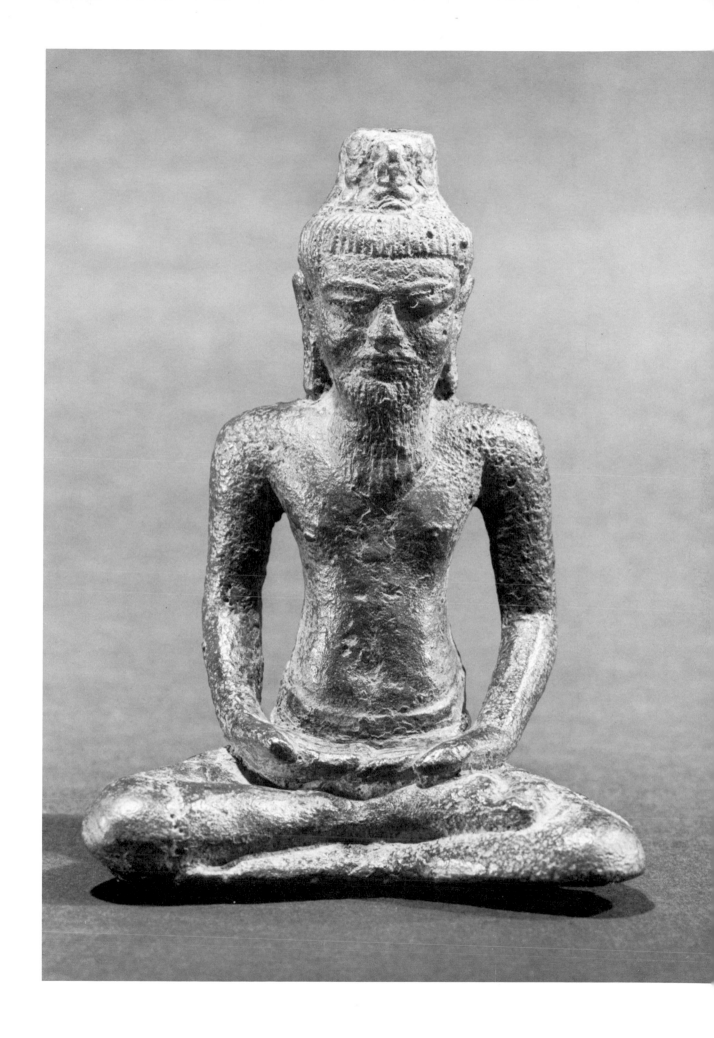

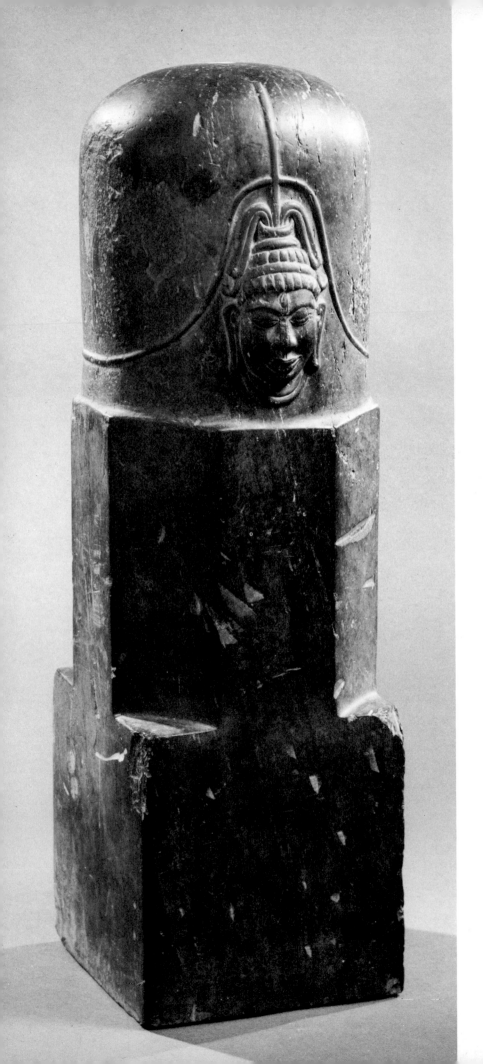

130. Ekamukhaliṅga (Phallus with One Face)
Buriram province (?)
8th–9th century
Gray sandstone
h: 27 in. (68.5 cm.)

This sculpture is a classic representation of the phallic emblem of the Hindu god Siva. At the same time, however, it is a symbol of all three members of the Hindu trinity: Brahma, Vishnu, and Siva. The sculpture is clearly divided into three sections, each symbolizing one of the three gods. The square base represents Brahma (*Brahmābhāga*), the octagonal middle part is the portion of Vishnu (*Vishṇubhāga*), and the rounded upper third represents Siva (*Rudrabhāga*). A head of Siva with his matted hair and the distinctive third eye is carved in high relief on this section of the sculpture.

While there is no doubt as to the identity of the subject, the style of the sculpture does present problems. The bold facial features are similar to those of a much damaged *mukhaliṅga* from Huei Thamo (Boisselier, 1966, pl. XLVII, fig. 2), but the style of the matted hair has almost identical parallels in several Dvāravatī sculptures in the Śrīrijaya style (Bowie, p. 31, no. 1, and *Khmer Sculpture*, p. 142 [M]). These sculptures, however, are Buddhist, and although at least one *mukhaliṅga* of the period is known from Thailand (Bowie, p. 48, no. 17), stylistically it is somewhat different from the present example. It has been brought to my attention that the sculpture was found near Prakon Chai but I have no way of verifying this information.

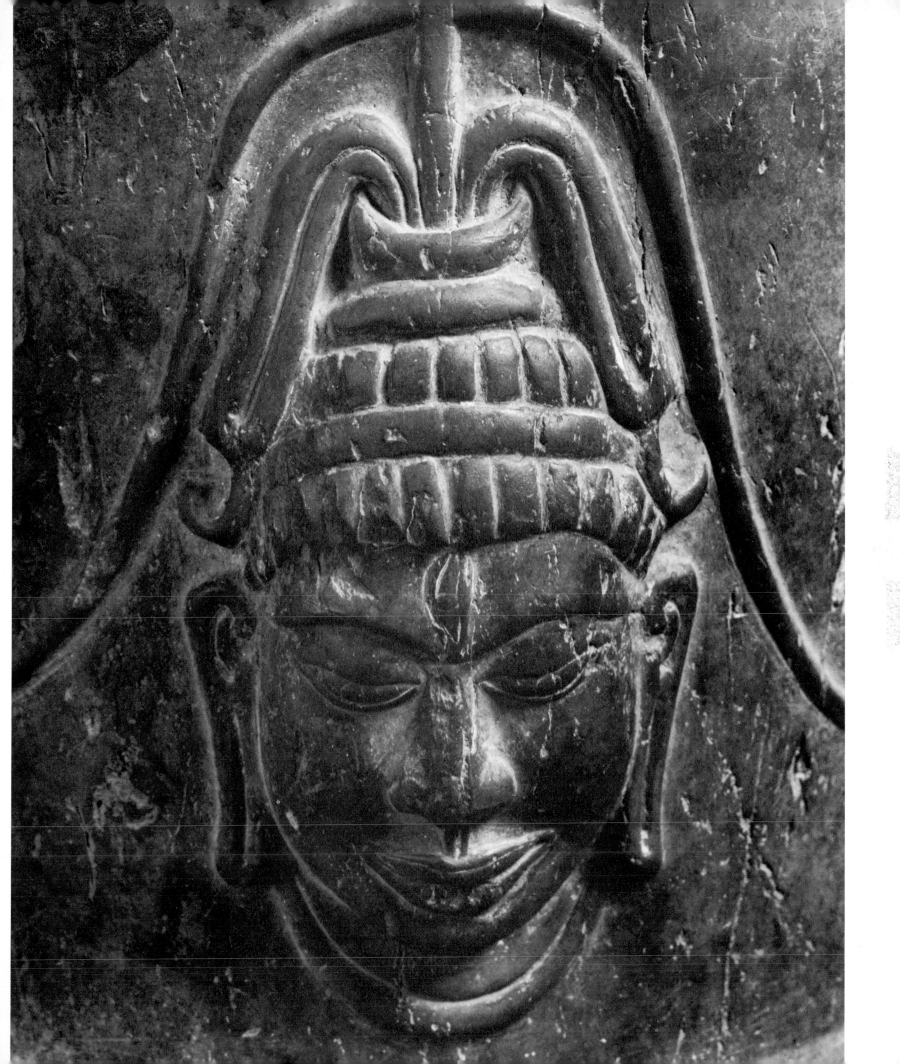

131. A Double-Sided Altarpiece

Lopburi style
12th–13th century
Bronze with green patina
h: 15⅛ in. (38.4 cm.)

One of the most elaborate Thai bronzes known, this double-sided altarpiece presents two typical Lopburi Buddha images. In the front, a crowned, meditating Śākyamuni is seated on a lotus atop a richly decorated pedestal. The gesture of his right hand (*bhūmisparśamudrā*), as well as the stylized Bodhi tree above, indicates that the occasion represented is the subjugation of Māra, the Buddhist god of desire who had tried to tempt the master immediately preceding his enlightenment. Three similar, though uncrowned, figures of the Buddha are portrayed against the Bodhi tree.

On the reverse is a standing figure of the Buddha Śākyamuni similarly framed by a flaming aureole with a cusped arch. Although not crowned, he is sumptuously adorned with ornaments. He stands on a lotus with his feet turned out and his right hand closed in a fist against his chest. Here also three seated Buddhas are represented in the tree above, but each against a stupa. Three other similar seated Buddhas are enshrined below the standing Śākyamuni. The exact significance of this repetition of identical Buddhas is not clear.

Stylistically, the principal seated Buddha in the front is closely related to a bronze in the Thompson collection in Bangkok (Bowie, pp. 80–81, no. 41), which is said to have been discovered in the Lopburi province. The crowned Buddha was popular both in Bihar and Kashmir in India (see no. 26) between the ninth and the eleventh centuries, and the Thai images were probably inspired by those from Bihar. The style of representation, however, seems more heavily influenced by Cambodian sculptures of the twelfth and thirteenth centuries.

Published: Dofflemyer, p. 49, figs. 3–4.

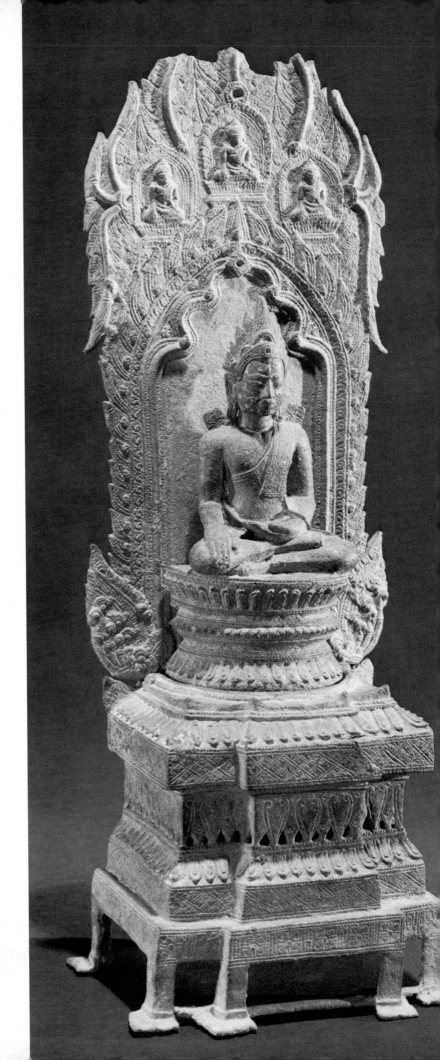

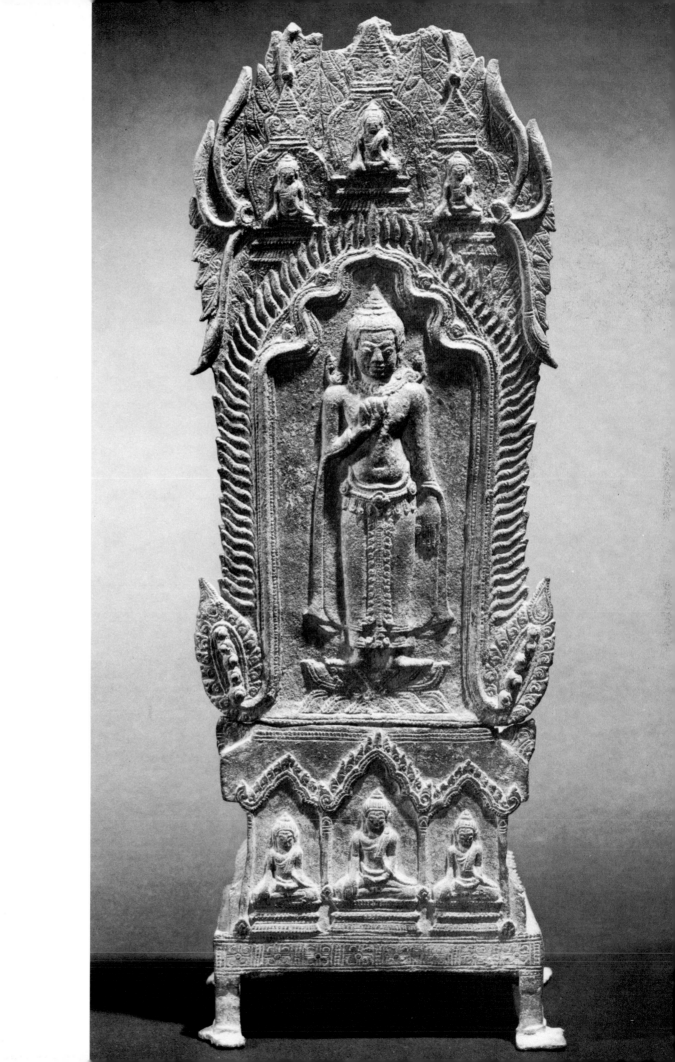

132. Buddha Sheltered by Muchalinda
Lopburi style
13th century
(a) Beige sandstone with paint
h: 37¾ in. (94.8 cm.)
(b) Bronze with green patina
h: 13⅛ in. (33.6 cm.)

This image type, which was particularly popular in Thailand during this period, symbolizes an incident from the life of the Buddha. It is said that once while Śākyamuni was meditating at Bodhgaya a storm broke out and it rained continuously for a week. The many-headed serpent king Muchalinda appeared at the site and provided shelter for the master by spreading his hoods. In sculptural representations, like those seen here, the Buddha is always depicted as seated on the coils of the serpent, which form an inverted pyramid, while the seven hoods of Muchalinda are spread out to shelter his head, forming a striking nimbus.

Although both sculptures were probably created in the same region, there are noteworthy stylistic differences. Typical of Thai Buddha images, the legs of both figures are so spread out that they form a remarkably expansive lap. The proportions of the figures are basically quite different, however, and the bronze has a more linear torso. Differences are also perceptible in the facial features. The nose, mouth, and chin appear more pinched in the bronze, and the eyes are clearly slanted. The face of the stone figure reflects a strong Khmer influence, which is quite common in the sculptures of the Lopburi school at this time. The treatment of the *ushṇīsha* is also quite different in the two sculptures and, interestingly, the fold of the *saṅghāti* across the left shoulder appears only in the bronze figure. This is almost an invariable feature of all Thai seated Buddhas of this period and its absence in the stone figure is unique. Much of the original pigment still adheres to the stone, while the bronze has acquired a rich green patina.

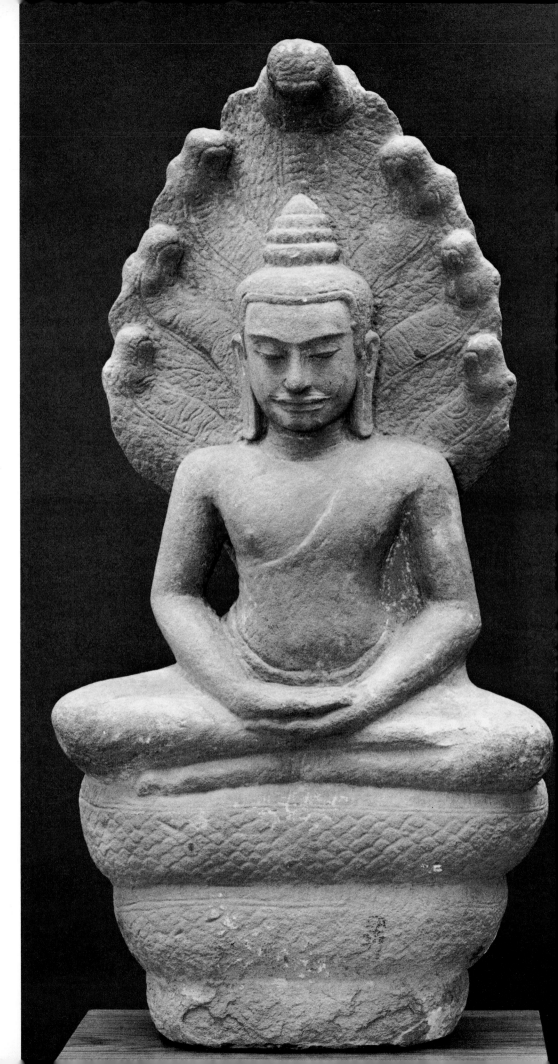

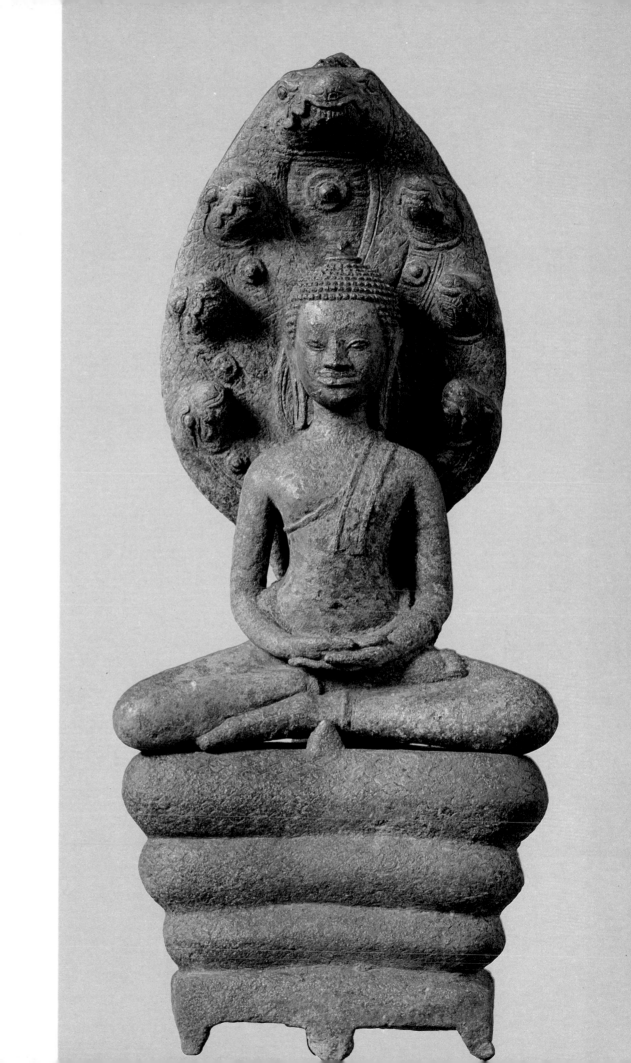

133. Buddha Śākyamuni
Lopburi style
13th–14th century
Beige sandstone
h: 18¾ in. (47.6 cm.)

Although bronze representations of
this Buddha type, probably created by
artists of the Lopburi school under
Khmer influence, are fairly common,
examples in stone are relatively rare.
An idea of how the full figure must
once have looked can be gleaned from
a bronze representation in the collection (no. 131, reverse). The upper
garment is so diaphanous that the
torso itself appears completely naked;
the lower garment is held together by
an ornamental belt. The ears are
provided with earrings and a jeweled
band separates the hair from the forehead. The left hand is extended along
the body, the right forms the
abhayamudrā against the chest, its palm
marked with the wheel, obviously
symbolizing the Buddhist faith. The
curls of the hair are like rows of pearls
and the *ushṇīsha* rises gently in a
stepped cone. Idealized as it is, the
face nevertheless has a very distinctive
expression that makes it almost
portraitlike.

The sculpture is stylistically
comparable to that of a meditating
Buddha in the National Museum in
Ayuthya (see Boisselier and
Beurdeley, p. 120, fig. 83), and a
slightly later bronze in the Wat
Benchamabopit in Bangkok (ibid.,
p. 133, fig. 94) may well have been
modeled after a sculpture such as this.

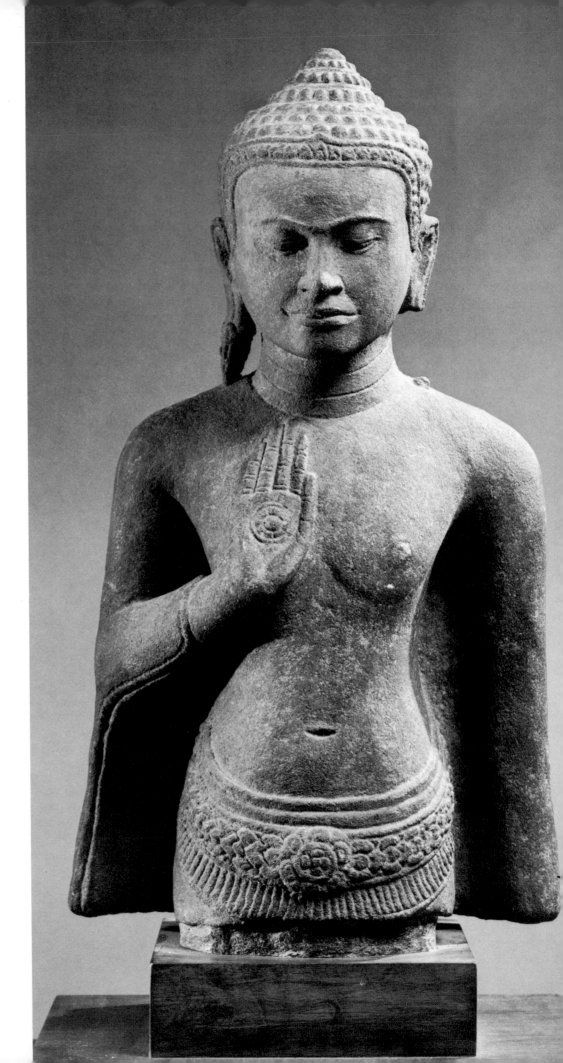

A Buddhist Altarpiece

Lopburi style
13th–14th century
Bronze with green patina
h: 21⅛ in. (53.6 cm.)

Less elaborate than the double-sided
example (no. 131), this too is a finely
crafted bronze of the Lopburi school,
again with the subject of Śākyamuni's
victory over Māra at Bodhgaya. The
tree above is so stylized as to be
scarcely recognizable and the thick
branches look almost like serpent
hoods, thereby suggesting the Muchalinda theme as well. The pedestal
below, decorated simply with lotus
petals and stamens, is supported by
squatting *yakshas*. The austere simplicity of the Buddha offers a marked
contrast to the busy flame-fringed
aureole. The hair is rendered as a grid
pattern of even squares, while the cone-
like *ushṇīsha* is conspicuously plain. The
face is distinguished by just a trace of a
smile, as we see in slightly earlier
figures from Bayon in Cambodia. At
the same time, however, the figure has
a noble bearing that is reminiscent of
the well-known Buddha of Grahi (see
Bowie, pp. 66–67, no. 30).

Published: Dofflemyer, p. 49, fig. 5.

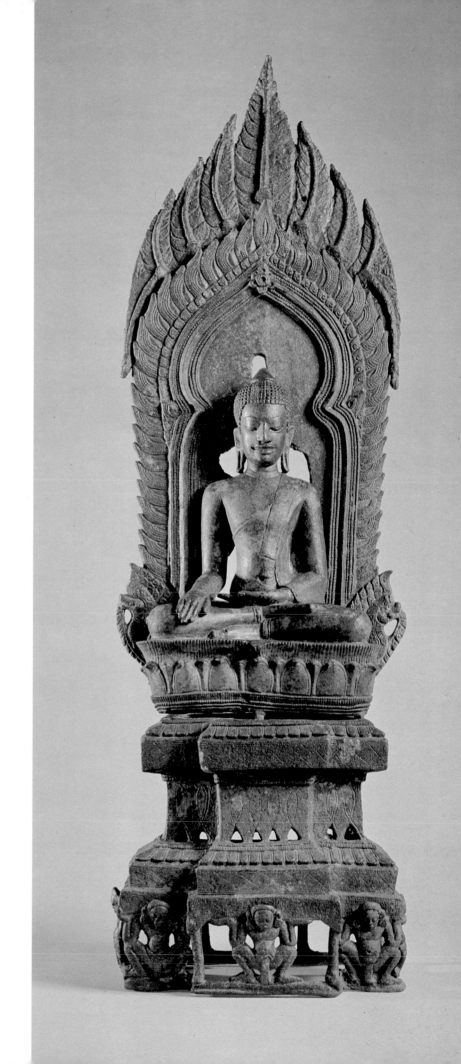

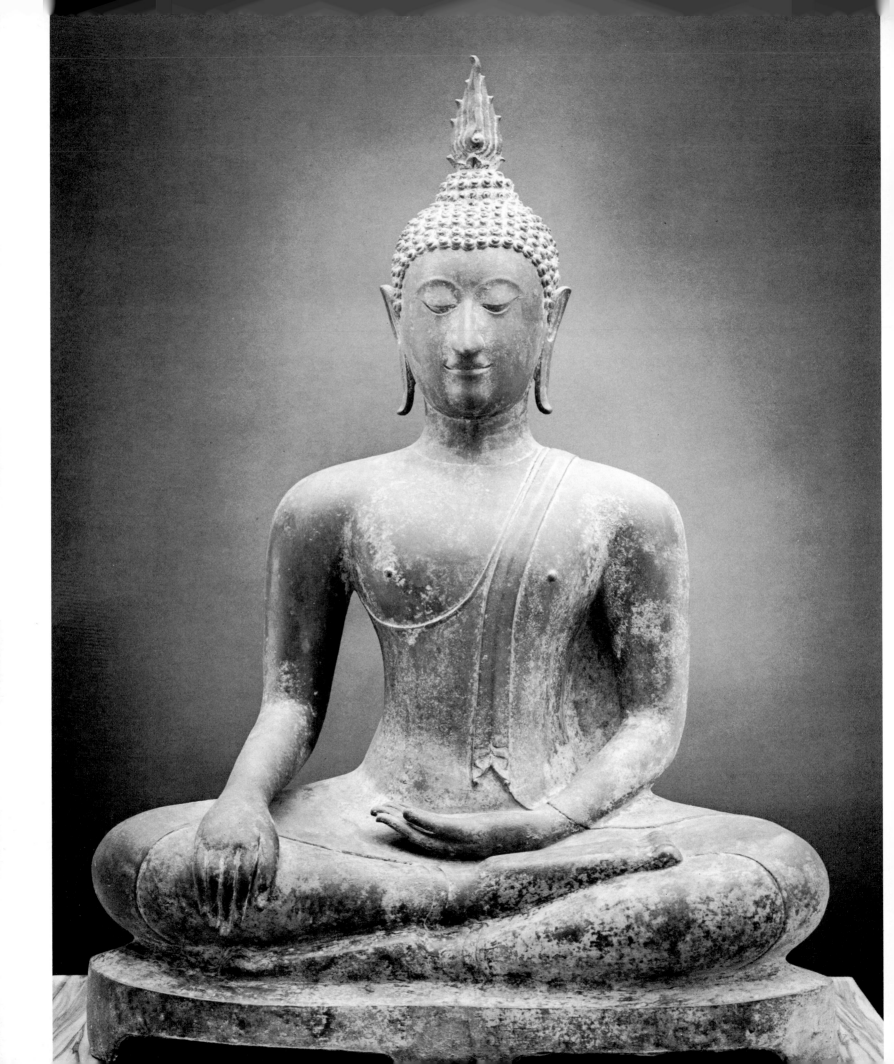

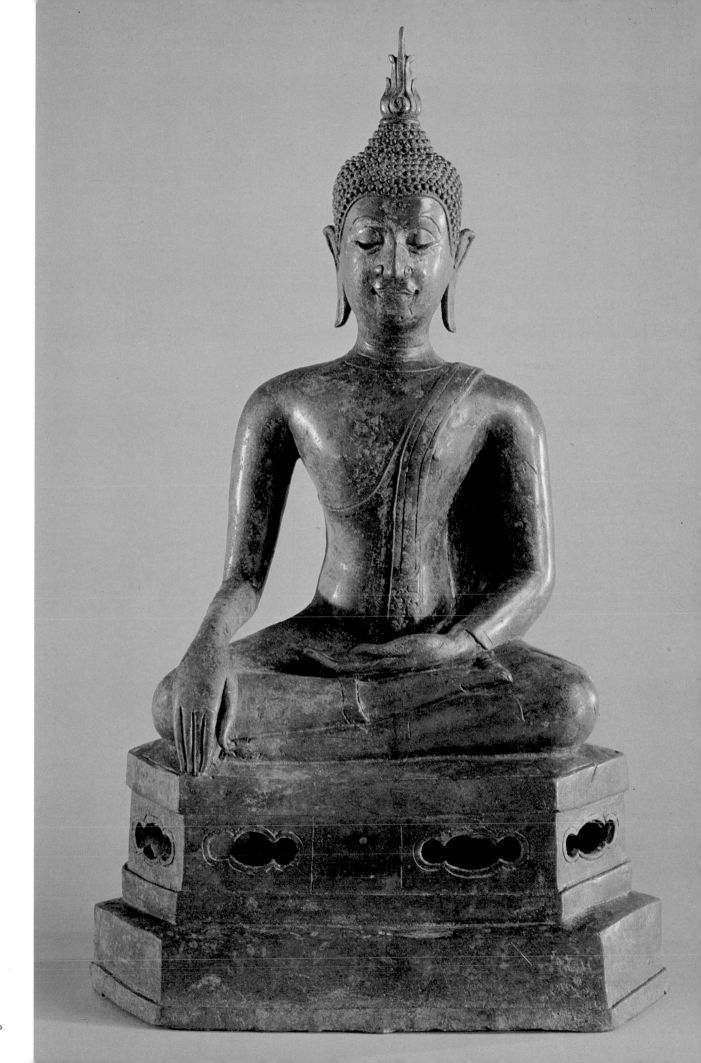

135a   135b

135. Buddha Subduing Māra

(a) Sukhothai style
14th–15th century
Bronze with green patina
h: 29 in. (73.7 cm.)
(b) Northern Thailand style
16th century
Bronze with green patina
h: 13 in. (33.0 cm.)

These two bronze images represent a
theme that was of abiding interest to
Thai devotees and sculptors. Both
portray Śākyamuni's conquest over
Māra, which is emblematic of the
master's enlightenment (*bodhi*),
whence he came to be known as the
Buddha or the Enlightened One.
Since the attainment of individual
enlightenment is the goal of every
Theravada Buddhist in Thailand, it
is not surprising that this particular
moment in the Buddha's life should
have remained one of the most popular
themes in Thai sculpture.

The Sukhothai style is generally
regarded as the most distinctive
expression of the Thai aesthetic. The
type of Buddha image represented by
(a) was rendered by the artists of
Sukhothai, probably in the early part
of the fourteenth century, and remained the norm for all succeeding
generations of Thai sculptors.
According to Boisselier, the Sukhothai
sculptors created "not a life-like
figure, but a hieratic image of other
worldly mien, and to this end they
emphasized everything that made the
exalted one a predestined man of
destiny" (Boisselier and Beurdeley,
p. 132).

The larger bronze (a) with its
ponderous volume, heavy limbs, oval
face with rather small eyes and a
looped chin, and the flame-sur-
mounted *ushṇīsha*, is a typical example
of a Sukhothai seated Buddha from
about the end of the fourteenth
century. Although basically of the
same type, the other bronze (b) has a
more distinguished face with a livelier
expression. Indeed, the slight smile
seems to be one of self-satisfaction
rather than beatitude. It is rendered in
the style of northern Thailand (cf.
Bowie, p. 115, no. 7, and p. 124,
no. 78).

Cambodia and Indochina

Almost all the basic research into the history of Cambodian sculpture has been undertaken by French scholars. Although their contributions are invaluable, the stylistic classification of Cambodian sculpture still presents many problems. Generally the history of Cambodian art is divided into two major periods known as Pre-Angkor (ca. 550–800) and Angkor (ca. 850–1350), with a brief, rather nebulous, transitional phase in between. There is no consistency in designating the styles: sometimes they are named after principal sites, such as Phnom Da or Koh Ker, at others they are named after specific temples, such as Banteay Srei or Angkor Wat. For the most part I have followed the French scholars and whenever possible have attempted to justify the attributions by citing similar published pieces. I am aware, however, that I have rushed in where most non-French scholars fear to tread.

136. The God Gaṇeśa
Phnom Da style (?)
7th century
Beige sandstone
h: 17¼ in. (43.8 cm.)

This well-executed representation is one of the rare images of Gaṇeśa, the Hindu god of auspiciousness, from the Pre-Angkor period. The figure has only two arms and he wears a short *sampot* with frontal pleats delineated with neat precision. Along the left thigh the garment forms just a slight wavy fold, anticipating an ornamental mannerism that was to be employed with stylish elegance in the sculptures of the Kulen style (825–875).

Typical of Pre-Angkor sculptures, the figure is modeled in the round, although it was probably viewed only from the front. Also characteristic is the relatively more precise articulation of musculature than is evident in the fifth–sixth-century sculptures of India that provided the models for Pre-Angkor sculpture. Two stylistically analogous sculptures are a torso from Prasat Pram Loveng and a Krishna from Vat Ramlok (Dupont, 1955, pl. xv, a and b).

137. Head of Vishnu
Phnom Da style
7th century
Beige sandstone
h: 8 in. (20.3 cm.)

Both Vishnuism and Sivaism were equally popular religious systems during the Pre-Angkor period in ancient Cambodia, and some of the finest sculptures of the age represent either Vishnu in his many manifestations or the composite deity Hari-Hara, a combined form of Vishnu and Siva. This superb head, distinguished by the simple cylindrical crown, must once have belonged to a magnificent image of Vishnu. It is rendered in what is characterized as the style of Phnom Da, the earliest and finest style of Pre-Angkor sculptures.

Typical of the style, the facial features are rendered with refined elegance and the face, with its wide, staring eyes, has a stern, though noble, expression. The modeling is astonishingly subtle, and the moustache adds a human touch, as if the head were an idealized portrait. What is most curious about such Pre-Angkor sculptures is their uncanny likeness to ancient Egyptian human figures, although the Pre-Angkor civilization was removed by more than two millennia from that of Egypt. The exact provenance of this head is not known, but it is possibly from the Vat Ba Sen region, where an almost identical head was discovered many years ago (see Dupont, 1955, pl. xxxvi, b).

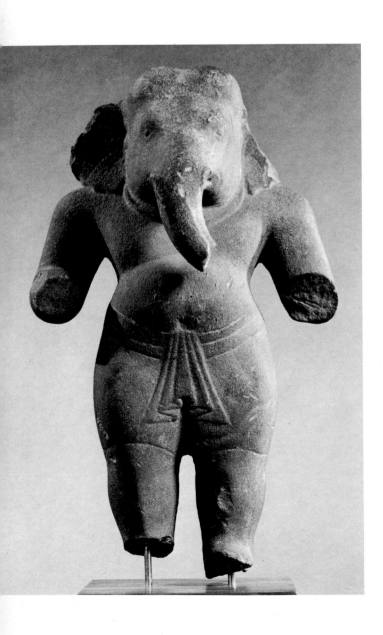

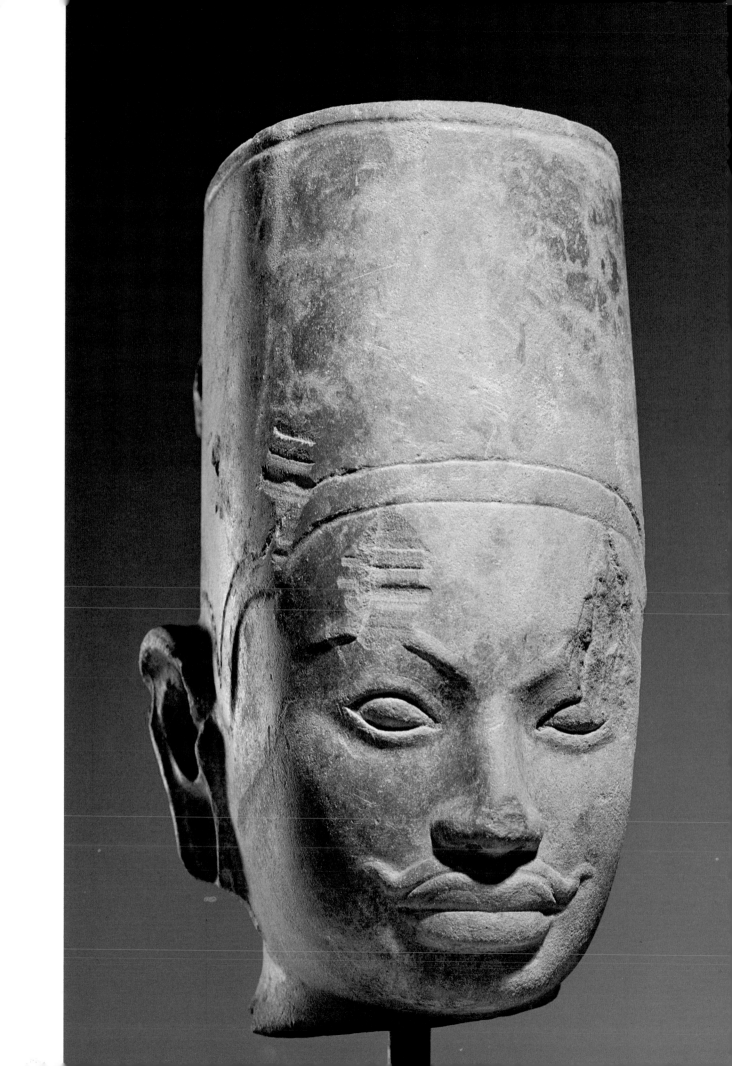

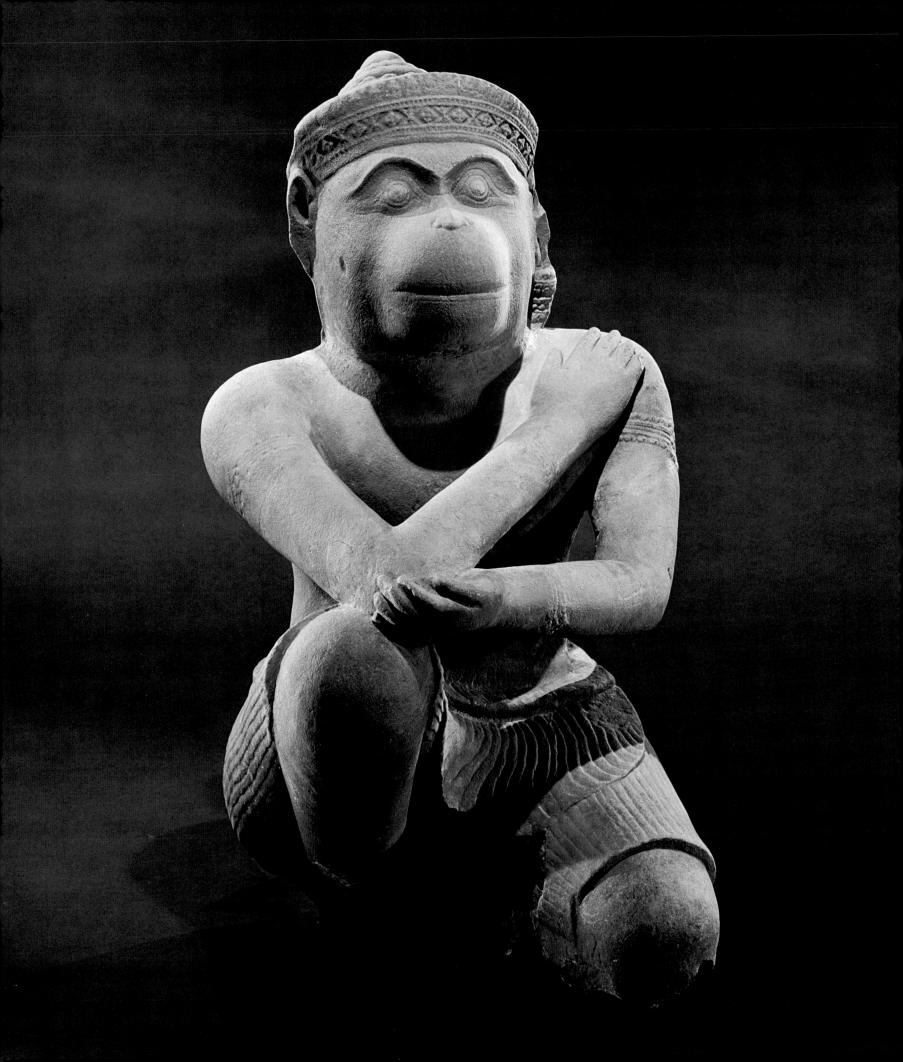

138. Hanumān

Koh Ker style
Ca. 924–937
Light brown stone
h: 43¼ in. (109.9 cm.)

For a discussion of the concept of Hanumān and two Indian representations of this monkey god, a devotee of Rāma, see nos. 70 and 71.

This is probably the most impressive sculptural depiction of Hanumān from Southeast Asia in a Western collection. As in the Chola bronze (no. 71) he is conceived essentially as a human being except for his head and tail. His legs, now broken, must have been disposed in a semi-kneeling posture. His arms are uniquely positioned, possibly reflecting his humility. This gesture seems to be a variation on one made by the dwarf Vajrapurusha in a Nepali bronze (no. 93). The best-known Hanumān sculptures of Cambodia are those on the terrace of the Banteay Srei temple where, along with heraldic lions, they serve as guardians. This Hanumān, however, is different iconographically and may have been placed before an image of Vishnu represented as Rāma.

Stylistically, the Hanumān is remarkably similar to a pair of wrestling monkeys representing Bali and Sugrīva, two well-known characters in the Hindu epic *Rāmāyaṇa* (see Boisselier, 1966, pl. LVI, fig. 1). Worked completely in the round, the combative monkeys are as monumental as the present Hanumān and display the same heavy proportions and ponderous volume. Analogous also are the design of the crowns, the addition of armbands, and the fall of the *sampot's* folds in front. Moreover, the tails of the three monkeys are delineated in almost an identical fashion, rising like serpents from the top of their *sampots* and ending at their crowns. The fighting monkeys sculpture is from Prasat Chen, near Koh Ker, and an inscription on the gateway of the temple tells us that the shrine was dedicated to Śrīpati, a name for Vishnu (see Briggs, pp. 120 and 122). Possibly this Hanumān was once associated with Prasat Chen.

139. The God Vishnu

Koh Ker style
925–1000
Beige sandstone
h: 37 in. (94.0 cm.)

Rarely is a freestanding Cambodian sculpture as well preserved as this example. The feet and hands of such sculptures are often broken (see no. 140), as indeed those of this sculpture were, but fortunately the limbs were found in situ and could be reattached. The representation here is of Vishnu, the Hindu god of preservation, who stands on a simple base in the *samapada* posture. Unlike Indian images of the deity, he has a beard and moustache and is given no ornaments except a crown. His only apparel is the *sampot* held together by an ornamental belt or sash. His upper hands hold the wheel and the conch shell and his lower hands grasp a boss, symbolizing the lotus seed, and the handle of a mace, which rests on the base.

In terms of both iconography and style, there are noteworthy differences between this Koh Ker Vishnu and earlier Pre-Angkor sculptures, particularly in the treatment of the crown, the presence of the beard and moustache, and the design of the *sampot*. The simple, tall, cylindrical crown of the earlier style (see no. 137) has been replaced here with one that remained standard throughout the Angkor period. The handling of the *sampot* with its prominent flap and double fishtail pleats is characteristic of the Koh Ker style. The easy naturalism of the Pre-Angkor sculptures has given way to a more simplified modeling that conveys a sense of hieratic grandeur rather than sensuous grace. Unlike Pre-Angkor figures, this one is free of auxiliary support, but the legs are still columnar and the feet awkwardly placed.

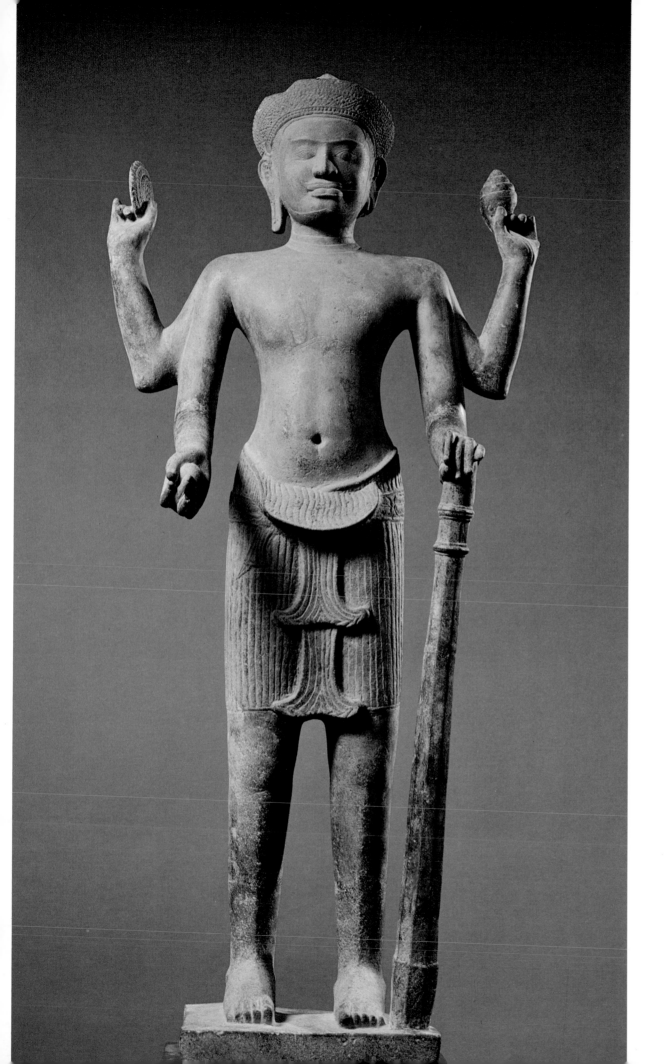

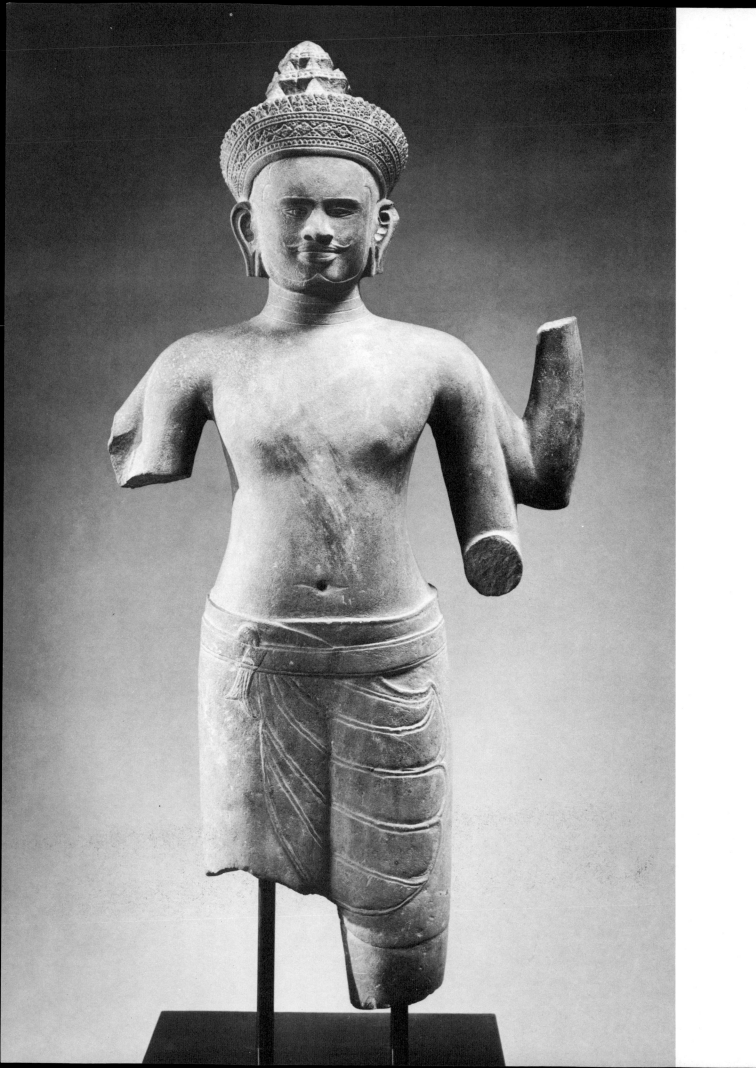

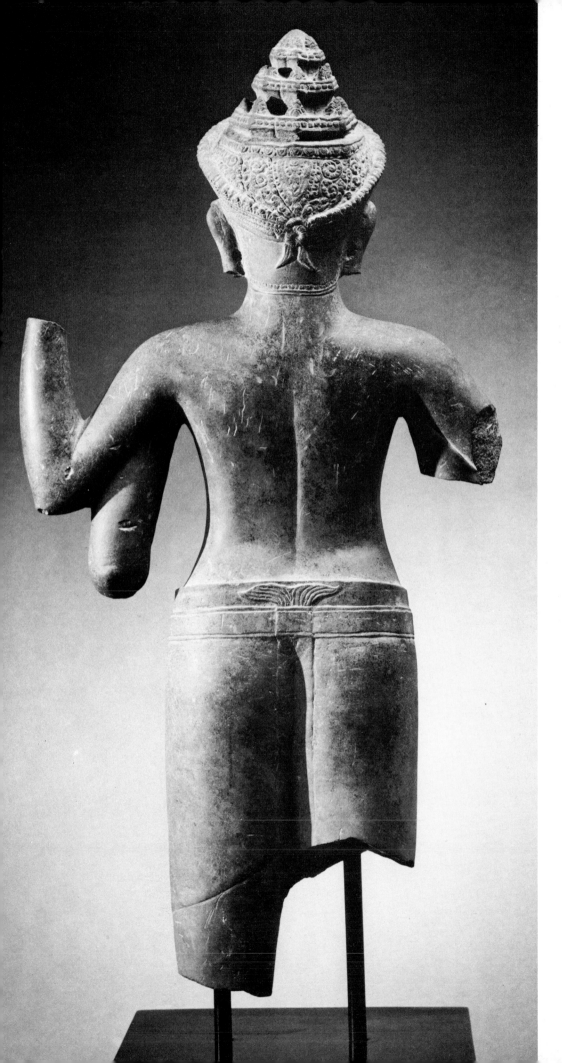

140. The God Vishnu
Pre Rup style
Mid-10th century
Beige sandstone
h: 31 in. (78.7 cm.)

The loss of the arms and legs makes this a more typical example of surviving Cambodian freestanding sculptures than the previous one. The sculpture is fully modeled in the round, continuing the Pre-Angkor style, and the superb delineation of the crown can best be appreciated from the rear. Had the hands remained, they would probably have held the four emblems exactly as they do in the more complete image in the Koh Ker style (no. 139). Their basic similarities notwithstanding, the two sculptures are distinguished by a number of subtle differences.

Compared to the Koh Ker–style figure, the torso of this Vishnu seems somewhat squatter, particularly because of the wider hips. The facial features are also recognizably different, the former still echoing the Pre-Angkor physiognomic type, while the broader face of the Pre Rup Vishnu is more like post-tenth-century figures. Although both have similar crowns, the Pre Rup sculptor displayed a more delicate feeling for details. Finally, the folds of the *sampot* in the Pre Rup sculptures are more ornamental and stylish. Indeed, the design of the *sampot* remained a primary concern of the Khmer artists and forms a basis for French archeologists to distinguish the various styles and their chronology.

233

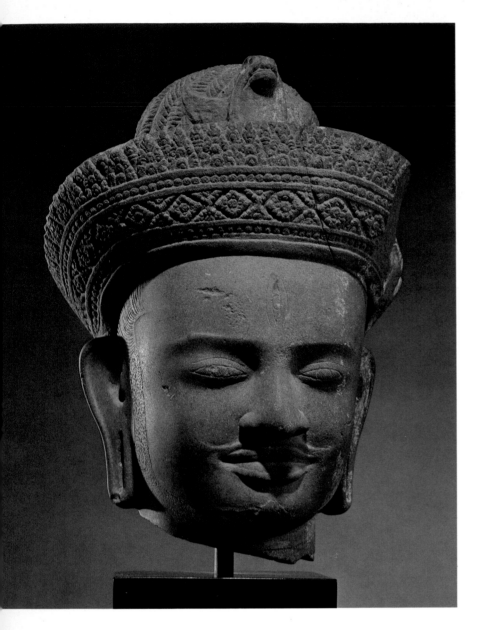

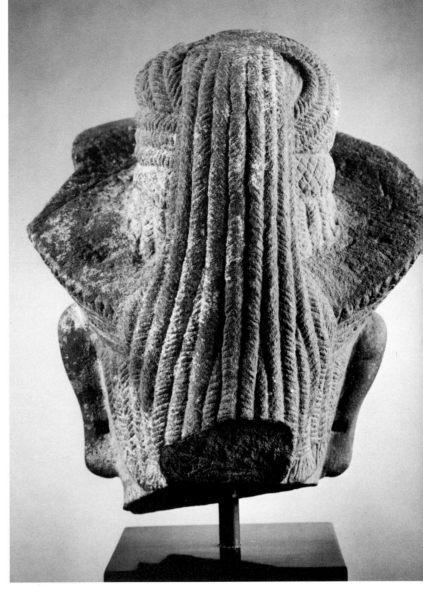

141. Head of the God Siva

Pre Rup style (?)
Ca. 950
Beige sandstone
h: 12¼ in. (31.1 cm.)

Although similar to the head of Vishnu (no. 139), both in terms of its features, including the beard and moustache, and its crown, this head once belonged to a statue of Siva. The third eye etched on the forehead and the elaborate and unusually matted hair embellished with a snake are distinctive features of Siva. The manner in which the hair is delineated at the back is particularly elegant and seems to be unique to this example. The face bears a slight trace of a smile, which makes the expression especially gentle and benign.

The exact attribution of this sculpture to a recognizable style is difficult. The face, as we have seen, is similar to that of the Koh Ker Vishnu (no. 139), as well as to that of a Siva in an Umā-Maheśvara group found at Banteay Srei (Giteau, 1976, p. 190, fig. 117). When first published (see below), it was assigned to the style of Pre Rup, presumably because of the stylish rendering of the hair, but this is by no means certain. The study of Cambodian sculpture is beset with such problems, but no matter what its style or provenance, the head remains a charming and refined example of mid-tenth-century Cambodian sculpture.

Published: Lee, 1969, no. 17.

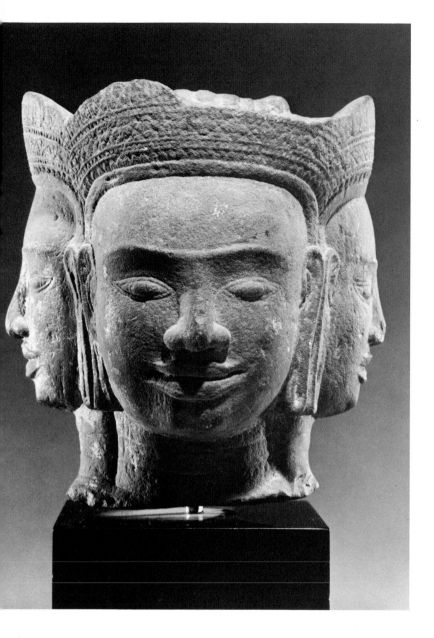
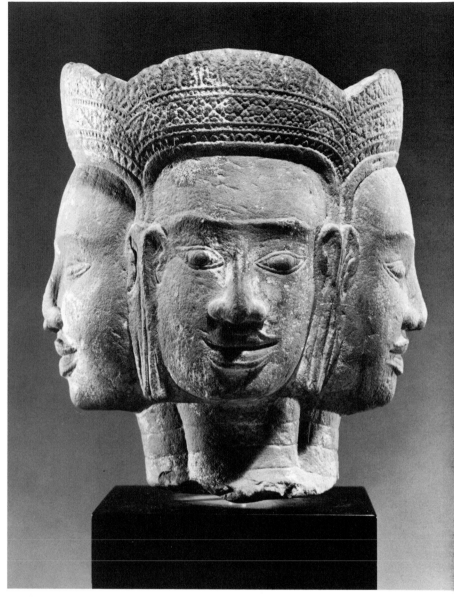

142. The God Brahma
Bakheng or Pre Rup style
10th century
Beige sandstone
h: 7⅝ in. (19.3 cm.)

These heads, unlike those of the Indian Brahma (no. 36), have no chignon, but in both sculptures a low-relief lotus joins the four heads at the top. A crown appears more often in Cambodian representations of this ascetic god than it does in Indian versions. Interestingly, the two side heads are rather compressed, which makes them unnaturally elongated. Otherwise, the faces are strikingly handsome with their precise features, long almond-shaped eyes, and serene expressions.

It is difficult to suggest an exact stylistic affiliation for this fragment, and though it seems closely related to sculptures of both the Bakheng and the Pre Rup styles (see Lee, 1969, nos. 10 and 17), the proportions and the expression are somewhat atypical of both styles.

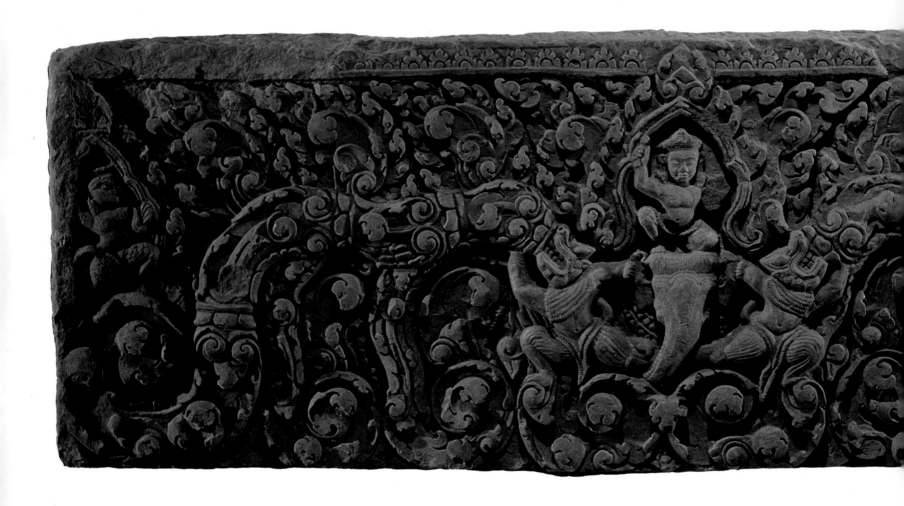

143. A Lintel

Banteay Srei style
950–1000
Pink sandstone
h: 20¼ in. (51.4 cm.)
w: 58¾ in. (149.2 cm.)

The color of the stone, as well as the depth and manner of the carving, relates this lintel to the style of Banteay Srei. Such luxuriantly decorated lintels adorn the entrances of most Angkor-period temples and, although the motifs basically remain unchanged, each lintel is quite distinctive. In monuments of the Pre-Angkor period the ornamental flair is less apparent and the predominant motifs are a combination of the *makara* and the *kāla* (*kīrttimukha*) head, both symbolizing abundance and auspiciousness. During the Angkor period the central *kāla* was frequently replaced by other figures, such as Indra riding his elephant, which is seen here. Indra is the king of the gods (*devarāja*) and since the Devarāja cult was popular in the

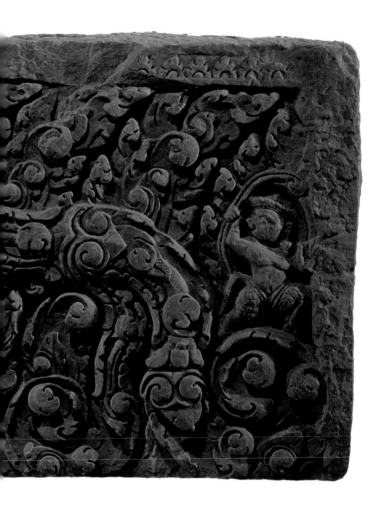

Khmer empire, his frequent presence on such lintels is not surprising. Also characteristic of the Angkor period is the transformation of the *makaras* into serpents, which are so stylized here as to be scarcely recognizable. Indra is flanked by two *rākshasas*, or demons, who lunge in opposite directions. At each end is a spirited *garuḍa*, each looking toward the center.

Almost every inch of the lintel surface is filled with leaping, curling forms infused with remarkable vitality and buoyancy. Charged with restless, nervous energy, the motifs are also rendered with a touch of whimsy that makes the design delightfully appealing.

144. A Guardian Lion

Region of the Royal Palace in
Angkor Thom
Ca. 1000
Beige sandstone
h: 37½ in. (95.2 cm.)

Squatting lions such as this, invariably rendered as freestanding
sculptures, are a familiar sight in most
Khmer temples, generally placed as
guardians on terraces or stairways.
Although the concept originated in
India, the lions are far more
conspicuous in Cambodian temples.
Since lions are not native to the region
and hence unfamiliar to the artists,
they are always treated conceptually,
and often the grinning or growling
faces are somewhat caricatured.

    The present example may have
come from the Phimeanakas temple
terrace, although it is difficult to be
certain. The fanciful head is more
demonic than naturalistic and the
mane on the broad chest is rendered
almost like a coat of mail. The
posture is essentially heraldic and the
sculptor seems to have been concerned primarily with expressing
physical strength through sheer
volume.

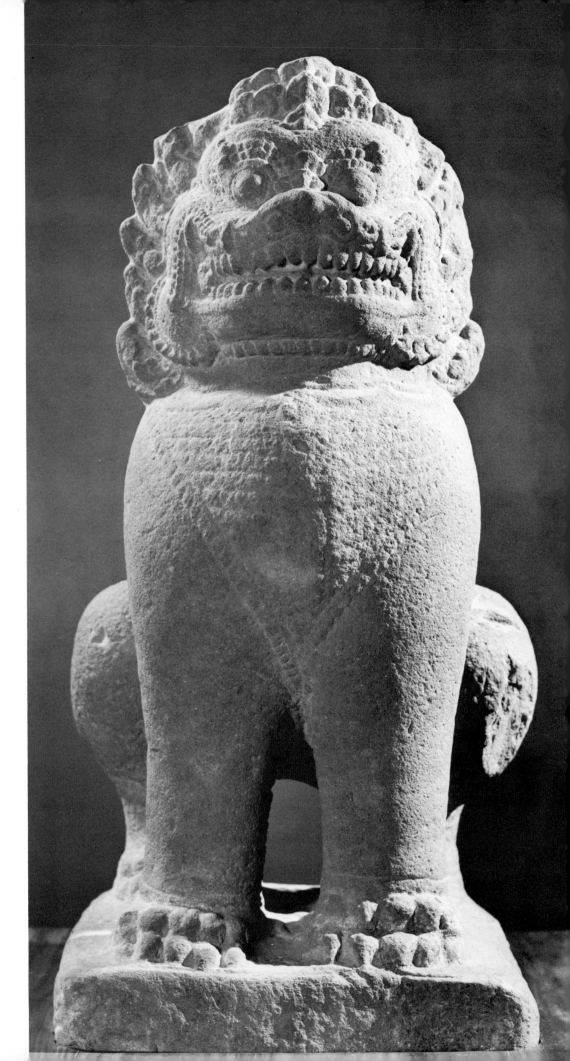

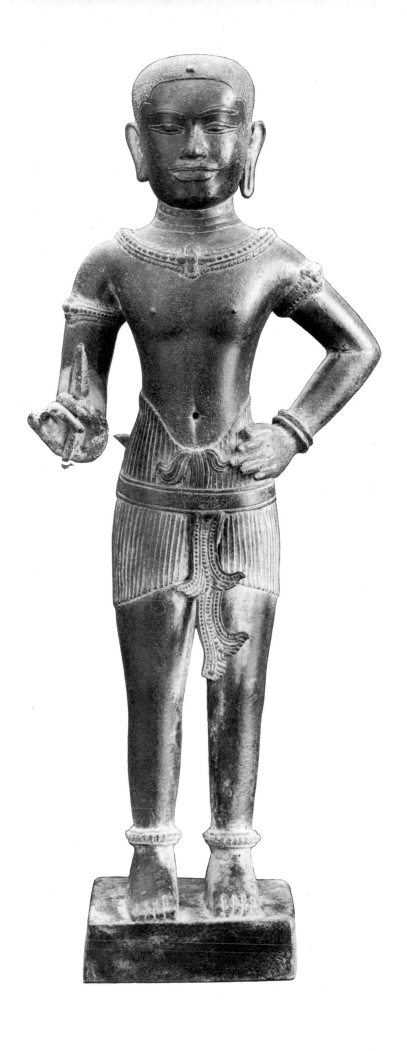

145. A Male Deity

Baphuon style
1050–1100
Bronze
h: 19¾ in. (50.2 cm.)

The figure stands on a plain base in
samapada posture with his left arm
akimbo and his right hand holding
what appears to be a lotus bud.
Wearing a *sampot* with stylishly
elegant pleats extending gracefully
down to his left knee, he is sparsely
ornamented. No crown adorns his
head and his hair is so lightly
indicated that his head seems fitted
with a shallow cap. His eyes, eyebrows, and lips are emphasized by
double lines and his moustache
appears to be incised. We cannot be
certain of the exact identification of the
figure, but he may represent the
bodhisattva Avalokiteśvara, who
generally holds a lotus.

A comparison with the Umā
(no. 146) clearly indicates that this
bronze is rendered in the soft and
elegant Baphuon style. The shape and
features of the two faces are remarkably similar, as is the modeling with
its emphasis on graceful proportions
and simplified form. Among other
well-known sculptures, an obvious
stylistic parallel seems to be the
monumental torso discovered at Basak
(Giteau, 1965, pl. XVI). Indeed, the
treatment of the garment with its V-
shaped curve at the waistline and the
placement of the sash on the lower hips
is almost identical in the two bronzes.
A face similar to that of this bronze
can be seen in the reclining Vishnu
from Mebon (ibid., pl. XV) which is
also dated to the second half of the
eleventh century.

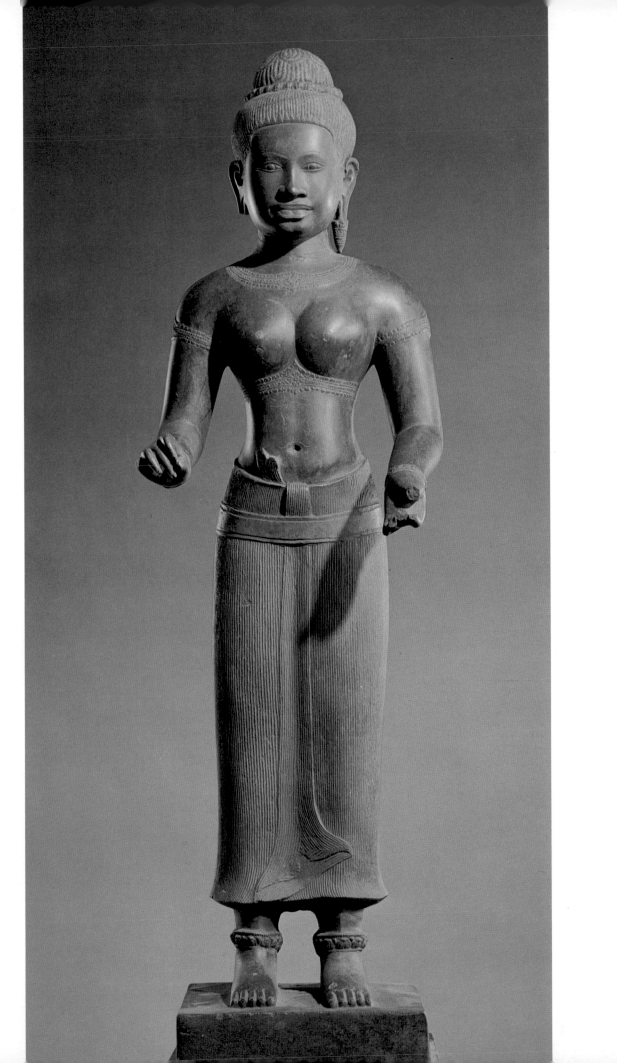

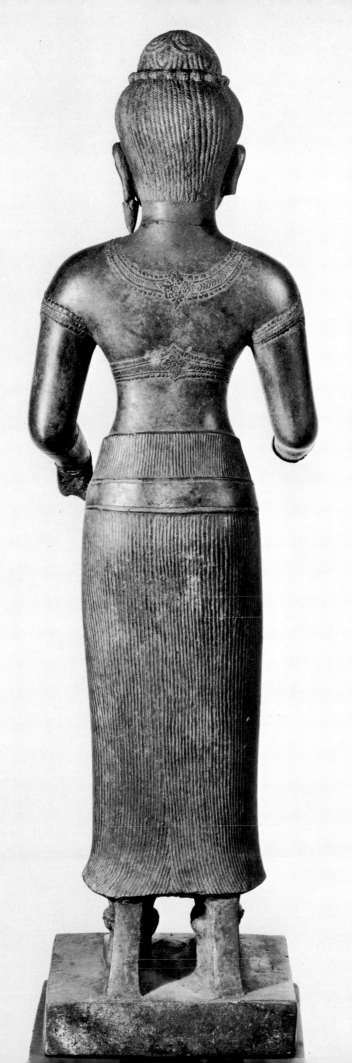

146. A Goddess

Baphuon style (?)
1050–1100
Brown sandstone
h: 36½ in. (92.7 cm.)

The goddess stands in *samapada*
posture on a narrow base. The fingers
of her left hand are broken and her
right hand may once have held a lotus,
but otherwise the sculpture is remarkably well preserved. Her long skirt
(*sarong*), held together by a simple
sash, is indicated by parallel vertical
lines and the central fold forms an
inverted lily pattern at the bottom.
Her jewelry includes conical ear
ornaments, a necklace, armlets,
bracelets, and anklets, and her hair is
gathered in a topknot held in place by
a jeweled band. An additional
ornamental band below her breasts
emphasizes their contour. The sculpture is equally well finished at the back,
where the legs are given additional
support. Usually such images are
identified as Umā, the consort of Siva.

Stylistically the sculpture is closely
related to three others, two of which
are considered to be of the Baphuon
style and the third of the Angkor
Wat style. All three figures are dated
to the second half of the eleventh
century. The two Baphuon-style
figures are in the Brundage collection
in San Francisco (see d'Argencé and
Tse, pp. 96–97, no. 43) and the
Angkor Wat–style figure is in the
National Museum of Phnom Penh (see
Giteau, 1976, p. 168, fig. 104). The
last sculpture, also representing a
goddess, is from the temple known as
Prasat Trapeang Totung Thngay.
The modeling and physiognomy of the
Pan-Asian sculpture are closer to those
of the Phnom Penh image, but the
ornamentation is more similar to that
seen in the Brundage figures. In fact,
the torso of the Phnom Penh piece is
completely bare, whereas the
Brundage figures are adorned with
necklaces, armlets, and even a chest
band, as is this Pan-Asian goddess.

No matter what its style, this
graceful and radiant figure is one of the
finest Cambodian sculptures in the
collection. The lightly polished brown
stone looks like rich velvet and gives
the sculpture an unusual warmth and
tactile quality.

147. The Goddess Prajñāpāramitā

(a) Angkor Wat style
1100–1150
Bronze
h: 12¾ in. (32.4 cm.)
(b) Bayon style
Ca. 1200
Bronze with green and blue patina
h: 21½ in. (54.6 cm.)

A number of such images of multi-headed and multi-armed goddesses are known, and they are generally identified as Prajñāpāramitā, presumably based on an inscribed bronze (see Coedes, 1923, pl. XXXV and p. 49). Prajñāpāramitā is the personification of the text and philosophy bearing that name, a treatise of fundamental importance to Mahayana Buddhism. In the Indian Buddhist pantheon she is regarded as the goddess of wisdom and the female counterpart of the bodhisattva Mañjuśrī (see no. 108), but in Cambodia she was considered to be the mother of all the Buddhas. Although the goddess was popular in medieval India, her multi-limbed form, particularly in the dancing posture (a), seems to be peculiar to Cambodia. In fact, no Indian text describes such a form and the image type may have been a Khmer creation. On the other hand, there was a Buddhist goddess called Chundā, also associated with wisdom, who was popular in East India and Java. Similar in concept and iconography, her images may have served as models for these Cambodian statues.

The two bronzes represented here are significantly different in iconography. In the earlier example (a) the goddess is seen dancing gracefully, with her principal hands displaying the *dharmachakrapravartanamudrā*, a gesture

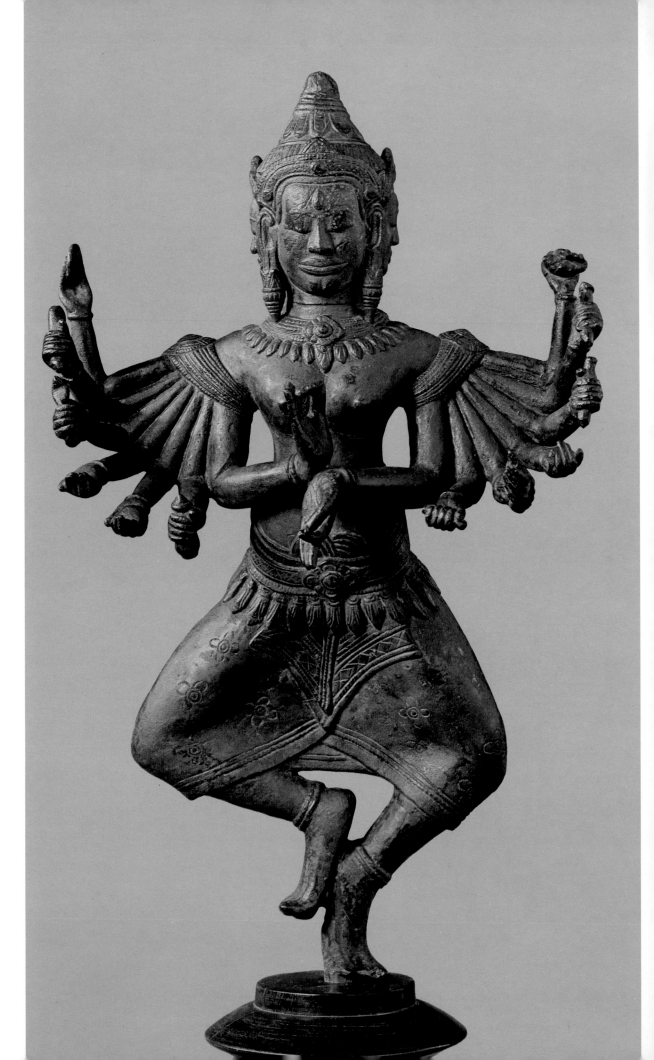

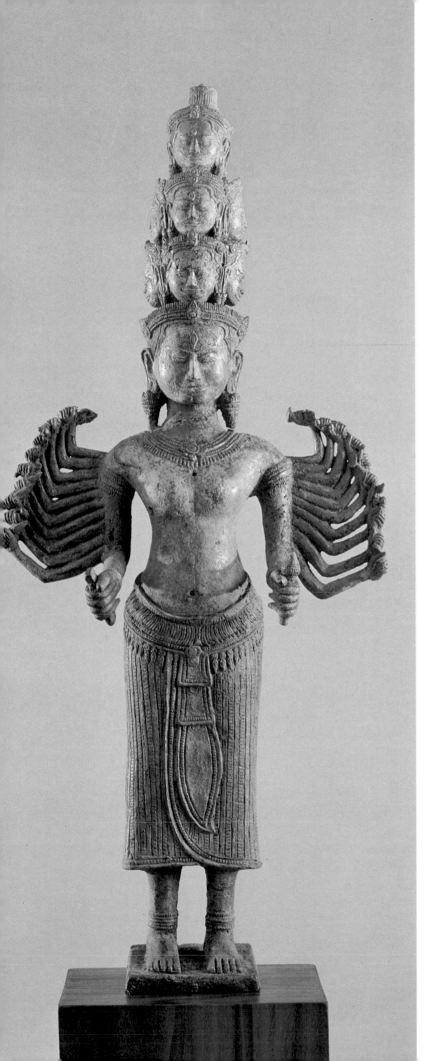

associated with both Prajñāpāramitā
and Chundā. Her twelve additional
hands hold various emblems such as a
wheel, a mace (?), a snake, a pot, a
manuscript, a thunderbolt (?), a bow
(?), an elephant goad (?), and a conch.
Three other objects, flat and circular,
cannot be identified. The larger bronze
(b) depicts the goddess in a more static
posture and she is given eleven heads
compared to the dancing goddess's
three. It may be pointed out that in
one of his forms the bodhisattva
Avalokiteśvara also has eleven heads.
In Cambodia there was a close
relationship between the one-headed
Avalokiteśvara and Prajñāpāramitā,
and the two are often seen flanking the
Buddha. The number of arms here (b)
has increased to twenty-two, the two
normal hands holding a lotus and a
manuscript. In both images the heads
are provided with third eyes, as is more
often true of Indian Chundā images
than of those of Prajñāpāramitā.

Apart from their iconographic
differences, the two sculptures differ
also in terms of stylistic minutiae. The
arms of the dancing goddess (a) are
integrated in a more organic manner
than in the other example (b) where
they look like bony wings tacked on to
the normal arms. The proportions and
facial features of the two bronzes are
also quite dissimilar, as are the treat-
ments of the garments and ornaments.
Finally, while one (a) is a lively and
rhythmic figure that delights us with
its unselfconscious and joyful movement, the other (b) is an impressive
bronze that exudes a sense of impassive
majesty and austere serenity.

Published: (a) Munsterberg, 1972,
p. 53; (b) Munsterberg, 1970, p. 233.

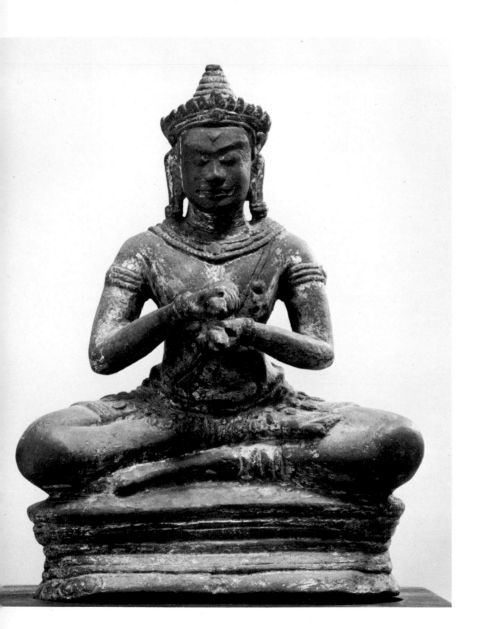

148. A Buddhist God
Angkor Wat style
1100–1150
Gilt bronze
h: 7 in. (17.7 cm.)

The exact identification of this handsome figure is difficult to determine. He holds a thunderbolt and a bell, which are the common attributes of two important Vajrayana Buddhist deities, Vajradhara and Vajrasattva. Normally Vajrasattva holds the thunderbolt with his right and the bell with his left hand, which is placed on his left thigh (see nos. 22, 52). Here, however, not only are both hands held against the chest, but the position of the emblems is reversed. Coedes (1923, pl. XXVII, fig. 1) identified a similar bronze—in which the hands are disposed in this fashion, but the emblems held in the usual manner—as Vajrasattva. Recently, however, Boisselier (1966, pl. LII, fig. 1) has identified a stone image of a Buddhalike figure with the hands disposed against the chest as Vajradhara, who is regarded as the supreme deity by some sects of Vajrayana Buddhism. It must be pointed out though that the attributes in the Banteay Chmar image published by Boisselier are broken, and that generally representations from Nepal, where the cult of Vajradhara was particularly strong, and those in Indian texts show the hands of the deity crossing one another to form the *vajrahumkāramudrā*.

Whatever the bronze represents, it is strikingly similar to the dancing Prajñāpāramitā (no. 147a) both in the delineation of details such as the jewelry and crown, and in the shape and features of the face. Possibly both bronzes are the products of the same school, if not of the same workshop.

Published: Munsterberg, 1972, p. 52.

149. A Goddess
Angkor Wat style
1100–1150
Gilt bronze
h: 14 in. (35.5 cm.)

This goddess, possibly representing Umā, the wife of Siva, is iconographically almost identical to the Baphuon figure (no. 146). The broken left arm must have been disposed like that of the earlier sculpture, but the right hand here extends much further from the body. The sheer sumptuousness and elegance of the bronze suggest that it might have been a royal commission. Also possible is that it is an idealized portrait of a royal or noble lady, for the Khmers were particularly fond of dedicating such images to someone's memory. The eyebrows and the irises appear to have been originally inlaid, perhaps with gold and semiprecious stones.

The treatment of the garment and the modeling of the figure are remarkably reminiscent of those of the Baphuon goddess. The crown and the jewelry, however, are particularly richly detailed, in a style more characteristic of Angkor Wat figures. Noteworthy also is the disproportionate size of the right hand and the somewhat heavier treatment of the buttocks. Because of the contrast between the almost emerald green patina of the torso and the gilt skirt, the bronze creates a dazzling effect.

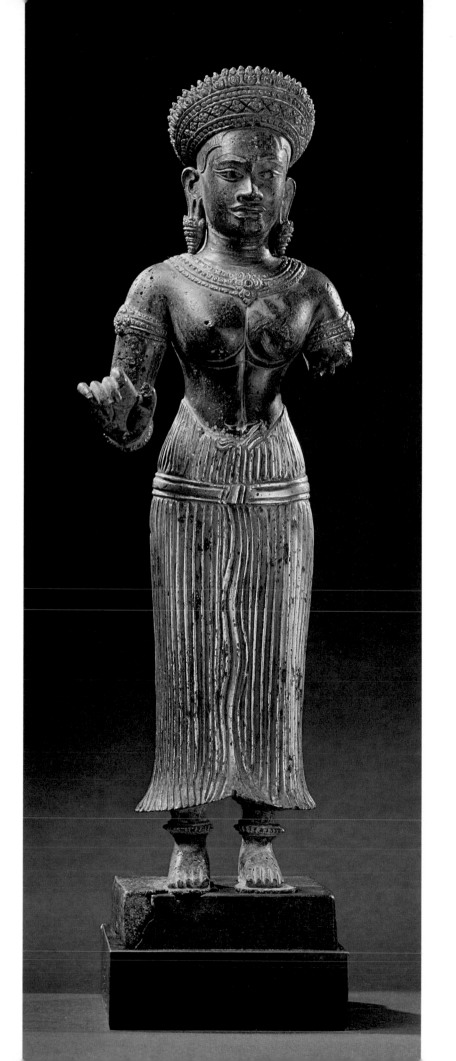

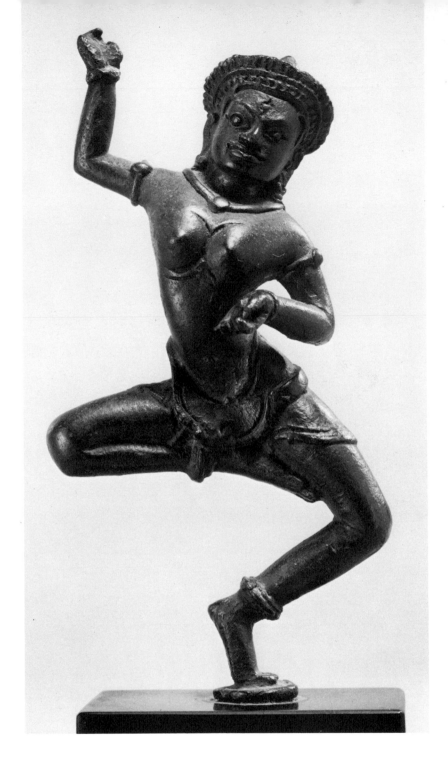

150. A Buddhist Goddess
Angkor Wat style
Ca. 1100–1150
Bronze
h: 5⅜ in. (11.1 cm.)

Balancing herself on her left foot, the goddess dances gracefully with her right leg folded under her body. She has the typical Khmer crown and her ornaments are of simple design. Except for the short *sampot* around her middle, the goddess is naked. Her forehead is marked with the third eye, and the emblem in her left hand seems to be a cup. The right hand might have held either a thunderbolt or a chopper (*kartri*); if the latter, then the goddess can be identified as Nairātmyā, the consort of Hevajra, whose cult was well known in Cambodia during the twelfth and thirteenth centuries. Interestingly, in most of his representations Hevajra is shown dancing in a similar fashion (see no. 153). Modeled with supple charm, this delicate figure is a fine realization of elegantly rhythmic form and poised movement.

Published: Coedes, 1923, p. 31, pl. XIX, fig. 3; Munsterberg, 1972, p. 47.

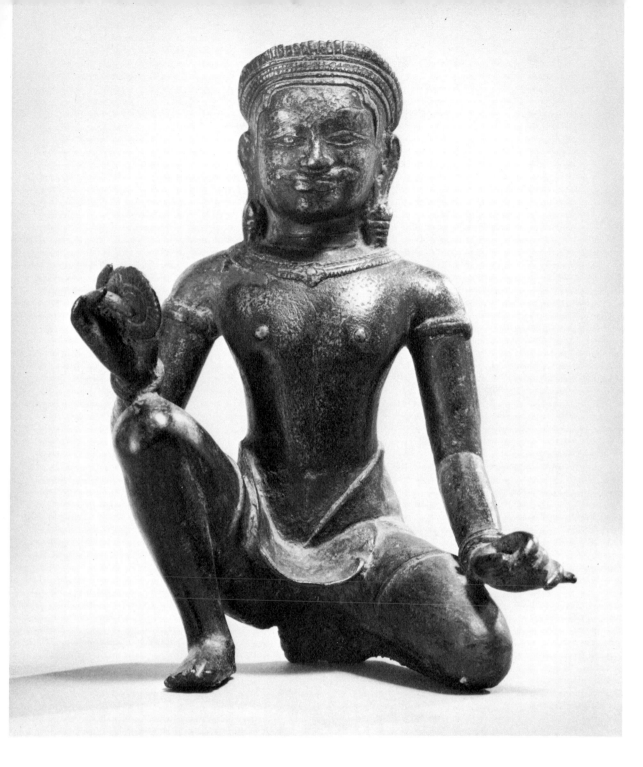

A Deified Devotee (?)
Angkor Wat style
1100–1150
Bronze
h: 6 in. (15.2 cm.)

This particular posture with the left leg folded back is peculiarly Khmer and to my knowledge is seldom encountered in Indian sculpture. Certainly no god in India sits this way, but devotees are often shown in a semi-kneeling posture that is not dissimilar (see no. 51). This bronze figure is crowned and bejeweled like royalty or a deity and is also provided with a moustache. His right hand holds a spoked disk and his left forms the gesture of exposition as it rests gracefully on his thigh.

Many such images, both in bronze and stone, were made during the Angkor period. Some of them, especially those figures who hold a measuring stick in their right hand, are identified with Viśvakarmā, the divine architect. Others, primarily because of the presence of the third eye, have been identified with Śiva. Since his right hand holds a wheel-like object it would be tempting to identify this figure as Vishnu. However, the object may very well be a metal marker of some sort, in which case this figure too may represent Viśvakarmā. More plausible than any of these identifications is that such semi-kneeling figures, because of their humble posture, portray deified devotees, who were particularly common in Khmer culture. Stylistically the bronze is similar to the dancing goddess (no. 150).

247

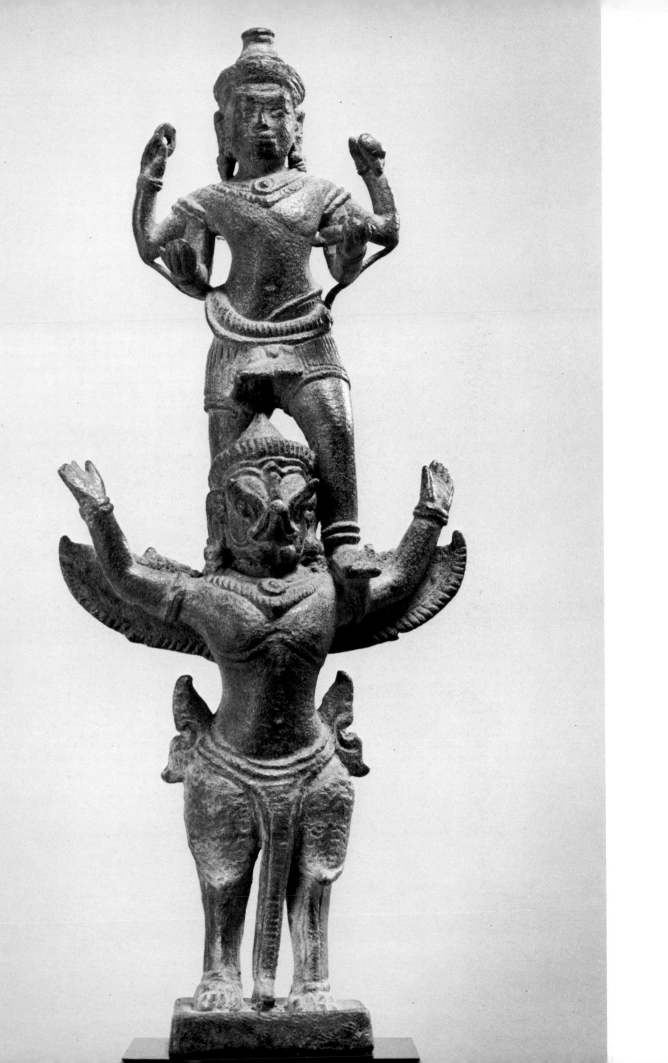

2. Vishnu Riding on Garuḍa
Angkor Wat style
Ca. 1150
Bronze
h: 10¼ in. (26.0 cm.)

Images in which Vishnu rides on his
avian mount, Garuḍa, are known as
Garuḍāsanamūrti. In both Indian and
Indonesian images, the god is normally
shown seated on the bird, as also seems
to have been the case in the Pre-
Angkor period, although not too many
early Garuḍāsana images have been
discovered. During the Angkor period,
particularly in the eleventh and
twelfth centuries, this subject seems to
have become especially popular, but in
most examples the god is shown
standing on the Garuḍa, as though
ready to enter into battle. The
majority of the bronze representations
are small and were probably intended
for domestic altars.
    In this particular example,
Garuḍa's arms, like his wings, are
spread out as if he were about to fly.
Vishnu stands over him with his left
foot placed on Garuḍa's left shoulder
and his right foot resting on the bird's
right wing. The head and hindquarters of the bird are avian, but the
torso and arms are human. Vishnu's
emblems are the wheel, the conch, the
seed of the lotus, and the mace which,
interestingly, is held horizontally (see
no. 65). As is usual with Khmer
sculptures, the bronze is well finished
at the back. For a stylistically similar
piece in the Bickford collection, see
Lee, 1969, p. 73, no. 35.

3. A Conch with Stand
Angkor Wat style
1150–1200
Gilt bronze
h: 16¾ in. (42.6 cm.)

Blowing a conch shell to ward off evil
is an integral part of worship among
Hindus, Buddhists, and Jainas alike.
Metal conches such as this were used to
encase a natural shell and to pour
ritual water during worship. The close
association with water is emphasized
by the three stylized aquatic animals
attached to the stand. The trifoliate
central panel of the shell is decorated
with a multi-armed dancing deity
who may represent Hevajra, in which
case the conch was certainly used in
Buddhist rituals. A similar conch of
about the same period is in the Boston
Museum of Fine Arts (see Lee, 1969,
p. 75, no. 37). For another such conch
depicting a more elaborate mandala
of Hevajra, see Boisselier, 1966,
pl. LVIII, fig. 2.

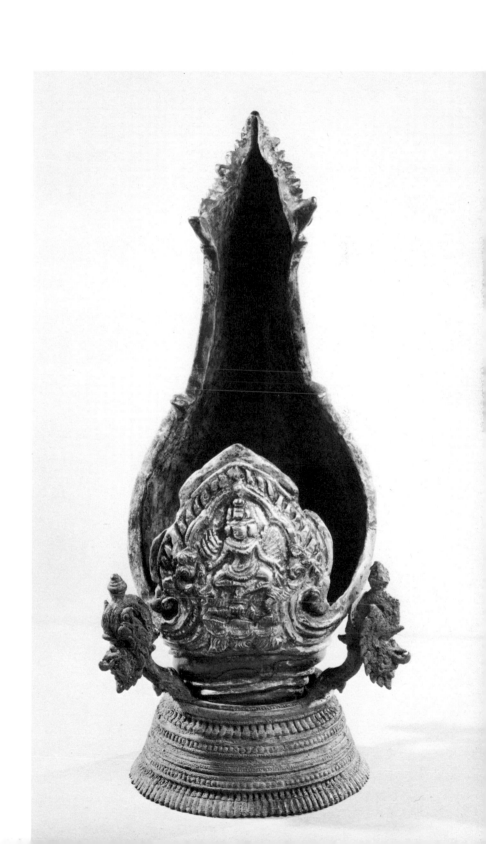

154. A Celestial Nymph

Angkor Wat style
12th century
Sandstone with pinkish tinge
h: 26½ in. (67.3 cm.)

This partly damaged relief depicts an *apsarā*, or celestial nymph, dancing within a niche. Her posture and hand gestures are quite typical of such dancing figures, which grace the walls of twelfth- and thirteenth-century Cambodian temples. Dancing was an essential part of temple ritual, and Khmer inscriptions often not only record gifts of such dancers to the temples but even preserve their names. The stone representations on the temple walls were obviously intended to be permanent offerings of dancers to the deities.

Richly bedecked in jewelry and floral ornaments and sporting a tall tiara, this rather squat *apsarā* dances with her right foot raised. The fingers of both hands are unnaturally slim and elongated and the folds of her stomach are indicated with incised lines. She is not quite as slender as the Bayon dancing *asparās*, and a twelfth-century date seems to be justified by the somewhat heavy structure of her physique, as well as by her broad facial features. Almost an identical relief, certainly from the same temple, is now in the Brundage collection in San Francisco (d'Argencé and Tse, no. 49).

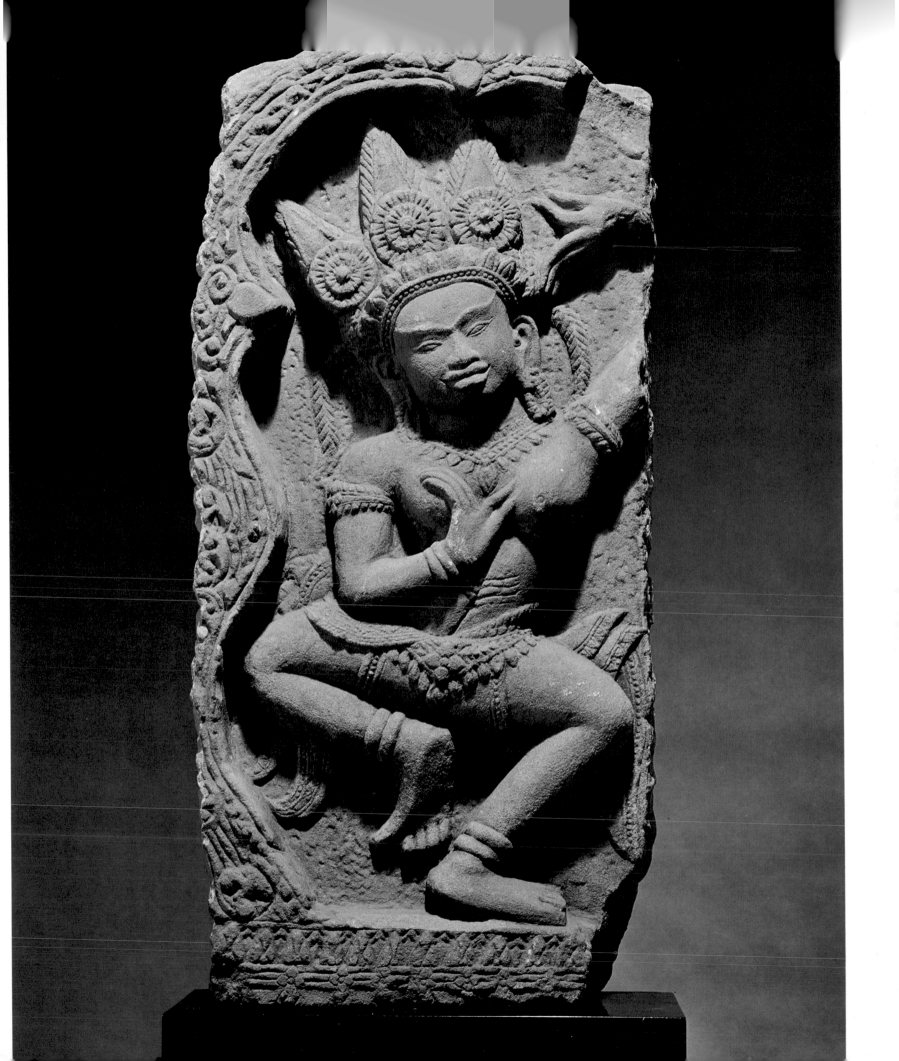

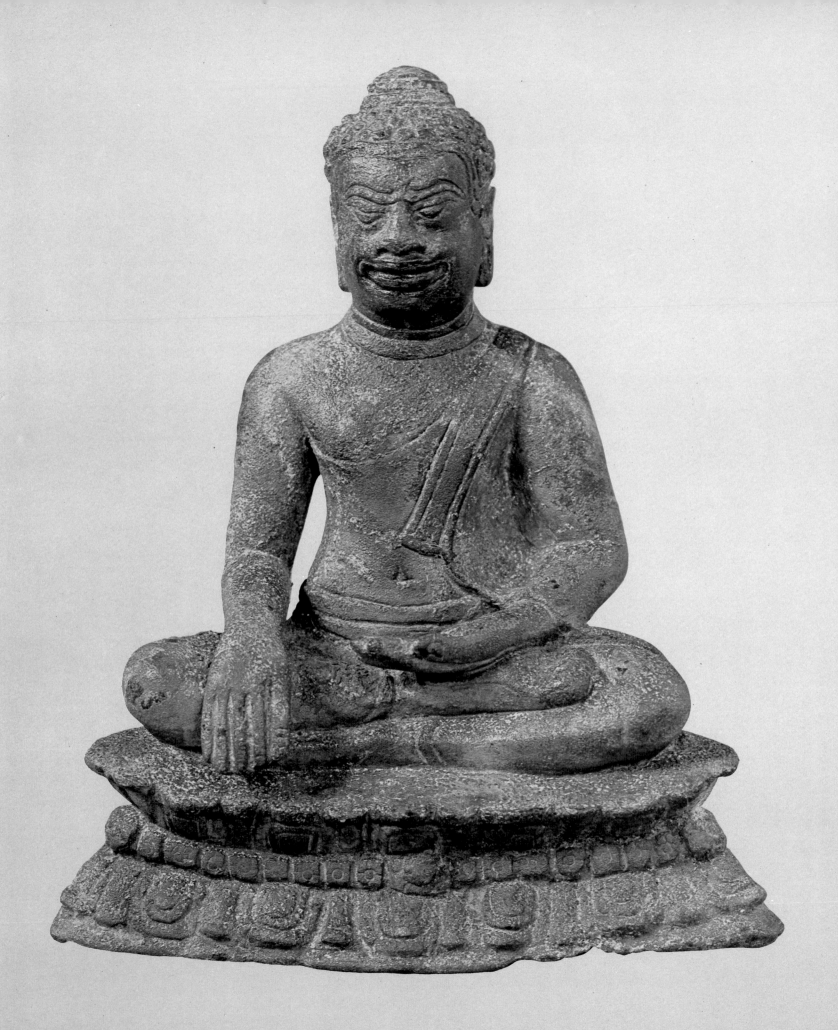

155. Buddha Śākyamuni

Bayon style
13th century
Bronze with blue green patina
h: 6½ in. (16.5 cm.)

Buddha Śākyamuni is here seated in meditation on a fully opened lotus. His left hand rests in his lap and his right forms the *bhūmisparśa* gesture. The fold of his *saṅghāti* is treated in the post-Bayon manner, a mode also commonly seen in Lopburi Buddhas of Thailand. What most distinguishes this bronze is the peculiar delineation of the face and the brilliant blue green patina, largely of azurite, that gives the surface a rich luster.

Although smiling, the Buddha does not display the placid serenity one notices in the usual Buddha images of the Bayon period. On the contrary, the features seem to relate more to the faces of grinning guardian figures, and the closest parallel I could discover is the Banteay Chmar Vishnu riding on Garuḍa (Boisselier, 1966, pl. XLIX, fig. 1).

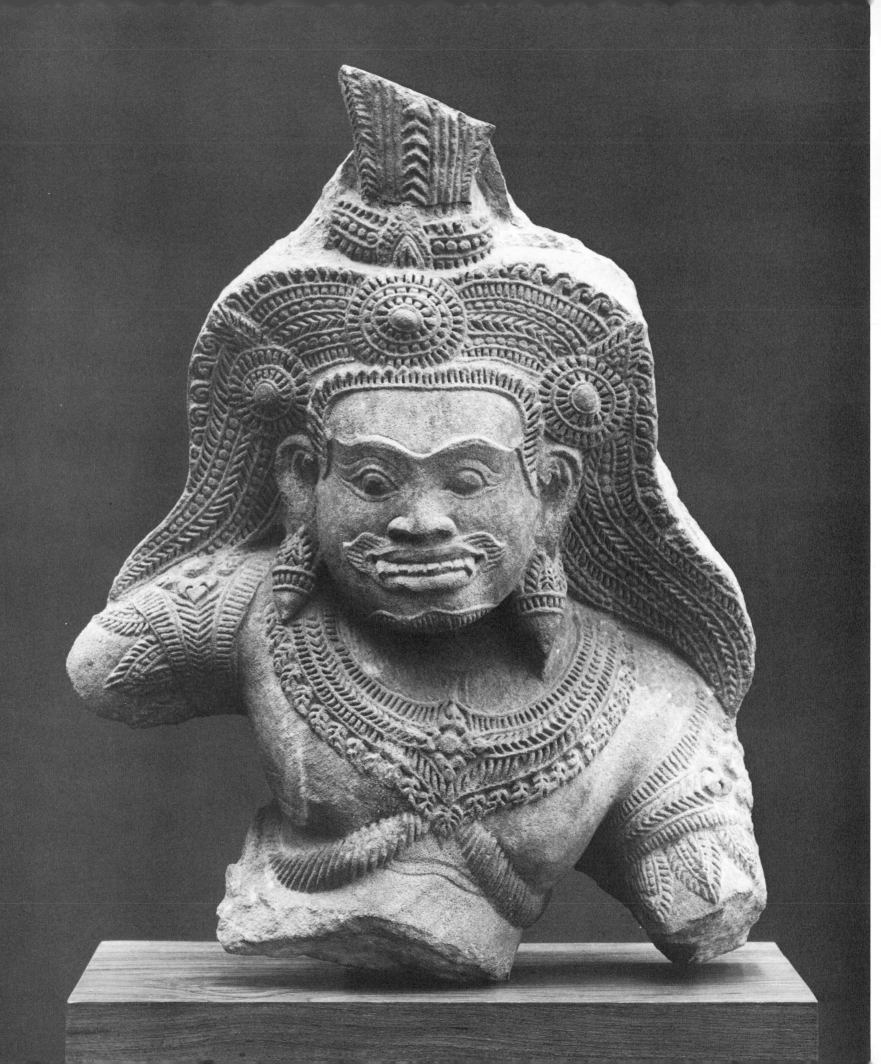

6. Asura Warriors

Bayon style
Early 13th century
Beige sandstone
h: (a) 17¾ in. (45.1 cm.)
(b) 17 in. (43.2 cm.)

In Indian mythology, the gods are
known as *devas* or *suras* and their
antagonists as *asuras*. The Sanskrit
word *asura* is commonly translated into
English as "demon," which is only a
close approximation. Since the walls
of Cambodian temples were freely
embellished with stories and motifs
from Indian mythology, representations of *asuras* are frequently encountered in relief sculpture. Khmer artists
were particularly fond of depicting
asuras and rendered them with great
imagination and whimsy, as we see in
these engaging, though fragmentary,
examples.

    Both sculptures are in the style of
those decorating the temple of Bayon,
the last great monument raised during
the long history of the Khmer empire.
As demonstrated by the more
impressive bust (a), the sculptural
style of Bayon is still bold and vigorous,
although not quite as dynamic as that
of Angkor Wat. A general carelessness
can be noted in the Bayon-style
sculptures, but the faces, as in these
examples, and the decorative details
are often rendered with admirable
sensitivity. Comparable sculptures
can also be seen on the Royal Terrace
at Angkor Thom (see Kalman and
Cohen, pl. 126).

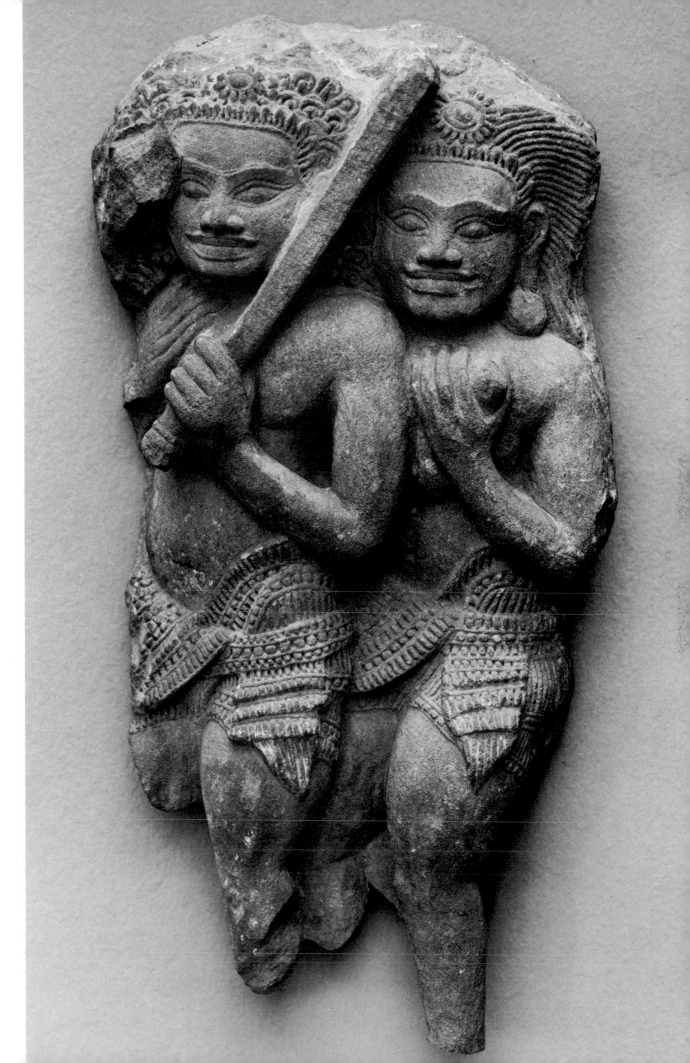

157. A Heraldic Lion

South Vietnam, Mison I style
10th century
Beige sandstone
h: 30 in. (76.2 cm.)

Between the fifth and fifteenth
centuries, parts of central and southern
Vietnam comprised the ancient
kingdom of Champā. Forms of
Hinduism and Buddhism were the
predominant religions and much of the
culture was strongly influenced by
Indian civilization. Mison was the
capital of the kingdom, and the name
is used to designate the style in which
the sculptures of this period were
rendered. This lion very likely once
formed the cornerstone of a pedestal
within a sanctuary at the site of
Tra-kiêu.

Lions have served as supports or
brackets for thrones, pedestals, and
buildings from ancient times in India
(see nos. 52, 53), and the motif was
transferred to most countries of Southeast Asia as well. A Cambodian lion,
serving a related function, also forms
part of this collection (no. 144). A
comparison with both the Cambodian
and an Indian lion (no. 34) clearly
reveals how different the Cham lion is,
both conceptually and stylistically.
While the slender form of the Indian
lion is more expressive of feline grace
and agility, the stout shape of the
Cambodian lion announces the
animal's unquestionable majesty. The
Cham lion is more fierce and animated, and although stylized, it is
astonishingly expressive of the
physical energy and strength of the
animal. An almost identical lion is in
the Musée Guimet, Paris (see Monod,
p. 181, no. 89).

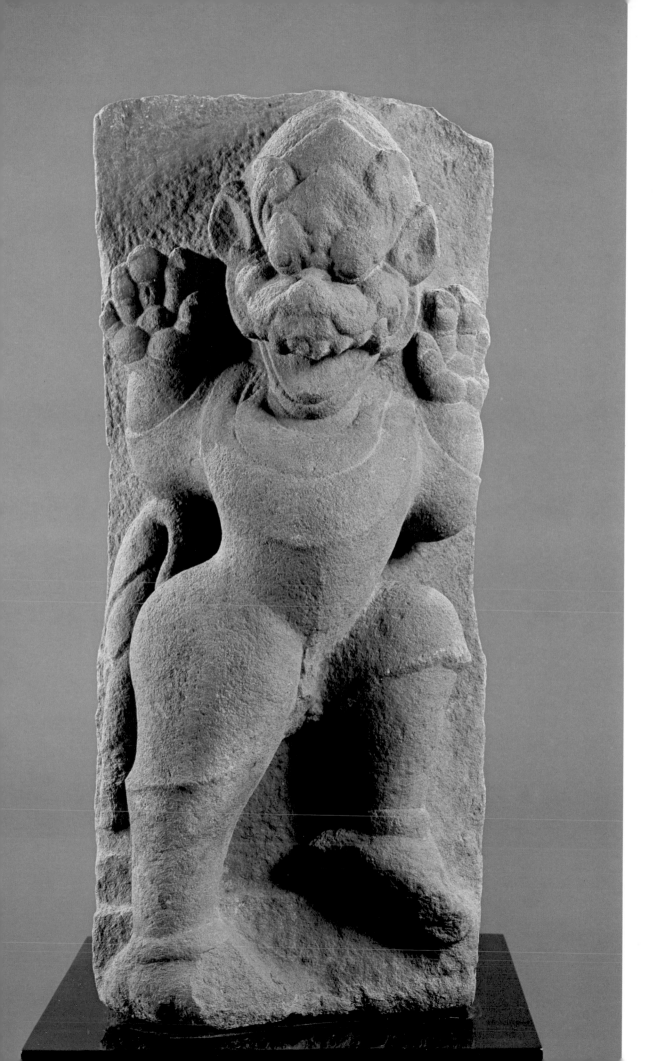

158. A Tympanum

Vietnam, Mison I style
10th century
Buff sandstone
h: 22 in. (65.8 cm.)

This semicircular tympanum, quite typical of Cham architecture, once graced a Saiva temple. Altogether five figures and a bull are represented and the divine status of three of the figures is indicated by their placement on three lotuses. The crowned male seated in a relaxed manner on the bull is Siva. His left hand holds a trident and his right, placed against his knee, may once have held a rosary. The two females face the central figure, sheltered by two parasols held by two diminutive male figures. Normally the two women would represent the wives of the central god, but Siva is generally given only one wife, Umā. However, the river goddess Gaṅgā is sometimes also regarded as his wife and perhaps the two figures here do depict Umā and Gaṅgā. It is also possible that the group represents portraits of a Cham king and his two queens deified as Siva and his consorts.

Although worn, the relief is a fine example of Cham sculpture of the tenth century. Typical of Cham sculptures, the figures are slight but elegant and have soft, tender expressions. The figure of Siva is remarkably close to another from Khu'o'ng-my now in the Tourane Museum (see Boisselier, 1963, fig. 102). At the same time, however, the design of the crown and the slim, graceful figures are more analogous to those from the site of Tra-kiêu (ibid., figs. 112, 117, 121).

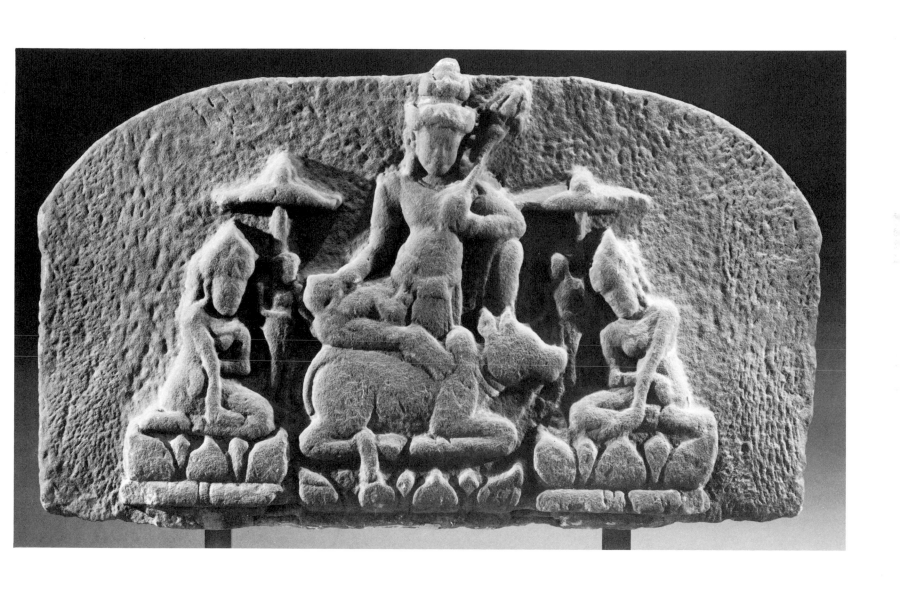

Bibliography

Agrawala, R. C.,
"Some More Unpublished Sculptures
from Rajasthan,"
Lalit Kalā, no. 10, October 1961, pp. 31 ff.

d'Argencé, R. L., and Tse, T.,
*Indian and Southeast Asian Stone Sculptures
from the Avery Brundage Collection*,
Pasadena and San Francisco, 1969.

Auboyer, J.,
Introduction à l'étude de l'art de l'Inde,
Rome, 1965.

Auboyer, J., and Régnier, R.,
Dieux de bronze en pays Tamoul,
Paris, 1974.

Banerjea, J. N.,
The Development of Hindu Iconography,
2nd ed., Calcutta, 1956.

Barrett, D.,
Early Cola Bronzes,
Bombay, 1965.

Barrett, D.,
Early Cola Architecture and Sculpture,
London, 1974.

Bénisti, M.,
*Rapports entre le premier art khmer et l'art
indien*,
2 vols., Paris, 1970.

Bernet Kempers, A. J.,
Ancient Indonesian Art,
Amsterdam and Cambridge, Mass., 1957.

Bhattacharyya, B.,
Indian Buddhist Iconography,
2nd ed., Calcutta, 1958.

Bhattacharyya, B. C.,
The Jaina Iconography,
2nd ed., Delhi, 1974.

Boisselier, J.,
La statuaire du Champa,
Paris, 1963.

Boisselier, J.,
Le Cambodge,
Asie du Sud-est, pt. 1, Paris, 1966.

Boisselier, J., and Beurdeley, J.,
The Heritage of Thai Sculpture,
New York and Tokyo, 1975.

Bowie, T., ed.,
The Sculpture of Thailand,
New York, 1972.

Briggs, L. P.,
The Ancient Khmer Empire,
Transactions of the American
Philosophical Society,
n. s. 41, no. 1, Philadelphia, 1951.

Bunker, E. C.,
"Pre-Angkor Period Bronzes from Pra
Kon Chai,"
Archives of Asian Art,
XXV, 1971–72, pp. 67–76.

Chandra, M.,
*Stone Sculpture in the Prince of Wales
Museum*,
Bombay, 1974.

Chandra, P.,
Stone Sculptures in the Allahabad Museum,
Poona, 1970.

Chow, F.,
Arts from the Rooftop of Asia,
New York, 1971.

Coedes, G.,
Bronzes khmers,
Ars Asiatica V, Paris and Brussels, 1923.

Coedes, G.,
*Les collections archéologiques de Musée
National de Bangkok*,
Paris and Brussels, 1928.

Coedes, G.,
Indianized States of Southeast Asia,
Honolulu, 1968.

Coomaraswamy, A. K.,
History of Indian and Indonesian Art,
New York, 1965.

Coral Rémusat, G. de,
L'art khmer,
Paris, 1951.

Davidson, J. L.,
*Art of the Indian Subcontinent from
Los Angeles Collections*,
Los Angeles, 1968.

Dofflemyer, V.,
"A Buddhist Thai Altarpiece and Five
Related Bronzes,"
*Los Angeles County Museum of Art
Bulletin 1975*,
XXI, pp. 44–56.

Dupont, P.,
La statuaire préangkorienne,
Ascona, 1955.

Dupont, P.,
L'archéologie mône de Dvāravatī,
2 vols., Paris, 1959.

Fisher, R. E.,
Mystics and Mandalas,
Redlands, Calif., 1974.

Fontein, J., et al.,
Ancient Indonesian Art,
Asia House, New York, 1971.

Getty, A.,
The Gods of Northern Buddhism,
Rutland, Vt., and Tokyo, 1962.

Giteau, M.,
Khmer Sculpture and the Angkor Civilization,
New York, 1965.

Giteau, M.,
Angkor,
Freibourg, Switzerland, 1976.

Gonda, J.,
Les religions de l'Inde,
3 vols., Paris, 1962, 1965, and 1966.

Gonda, J.,
Aspects of Early Viṣṇuism,
2nd ed., Delhi, Patna, and Varanasi,
1969.

Griswold, A. B.,
Dated Buddha Images of Northern Siam,
Ascona, 1957.

Griswold, A. B., et al.,
The Art of Burma, Korea and Tibet,
New York, 1964.

Groslier, B. P.,
The Art of Indochina,
New York, 1962.

Harle, J. C.,
Gupta Sculpture,
Oxford, 1974.

Härtel, H.,
Indische Skulpturen,
Berlin, 1960, I.

Härtel, H.,
Museum für Indische Kunst Berlin
(Katalog 1971), Berlin, 1971.

Holt, C.,
Art in Indonesia: Continuities and Changes,
Ithaca, N.Y., 1967.

Indische Kunst (exhibition catalog),
Würltembergischer Kunstverein
Stuttgart,
Stuttgart and Hamburg, 1966.

Ingalls, D. H. H., trans. and ed.,
An Anthology of Sanskrit Court Poetry,
Cambridge, Mass., 1965.

Ingholt, H., and Lyons, J.,
Gandhāran Art in Pakistan,
New York, 1957.

Joshi, N. P.,
Mathura Sculptures,
Mathura, 1966.

Kalman, B., and Cohen, J. L.,
Angkor : Monuments of God-kings.
New York, 1975.

Karmay, H.,
Early Sino-Tibetan Art,
London, 1975.

Khmer Sculpture (exhibition catalog),
Asia House, New York, 1961.

Kramrisch, S.,
Indian Sculpture,
Philadelphia, 1960.

Kramrisch, S.,
The Art of Nepal,
New York, 1964.

Kramrisch, S.,
Art of India,
3rd ed., London, 1965.

Le Bonheur, A.,
La sculpture indonésienne au Musée Guimet,
Paris, 1971.

Lee, S. E.,
Ancient Cambodian Sculpture,
New York, 1969.

Lee, S. E.,
Asian Art from the Collection of Mr. and Mrs.
John D. Rockefeller 3rd,
New York, 1970.

Lee, S. E.,
Asian Art (Rockefeller Collection),
New York, 1975, II.

Le May, R.,
A Concise History of Buddhist Art in Siam,
Cambridge, 1938.

Lippe, A. de,
The Freer Indian Sculptures,
Washington, D.C., 1970.

Lowry, J.,
Burmese Art,
London, 1974.

Luce, G. H.,
Old Burma–Early Pagan,
3 vols., New York, 1970.

Mallman, M. T. de,
Introduction à l'iconographie du tântrisme
bouddhique,
Paris, 1975.

Monod, O.,
Guide du Musée Guimet,
Paris, 1966, I.

Munsterberg, H.,
Art of India and Southeast Asia,
New York, 1970.

Munsterberg, H.,
Sculpture of the Orient,
New York, 1972.

Nagaswamy, R.,
"Some Ādavallān and Other Bronzes of
the Early Chola Period,"
Lalit Kalā, no. 10, October 1961, pp. 34ff.

O'Connor, S. J.,
Hindu Gods of Peninsular Siam,
Ascona, 1972.

Pal, P.,
The Art of Tibet,
New York, 1969.

Pal, P.,
"Some Rajasthani Sculptures of the
Gupta Period,"
Allen Memorial Art Museum Bulletin,
XXVIII, no. 2, 1971, pp. 104–18.

Pal, P., ed.,
Aspects of Indian Art,
Leiden, 1972.

Pal, P.,
The Arts of Nepal,
Leiden, 1974, I.

Pal, P.,
"Bronzes of Nepal,"
Arts of Asia, IV, no. 5, 1974, pp. 31–37.

Pal, P.,
Buddhist Art in Licchavi Nepal,
Los Angeles, 1974.

Pal, P.,
Bronzes of Kashmir,
Graz and New York, 1975.

Pal, P.,
Nepal/Where the Gods Are Young,
New York, 1975.

Pal, P.,
"South Indian Sculptures in the
Museum,"
Los Angeles County Museum of Art
Bulletin, 1976,
XXII, pp. 30–57.

Quaritch Wales, H. G.,
Dvāravatī,
London, 1969.

Rawson, P.,
The Art of Southeast Asia,
New York and Washington, D.C., 1967.

Rosenfield, J. M., et al.,
The Arts of India and Nepal, The Nasli and
Alice Heeramaneck Collection,
Boston, 1966.

Rosenfield, J. M.,
The Dynastic Arts of the Kushāns,
Berkeley and Los Angeles, 1967.

Rowland, B.,
The Art and Architecture of India,
3rd ed., Baltimore, Md., 1967.

Saraswati, S. K.,
A Survey of Indian Sculpture,
Calcutta, 1957.

Saraswati, S. K.,
Early Sculptures from Bengal,
Calcutta, 1962.

Shah, U. P.,
Sculptures from Samlaji and Roda in the
Baroda Museum,
Baroda, 1960.

Sivaramamurti, C.,
South Indian Bronzes,
New Delhi, 1963.

Smith, H. D.,
Vaiṣṇava Iconography,
Madras, 1969.

Snellgrove, D., and Richardson, H.,
A Cultural History of Tibet,
New York and Washington, D.C., 1968.

Stern, P.,
Les monuments khmers,
Paris, 1965.

Trubner, H., et al.,
Asiatic Art,
Seattle, 1973.

Wagner, F. A.,
The Arts of Indonesia,
New York, 1959.

Zimmer, H.,
The Art of Indian Asia,
2 vols., 2nd ed., New York, 1960.

Los Angeles County Museum of Art

Edited by Nancy Grubb.
All photographs by Los Angeles County Museum of Art
Photography Department except nos. 67b, 128b, and 146b,
which are by Helga Photo Studio, Inc., New York.
Designed in Los Angeles by Rosalie Carlson.
All text set in Baskerville by
Westerham Press Ltd.
Catalog printed on Satin Text
by Westerham Press Ltd., Kent, England.